ROBERT H. GODDARD

PIONEER OF SPACE RESERACH

THE DA CAPO SERIES IN SCIENCE

ROBERT H. GODDARD

PIONEER OF SPACE RESERACH

MILTON LEHMAN

New Introduction by

Frederick C. Durant III

A DA CAPO PAPERBACK

Library of Congress Cataloging in Publication Data

Lehman, Milton.
  Robert H. Goddard.

(The Da Capo series in science) (A Da Capo paperback)
  Previously published as: This high man. 1963.
  1. Goddard, Robert Hutchings, 1882-1945.
  2. Rocketry — United States — Biography. I. Title.
  II. Series.
  TL789.85.G65L43   1988   629.4′092′4 [B]   88-18956
  ISBN 0-306-80331-3 (pbk.)

This Da Capo Press paperback edition of *Robert H. Goddard: Pioneer of Space Research* is an unabridged republication of the book entitled *This High Man: The Life of Robert H. Goddard* published in New York in 1963, here supplemented with a new introduction by Frederick C. Durant III. It is reprinted by arrangement with Mildred Lehman.

Published by Da Capo Press, Inc.
A Subsidiary of Plenum Publishing Corporation
233 Spring Street, New York, N.Y. 10013

That low man seeks a little thing to do,
     Sees it and does it:
This high man, with a great thing to pursue,
     Dies ere he knows it . . .

—Robert Browning, A Grammarian's Funeral

To Mildred,
And for Ann, John, Betsy, and their generation

INTRODUCTION TO THE
DA CAPO EDITION

Twenty-five years have passed since the appearance of this splendid biography of our American rocket pioneer. So much has happened in the technology he pursued: space exploration. Men have spent the better part of a year in earth orbit and traversed the surface of the moon. Weather and communications satellites are now vital elements of the global economy. Daily they touch the lives of each of us.

Historians recognize three men of science as pioneers of rocket theory: K. E. Tsiolkovsky (U.S.S.R.;1857-1935), Robert H. Goddard (U.S.A.; 1882-1945), and Hermann Oberth (Germany; 1894-   ). All three inspired the youth of their countries to dream of flight into space, and to work towards its accomplishment. However, Robert Goddard was the only pioneer who also invented, built, and launched rockets.

On the 16th of March, 1926, Goddard launched the world's first liquid propellant rocket. It burned liquid oxygen and gasoline, and weighed nine pounds. The rocket reached an altitude of 41 feet and landed 184 feet away. Nevertheless, this may be considered a bench mark in flight history; perhaps as great as that of Orville Wright. Wright's first flight achieved a distance of just 120 feet. Collecting the pieces of his rocket, Goddard made a few modifications and launched it again in eight days.

Forty-three years later the multi-engine, three-stage Saturn 5 rocket boosted three astronauts to the moon. The basic principles involved—the use of metered liquid bi-propellants forced into a combustion chamber to burn and exit at supersonic speed through a tapered exhaust nozzle, and the concept of multiple, or staged, rockets—were detailed in two U.S. patents issued to Goddard in July 1914. In 1926 these principles were demonstrated in actual flight.

During his lifetime Robert Goddard designed, built (with a few technician assistants), and launched thirty-five rockets of increasing sophistication. He improved his sounding rockets' designs, developing turbopump systems; gyrostabilization; aerodynamic and jet-deflector flight controls; automatic sequencing launch systems; flight trajectory tracking and recording devices; gimbal-mount clustered rocket motors; parachute recovery—and many other techniques later to be developed further by others. But he did it first!

There is no greater proof of Goddard's originality than his U.S. patents. In addition to the two issued in July 1914, fifty-six more would be issued to him in his lifetime. Thirty-five patents pending were issued after his death in 1945. An additional 131 (!) based upon his notes, sketches, and photographs, were applied for by his widow, Esther C. Goddard. In 1960 the U.S. Government paid the sum of $1,000,000 to acquire the rights to use these 214 patents.

Author Milton Lehman spent seven years in the research and writing of his biography. It was a monumental task and he succeeded admirably. Lehman had been a combat correspondent during World War II and received the Army's Legion of Merit for his distinguished reporting on the Anzio beachhead in Italy. He was editor of *The Stars and Stripes* (Mediterranean).

Married to Mildred B. Kharfen, he enjoyed an active family life with their three children in Bethesda, MD. His death in 1966 at age 48 was untimely.

The depth of Lehman's research was extraordinary. There is no doubt that he was challenged by the task of presenting accurately the accomplishments and character of Robert Goddard. Mrs. Goddard was, naturally, of great assistance, for she had typed all records of Dr. Goddard's research and test activity, as well as photographing flights. She also pointed the way to others who had known and worked with Dr. Goddard, or whose areas of competence and knowledge were relevant. Lehman listed 149 individuals whom he interviewed from 1956-1963. The great majority of these men and women, who were contemporaries of Robert Goddard, are now gone. This is one reason why this book is valuable. Another is because it is so readable.

When I taught rocket history to classes of young people at the Smithsonian Institution, I urged all students to obtain this book. It is an inspiring example of brilliant innovation, of the pursuit of a dream. Robert Goddard created the building blocks which others would later invent independently.

The reader will find that another independent thinker and doer, Charles Lindbergh, would play a major role as a catalyst in Goddard's career, and as an encouraging friend. Some years ago I was privileged to have several long discussions with Lindbergh on the island of Maui. I was struck by the intertwining of the lives of these two men, each brilliant, self-confident, and forcefully persistent. Each was aided by a loving wife. Lindbergh encouraged me to write on the relationship between himself and Dr. Goddard, offering access to archives of his papers at St. Louis and New Haven. My paper on their relationship is presently being written.

It should be noted that serious students will find primary source material on Dr. Goddard at the Robert H. Goddard Library archives (Clark University, Worcester, Massachusetts, and at the Library of the Smithsonian Institution's National

Air & Space Museum in Washington.) Mention must be made, too, of *The Papers of Robert H. Goddard,* (McGraw-Hill, New York, 1970). This monumental, three-volume (1700 pg.) reference set was edited by the late G. Edward Pendray and Esther C. Goddard. Publication was made possible by The Daniel and Florence Guggenheim Foundation.

The public may see the few surviving actual rockets built by Goddard at the National Air & Space Museum. Many rocket parts and memorabilia are in the Roswell Museum, New Mexico. There is also an excellent recreation of Goddard's Mescalero Ranch workshop and his actual launching tower. Both Worcester Polytechnic Institute and Clark University have collections of rocket parts. At nearby Auburn, there is a granite marker at the site of the 1926 rocket flight. A granite tablet beside the road explains the significance of the marker.

During the period 1920-1929 Goddard's research was sponsored, in the main, by the Smithsonian Institution. In addition to his periodic reports of expenditures and accomplishments, he wrote four unsolicited reports: March 1920, August 1923, March 1924, and August 1929. They are fascinating! In these reports, which he asked the Smithsonian to hold but not make public, Goddard revealed his visions of space exploration. He considered both manned and unmanned vehicles to explore the moon and planets, messages to possible extraterrestrials, solar power, ion (electric) propulsion; even flight to the stars. Goddard wished to make certain that his convictions would be documented, although such concepts were then totally unacceptable to the scientific academic world.

Apparently it did not disturb Goddard that, despite his steady progress, his long-term dream of space exploration lay far in the future. In 1932, at age 50, he revealed his inner drive in a letter to H. G. Wells. He wrote of his research: ". . . . . There can be no thought of finishing, for 'aiming at the stars,' both literally and figuratively, is a problem to occupy generations, so that no matter how much progress one makes, there is always the thrill of just beginning. . . . . ."

Robert H. Goddard died thirteen years later, on 10 August, 1945. Today's accomplishments in space exploration are, indeed, "just the beginning."

— FREDERICK C. DURANT, III
Chevy Chase, MD
May 1988

Mr. Durant is an engineer and historian, involved with rocket and space flight for more than forty years. As Assistant Director of the Smithsonian Institution's National Air & Space Museum, he organized the Astronautics Department and headed it for 16 years.

CONTENTS

Sources and Acknowledgments:

ILLUSTRATIONS

Five eight-page photographic sections, covering the major periods of Robert Goddard's life, appear between the following pages:

In addition, line cuts of Dr. Goddard's patents and a schematic comparison of a Goddard rocket and the German V-2 appear on pages 68, 69, 359, 391.

PREFACE

*"Am I a man who dreamed of being a butterfly,
Or am I a butterfly dreaming myself to be a man?"*

The ancient wisdom of the Orient, subtly questioning, in these lines of poetry, the relationship between reality
and dreams, seems a fitting introduction to Milton Lehman's
biography of the pioneer astronautical scientist, Robert H.
Goddard. In the following chapters about this extraordinary
man, one is constantly aware of the fact that we live in a
world where dreams and reality interchange.

Sitting in his home in Worcester, Massachusetts, in 1929,
I listened to Robert Goddard outline his ideas for the future
development of rockets—what might be practically expected,
what might be eventually achieved. Thirty years later, watching a giant rocket rise above the Air Force test base at Cape
Canaveral, I wondered whether he was dreaming then or I
was dreaming now.

The Orient enters this introduction, too, because Goddard's lifetime interests root back to the invention of gunpowder, firebolts, and skyrockets, often attributed to Chinese
of more than two thousand years ago.

Goddard's early experiments in the field of astronautics were made with solid-propellant rockets; but some of his greatest accomplishments relate to his transition from solid to liquid fuels. With this transition rockets advanced from an era of fireworks, lifesaving, and minor military roles, to one of intercontinental warfare and spatial flight.

This is a story of individualism, of one man's effort and almost superhuman vision in a field of science so fantastic in his day that anyone venturing much confidence in its future was considered unscientific by most scientists. It is a story of a young wife's dedication and persistence; of two business-men, father and son, with the perception, courage, and gen-erosity to finance a spatial project that appeared to most people of the time a fool's dream. Here one views the early history of missile development in changed perspective by meeting such divergent pioneers in that development as "Aunt" Effie, Ambassador Guggenheim, Dr. Abbot and H. G. Wells.

Robert Goddard's dual approach to astronautics is a fas-cinating study, now cautious and realistic, now adventurous and fictional. On one day he would be a conservative scientist, confining the objective of his "high-altitude research project" to measurements relating to the earth's upper atmosphere. On another, he would let his mind run freely through fic-tional accounts of interplanetary warfare, or put down in writing new ideas for human emigration to distant areas of space.

Goddard's ideas are partially recorded on thousands of pages of his journals, notes, records and reports, assembled through years of devotion by his wife before the writing of this book. These pages might be considered as belonging to an open volume, with a preface of fact on one side and thick chapters of fiction on the other. Year by year, time keeps turning pages of fiction over into the preface of fact. Satellites are now orbiting our earth; missiles have struck the surface of the moon; space probes have hurtled out beyond the gravitation that we humans feel.

But man's rockets have penetrated an infinitesimal portion of the known universe. Even when we gather confidence from our accomplishments to date and look forward to sometime visiting other members of the solar system, we use a scale of miles to help our planning—about 240,000 to the moon, about 50,000,000 to the planet Mars. When we expand our thinking to orbits around a different star, we change this scale of miles to one of light years—9 light years to the Dog Star, Sirius, 900,000 to Andromeda's "nebula." Goddard's imagination carried man through galaxies.

An intercontinental ballistic missile travels between 200 and 300 miles a minute in its high trajectory. At such speed, man would take less than a day to reach the moon, several months for a trip to Mars, and over 100,000 years to approach the nearest star. "Spaceships" will operate at speeds above those of our ballistic missiles; but even at the velocity of light, which flashes from earth to moon while two human steps are taken, and which scientists claim will remain unattainable by man, the extent of a lifetime would limit us to nearby areas of space. Yet our supermen of fiction adventure to the stars.

Thus, living in our dreams of yesterday, we find ourselves still dreaming of impossible future conquests, as Robert Goddard dreamed, as men have dreamed throughout the ages. Will new, scientifically established obstacles, unlike the angry gods, storm waves, and sonic barriers of generations past, place a final limit to the achievement of mankind? Or may we eventually discover that limits are relative to years, that dreams and reality transpose with time, as do energy and matter?

In this biography of Robert Goddard, one is kept aware of the human challenge to all limits.

CHARLES A. LINDBERGH

1. THE CHERRY TREE

The sun came up over the barren prairie in New Mexico in December of the year 1930. The wind, dry and soft, played over the silent flatland, open to space.

The land was called Eden Valley. It was a vast monotonous depression, level as a floor for miles, far from any highway, remote from the nearest town. To the southwest, near the horizon, foothills rose abruptly to El Capitan, purple in the distance and streaked with snow. To the east lay the sun-lit slopes of the Caprock and, beyond it, the Staked Plains where the Comanche Indians had once marked waterholes. Here the Spanish explorers Coronado and Castillo had found their stakes and crossed safely, followed by later explorers who died without leaving marks or evidences. Now came another explorer.

A small caravan, raising dust, arrived from the south, a model T Ford towing a trailer in which, extended over its tailgate, lay a long bundle, trussed down and covered with quilts and oilcloth. The Ford moved slowly over the rough

1

land to avoid jostling its cargo. After it came a black vintage touring sedan.

The vehicles stopped. Five men emerged and walked quickly to the trailer, unleashed the bundle, threw back the quilts.

"Easy with her," one said. Out of the trailer bed they lifted a slender cylinder containing an involvement of tanks and tubing. It was 11 feet long, 9 inches in diameter at its thickest, 33.5 pounds in weight. From its glistening nose cone to its flaring stabilizer vanes one quadrant was painted a gaudy Chinese red. The men handled the device with considered respect, having spent months preparing it for this moment.

This was the fledgling rocket, a symbol of aspiration, being hand-carried gently past a wooden shelter to a steel-webbed tower reaching sixty feet above the valley floor. The converted tower, designed originally for a windmill, had been brought to the prairie and erected a few months earlier. It was guyed by cables and anchored in concrete.

The crew of machinists worked inside the tower, setting up the fragile machine. The man whom they called "the doctor," or "the professor," stood by, watching, as they went about the familiar rites. Robert Hutchings Goddard was forty-eight years old, a professor of physics on leave from Clark University in Worcester, Massachusetts. In pursuit of space, Goddard had come far from his native New England. He was middling-sized, slightly stooped, with the thin body and the hollow-chested appearance that tuberculosis often gives. He was bald, with dark eyebrows and mustache. His brown eyes were intense, and subject to change. They projected a warmth that could quickly turn to austerity, an openness that could turn to retreat.

From early manhood, he had been possessed by a dream of bringing man into an era of journeys beyond the earth. He had quietly offered calculations and experiments to prove that the enormity of space exploration was possible. In his secret papers, dating from 1906, were his concepts of space travel—speculations on solar, atomic and ion energy for propulsion; suggestions on the positioning of pilots and methods of re-entering the earth's heavy atmosphere; discussions of lunar landings; plans for an intergalactic solar sail. In 1926, in an obscure test at a Massachusetts farm, he had flown the world's first liquid-fuel rocket, a modest sire for the space age. It was a short flight, to be sure, rather like the first aircraft efforts of the Wright brothers. But even as he struggled to get that primitive engine to lift, he was driven by the conviction that man in time would travel by rocket to explore the universe. He had already considered the freezing of human protoplasm to prolong life for such incredible journeys.

Of all explorers of the twentieth century, Goddard was one of the boldest, but also among the most elusive and contradictory. He was a revolutionary with a flaming mission who banked his fires behind a respectability becoming a Boston trustee. In a field so complex that it would call for teams of scientists and technicians, he remained a solitary, mustering a few mechanics to help him. Among the voluble rocket fraternity, he was considered a curious and withdrawn genius who would neither join the team of others nor permit them to join his. But removed from the rocket brotherhood, he faithfully attended the weekly meetings of Rotary International.

Goddard presents us with a double image, a range of contradictions. These contradictions, however, were essential and vitalizing. They provoked in him an insistence on standing alone in a province of technology that one day would summon the physical scientists and most of the social scientists as well.

Among those who saw most of him and possibly knew him best were his crew members in New Mexico that morning in late December 1930. Like the mechanics and machinists whom he hired later, they were somewhat aware of his physical frailty and also his strength of purpose. They were warmed by him and protective toward him. At daily tasks, they found him altogether approachable, wearing shabby clothes for comfort, gently humorous, easy to talk with on matters at hand. But they had learned not to probe too deeply with this man, to respect his unstated ground rules that included his highly developed sense of privacy and restraint.

The doctor and his men were absorbed in checking and installing their flight equipment. It was midafternoon before they were ready. Almost New Year's Day, it was hot inside the sheet metal wrapped around the base of the tower as a windbreaker. But they went on methodically with their tasks as if they were back in their familiar New England. Long rehearsed, they had little need for instructions.

Henry Sachs, the crew chief and instrument maker, and Al Kisk, Goddard's brother-in-law, had climbed the tower. They fastened cables to the striped rocket to hold her steady until the hoped-for moment of release. Below them, Lawrence and Charles Mansur paid out wire from the tower to the control shelter they had recently built one thousand feet away and buttressed with sand bags. When—and if—the rocket flew, Larry would be farther out on the prairie, measuring its approximate speed and altitude with the aid of his recording telescope and stop watch.

Goddard, perhaps alone, concealed anxiety. His men seemed confident of success. He did nothing to short-circuit their optimism. For years he had tested his small rockets, seeing them as embryos of rocket ships to come, the new prime movers for outer space. Unlike motors of the past, which were harnessed to the wheel and wheel-like screw and propeller for locomotion on land, water and in the air, Goddard's reaction motor would presumably thrust itself ahead, into the airless voids of space.

The principle was simple enough. Obvious even. But reducing theory to a workable device had proved enormously difficult. There would be hundreds of experimental tests ahead, and more than could be accomplished in a lifetime. After each small advance had come failures and breakdowns. Although acclaim accompanies scientific success, the scientist accepts failure as a means of learning.

The mechanics themselves grew impatient whenever the machine broke down or failed to rise. But they listened quietly when Goddard explained the importance of error, the lessons to be learned when a valve jammed, or a nozzle burned through, or a rocket chamber exploded. Usually he managed to restore their morale. But what of his own? He had never thought his rocket would take so long to reach great altitudes.

This flight test in late 1930 already mattered too much, too much depended on it, the doctor doubtless mused. He hoped to record a flight for his new sponsor before the year ended, and already it was December 30. Again, he could feel the build-up of tension, the need to demonstrate, as if by magic, the extraordinary power of his rocket system.

It was a familiar sensation, reaching back to 1916, when he first sent his calculations, neatly boxed, with a plea for support to Smithsonian Institution scientists. They had extended financial aid to explore the atmosphere beyond the reach of balloons and aircraft. They seemed to regard him as a sort of meteorologist, not minding his statement—it was almost a footnote—that it was theoretically possible to send a rocket to the moon. Enthusiasm, they possibly felt, was a good thing in pioneering research.

Henry Sachs wouldn't believe in moon rockets either, the professor realized. All the day before, Sachs was improving the rocket igniter, following a scrawl Goddard had penciled on an envelope back. Now he was fitting a garden hose, fresh from the local hardware store, to the rocket's liquid-oxygen tank. Solemn, practical Mr. Sachs knew he was building no moon rocket. The highest their rockets had gone so far was less than one hundred feet.

Back in Auburn, Massachusetts, four years before, their first liquid-fuel rocket had barely cleared its launching frame. A crude and naked assembly of pipes and chambers, it had reached only forty-one feet, rising from the farmland like a bizarre hatrack. Sachs had seemed amazed that the contrivance had flown at all. You could throw a baseball a lot higher, he'd observed.

But Goddard knew, from this brief, unheralded trial, that he had finally reached the beginning of altitude. The rocket engine was already the most efficient motor yet contrived. In laboratory tests, he had demonstrated the probability of velocities greater than sound. With more fuel, more oxygen and a more dependable combustion chamber, the rocket had a potential velocity sufficient to enable a vehicle to escape the earth's gravity.

It was enough to embolden the professor, whatever his difficulties might become. Elated, he had kept his emotions to himself in proper Yankee fashion, not even allowing to his young wife Esther the extent of his dream. She had attended the 1926 flight as his photographer and calmly approved his results. Now, in 1930, he anticipated her arrival before the intended launching.

Esther drove into the valley alone, her motion picture camera ready. She had firmly declined his offer to have one of the men come back to the ranch house to get her. It would be a waste of time, she said. From the outset of their marriage, six years before, she had tried to adapt herself to his ways, which she persisted in regarding as ordinary academic behavior. She was offended when others disagreed, made his "moon rocket" a butt for editorial cartoons and Sunday supplements, or when a colleague at Clark University would say, with an attempt at wry good humor: "Well, Robert, how is your moon-going rocket?"

Personally, he hadn't minded this foolishness, at least not

much, Goddard told her. What really mattered was the effect on his reputation. Unhappily, it was not always possible to avoid sensation. In 1929, the blast of one of his rockets had attracted the press and the fire marshal to the secluded farm in Auburn. The reporters said the professor was trying again to fly up to the moon, which he wasn't, and that one of his rockets had blown up, which it hadn't. The marshal had simply called the rocket a fire hazard, which it was, and ruled it out of the sovereign state of Massachusetts.

At the post mortem one morning in 1929, Larry Mansur tried to sum up their feelings with a wheeze. "They ain't doing right by our Nell," he said. Thereafter, the generic name for the rocket was "Nell," although Esther never cared much for it.

Now the professor helped his slender blonde wife out of the car with her camera and gear. Flight preparations would soon be over and the test could start. Standing beside her, he watched Larry and Henry Sachs filling the rocket's tanks, first the gasoline, then the liquid oxygen, the "lox," which they kept in a thermos container.

For the Yankee professor, "lox" was hard to come by and expensive on a slim budget. Paying $1.00 a liter, he was the only customer for the subzero liquid from the Linde Air Products Company, which made it available as a by-product of gas for oxyacetylene welding. Small supplies of the "lox" were sent to him by truck from Linde's plants in Texas and Oklahoma.

Even without liquid hydrogen, which was neither practical nor as yet available as fuel for his experiments, his calculations showed that liquid oxygen, as oxidizer, was the most powerful and efficient of combustion agents. He could anticipate the roaring inferno when the gasoline and oxygen united. If the combustion chamber would hold this time, they might record a notable flight.

Feeling the hot sun on his back, the professor made a final

check of the rocket, examining its controls, its connections, its pressure tanks. He saw that the aluminum sheathing over the oxygen tank was already frosted over, that the wires were well anchored and unobstructed from the tower to the control shelter. He signaled to Larry Mansur that it was time to go out to the observation post at 3,060 feet and set up his recording telescope. Just in case.

With his wife, Goddard then joined the rest of his crew at the control shack. He watched Esther adjust her movie camera on its tripod, pointing it toward the tower from a hole cut in the shelter wall.

All was ready now. He looked at his watch. It was shortly before three o'clock. The sequence began.

When the pressure-generating tanks built up to 200 pounds, Goddard quietly ordered: "Ignition!" Al Kisk fired the igniter.

For a moment, through the open slot in the shack, he studied the flame shooting out from the base of the rocket, was aware that Esther's camera was running. He brought the second pressure gauge on the fuel tank up to 225 pounds. Now he could almost feel the rocket straining at its cables.

In another moment, or perhaps a few seconds, Sachs, watching the lift indicator, moved the release lever. Al Kisk, seeing that the lever had moved, pulled the releases.

This was the magic moment. The slender rocket worked up out of the tower, slowly at first, like a heavy man pushing himself up out of a chair. As the rocket neared the top of the tower, it climbed faster, gaining speed. Its jet was still pointed and strong. Its nose came out of the tower, and then the rocket was out completely. It was leaning a bit to the southwest, but it was already higher than on any earlier flights. Probably 1,000 feet up and still climbing, though slanting off more. It was still making altitude and barely turning. Its red stripe was visible. But now it was slanting over.

At this point, the apex of its flight, Goddard's rocket was 2,000 feet above the prairie floor, by far his best altitude yet. The doctor watched for its parachute to emerge from the nose. Something in the rocket had jammed. He heard Esther's hand-wound camera run down and stop. She had her movie film of the ascent. With his crew, Goddard followed the rocket's jagged descent. It came down shrill and whistling, banging into the dry lands a half mile away.

Near the launching tower, Sachs was shouting at Kisk, who was already in the touring sedan, heading toward the fallen machine.

"All right," said the professor. "After we pick up the pieces, we've got a few things to do. First, we have to re-figure that parachute release. And then we'd better start testing our gyroscopic controls."

II

Massachusetts, by the turn of the nineteenth century, was a commonwealth of uncommon challenge and possibility. The Industrial Revolution, immediately following the stimulus of the Civil War, had come from England to New England and was flourishing. Through science and technology, man was gaining dominion at last over his hard environment. Nowhere else in the New World was there more optimism than in this prospering region.

Reports of conquests at home and abroad in fundamental science were followed shortly by news of inventions. After Britain's Michael Faraday explored electrical induction and Joseph Henry advanced electromagnetism, Bell devised the telephone, Morse the telegraph, Edison the incandescent lamp. After Germany's Heinrich Hertz detected radio waves, Italy's Marconi produced his wireless communicator. While science was busily shaking classical doctrines, among them the concepts of the essential elements of matter and the behavior of light waves, applied inventors put the new doctrines to work.

Two cities in Massachusetts gave the state its essential character and became a fulcrum for novel ideas. Unknowingly, each for a time harbored one of the new century's great and least-known innovators.

One city was Boston in whose suburb, Roxbury, Goddard spent most of his childhood. Boston was the intellectual, social and financial hub of New England, sending often stormy eddies across the land. Here Horace Mann reformed public education; William Lloyd Garrison gave fighting force to the press; Puritanism was set back on its heels by Unitarian reform. Perhaps ultraconservatism had invited rebellion. But after each engagement, Boston's liberal conscience, Thoreau and Emerson, remained; after every skirmish, the core of New England individualism remained. Then and later, Boston was a city of pristine and often magnificent standards.

The second city was Worcester, where Goddard was born and where, after Boston, he grew to manhood. There, each morning, factory whistles summoned citizens to produce a cornucopia filled with practical wares: razors and envelopes; wallpaper and corsets; weaving looms and machine tools; grinding wheels and shoes; trunks and silverware; and, for the opening of the West, nails and barbed wire and plows. Its local heroes included Eli Whitney with his cotton gin; Ichabod Washburn with his techniques of drawing wire from steel; and, perhaps for flippancy, J. C. Stoddard with his remarkable steam calliope. These and other inventors like them were well buttressed by patents. What counted in Worcester was not theory but practice. Wealth, not philosophy, was its measure of success. The city prided itself on being the "industrial heart" of the state.

If Boston was academic and sometimes outgoing in spirit, Worcester was self-protective and ingrown. Between them, the two cities set in Goddard the dual strains which persisted throughout his life. One of his central problems was to transmit his ideas freely, in the manner of Boston, while protecting and proving them, in the style of Worcester.

III

Goddard came from prudent Yankee ancestors, his family tree burying thrifty roots deep in New England. Among his forebears were ministers, deacons, tradesmen, machinists, farmers and occasional mavericks. The New England Goddards were descended from Edward Goddard, a farmer in old England's Norfolk County, whose son William, a London grocer, transplanted the line in 1666 to Watertown, Massachusetts.

On his mother's side, too, Robert's kinsmen were founders of Massachusetts, going back to Stephen Gates, who came to America in 1683 on the ship *Diligent* out of Ipswich, and to John Hoyt, an original settler of the town of Salisbury. Another, Michael Gill, was a printer and a revolutionary, one of the leading spirits of the Boston Tea Party.

Of all these forebears, whose lives were often recounted to him, the youngster was most enthralled by the enterprising mavericks within his ancestral tree. He was especially taken with the legend of Captain Levi Pease, his grandfather thrice removed and a pioneer of early American transportation. The story of Captain Pease in many ways ran parallel to Robert's own adventure, more than a century later.

After earning his captaincy in the Revolution as a purchasing agent and general's aide, Pease set himself up briefly as a blacksmith in Somers, Connecticut. But he was too restless and imaginative to remain in a trade. He decided that others in the new country were equally restless and that they would promptly provide capital for his venture—to introduce the stagecoach to New England.

In 1783, with a fellow blacksmith named Reuben Sikes, the enterprising Pease obtained "two convenient wagons" and eight horses. His first effort was to establish a coach line between Boston and Hartford, a distance of a hundred miles. Passengers desiring to alight en route were advised to signal the driver by pulling a cord tied around his leg.

Unfortunately, neither capital nor passengers were quick to materialize for the new transport system. Society, as Goddard would also find, is slow to accept its innovators. But with or without passengers, Pease and Sikes resolved to run their coaches on schedule. "I will have plenty of paying customers," Pease was later quoted in a local history, "when people learn they can depend on me."

Pease expanded the coach line, promoting its services with a notice in the Worcester *Spy* calling attention to the "unparalleled speed" of his stages. "A merchant may go from Boston to New York and return again in less than ten days, which is truly wonderful," he added. In time, New England agreed it was wonderful and accepted the stagecoach as its own. As a contemporary account observed, the line "ran in fair weather and foul" and "earned the reputation of being 'as punctual as the stars in their courses.' "

By 1786, Levi Pease had determinedly carried his well-cushioned "clipper" stages all the way south to Savannah, Georgia, complete with way stations and ticket agents en route. He drove one of the stages himself until he was an old man.

The lesson of Levi Pease adhered. Dependability, as Grandmother Goddard would one day point out, was the enabling partner of imagination; one reinforced the other. For this happy combination, Robert could look to Worcester and to his own father, Nahum Danford Goddard.

From childhood on, Nahum Danford was determined to be

more practical than his own father, Nahum Parks Goddard, a rather improvident Civil War veteran who earned a meager income as a musician. When the family moved from Boston to the ancestral farmhouse at Worcester, Nahum Danford carried with him the commendation of a Boston businessman named W. B. Browne, who spoke of him as "a young man of excellent character and good English education . . . who by his faithfulness and integrity and energy will give good satisfaction."

When Nahum fell in love, he was a young bookkeeper in the Worcester firm of L. Hardy Company at Webster Square, a manufacturer of machine knives used for cutting paper, textiles, leather and other materials. The company was then owned by Henry A. Hoyt, a crusty merchant with an only daughter.

The Hoyts lived across the road from the Goddards in a more imposing home, with larger and better-tended acres, guarded by two sizable watchdogs. Their daughter, Fannie Louise, was seventeen years old, golden-haired and pretty, with an appealing fragility. Henry Hoyt was not pleased when he learned that his bookkeeper had won his daughter's fancy. He regarded Nahum's fiddle-playing father as flighty and could find no virtue in having his daughter marry beneath the Hoyts' financial status. Over his protests, Nahum and Fannie were married on Nahum's twenty-third birthday, January 3, 1882. At their wedding, no one was more dry-eyed than Henry Hoyt, the employer of the groom and father of the bride, whom he shortly disinherited.

The Goddards cheerfully took Fannie Louise into their home on Maple Hill, setting aside a room for the new couple. She found herself in crowded, but lively and affectionate surroundings. The nominal head of the family was her father-in-law, who divided his time between Worcester and Boston, playing in bands and quadrille ensembles for fashionable comings-out and goings-on, and shuttling between the two cities to give violin lessons to dutiful disciples. But the actual and evident head was her mother-in-law, Mary Pease Upham Goddard, who seemed born to take charge.

Madame Goddard, a strong-willed matriarch, had come from a family of thirteen children. With good humor and firmness, she cared for the multiple needs of the household. She looked after her husband, her son and his wife, an Aunt Czarina and her elderly mother-in-law Elvira Ward, who owned the house and wanted considerable attention in her declining years.

IV

Into this genteel and conventional establishment, Robert Goddard was born on October 5, 1882. Grandfather Hoyt across the way unbent enough to call on his grandson, but after a few visits he resumed his detachment.

Early the following year, Nahum gave up his job with the L. Hardy Company and returned to Boston with his family, renting and then buying a house on Forest Street in suburban Roxbury. In Boston, he found employment with S. C. Ryerson, also a manufacturer of machine knives, and later managed with another employee, Simeon K. Stubbs, to buy out the small firm.

Nahum invented a machine knife useful for cutting rabbit fur, developing a market among the hat manufacturers of Danbury, Connecticut. He also devised a flux for welding steel and iron, which he called "The Goddard Welder" and sold to New England machine shops. A short, dapper man sporting a large mustache, he was the firm's traveling salesman, at home in Boston drawing rooms or in Pullman smoking cars, usually preferring the latter.

While Boston's new trolley cars were going underground as subways, and electric lights were beginning to flicker on the city's streets, Nahum was installing in his home such fascinating new conveniences as incandescent lamps and a phonograph. He enjoyed his son, and stimulated Robert's precocious interest in invention, which was already vaulting ahead of childhood's natural curiosity. At the Goddard dinner table, Nahum often observed: "I wonder what they'll think up next."

When he was no more than five years old, the boy was already engrossed in the thinking up. He was enchanted by electricity, which was one of the wonders discussed at home. When his father told him that scuffing along a carpet produced electric sparks, he tried it himself. When he heard that the mysterious power of electricity could be stored and delivered through a battery, he took one apart. He tried to combine the two effects.

"One day," he wrote, "I obtained the zinc from one of these Leclanché batteries and scuffed along the gravel walk outside my house. I mounted a low fence and jumped." Nothing happened from this scuffing and jumping as he held the zinc rod in his hand. "Then I repeated the experiment, scuffing over a longer distance, and endeavored to convince myself that I jumped higher. My mother caught sight of this investigation and called out to me that I should be careful.

" 'Sometime it might work,' she said, 'and then you'll go sailing away and might not be able to come back.' "

His mother's words brought him momentarily to earth. He hid the zinc rod and forgot about altitude.

In many respects, Robert was shaped by Roxbury's conforming, middle-class background. The Goddard home, a large frame house, was on a comfortable street shaded by horse chestnut trees. The boys in the neighborhood called him "Robbie," regarding him as a lively, although somewhat sickly, companion. When he could, he joined in their youthful adventures, skating in winter in the Hemenway yard, which was flooded and frozen over, and tobogganing on the white slopes of the neighboring Curtis place. One summer, he persuaded young Ray Hemenway and Fred DeCock to help him dig a tunnel to China in his backyard. The boys dug for a week under his direction.

Through most of the year, school and church formed the pattern of his days. On weekdays, he went to Roxbury's Mount Pleasant primary school, and then to the new Hugh O'Brien elementary school, named for the first foreign-born mayor of Boston.

On Sundays young Robert was taken to the small, wooden Episcopal church of St. Ann's. When the family's fortunes improved, he attended the more splendid, turreted St. James's Church. He sang in the choir at both churches.

The adults who had stood at his cribside hovered, through his growing years, over the frail, handsome youngster. When Robert was twelve, there was a brief prospect of distracting the elders' attention. A brother, Richard Henry, was born. But the infant had a spine deformity and died in less than a year. Thereafter, concern for Robert's health was magnified.

His grandmother, Madame Goddard, was especially possessive. She also was determined that her grandson should survive in a day when only the physically fit were expected to survive. A glorious age was coming, she believed firmly, and Robert must be prepared for it. Her resolve was underscored at Sunday school, where he was obliged to copy the craggy verses of Archbishop Nicholas French:

> "While they who bid stern duty lead,
> Content to follow they,
> Of duty only taking heed,
> Find pleasure by the way."

His cheerful father, however, was not one to abide dreary New England precepts. A man of few but firmly fixed convictions, he taught his son by example that it was better to work for oneself than for someone else, that it was unprofitable to mind other people's business, that it was much wiser to mind one's own. Among his neighbors, he was considered unusually concerned about keeping his house and private affairs under lock and key.

Nahum liked to illustrate his philosophy with a traveling man's tale which Robert often retold. On one of his train trips to Canada for Stubbs and Goddard, he sat beside a proper Bostonian. En route, one of the kerosene lamps lighting the coach tipped over, starting a blaze. While agitated passengers rushed to put out the fire, Nahum's Bostonian merely pulled the emergency cord and sat back calmly to wait.

"Why don't you help us, sir?" a passenger indignantly exclaimed.

"Because," said the Boston gentleman, "this is the railroad's problem."

Thereafter, "lamps to Canada" became a family phrase, a reminder that life is simpler for those who let the railroad tend to the railroad's business.

Recalling Nahum's companionship, Robert described a summer trip they took to Worcester when he was thirteen:

"My father and I were great pals, and spent the time tramping through the country, I with a small air rifle and he with a camera. At times I used to watch him fish for horn pouts, and sometimes took a hand at it myself. It was my first genuine experience in the country, my world having been previously limited to our large backyard in Boston. The beauty of trees and pond, the interest aroused by the wild life, and the mystery of a road to the spring, that lost itself in the woods, all combined to make a deep and lasting impression."

As Nahum valued his own independence, so did he respect his son's. He supplied a warm and ready audience for the boy's enthusiasm, as well as the paraphernalia for his puttering, including a telescope, a microscope and a subscription to the authoritative *Scientific American*. At times Nahum lent a restraining hand. After the battery experiments, Robert wrote in his autobiographical paper, came a "real enthusiasm" for what he hoped was a splendid commercial idea. It had to do ". . . with a brand of washing powder called 'Soapine.' I spent considerable time in the summer of 1893 planning on a large wooden whale, to be carried through the streets on wheels . . . for advertising purposes. I took the matter up with a local carpenter, and everything appeared to be going smoothly until I approached my father on the matter of financing the undertaking, when the plan fell through."

If one plan failed, the boy quickly replaced it with others. He kept up a lively correspondence with scientific supply houses. He experimented with kites, sending away for the newest models, and on a trip to Worcester flew the first box kite anyone there had seen. He sent for optical devices which he tried out on his great-grandmother Elvira. "She was paralyzed and therefore excellent for my experiment," he wrote. "She could not get away."

The world of invention was bright and beckoning. In 1895, when he was thirteen, Robert read a newspaper report describing the "talking wires" of Alexander Bell:

"Very satisfactory experiments in vocal telegraphy were made by Professor A. G. Bell between Boston and Salem, and North Conway, the longest distance being 143 miles. Conversation directly was carried on between Salem and Boston, the voice at one end being actually heard at the other. . . . The fact seems now to be fully demonstrated that talking by wires can be made a practical thing."

To his enterprising mind, anything seemed possible, the less probable the better. He tried his hand at perpetual motion, contriving an elaboration of small boards and a large quantity of string. While trying to make it go, he showed the contrivance to a confidant, young Percy Long, the son of a family friend. The two boys were often together during winters in Roxbury and summers in Worcester and, while their elders visited, they talked out the long bold thoughts of youth. Although Percy was as unmoved by the Goddard machine as it was unmoving, he reported that Grandmother Goddard had eyed it in respectful wonder. Robert's devotion to "Gram" was no doubt based in part on her unblinking faith in his efforts.

Goddard's casting in all directions was, as yet, unencumbered by much knowledge. Later, after a long spell of illness, he referred again to his aborted perpetual motion device in an earnest essay he called: "The Disadvantages of Slight Education":

"Very often, a hunter after that exceedingly shy game, perpetual motion, has prided himself on the fancied secrets he, alone, is acquainted with; and has worked day and night, squandered his money, and then passed his last days in an asylum. . . . No doubt, if he had taken a course of mechanics in a modern school, he would have found that nature's laws are not to be violated. . . . The best plan for all of us to follow is to leave our researches and investigations until knowledge and experience are attained, after which our work will either be crowned with success or buried once and for all as an impossibility."

Toward the end of grade school, Robert suffered a variety of ailments diagnosed as colds, pleurisy, and bronchitis. He began to fall behind his contemporaries. When he entered high school in 1898, he enrolled for a curriculum of general science, but recurring illness kept him out of school through most of the term. He tried self-education. In the public library he found books on magic and electricity, on elementary chemistry and chemical analysis, on the atmosphere and the crystallization of substances. A book on carbon and diamonds gave him the notion for another project, to make artificial diamonds from graphite.

"I decided to heat some graphite in a small mass of iron by

an oxy-hydrogen flame, and dump the mass into water, subsequently examining it for possible diamonds . . . ," he wrote. While thus engaged in his attic "laboratory," a glass tube of hydrogen gas, thrust into the flame of an alcohol lamp, suddenly exploded with such force that glass was driven into the ceiling and through the attic doorway. Startled by the explosion, their servant girl screamed out that she had been killed. The family calmly assured her that she was not, and pledged Robert to refrain from the manufacture of diamonds.

During his last year in Roxbury, the restless novice decided that aluminum had more inviting prospects than diamonds. Charles M. Hall had recently patented his electrolytic method of extracting the pure, lightweight element. There was widespread speculation on its potential uses. Robert explored it for possible use in flight.

"Perhaps because the sky appeared so attractive," he later wrote, "I spent considerable time in thinking how delightful it would be to have a small balloon, attached to a thread and 'flown' like a kite." For fifty cents, he bought a quarter pound of the metal from the new Aluminum Company of America. Over the family's wood-burning kitchen stove, he tried to melt it in a stout ladle.

For weeks, Goddard's diary was studded with reports of his efforts to manage aluminum:

Jan. 8:—"Tried to melt it nearly all-day but could not."

Jan. 10:—"After school at night tried to melt aluminum again but could not."

Jan. 11:—"After school at night tried to melt aluminum in furnace but could not."

Jan. 15:—"Went to Plumbers but he could not melt aluminum. Tigley told me to buy it in a sheet. Sold aluminum back again for 50¢."

Jan. 18:—"After school at night, went & bought 3 ft. of sheet aluminum for 54 cents at Wilkinsons."

Jan. 19:—"After school worked on aluminum . . ."

Jan. 20:—". . . Went to Plumbers but he could not join aluminum sheet . . ."

Jan. 24:—". . . tried to have Bramhall bend aluminum . . ."

Jan. 27:—". . . cemented aluminum . . ."

His patience had by no means run out; his enthusiasm was barely tested. Finally, by February, he bent the metal into a pillow-like shape, furnished it with a valve, and sealed the edges with litharge and glycerine. Most of the chill, rainy afternoon of February 19, he spent on Dudley Street with a druggist's clerk he had persuaded to help him. They tried to inflate the aluminum pillow with hydrogen and then to launch it. The balloon refused to rise.

The clerk, he wrote, "caught a very severe cold, but I was too excited to do that."

He recorded the experiment that night in his diary:

"Aluminum balloon will not go up. Tried to put gas in it, but could not. Aluminum is too heavy. Failior crowns enterprise."

Thus he observed at the age of sixteen, blithely misspelling an early failure in a lifetime to be spent at trial and error and trial again.

v

The old century had only a short time to go. For the Goddards of Boston, it seemed about to end in disaster. In 1898, Nahum summoned eminent physicians to examine his ailing wife. Fannie Louise had tuberculosis—"consumption and complications," the bearded specialists said. She required total bed rest, nursing care, and clear air. The higher farmlands of Worcester, they agreed, might help.

Before the doctors left, Nahum asked them to examine his thin, long-legged son, grown to adolescence but already two years behind in school. The specialists allowed that the boy's trouble lay in his stomach possibly, in his kidneys probably, and mentioned the usefulness of an exploratory kidney operation, which Nahum and Fannie politely declined. They settled for an abdominal belt for Robert and another withdrawal from school.

Whatever the possible state of his kidneys, the boy found an escape from his family's urgencies. In the Boston *Post,* he came on a provocative fiction series and shortly obtained the novel, *The War of the Worlds,* in which he was soon absorbed. He would re-read it many times through the years, often around Christmas, as a rather extraordinary Yuletide gift to himself. The local newspaper had adapted the novel as "The War of the Worlds—In and Around Boston," in place of the original London locale.

The book's renowned British author, H. G. Wells, was then in vogue for his graphic tales based on the old, tantalizing vision of space flight. His work, as future science fiction writers would say disparagingly, was a prime example of the "whoosh-and-you're-there" school of science fiction. The book was later adapted by Orson Welles, no kinsman, into an American radio broadcast that panicked the listeners and sent families off in their cars in search of safety.

Young Goddard, back in 1898, was immediately caught up by the novelist's opening paragraph:

"No one would have believed, in the last years of the nineteenth century, that human affairs were being watched keenly and closely by intelligences greater than man's and yet as mortal as his own . . ."

It was heady stuff. Wells's description of Martians, somehow landing after a journey of roughly 140,000,000 miles, was impressive. The bellicose Martians, as Wells described them, were frightful, polyp-like blobs of brain matter, equipped with astonishing mechanisms for movement and battle. Goddard spoke of his discovery of Wells's Martians as

". . . an event . . . which provided me with all the speculative material I could desire. . . . It gripped my imagination tremendously. Wells' wonderfully true psychology made
the thing very vivid, and possible ways and means of ac-
complishing the physical marvels set forth kept me busy
thinking."

Goddard's sense of "true psychology" remained for most
of his life on this same child-like plateau. He would always
shy from deep introspection and the growing science of psychology. In 1932, when he was fifty and building the incipient space vehicle, he congratulated Wells on one of the
novelist's last birthdays:

"In 1898, I read your *War of the Worlds*. I was sixteen
years old, and the new viewpoints of scientific applications,
as well as the compelling realism . . . made a deep impression. The spell was complete about a year afterward, and I
decided that what might conservatively be called 'high altitude research,' was the most fascinating problem in existence. . . .

"How many more years I shall be able to work on the
problem, I do not know; I hope, as long as I live. There can
be no thought of finishing, for 'aiming at the stars,' both
literally and figuratively, is a problem to occupy generations,
so that no matter how much progress one makes, there is
always the thrill of just beginning. . . .

"What I find most inspiring is your optimism. It is the best
antidote I know for the feeling of depression that comes at
times when one contemplates the remarkable capacity for
bungling of both man and nature. . . ."

Wells's reply was brief and almost perfunctory:

"Dear Mr. Goddard:

"Thank you for your fine letter. It's the sort of greeting
one appreciates from people like you.

"Yours,

"H. G. Wells."

In 1898, when his mother's illness would bring
Nahum and his crowded ark back to Worcester, Robert's
grandmother spoke up with her usual firmness. Considering
Fannie, Nahum and the impending move, she announced
her intentions for Robert.

"He's going to be my boy now," she said.

At the old farmhouse on Maple Hill, Robert's parents
moved into the upstairs quarters, leaving the downstairs to
their tenants, the George Boswells. Later, when the Boswells
moved, Robert and his grandmother—Nahum Parks, his
musician grandfather, had died in Boston—also settled on
the first floor, where the boy was presumably isolated from
his mother's illness. His room was so close to his grandmother's that she could hear him breathing at night.

He continually admired his father's resilience. Although
Nahum bluffly tried to conceal his disappointment at selling
his Roxbury home and his share in Stubbs and Goddard, it
was scarcely a victory to return as shop superintendent to
L. Hardy, which Grandfather Hoyt had sold to new owners.

Living in the country had its advantages for Robert, although he was aware of distinctions between the suburbs
and the way wealthier Worcester families lived. Downtown
Worcester meant substantial homes and imposing churches
used mainly on such special occasions as births, weddings,
deaths, Easter and Christmas. The Goddards' frame house,
however, had no lavish trappings. In its kitchen were an
iron sink and pump, and behind the establishment a well,
an outhouse, and a woodshed. A coal-burning dining room
stove helped supply the downstairs with heat and, where
needed, Franklin stoves had been installed. The one in the
parlor was lit on Sundays, before company came.

The Goddards never moved downtown into one of the

"better" homes. It mattered little to the boy. H. G. Wells had opened for him another door. On October 19, 1899, he climbed a cherry tree in his backyard and dreamed a fantastic dream of the future.

VII

Like other autumn days on Maple Hill, the afternoon of October 19 was quiet. After his long rest-time in bed, Robert was glad to be out of doors. He stood for a few moments on the back porch. In the yard, enclosed by chicken wire, near the tool shed, was "Uncle" George Boswell's collection of cocker spaniels, two dozen of them, yawping and sprawling over one another, some nuzzling up to their mothers who lay sunning themselves beside the fence.

He went past the spaniels to the shed where the sight of "Uncle" George's immaculately arranged tools was "always a feast to my eyes." There he kept his own tools, oiled, sharpened, each in its proper place. He picked up his bench saw, his hatchet and a small ladder he'd nailed together, and headed down to the fruit orchard to do some pruning. He stopped before a gnarled cherry tree at the edge of a narrow brook.

There, in past summer vacations, he had contrived a plan for a Goddard Frog Hatchery, with himself as proprietor of the profitable enterprise. The brook would run a wheel to power an electric generator, which in turn would heat incubators. An elaborate arrangement of pools and waterways would meet at a brightly painted wooden frog house. He had made detailed sketches after studying a library book on mechanical drawing, but he had not yet approached his father for the necessary financing. The plan was still confined to his notebook.

He propped his ladder against the cherry tree and climbed into its foliage. He hooked his saw and hatchet on a broken branch, then paused, enjoying the smell of meadow and woods below, hearing the sound of brook and birds. Lying in the tree, as if in a womb of branches and leaves, he could lose all sense of time and space and immediacy.

While he was suspended there, a fantasy took shape in the mirrors of his mind, an image sharp enough to shut out the surrounding scene. A mechanical device materialized from nowhere, functioning perfectly. Faster and faster it whirled until it began to lift, twirling and spinning above Worcester and sickness and spaniels and fruit trees, upwards into space.

The boy was transfixed. When he collected himself, he began to prune one of the dead branches. But after a few cuts with his saw, he climbed down. He walked back to the tool shed and the house.

Goddard marked the day, October 19, in his diary every year thereafter, referring to it as "Anniversary Day." That evening, however, he wrote simply: ". . . trimmed large cherry tree . . ." He amplified the experience in his autobiographical notes:

"On this day I climbed a tall cherry tree at the back of the barn . . . and as I looked toward the fields at the east, I imagined how wonderful it would be to make some device which had even the *possibility* of ascending to Mars, and how it would look on a small scale, if sent up from the meadow at my feet. I have several photographs of the tree, taken since, with the little ladder I made to climb it, leaning against it.

"It seemed to me then that a weight whirling around a horizontal shaft, moving more rapidly above than below, could furnish lift by virtue of the greater centrifugal force at the top of the path.

"I was a different boy when I descended the tree from when I ascended," he wrote. "Existence at last seemed very purposive."

2. IF THERE'S NO LAW
AGAINST IT

In 1899, young Goddard had no clear concept of the vehicle, the rocket, through which space flight would come to pass. His first idea was that centrifugal force might somehow be used. His diary shows that early that year he had been speculating and experimenting with centrifugal force. On March 11 he wrote, ". . . made wheels for a centrifugal experiment." But when he confided this to Percy Long, his skeptical friend of the perpetual motion machine, he met discouragement. Percy had become a Harvard freshman and was loftily condescending. Dreams were one thing, science was something else, and neither Mars nor any other planet could be reached through schoolboy fantasies. Robert would learn this in time for himself, said Percy.

Percy Long was no scientist; after Harvard, he would devote himself to revising Webster's dictionary for the G. and C. Merriam Company of nearby Springfield. But Percy had raised an early voice of doubt, a voice that Goddard was often to hear. Later, remembering their talk, he wrote in his autobiographical notes:

"I laid the centrifugal problem before him. He said it was inoperative, but could not explain it so as to convince me— a circumstance which was, perhaps, fortunate."

There is no record of Goddard's having read a short story, "The Brick Moon," which was drawing attention around this time. The story was written by Edward Everett Hale, the orator and clergyman who had spoken at length before Lincoln briefly addressed a Civil War audience at Gettysburg. "The Brick Moon" was first published in the *Atlantic Monthly* in 1869, and in short story collections in 1870 and 1899. The tale was not as celebrated as H. G. Wells's *War of the Worlds* or Jules Verne's *Journey from the Earth to the Moon,* both of which Goddard read and recorded in his diary. In "The Brick Moon" Hale, like Goddard, imaginatively employed centrifugal force. It was his means of "launching" a manned satellite into orbit around the earth.

Goddard's former fellow students were going ahead in school. His own ailments, diagnosed and otherwise, had left him like the lame boy in the "Pied Piper of Hamelin," hobbling to reach the mountain into which his classmates had disappeared. Perhaps he dreamed of devising ways to soar over the mountain, covering distance and time as well.

The doctors, meanwhile, extended his absence from school. Each morning, hearing the door close as Nahum set out for work, he resolutely constructed a world of his own. He assigned himself a mass of hard reading in the physical and chemical sciences, some from Cassell's encyclopedic *Popular Educator* and *Technical Educator,* given to him by his father; some from textbooks borrowed from the Worcester Public Library. In his notebook he copied an aphorism: "If there's no law against it, why then 'twill happen some day."

It was a lonely time, although he was reading voraciously. In his diary he recorded his restlessness: scuffing shoes, kicking rocks down the road, climbing trees, peering through his telescope at night, collecting butterflies.

His immediate prospects for returning to high school seemed dim. In the fall of 1900, when he felt stronger, he enrolled in morning classes at Becker's Business College, a small institution which drilled its students in the commercial arts. After he had attended the school for a few months, his health failed again.

At Becker's, he acquired a fine Spencerian script, which eventually deteriorated to a scrawl under the onslaught of a mind that thought too fast for meticulous penmanship. He also fancied himself as a successful man of affairs.

For a time, he engaged in a curious masquerade, wearing a beige cotton jacket and a green celluloid eyeshade in the style of a bookkeeper. He addressed a series of business letters to his father as "Gentlemen of the Company" and signed himself "The Manager." Nahum was amused and tolerant of his son's proposals, such as purchasing "suitable land in the western part of the state" to establish the grandiose frog hatchery, or building a motorless airship which "could carry fast mails, if nothing more." But it seemed unlikely to Nahum that Robert would ever find himself in a routine business or trade. There was nothing routine about the boy.

In the well-ordered files at Robert's desk, an envelope marked AERIAL NAVIGATION DEPARTMENT grew thicker. He often climbed the cherry tree in the back acres, thinking again of space flight. The planets Mars and Venus were scarcely more remote than his own longings.

II

Toward the close of the nineteenth century, man was mastering the earth's envelope of atmosphere. In 1896, Dr. Samuel P. Langley, then Secretary of the Smithsonian Institution, had sent his unmanned, quarter-scale, steam-powered "aerodrome" into a flight of 4,200 feet. After circling over the Potomac River near Washington, the model landed gently on the water. During his early experiments Langley was writing learned treatises on "The Internal Work of the Wind" and "Experiments in Aerodynamics," which were published by the Smithsonian.

Young men around the country wrote to the Institution for Langley's scientific papers, studied them, and watched bird flight in their backyards until their necks ached. Among them was Goddard, the reluctant invalid, sitting on his porch, wrapped in blankets, examining the wing structure of a captured monarch butterfly and the soaring methods of swallows and chimney swifts.

He was determined to tutor himself, an enterprise in which he accepted no man's view as sacred. The more he watched, the more he saw, and he watched intently. He became engrossed by chimney swifts which "possess the greatest powers of flight of any bird I could observe." In a letter to *St. Nicholas Magazine,* which offered to publish the comments of young readers, he took exception to Dr. Langley's view that a bird, endeavoring to turn, "flaps one outer wing harder than the other, thus tilting the bird."

Chimney swifts, Goddard found, "push the wing nearest the center of the curve downward and the other upward, thus pushing against the air just as a man might push against the outer baluster in running down a spiral staircase." The rear feathers of its wings, said the bird watcher, gave the swift its remarkable flight control. Later designers of aircraft agreed. They would call the airplane's equivalent of these finial bird feathers the "aileron."

St. Nicholas, however, politely rejected its young contributor from Worcester. Edward F. Bigelow, an editor for the magazine, advised Goddard that he had "never given much consideration to the problems of flying machines," although he felt sure that birds were bestowed with a special intelligence by nature, which governed the use of their bodies in getting wherever they intended to go. "Machines," Mr. Bigelow wrote, "will not act with such intelligence."

Robert was not convinced. If man could devise a machine to match the bird, why couldn't he also fly the machine and provide it with his own intelligence? And if man could rival the airborne bird, why couldn't he surpass it and conquer space beyond the atmosphere? Was there really a law against it?

Cassell's *Popular Educator* suggested no such adverse law. Instead it offered, in passing, the three venerable laws of motion of Sir Isaac Newton. It was at this time that Goddard read and reread the precepts from *Principia Mathematica*. Sir Isaac's Third Law on action and reaction was especially interesting:

"Law III. *To every action there is always opposed an equal reaction: or the mutual actions of two bodies upon each other are always equal, and directed to contrary parts.*

"Whatever draws or presses another is as much drawn or pressed by that other. If you press a stone with your finger, the finger is also pressed by the stone. If a horse draws a stone tied to a rope, the horse (if I may so say) will be equally drawn back towards the stone; for the distended rope, by the same endeavor to relax or unbend itself, will draw the horse as much towards the stone, as it does the stone towards the horse, and will obstruct the progress of the one as much as it advances that of the other. If a body impinge upon another, and by its force change the motion of the other, that body also (because of the equality of mutual pressure) will undergo an equal change, in its own motion, towards the contrary part. The changes made by these actions are equal, not in the velocities, but in the motions of bodies; that is to say, if the bodies are not hindered by other impediments. For, because the motions are equally changed, the changes of the velocities made towards contrary parts are reciprocally proportional to the bodies."

In his reading, Goddard had accidentally come upon the key to motion in space. He read the Third Law again. It suggested an experiment.

"I began to realize that there might be something after all to Newton's Laws," he wrote. "The Third Law was accordingly tested, both with devices suspended by rubber bands and by devices on floats, in the little brook back of the barn, and the said law was verified conclusively. It made me realize that if a way to navigate space were to be discovered, or invented, it would be the result of a knowledge of physics and mathematics. . . ."

III

In September 1901, shortly before he was nineteen, Robert enrolled as a sophomore at Worcester's new South High School on Richards Street. The eager, hard-working student was received as a minor phenomenon by his younger classmates, who described him as a "shark" and twice elected him as their class president, an exalted post for which he equipped himself with a volume on parliamentary law.

He studied as though he had no time to lose, exploring the school library where he borrowed texts on composition, mathematics, mechanics, astronomy. In geometry, "Any proposition I could think of, I would try to prove." In English, he delighted his teachers with lofty New England precepts. He elaborated on Ralph Waldo Emerson's portrait of the scholar as one who took "into himself all the ability of the time, all the contributions of the past, and all the hopes of the future." In another essay, he dealt with "The Spirit of Inquiry":

"Science is a large part of the foundation of our civilization. It gives us the key to a clear understanding of the laws of nature, whose phenomena we no longer view with terror but with respect and admiration. It brings humanity closer together by means of the railway and the telegraph and the printing press; thus ideas and thoughts are more readily interchanged. . . . Yet science is in its infancy. It is but an outgrowth of man's energy, while the spirit of inquiry is part of his being. . . ."

Goddard approached science and nature with towering respect. "It is of value to study nature in connection with applied science," he wrote, "because nature rarely makes mistakes, and her creations are doubtless the most perfect of any kind that can be made under the existing conditions— the lightning bug, the soaring bird, and the fish. Thus we may try to realize what nature would do under the changed circumstances we desire, or under circumstances with which nature never had to cope."

If Goddard's prose was somewhat high-flown, it soon aroused the interest of Calvin H. Andrews, a stocky, energetic teacher of physics, a subject which students considered the most difficult at South High. Andrews' favorite advice to his disciples was: "Observe, observe, observe!" Robert found the course "enjoyable at the hands of this very delightful and capable teacher." Andrews responded warmly to his pupil's unbridled curiosity. They formed a lasting friendship.

In December 1901, after the Worcester *Gazette* announced that Guglielmo Marconi had sent a wireless message across the Atlantic Ocean, Andrews helped his students devise a Marconi "coherer"—a glass tube with two metal plugs inside and metal "tails" extending beyond it. Between the plugs were iron filings. When high frequency waves passed through the tube, the filings clung together, or cohered, thus permitting a battery current to flow through them and ring an electric bell. When the bell rang, the filings came apart, or "decohered." Through such impulses and agitations, the coherer's demonstrable effects delighted young Goddard and his classmates.

Storing up his knowledge of Marconi's accomplishments, Goddard went on with his own problem in a brief manuscript he called "The Navigation of Space." He submitted it to a journal called *Popular Science News*. It was promptly rejected. D. P. Doremus sent along a formal reply on January 27, 1902: "The editor regrets that he cannot use your valuable article in the near future. . . ."

Goddard's second aborted try at publication contained a major modification of his reading of Jules Verne. Unlike Verne's suggestion of a giant cannon firing a shell to the moon, the student modestly proposed to fire skyward the "cannons" themselves, a nest of them. Each cannon in turn would eject a successively lighter, smaller one, with the uppermost traveling to great altitudes. It was his pioneer proposal of the multi-stage space craft.

Again, Goddard displayed his curious duality: the bold dream and the personal caution, which, taken together, propelled him. He had ended his article on the conflicting note of doubt and hope, a disclaimer he felt was sound and scientific:

"We may safely infer that space navigation is an impossibility at the present time. Yet it is difficult to predict the achievements of science in this direction in the distant future."

Although he would grow increasingly reluctant to submit his visions for publication, he began to discuss them tentatively with his trusted teacher of physics, spending free hours at the high school laboratory and at Calvin Andrews' home in nearby Boylston. Together they covered the essentials of dynamics and mechanics and then moved into the heady province of space flight.

The teacher considerately muffled his own doubts as their

dialogue proceeded, framing his reservations as questions, which further aroused his disciple's imagination. Encouraged, Robert speculated with Andrews about meteor swarms in space, planetary landing fields, the likelihood of inhabiting Mars with its rumored canals, whether man could live in suspended animation. He began an intensive study of propelling devices similar to a machine gun. He wondered whether Sir Isaac Newton had been alert to the chance of reaching habitable planets which, as Goddard wrote, were "near our age and size, probably with strange costumes and still stranger manners. . . ."

The student was welcomed at his teacher's house. He attended weekend picnics at which Mrs. Andrews served coffee and sandwiches and heard, as she said afterward, "conversations that were usually over my head." When Andrews invested in a Stanley Steamer, he called Robert to see and help him drive it. On many summer evenings, they liked to sit on the Boylston porch, overlooking a substantial sweep of lawn, "speculating about the crickets, the fireflies and the stars," as Mrs. Andrews remembered. On an especially hot evening, the teacher pointed out that the crickets were chirping faster than usual. Robert and Andrews knew that the heat affected the rate of chirping. They drew up a cricket chirping chart which proved remarkably accurate in reckoning temperatures.

Before the year was out, Robert wrote in his diary that "the teacher of science has the power to influence the future course of a student." Andrews, although thirteen years older than his pupil, would say later: "My student has passed me by."

IV

Goddard was periodically brought back to earth by his family's welfare. His mother grew weaker despite specialists, nurses and the devotion of her husband and son. When he returned from school, Robert ritually climbed the stairs to visit her. As his graduation approached, she was happy to hear that he was chosen to deliver the class oration. He had humored her by agreeing to take dancing lessons. Although he found them tedious and time-consuming, he became fairly competent in the art. Often, he stayed with her until his father, easily shrugging off business pressures, came home. Like Nahum and Gram, Robert learned to communicate his own concerns lightheartedly. In a final "Report of the Manager" to the "Gentlemen of the Company," he wrote to his father with deliberate playfulness:

"The Manager is doubtless gaining in ability to reason, and to think quickly and accurately, yet . . . improvement may be made . . . the path to success surely lies over rough and stony ground, full of disappointments, failures and longings destined to unfulfillment. . . ."

His coming graduation introduced one innovation, a girl, for which science had ill prepared him. His English teacher, Miss Marietta Knight, had asked him to prepare his class oration on any subject he liked. He suggested a discourse "On Taking Things for Granted." It seemed to him an abysmal folly to take anything for granted in an age of magnificent possibilities. Miss Knight said that would be nice.

She also selected a female honor student, Miriam Olmstead, to speak at the exercise. Miss Olmstead's theme, "The Wealth of One Field," was to describe the wealth of nature to be found within the compass of a single New England field. In nature, Miriam suggested, one could feel intensely free, hearing the high song of youth, finding cuckoos in the apple tree, seeing birches reflected in clear pools and sandpipers wading along the water's edge.

A week before commencement, Miss Knight called her

two blue-ribbon speakers together to rehearse their talks. They met in Mechanics' Hall, a vast, bleak auditorium and a center for Worcester's public gatherings. The students were well prepared for the rehearsal but not in the least for each other. Miss Olmstead declaimed first. She was a shy, luminous young lady, with the beauty of some creature from the Italian Renaissance. Or so Robert thought as he listened. He almost forgot his own speech.

When Robert rose, Miriam grew equally fervent. She listened breathlessly to his endorsement of individualism, to his conviction that true wealth and happiness sprang from the bold and exploring mind. "It has often proved true," he was saying, "that the dream of yesterday is the hope of today, and the reality of tomorrow."

v

On meeting Miriam, he felt stirrings of young manhood, unfamiliar and long delayed. He wondered why he had never noticed her before. There were lost years to make up. For a time, his dream of space was blurred.

It began like a spring idyll. On a warm June evening in 1904, when South High's senior class held its graduation dance, they had their first date, the valedictorian and the salutatorian of the class.

He escorted her by trolley to the embellished auditorium, stopping in the town square to buy a corsage of red roses. Their classmates, Miriam recalled, were "surprised and pleased to see them together." That night Robert set down in his diary a most unscientific entry: "Miri . . . Magnificent time!!!!" He transformed Miriam into "Miri," the name of his love.

At the commencement exercises, they heard other classmates discuss "The United States as a World Power," which it was becoming under President Theodore Roosevelt, and the quality of American citizenship, which was essential to such power. They listened to the class song. A few months before, three melodies, submitted anonymously, were chosen from many for the final selection. The winning tune was by Robert H. Goddard, as were the two others. With lyrics supplied by a classmate, Sadie McCauley, the song resounded earnestly through the crowded auditorium:

> "Out upon life's changing ocean
> We have launched our barks to-day,
> Deep and wild the sea before us,
> Rough and stormy lies the way. . . ."

Courtship followed that summer, grave and measured in New England style. Robert and Miriam walked in Hadwen Park, an expanse of greenery enclosing trails, a pond and the bandstand where his grandfather had played, overlooking the city's cemeteries. On these adventures, they were capably chaperoned by Miriam's mother, who sat sewing under a tree while he led Miri to a cloistered spot where South High's biology class had gone bird watching. There, holding her hand, Robert said he hoped they would become "more than friends." It was, in the accustomed ritual, "an understanding."

The understanding led to a curious and tentative romance. Like Robert, Miriam had pronounced ideas of her own. She, too, had grown up near sickness. Her late father, Dr. James Olmstead, Jr., had been superintendent of the Connecticut Hospital for the Insane and had settled his family in a house on the hospital grounds.

While Goddard was drawn to the hard science of physics, Miriam was fascinated by biology and metaphysics. She introduced him to the hidden labyrinths of Browning and Wordsworth, Thoreau and Whitman.

The genii of physics and metaphysics looked on dubiously.

VI

While Robert considered his sparkling Miriam, his vision of space lost some of its sheen. "My own dream did not look very rosy," he recalled at the end of his high school years. "I had on hand a set of models which would not work, and a set of suggestions which I had learned enough physics to know were erroneous."

One Sunday morning, he bundled together a mass of notes, carried them to Gram's dining room stove and cremated them ceremoniously. Although the fire was banked as he disposed of his dream, it flared up swiftly. But only the papers went up in smoke.

"The dream would not down," said Goddard, "and inside of two months I caught myself making notes of further suggestions. For even though I reasoned with myself that the thing was impossible, there was something inside me which simply would not stop working."

3. ONE-DREAM MAN

Robert's diary that summer spoke, in one breath, of his plans for space flight; in another, of "Miri." Miriam posed new and unexpected hazards. She urged on him such works as Ralph Waldo Trine's *In Tune with the Infinite;* he preferred to reread H. G. Wells's *The War of the Worlds,* which he considered less elusive. She also demonstrated an unfamiliar quality, a mystical outlook he could detect neither in his mother, nor in his grandmother. Miriam's unfamiliarity made him apprehensive.

He did not question that Miriam expected marriage to follow college, although he tried to persuade her that first he must earn his doctorate, then put aside $1,000 as a reserve, and then get on with his research.

In his diary he set down in French a maxim she endorsed, although he rather disliked it himself. *Être et pas avoir.* (To be, yet not to possess.) At first, he regarded her desire for independence as he hoped others would regard his own. "After all," he observed, "a man who would hold himself back from marriage is in the same class with him who runs away from battle."

At the moment, he had no intention of running from battle. One problem of marriage was assuredly money. He began making sketches of novelties which, he trusted, would bring commercial returns. He fashioned a toy "fire fly" with a wooden body and a glass tube as its abdomen, filled with phosphorescent oil "which is made to glow." He contrived, among other devices, a reusable pen wiper, a "necktie press," an attachment to remove impaled leaves from garden rakes, and a mobile advertising sign powered by electromagnets.

After these fleeting inventive efforts, he tried to find a workable compromise between industry and the "dream that would not down." That fall Miriam enrolled as a biology major at Smith College in Northampton, already a respected institution for young women. He decided on a "practical education, from an economic standpoint," at the Worcester Polytechnic Institute which, he said in a freshman theme, was "pointed out as the goal toward which I must aim."

Worcester Tech was founded in 1865 by Ichabod Washburn, the Worcester wire manufacturer, and John Boynton, one-time farmer, peddler of tinware and manufacturer, to meet the city's emerging need for skilled engineers, mechanics and technicians. In the view of Boynton, education was meant to be usefully and profitably applied.

Goddard, thinking of Miriam, tried to accept this sensible view of education. He would put aside his dream a while longer. In his diary he recalled their visit to an astrologist, arranged by Mrs. Olmstead. Robert reminded himself of his horoscope as offered by this strange practitioner:

" 'Position, living salary, real estate when old, travel, fame. Take physics as special study. Get things to come to you.' . . . I have the life that is made or ruined by a woman. I must always follow her advice in everything I do."

He enrolled in 1904 at "the Tech," as Worcester called it,

after Grandmother Goddard obtained a loan for his tuition from E. T. Smith, a local wholesale grocer.

II

Professor A. Wilmer Duff, head of the department of physics, was accustomed to the attitudes of Worcester's young students of engineering. They looked to him for crisp, matter-of-fact answers, readily translated for the uses of industry. Goddard, however, was always raising questions. Electing a course in general science, he came to physics with an expanding appetite.

Alert and witty, the brush-mustached Dr. Duff had earned his doctorate at the University of Edinburgh and brought to the Tech the stern requirements of European scholarship. He was fascinated by Goddard's ferret-like curiosity, took him on as his laboratory assistant, and recommended him as a tutor to help him pay his way. Goddard's drive for knowledge, Duff suspected, concealed more than it revealed. It was at least a match for the teacher's own astringencies. While at the Tech, Goddard copied into his diary some lines from his reading:

"Anything is possible with the man who makes the best use of every minute of his time."

"Every piece of work which is not [so] good as you can make it should rise up against you in the court of your heart and condemn you for a thief."

"You cannot run away from weakness; you must fight it out or perish. And if that be so, why not now, and where you stand?"

Goddard's plans for practicality lasted only a few months. When his freshman English professor, Zelotes W. Coombs, assigned a theme on "Travelling in 1950," it set off a familiar reaction. Goddard responded with a scheme for earth travel, revealing again his talent for blending science and fiction. He pondered the problem at length. What, in fact, were the impediments to surface transit? One was friction, the grinding of wheels on tracks and roadbeds. Another was the resistance of air. How could he eliminate these obstacles to obtain great speed?

The train Goddard projected for the year 1950 seemed fantastic to his engineering classmates. It was intended to run inside a steel vacuum tube, its cars suspended, floating and driven by the attraction and repulsion of electromagnets. There would be no wheels, no tracks, no air in the tube to hinder the train's progress.

Theoretically, this freshman of physics observed, the train's electromagnetic speed would be limited only by the force of acceleration on the passengers, who would be strapped securely in reclining and reversible seats. At the outset of each trip, the train would accelerate rapidly, reach maximum velocity at its midway point, and decelerate for the last half of the journey. Some two hundred miles between New York and Boston would be covered in ten minutes' time, an average speed of 1,200 miles per hour.

The idea of "the fastest possible travel for living bodies on the earth's surface" always appealed to Goddard. It was an ambitious reach beyond the stagecoach of his ancestor Levi Pease or the usual all-night journey by steam locomotive between the two cities. A few years later, he recast his idea in a science fiction story he called "The High Speed Bet" in which he barely concealed himself as his hero, Maurice Sibley, who routed the skeptics by building and demonstrating the novel apparatus.

In time future inventors would propose a variety of similar schemes. Among them were the Americans Emile Bachelet and Dr. Irving Langmuir of the General Electric Corporation. In the 1940s Langmuir suggested that speeds up to five thousand miles per hour from New York to San Francisco were perfectly possible in a vacuum tube. By 1950 patents on the vacuum tube system of transport were granted in Goddard's name.

At Worcester Tech, various faculty members regarded Goddard's projects as unworkable, if not bizarre, while one of his classmates, writing in the school yearbook, observed that: ". . . he fairly revels in the weirdest of physics and kindred stumbling blocks to the less fortunate of us." But bizarre or weird as his schemes might seem, Duff rarely found a flaw in his physics.

Within the year, Goddard's interests were vaulting again. He never forgot the cherry tree in the backyard at Maple Hill, marking October 19 each year in his diary. He bought a number of green cloth-covered notebooks to record in copious detail his speculations on space flight, dating his concepts as they occurred to him. One day, he felt, there would be a question of priorities. With Professor Duff and a few other faculty members, he began to discuss, somewhat more openly, the fragments of his ideas. But he kept his goal to himself.

III

Even for an inventive man, the affair with Miriam was traveling at frightening speed. In almost daily courtship by mail and in visits between Worcester and Smith College, they exchanged such tender gifts as the poems of Browning for a gold-plated locket. Her mother and his parents had quietly approved of an eventual marriage, after a proper courtship. But the courtship ran on and Miriam grew restless. "Five years is a long time," she told him, a distressing comment which he recorded in his diary.

During the Thanksgiving holidays of November 1905, in the parlor of his grandmother's house, Robert gave Miriam a small diamond ring. They were engaged. His family, after a respectful wait, came in to welcome her and admire her trophy, which they had already examined. That night Robert omitted his diary entry. He did not resume his daily record for almost a month.

The following summer Robert and Miriam, through some mix-up, took the wrong train out of Worcester for Chesterfield, New Hampshire, where Miriam had arranged to study German and board with an erudite pastor. After a roundabout train trip to Keene, New Hampshire, and then a stagecoach ride, they managed to get to Chesterfield, where Robert took quarters down the road from the parsonage. It was the high tide of their romance. After Miriam's lessons, they spent long afternoons walking, talking, riding through the countryside in the pastor's surrey.

"Happiest two weeks at a stretch I ever had," he wrote that summer, remembering her "in evening near yellow lamp, her dress blue and white lace, with the fire-light shining on her. . . ." One day, Miriam spoke of a short story she was reading in German, "Alles Hat Ein Ende." Perhaps she was warning him. At the time he could see no reason why love, too, might end.

That fall, Robert got out an odd photograph he had made of himself and Miriam in his grandmother's parlor. In a whimsical mood, he had set his camera for a double exposure, producing a picture in which Miriam and Robert sat on a love seat in one corner of the room, looking quizzically across at another view of Robert and Miriam.

IV

At the Tech, seemingly unrelated facts clung to his mind like the iron filings of his high school coherer. He took the usual undergraduate courses, but displayed an unusual intensity, whether in mechanics or chemistry, calculus or astronomy. He was like a spaniel scooping away the fall leaves to find his way to some buried bone. The work of the British chemist, Sir William Ramsay, aroused him. Sir William had shown that the atom was not the ultimate particle, that it was subject to further subdivision. The electron theory of matter, posed by the physicist Sir Joseph Thomson, seemed to suggest an enormous potential source of power: an artificial breakdown of matter. There was no end to his questioning.

During his undergraduate years, fellow students considered Goddard a brilliant but acceptably genial class leader. They found fewer eccentricities in him than in their faculty, one of whom, making his way to a campus meeting, stepped on the tail of a wayward cat and absently apologized to the animal.

The professors, accustomed to engineers, found in Goddard a curious half-breed. After a battering of questions, Dr. Leonard P. Kinnicutt, his chemistry professor, demanded: "What are you trying to get at, Mr. Goddard?" It was much the same inquiry he had heard from Dr. Duff and his department. What was he trying to get at? Once again, he felt it was safer to keep his distance.

In the classroom, he held to his reserve. But in his private notebooks, Goddard was deliberately building a monument to optimism. From the outset, he considered possible hazards to space journeys. Would meteors endanger the traveler or could his hypothetical vehicle move safely among meteor swarms beyond the earth's outer voids? He groped for a mathematical answer.

Then, would landing on distant planets imperil a space traveler? Again, he saw more questions. A space ship in transit would build up enormous speeds, 5,000, 10,000 miles per hour, requiring an ingenious slowdown to avoid catastrophe. What sort of landing process would be essential? Perhaps, he reasoned, a spaceship could orbit its target planet at ever decreasing speeds and altitudes, employing gravity and atmosphere, if any, to reduce its speed, before an approach through a long and sweeping tangent.

Another problem in leaving this world for others was life itself. Our satellite moon was only a stepping stone, some 240,000 miles away. If one found a way to the moon, how long would the flight take? A few days? And to Mars, which was never closer to earth than 35,000,000 miles, how long for a Martian voyage? A week, a month? And if man could venture beyond this solar system to distant suns, how many years or decades or generations would be spent in such flights?

Here was a problem of man himself, given a dependable vehicle: to survive voyages far longer than any normal lifetime, even at the most abnormal speeds. So, then, came the final question—death. How to delay it, to alter its course? Death was no stranger. He had sensed its presence for years, on the second floor of Maple Hill, where his invalid mother was slowly failing.

Thinking of death, he speculated on how tissue and protoplasm might be conditioned against decay, how life could be sustained indefinitely. Late one evening, after visiting with his mother, he came down to his room past his sleeping grandmother, and wrote in his notebook:

"If there were some substance like formaline, which would permeate every tissue, and kill all bacterial life except the spores, and besides, the body were placed in a sealed glass containing nitrogen, and, perhaps, the temperature remained constant, and a little above freezing, there seems no reason why the body might not remain in this passive condition indefinitely, since decay is absolutely arrested from the moment the passivity is assumed, although the same amount of moisture is present, as when the body is active. . . ."

He paused over the exceptional notion. Could one achieve an indefinite suspension of life and then, at will, restore it, return blood to the veins, recirculate the fluids, restart the respiratory and circulatory systems? "If this plan is feasible, and there seems no reason now why it should be impossible," he observed, "a person can live a thousand years, and retain his youth for unlimited years."

The floodtide of spring was returning to Worcester when these thoughts came to him. He cautiously questioned his chemistry professor, Dr. Kinnicutt, who said that his speculations were interesting, but that lowering the temperature of the blood would cause certain death through the process of dialysis.

Robert accepted the verdict, but the idea still nagged. "It may be profitable to study seeds," he recorded next. Seeds might be frozen or buried without losing their power to germinate. And if this were so, could not protoplasm be concentrated, reduced to a granular or seed state for safekeeping? Could the decay of tissue be postponed through freezing?

Death and life, departure and landing. . . . Yet the first problem was still the vehicle, to get something into space. What sort of device would work?

"It became apparent," he wrote, "that bags of gas and moving propellers could never lift objects to really great heights—to 40, 50, 100 miles or more above the surface of the earth. . . ."

Examining the prospects, he wrote: "At present the thing is impossible. There may be some trick of applying things that are known, or there may be something that is not known, that may change this, but at present the thing is impossible. . . ."

Then he reasoned: "The less work I do on any one thing, the more things I shall think of. . . . In this way, if the thing actually is impossible, it will die a natural death; if it isn't impossible, I shall be most likely to get it first."

As he explored his theories, he seemed to be arguing with himself, setting up potential methods and then knocking them down. At first, he referred to his spaceship as a "car," to be propelled or hurled into outer space. And then, for a few years, he thought of it as a "gun," recoiling upward from the earth.

Could one really devise such a space vehicle, a nest of guns one inside another? The guns in turn would add increasing thrust; each gun, once discharged, would be "disengaged and dropped en route." He had explored the idea earlier. Once again, he considered his notion of a multistage vehicle.

Probing his own ideas, he went through periodic occasions of gloom. In 1906, on a March afternoon, he wrote and then pushed back his notebook: "Decided today that space navigation is a physical impossibility." But soon he returned to his recoiling gun, even though his mathematics told him it would require 56 tons of explosive to lift 500 pounds to a height of 2,000 miles.

How could he intensify its recoil? The gun must be redesigned. With a larger explosion chamber and a smaller opening to expel its gases, he might build up a considerable thrust. The gun, moreover, could be given a head start on its journey, carried upward by balloons or airplanes.

He speculated about new energy sources once the space gun was under way. "If sufficient energy cannot be stored," he wrote, "the only possible scheme will be to utilize the energy of the sun." The gun might be equipped with a concave mirror to catch the sun's rays, focussing them inward toward a solar boiler. If the vehicle could take on power in space, its initial weight might be lessened, its range increased.

Another possibility was an electrical gun, discharging ions.

He speculated on the method, wondering whether it would really work. It might be better to start with more conventional power.

His graduation thesis at the Tech was called: "On Some Peculiarities of Electrical Conductivity Exhibited by Powders and a Few Solid Substances." Professor Duff had encouraged the subject, seeing in it a sound approach to the development of radio. His student was apparently preoccupied with something, but whatever it was, he was unwilling to unburden himself. Perhaps Duff wondered about this as he considered the thesis. It was a well-informed paper. The lad really understood the principles of physics and how to apply them. He ought to be successful in radio engineering. In radio, there was promise enough for any ordinary lifetime.

But Goddard's undergraduate years were already extraordinary. In 1907, at Duff's suggestion, he had offered a proposal for the "balancing of aeroplanes" to the *Scientific American,* which published it. "So far as I have been able to learn," he said later, "this was the first suggestion of a gyro-stabilizer for aeroplanes."

His most important observations, however, were still in his guarded green notebooks and not for publication. The speculative harvest of his college years, they included the groping conceptions and misconceptions which would lead within a year to his rocket experiments.

v

Four years had passed since their meeting at Mechanics' Hall. There was little hope left for the affair when Robert and Miriam were graduated from college. He received his degree, "first prize, $75 and a handshake," he wrote in his diary, before setting off for Northampton and

Miriam. There, they talked through earnest and agonizing evenings before he added this entry:

"Our minds have grown apart in the last four years, and it will take time to bring them together."

Miriam guessed, perhaps correctly, that she had found a master at delaying tactics. That summer she left for a chaperoned tour of Europe, spoke distantly of buying a lace dress and trousseau, and suggested that Robert might meet her in Europe for their marriage.

Her suitor was more conservative than she had reckoned. There was an order, an agenda to life, he told her. His family must attend the wedding. He said he hoped she would return soon. He intended to complete his graduate studies at Clark University, live at home, and accept a modest instructorship at the Tech to support himself.

When Miriam returned from Europe in the autumn of 1909, he sensed a new conviction about her, a sureness and independence of spirit. During the year, she had studied at the Comparative Anatomy Department of the University of Freiburg-in-Baden. She spoke, as if enthralled, of listening to the lectures of Professor August Weisman on the continuity of the germ-plasm theory; she had reconstructed the skull of a dog embryo and written a description of it for publication in Germany. She didn't care much for Worcester and was only mildly interested in Robert's rocket activities. Incidentally, how was he making out with his space machine?

He wasn't making out too well, he had to admit, either with the space ship or with Miriam. Before she applied for a position in New York City at the research laboratory of the Department of Health, she stopped over tentatively in Worcester to see him. She wore an old hat, saying she planned to throw it away when she reached Manhattan.

"Oh, don't do that!" he advised her. "Save your old clothes. You might need them!"

When Miriam took the next train for New York, he already knew it was over. "The years forever fashion new dreams when old ones go," he had written in his diary. It was more a question than a statement. The space pioneer, feeling his old isolation, then observed:

"God pity a one-dream man!"

VI

At Clark University in Worcester, Goddard earned his doctorate and became a notable, if occasionally notorious, professor of physics. His association with the school began in the fall of 1908 and lasted through the many years of his rocket trajectory.

In the early 1900s, Americans were still streaming to the greater and lesser universities of Europe for advanced degrees. Clark, founded in 1887, was among America's first graduate schools for science. The Worcester university was a bold experiment: to match foreign graduate schools by offering high academic standards.

The university's first president was Dr. G. Stanley Hall, a pioneer psychologist from Johns Hopkins, who placed Clark's major emphasis on the physical and psychological sciences. He had successfully convinced the school's benefactor, Jonas Clark, to support his proposed graduate curriculum, in itself a psychological achievement. Meagerly schooled, Clark had intended to found an undergraduate institution for poor boys. When the school's main building was designed, it was said that Jonas Clark ordered it built on the model of Worcester's Denholm and McKay's department store. If President Hall's experiment failed, the building could be converted for merchandising.

During its early years, Clark presented Worcester with a brilliant array of scholars. In 1909, during Goddard's first year at Clark, President Hall introduced, for their maiden lectures in the United States, Dr. Sigmund Freud, the Viennese founder of psychoanalysis, and his colleague Dr. Carl Gustav Jung. The city was shocked by the visitors' frankness on "sex." In his usually detailed diaries, Goddard, the space dreamer, did not mention the visit of these eminent pioneers of the mind and emotion.

Dr. Hall's physics department was headed by Professor A. A. Michelson, the first American scientist to win a Nobel prize, and then by Dr. Arthur Gordon Webster. Michelson had conducted fundamental research into the velocity of light and, through his studies, was able to determine the distances to the stars. His work also formed a starting point for Einstein's later studies in relativity.

Dr. Webster, Michelson's successor, was an outstanding mathematical physicist, born of New England stock and trained in the classical German method under von Helmholtz at the University of Berlin. He was the author of basic textbooks on dynamics and electromagnetism. In the three decades that he taught at Clark, he saw fit to accept and prepare only twenty-seven candidates for their doctorates. Among them was Goddard, who would succeed him.

The professor and his singular scholar were opposite numbers both in personality and approach. Webster was flamboyant in his views, outspoken on virtually all subjects in all fields that attracted him. He successfully urged his accomplished students to publish their findings on the dire threat that if they didn't, he would do so himself. He set little value on practical or applied science, regarding it as a low order of activity, not much better than engineering.

Dr. Webster conducted his classes with strict formality. When the bell rang, he would enter the classroom, nod briskly and begin his highly polished lectures. Upon concluding his discourse, he went at once to his office where students, if they wished, could seek out his assistance.

Unlike his fellow professors, Webster never gave formal

examinations, but customarily visited the physics laboratory, encouraging his students to unburden themselves of difficulties, physical or spiritual. One observed: "He brought to us an ideal of comprehensive and exacting theoretical scholarship at a time when contemporary physics in America concerned itself largely with commerce." When another applied for study at the University of Berlin, he was sternly advised by the German department head: "I cannot teach you anything which you have not already had with Professor Webster."

From his mentor, Goddard received a deeper grasp of the fundamentals of physics, the nature of motion and matter, the principles of electricity and mechanics, of heat and light and sound. He attended the physicist's campus lectures on Faraday and Maxwell, on Kelvin and von Helmholtz, gaining new insights into his own explorations. Through Webster, he learned the poetry of mathematics and science, observing in his diary:

"The most wonderful thing in nature is the uniformity, that $2 + 2 = 4$, and that all the atoms of the same element are alike, and the constant development towards higher perfection, even if temporal and at times uncertain. . . ."

Unlike Webster, a fundamental physicist who saw in physics a quest important in itself, Goddard found it a means of reaching outer space. He resolved to test his vision, to produce the space machine, the unheard-of machine, or at least to make a start toward its production.

The compulsion grew. In 1909, during his second year at Clark, he marked in his diary the "Tenth Anniversary" of his cherry tree dream. He was then twenty-seven years old.

If there was any important flaw in his thinking, he looked to Webster to help him dispose of it. The professor had already cleared Goddard's blurred impression of Newton's reaction principle. According to the Third Law, nothing was needed by a reacting device to react against, not gravity, nor magnetic fields, nor even the air. Goddard finally turned to a reaction device, to a rocket, as a means of rising above the earth's atmosphere.

At first, Goddard was no less dubious of the rocket's potential than his physics professors had been. He had begun with an enterprising study of conventional rockets, which he found were inefficient. If the rocket's energy could be more fully utilized, stepped up from 5 to 50 per cent in efficiency, then it might really go places. In his effort to create a better rocket and find adequate fuels to propel it, he resolved to "set down suggestions" and "when expedient, work the subject up."

On February 2, 1909, he wrote down a tentative suggestion for a liquid-fuel rocket. It would employ the perfect blend of liquid hydrogen, the ideal fuel, and liquid oxygen, the flawless oxidizer. Although neither liquid was available in fact, both were readily at hand in Goddard's imagination when he outlined his theoretical breakthrough:

"Try, if possible, an arrangement of H&O explosive jets, with compressed gas in small tanks, which are subsequently shot off—giving perhaps 40 per cent or 50 per cent. To get even 50 per cent efficiency, it will probably be necessary to have small explosive chambers and jets, into which the explosive (not too violent) is fed. They should also be small in number. Otherwise a large mass of metal will be needed for the large high-pressure chambers, which will cut down the efficiency per pound greatly. . . ."

His first tests used more commonplace but, at least, "expedient" fuels, exploring homemade rockets charged with gun powder. These after-hour ordeals failed for lack of effective apparatus, although one produced a lively, pyrotechnical display. As he described it afterward:

"The only result of an experimental nature during this period was the filling of the physics laboratory with smoke one day when I ignited a mixture of charcoal and potassium nitrate in an attempt to find the reactive force of a home-made rocket. I have a feeling that my explanations were not entirely satisfactory to the instructor who came to investigate."

He summed up his various conceptions: the cartridge-loading rocket, the solar rocket, the ionized rocket, the hydrogen-oxygen rocket. He speculated about exploiting the energy of the atom, if it could ever be released, for rocket propulsion. Judging his brain children, he found them wanting:

"Impossible on the face of it" . . . "proved impossible elsewhere" . . . "not shown impossible in all its phases, but probably is so" . . . "may or may not be found impossible, due to difficulties" . . . "not of use in itself, but may be of use if combined. . . ."

In December 1909, he was still skeptical:

"1. Ions, not much hope.

"2. Gun, certainly very expensive.

"3. Jet method: expensive, and too difficult to carry out and to show enough interest to others.

"In short, all of these promise to be so expensive and difficult that it is hardly worth while spending time on them, unless there is certainly no other way."

He underscored the words: *"unless there is certainly no other way."*

In June 1910, Goddard received his Master of Arts degree for his thesis: "Theory of Diffraction." It bore little relationship to his consuming interest in altitude, nor did his doctoral dissertation, under Webster, which he began that fall: "On the Conduction of Electricity at Contacts of Dissimilar Solids."

He chose the latter topic, he admitted, "not because I was particularly interested, but because I considered that my previous studies on the conductivity of powders at

Worcester Tech would be of help—a belief which, after only two weeks' work, I found not fully justified."

Goddard, inadvertently, had become involved in an advanced view of solid state physics. Under Webster's requirements, he was soon working his way uphill through the properties of crystal rectifiers, or detectors, which were later to provide a short cut past the vacuum tube to form the basis of mid-twentieth century radio. His tangential study touched an area that a generation later included the development of the transistor and other related devices.

Webster readily approved of his student's original thesis, submitted in June 1911, but was especially pleased by his oral examination. Under a barrage of questions, Goddard was lucid on every point. "It was a spectacular performance," Webster said.

VII

After his examination, Dr. Goddard took the electric trolley from Clark toward Maple Hill. He was exhausted and slept all day, dreaming "the whole thing through" and awoke drenched with perspiration, in time to take his grandmother to a band concert at Hadwen Park.

The fortunes of his father at the L. Hardy Company had improved and Nahum, wishing to make his ailing wife as comfortable as he could, had built and furnished a house for her on Bishop Avenue, on the next ridge across from the old farmhouse. It was a frame house, painted brown, with porches on three sides and on both floors, making it convenient for Fannie Louise, now encumbered with arthritis as well as tuberculosis, to enjoy the open air. He had also purchased a Brush automobile, opening at the rear, so that she could be transferred easily from her wheelchair.

Robert continued to live at the farmhouse with his grandmother, who cared for him solicitously and listened to his ideas admiringly. "I shall never leave my home," she said. "This *is* a good little home, isn't it, Rob?"

That summer he rested, rode in the new car with his family, watched a motorcycle climb on Dead Horse Hill and attended Worcester's annual New England Fair, where he saw the first airplanes to land in the city. He watched an air race between a Bleriot monoplane and an Army biplane, which the Bleriot won. The *Evening Gazette* ecstatically but accurately reported the spectacle:

"It seemed as though half of Worcester County was in the city to witness the first appearance of the birdmen in the Heart of the Commonwealth since the invention of the heavier than air machines. Well over 40,000 people were packed into the fair grounds, and every hill in or near Worcester was swarming with humanity eager for their first glimpse of a real airship in flight."

In Worcester's excited audience, one spectator would later sharply alter the importance of the wing and propeller.

VIII

He spent an additional year at Clark as an honorary fellow in physics and then accepted a research fellowship at the Palmer Physical Laboratory of Princeton University in 1912. Dean W. F. Magie of Princeton assured him that "if any teaching comes to you, it will only be incidental. . . . Come along with any ideas you may wish to exploit and we will try to furnish you the opportunity to develop them."

Goddard was still hesitant about baring his rocket idea, the only one he really "wished to exploit." He needed a laboratory and time for research. But rather than speak of rockets, he proposed to carry forward an aspect of his radio studies, which he labeled formidably as "the positive result of force on a material dielectric carrying displacement current." It was an intricate, out-of-the-way problem, but acceptable to Dean Magie.

Goddard took rooms in Princeton, bringing his grandmother along to keep house for him. She had looked after him since his adolescent illness with a concern he comfortably accepted.

His project in the Palmer Physical Laboratory was precise and exacting. "Normally," he wrote later, "such a piece of work should require from two to three years to be carried out satisfactorily, as it was one of great delicacy. The force on a strip of hard rubber, as insulator, was under one six hundred millionth of a pound; a current of 3,000,000 alternations per second, maintained constant, was necessary; and no appreciable air currents could exist in the apparatus."

Each day, Goddard pursued his displacement current experiment in a sort of self-devised gas chamber, its doors and windows "stopped with cotton and a hydrogen generator introducing sulphuric acid fumes into the room." In the course of his work, he constructed an ingenious measurement device, a continuous tube oscillator, to measure high-frequency oscillations. The tube he constructed, a by-product of his experiment, became the basis of his oscillator patent, No. 1,159,209, applied for August 1, 1912, and issued November 2, 1915. The patent was an early form of the radio tube principle employed in Dr. Lee De Forest's celebrated audion tube, which made long-distance radio possible. In 1936, Goddard's patent would be cited as "prior art" by a young man named Arthur A. Collins, whose manufacture of radio transmitters was then being challenged by the Radio Corporation of America for infringement of patents by De Forest and Dr. Edwin Howard Armstrong.

"My nights were free," Goddard noted, "and I used them to try out the new tools of mathematics to learn, if possible, just how high the best conceivable rocket could go. . . . I worked on the theory of rocket propulsion, assuming that . . . an efficiency of 50 percent could be secured, which I later found by experiment to be true. . . ."

On November 5, 1912, Goddard joined Princeton students in a firelight parade to Woodrow Wilson's house. Former president of the university, then governor of New Jersey, Wilson had just been elected President of the United States. In March 1913, Goddard joined the student body and saw the President leave for his inauguration in Washington. It was a rare distraction for him. No sooner had the train left the station than he returned to his rooms and his rocket problem.

This problem was clear in his mind. He must "attempt, by theoretical means, to estimate what initial masses would be necessary to project a pound mass to various altitudes," as he later stated. "Books on steam turbines were consulted, and it was assumed that an efficiency of 50 percent was possible, that is 50 percent of the energy of the powder being transformed into kinetic energy of the gases expelled. It was also considered that charges could be fired successively in the same chamber.

"The result of these calculations, in February 1913, indicated that extremely great altitudes were possible, and that about 200 pounds initial mass would be required to project one pound entirely away from the earth, using nitrocellulose at 50 percent efficiency, or at higher efficiency, but with the mass of the mechanism sufficient to reduce the efficiency to this effective value. . . ."

Goddard filled pages with the abbreviated language of mathematics, the precision of proof for his rocket theory. He saved these pages of hieroglyphics, used them for a while, and then packed them away.

IX

Goddard was very tired. He had an annoying cold. At Easter vacation in March 1913, he went home to Worcester, to his father's house. Nahum looked at his son and frowned. He didn't like the sound of his cough.

"After I had been home for a day or two," Goddard recalled later in his autobiographical notes, "the cold became very much worse, and I had unpleasant spasms of coughing. These appeared to be less after my mother applied the old family remedy of snuff-and-lard to my chest. But the family doctor was nevertheless called for. He came and afterward brought a specialist with him, and both looked very grave, for no reason so far as I could see. I learned the reason when they told me I had tuberculosis of both lungs."

Following the diagnosis, he dictated a letter to his grandmother in Princeton, asking her to pack up every note and scrap of paper she could find in his quarters.

He didn't hear the doctors outside his room as they exchanged gloomy prophecies. If he had, he would not have believed them anyway. They declared, he later learned, that he had ten days, perhaps two weeks, to live.

4. A METHOD OF REACHING

When the physicians left, his mother in her wheelchair sat silently beside Robert's bed. Fannie Louise and her son, now thirty years old, were rejoined through the same baleful disease, the same solemn words of the physicians, the same indeterminate prospect. As the days passed and then the weeks, the doctors could not explain his staying power. The family physician said he "never saw a case like it," that "he was lucky to be alive." His will was beyond the detective power of thermometers and stethoscopes.

On March 22, 1913, two weeks later, Goddard wrote on a penny postcard to his grandmother at their boarding house in Princeton: "The doctor just came. Said my lungs were better and was glad I could breathe as deeply as I do—which is as deep as usual. Temp 101.8, but probably less than last night at this time. . . ."

After the immediate crisis, he began to treat his own case, the experimenter experimenting on himself:

"I reasoned that fresh air and oxygen were desirable in

the lungs, and I asked the family physician if deep breathing might not be a good thing. He seemed rather skeptical, as, he said, it might stir up matters. But I considered that slow breathing would not stir up half what a racking cough would, and I resolved to make a try. I also refused to sleep out of doors, in the damp cold March air, but remained in the room with the steam heat on and the windows open."

For weeks he lay in bed at his father's new house on Bishop Avenue, cared for by a nurse, Miss Margaret Doyle. Death was possible. What seemed impossible was to go at the verge of discovery, without leaving a trace.

"I was not particularly happy," he wrote to a friend afterward, "for I had worked out all this rocket theory on bits of scrap paper, while at Princeton, and I knew nobody could ever read my writing. . . ."

Although the doctors ordered complete rest, he was soon at work on his equations to show with certainty that a rocket could conquer space. His life and dream were now crystallized by sickness.

His packet of notes, brought from Princeton by Gram, were under his pillow. Before his fever dropped, he allowed himself an hour a day with his papers. "Even this was constructive and a pleasure to look forward to," he observed, adding: "It gave me an opportunity for the next step: to puzzle out the type of construction . . . needed to make a real rocket that would embody as nearly as practicable the ideal conditions of the theory."

In Worcester, a United States patent was a respected flag of discovery, a sign to others that one had been here. By May 1913, as he lay in bed, he was quietly converting his mathematics into his first rocket applications, entrusting them to his father for delivery to Southgate and Southgate, one of the city's reputable patent firms. Perhaps Nahum, humoring his ailing son, recalled the earlier letters from "the Manager" to "the Gentlemen of the Company." Doubtless Robert, setting out to develop the rocket, had little idea of the Manager he must now become, of the length and strange bypasses of the trail he was taking.

He began to record in his diary his slow recuperation: "Sat in chair, side of bed," and, again, "Walked to and sat in chair." Within another few weeks, the mailman Benjamin Cooper was greeting him each morning as he sat bundled on the Bishop Avenue porch. "He was very methodical," Cooper recalled. "When he began to feel better, he started walking up Brookline Street, a rather steep hill. Each morning, he'd walk as far as he could and mark the distance he'd gone with a stick. The next morning, he would try to go beyond the mark. Finally, by fall, he was able to make his way to the top of the hill."

As he walked, Goddard stopped on occasion to lean against a tree, a rock, the bank of a stream, touching everything as if to draw from nature new sources of strength. Thinking of space, he clung to the earth. In August 1913 he wrote in his diary:

"I feel as if I blended into the landscape, without hope, ambition, feelings or regrets. . . . I like nothing better than to go way off and lean against a tree or rock and become just a part of the landscape."

Several months later he wrote: "Through the fall and winter of 1913 and the spring of 1914, I was able to take daily walks over the beautiful wooded hills about the 'hermitage,' . . . and to think over my main problem. . . ."

Gaining energy, he reached for nature greedily: "saw bird's nest and partridge tracks". . . "heard a song sparrow, saw a grasshopper, butterfly" . . . "leaned against ash tree, woods pretty" . . . "saw a bat flying near pine trees in the grove" . . . "walked up on top of hill, stood under big maple, seemed solemn and impressive, like a church, trunk and branches columns, green and sky windows overhead. . . ."

His pulmonary tuberculosis, although remaining dormant, left him in frail health. He always regarded himself as an undependable and somewhat tenuous mechanism. "It's appalling how short life is," he wrote, "and how much there is to do one would like to do. We have . . . to take chances and do what we can."

II

As soon as he felt able, he made his first trip downtown to the offices of Southgate and Southgate, at 25 Foster Street. The law firm's most profitable account was Crompton and Knowles, the prominent Worcester loom works, which protected its novel textile machinery with a multitude of patents. Goddard was one of the city's few professors to seek the firm's counsel, arriving with a cluster of rocket proposals.

The professor was turned over to the lanky junior partner, Charles T. Hawley. After examining Goddard's patent proposals, Hawley observed that the ideas were ingenious enough, but that Goddard, like most young inventors, had tried to put altogether too much into a single patent application. This seldom saved money on patent fees, the lawyer said flatly. Usually it complicated matters. Lawyer Hawley would try to perform the necessary surgery.

The new client liked his lawyer's no-nonsense style. Ten years older than Goddard, Hawley came from Vermont, where reticence and restraint are carefully cultivated. For three decades, the two men would work together preparing claims for patent applications. After the inventor's death, Hawley would spend another decade on Goddard's voluminous notes for additional patents in his client's name. In correspondence they addressed one another as "Dr. Goddard" and "Mr. Hawley," with "Dear friend Goddard" an intimacy the attorney allowed himself during the scientist's later years.

On February 25, 1914, a letter from Southgate and Southgate informed Goddard that both his rocket patents had been allowed by the patent office. The patents were basic to rocket development. They introduced the essential features of every modern rocket, whatever its thrust or trajectory: the use of a combustion chamber with a nozzle; the feeding of propellants, liquid or solid, into the combustion chamber; and the principle of the multiple or step rocket. These concepts, broadly stated and often ambiguous, dated from Goddard's speculations beginning in 1908. They foreshadowed the future era of rocket flight just as the concepts of the Wright brothers and Langley foreshadowed the age of the airplane.

Goddard's patent No. 1,103,503, issued on July 14, 1914, described in detail a cartridge-feeding mechanism employing a breech block to inject successive charges. This was a method he would eventually discard as potentially workable but impractical. Among his claims in this patent, he also staked out priorities for other likely methods, giving special emphasis to "a modification" for pumping liquid fuel and oxidizer from tanks into the combustion chamber.

Two paragraphs from the patent are of particular significance, establishing the fundamentals of modern rocket construction:

"In this form I provide a combustion chamber having a refractory lining and a rearwardly extending tapered tube. . . . Within the rocket casing I provide two tanks. These tanks contain materials which when ignited will produce an exceedingly rapid combustion. This result may be attained, for instance . . . with gasolene and . . . liquefied nitrous oxid. As the latter substance is a liquid only at low temperatures it is necessary that this tank should be filled immediately before the discharge of the apparatus.

"In order to retain the low temperature of the liquid oxid, I enclose the tank within a second tank. The space between the tanks may be filled with a suitable non-conductor. . . . Force pumps are connected to the tanks . . . and combustion chamber by the system of pipes shown. . . . These force pumps may be of any preferred form and may be operated by any suitable mechanism . . . so proportioned that the proper mixture of gasolene and nitrous-oxid will be at all times fed to the combustion chamber. In this form the combustion is continuous and the propelling force is therefore constant."

Although Hawley had firmly counseled him against packing too much into a single patent, Goddard had added the claim on tanks and liquid fuels almost as an afterthought. It was readily accepted by the patent examiners in Washington, who could find no similar proposal in their thin file of rocket priorities. The inventor had posted his flags.

Possibly Goddard failed at the time to appreciate fully the extent of his rocket claim. With patent No. 1,103,503, he had opened the way to the liquid fuel rocket, to his own historic flight near Worcester and the dawn of the space ship.

His other pioneer patent, No. 1,102,653, was issued to Goddard on July 7, 1914, a week before his liquid-fuel patent was granted. It embodied his concept of the multistage or step rocket, vital to the future lifting of satellites or space craft. What had begun in his mind as science fiction was translated, with Hawley's help, into the harder language of patent law:

"What I do claim is . . . in a rocket apparatus, in combination, a primary rocket, comprising a combustion chamber and a firing tube, a secondary rocket mounted in said firing tube, and means for firing said secondary rocket when the explosive in the primary rocket is substantially consumed. . . ."

Beginning with their first meeting, in which these two patents took form, Hawley asked no questions beyond the

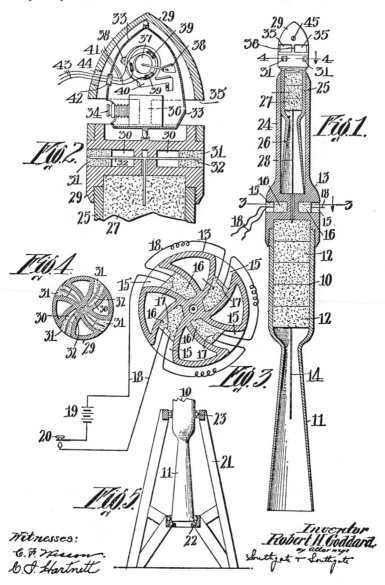

R. H. GODDARD.

ROCKET APPARATUS.

APPLICATION FILED OCT. 1, 1913.

1,102,653.

Patented July 7, 1914.

Fig.1.

Fig.2.

Fig.4.

Fig.3.

Fig.5.

Witnesses:
C. F. Nixon.
C. S. Hartnett

Inventor
Robert H. Goddard,
by attorneys
Southgate & Southgate

R. H. GODDARD.

ROCKET APPARATUS.

APPLICATION FILED MAY 15, 1914.

1,103,503.

Patented July 14, 1914.

2 SHEETS—SHEET 2.

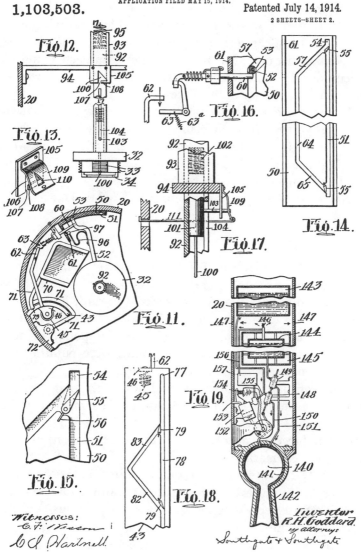

Fig. 12.
Fig. 13.
Fig. 11.
Fig. 16.
Fig. 17.
Fig. 14.
Fig. 15.
Fig. 18.
Fig. 19.

Witnesses:
C. F. Mason
C. L. Hartnell

Inventor
R. H. Goddard
by attorneys
Southgate & Southgate

business at hand. He believed then and thereafter that Goddard's objective was to produce a sensible, scientific means for high-altitude research. With all his Yankee shrewdness, or perhaps because of it, the lawyer never suspected, and his client never volunteered, that the Goddard rocket was an incipient vehicle for outer space.

"Since there was little prior art, the early patents were unusually broad in their claims," the attorney said in later years, after Goddard's first claims had expired. "They were original concepts, what we call 'blue-sky' patents. They covered the universe, pretty near."

And so they did, in ways unimagined by Mr. Hawley.

III

A few weeks before the rocket patents were granted, the Archduke Francis Ferdinand of Austria was assassinated at Sarajevo. A few weeks afterward, Europe was engulfed in war. In Washington, President Wilson, formerly of Princeton, was committed to an official policy of neutrality. But already emotions and events were pointing the way to America's eventual involvement.

The convalescing Goddard had long felt that he had something unique to offer his country. His mission, if he survived, was to create a means for space travel. His rocket concepts, however, also had implications as weapons of war. Again, he left markers behind.

On July 25, 1914, he wrote to the United States Navy, enclosing copies of his crisp new patents. Within three weeks, he had a brisk reply dated August 12 from Josephus Daniels, Secretary of the Navy:

"The Navy Department is very much interested in any weapons for use against air craft, or for use from these vessels. It would be interested in considering your invention if you would give more specific data and descriptions. It would be still better if you would submit actual samples of your rockets for a test. . . ."

The Germans, as Goddard pointed out in his letter to the Navy, had recognized the military application of the Wright brothers' airplane well before the United States. He wished to avert such an oversight with the rocket. He proposed that the Navy consider the rocket for airborne artillery, emphasizing that it would eliminate the problem of recoil. He also underscored its potential usefulness as a ground-based antiaircraft weapon.

After the reply from Washington, Goddard put the correspondence aside. The Navy wanted "samples." He was still under doctor's care. He needed time to recover from his illness, to catch up with his theories and to produce some samples for himself.

IV

In the summer of 1914, a neighbor said: "He is almost beginning to look like one of us." It was an overstatement. Goddard's long illness had left him bald and reduced his weight to 136 pounds, so that his suits hung loosely on him. He listened absently to the latest prognosis of a visiting specialist from one of New England's larger tuberculosis hospitals, in Rutland, Massachusetts. More than a year before, the specialist's report had led the hospital to refuse him admission as a patient on grounds that he had no chance for survival. Now the doctor from Rutland was more encouraging. Goddard might try working "moderately, avoiding overfatigue," he said. "If you can go five years, you might never have a recurrence."

The physicist had his fill of physicians and their changeable verdicts. He much preferred his daily walks up Maple Hill to visit his once indomitable grandmother, noticeably worn after her return from Princeton. Robert arranged for a

dependable housekeeper and looked after her needs as un-
obtrusively as possible. Gram had persistently declined
Nahum's suggestion that she leave the old house and move
in with him. She, like her grandson, had a full measure of
Yankee self-sufficiency. He was refreshed by her high spirits
and told her more and more about his astonishing rocket,
what it would accomplish some day. Before going home to
Bishop Avenue, he would stop in her parlor to play old familiar tunes on the piano. Often he left Maple Hill by way
of the backyard and the brook, pausing to examine the
cherry tree.

In the fall of 1914, Goddard was eager to return to Clark
and the laboratory. He had declined offers from Princeton
and Columbia universities, and several small colleges where
his energies would be absorbed by teaching. He needed
time for research. He mentioned the usefulness of a combined research and teaching schedule to two companions who
called on him during his sickness, Dr. John C. Hubbard, professor of physics at the Clark undergraduate college, and Dr.
Harold F. Stimson, Dr. Webster's laboratory assistant. At
one of their meetings, Goddard whimsically proposed nam-
ing the trio after another trinity—a suggestion that would
surely have appalled Worcester's propriety. In his play on
words Goddard was God, the father; Hubbard was "J.C.,"
the Son; Stimson was "H.S.," the Holy Spirit.

"Underneath, Bob was a free thinker and childish, just
like me," Stimson said years later, when he was research chief
at the Bureau of Standards. It was an apt definition of scientific genius.

Hubbard and Stimson, concerned for Goddard's morale,
endorsed their friend's special requirements. If President
Edmund C. Sanford was possibly unclear about the future
of rocket propulsion, he was a gifted experimental psychologist who believed that universities should offer unusual
opportunities to unusual talents. He was also personally

moved by Goddard's determination. He assigned him as a part-time instructor and research fellow in Hubbard's physics department.

"By the fall of 1914, I was able to teach part-time at Clark University, and thanks to Dr. Hubbard and President Sanford, taught Starling's Electricity and Magnetism three hours a week, and had a conference hour with Dr. Hubbard once a week, on the lab work," Goddard wrote in his autobiographical notes. "This gave me considerable leisure time, and besides walking, I worked out the theory and calculations for smokeless powder and for H and O completely, and began experiments on the efficiency of ordinary rockets."

Behind the closed door of the redolent Physics Shop, the new instructor explored the limitations of old rockets and studied ways to redesign and improve them. Enforced theorizing had preceded his scientific pilgrimage; now he was free to experiment. He suspected, not always correctly, where the troublesome reefs and shoals lay in still uncharted seas. Thus far, at the age of thirty-two, he was recovering his strength and gaining weight; his Clark workshop was well equipped; his optimism was boundless. Shortly after the university's registration day, he began to assemble New England's first arsenal of rocketry, both historic and developmental. In return for his letters to scientific supply houses and industrial firms, he received a succession of packages which he opened expectantly.

His growing rocket collection, beginning with his own tentative devices, now included an exciting array from the past and present—cardboard-and-paper sky rockets, the kind developed by the ancient Chinese, improved by the Italians, and used on the American Fourth of July for generations; ship-signaling rockets which produced an intense, long-burning flare; rockets of powder-and-metal invented by Colonel William Congreve, the son of an official of the British Royal Arsenal at Woolwich. Sir William's superior powder rockets were used by His Majesty's Navy in 1806 against Napoleon. They harried the Little Emperor all the way down to Elba. The British also employed the Congreve rocket in 1814 against the upstart United States at Bladensburg, Maryland, and next against Fort McHenry near Baltimore. But this time, the Congreve weapon was not enough. The British defeat at Fort McHenry was chanted thereafter in Francis Scott Key's *The Star Spangled Banner,* which sang of "the rocket's red glare, the bombs bursting in air" as symbols of American survival.

Goddard's next rocket shipments were no less enticing. They included metals, ranging from steel to aluminum and their newer, lightweight alloys; and a variety of the more promising explosives. The Du Pont Corporation sent him samplings of its smokeless powders. Correspondence with Hudson Maxim, brother of the inventor of the gun silencer, led to a shipment of Maxim's new gun powder, "motorite." In these weeks, Goddard was often so absorbed in experiments with steel rockets using smokeless powders that he forgot to remove his smudged machinist's apron before addressing his class in magnetics.

He spent most of the year preparing rockets for tests, both the older models and new ones he built in the shop. One evening, when the students were gone, he sent up a rocket from a wooden lean-to abutting on the physics building. A modified Coston affair, its blast and rainbow of colored smoke aroused the janitor, who came to investigate. Goddard managed to calm or possibly numb him with a learned discourse on rocket theory, offering the untenable conclusion that his trial rocket was certainly nothing to get excited about. Rockets, he said, and would say again, tended to be noisy contrivances.

Nevertheless, he took care to postpone further flight tests and began conducting, with as little disturbance as possible, a series of static tests of the relative efficiency of different fuels and rocket designs. He was comforted to find that his earlier estimates were confirmed. Powder rockets, from the Chinese to Congreve, were highly inefficient machines, converting about 2 per cent of their fuel energy into the thrust of their jets. When he improved these devices with De Laval nozzles, the sort usually employed on steam turbines, the thrust rose to 16.7 per cent. With every improvement he made in the nozzle, the fuel efficiency rose. By midsummer of 1915, he was obtaining an average rocket efficiency of 40 per cent, with ejection velocities up to 6,730 feet per second.

That summer, when school was out, he happily returned to flight tests, inviting his friend Stimson to witness the dazzling display. He chose the isolated and foliage-surrounded Coes Pond, firing off his small rockets in the early morning hours. His most successful performers were original designs, or radical modifications of earlier powder systems. There was enough whoosh, sparkle and bang to suit the "childishness" of any man. But Goddard was scientist enough to record accurately that his liveliest powder rocket, which lofted across the pond, had attained an altitude of 486 feet and an ejection velocity of nearly 8,000 feet per second before striking the opposite bank.

The flight tests at Coes Pond were soon completed, with their various clues and miscues for the future. But the vision still lingered. In his diary on August 8, Goddard recorded a bizarre fantasy:

". . . dreamed at 6.15 am. of going to the moon, and interested, going and coming, on where going to land respectively on moon and earth. Set off red fire at a pre-arranged time (and place) so *all* can see it, it was cold, and not enough oxygen to breathe, and saw earth once during return—South America? Used combination crowbar and ladder, used tripod arrangement, to hold, in position . . . during the transit. The light was rather dim. Not enough oxygen when I opened my helmet to see if so."

What does one make of this curious dream? Was it a subject for psychologists such as President Sanford, or President Hall, or Hall's invited guest, Dr. Sigmund Freud of Vienna? Was it merely an astronaut's nightmare, half a century in advance? Taken literally, was it simply a scientist's hope of developing a powerful rocket that *all* could see?

Goddard's immediate task was to learn what kind of nozzle would produce the highest velocity of gases in thin air. He was excited by the chance to demonstrate the theory that the rocket would operate without any air to push against, into the airless voids of space. Dr. Webster, who tolerated but was not yet engrossed with his former student's work, was one of the witnesses at his rocket demonstration. He believed that Goddard had somehow gone off the track, that he was wasting his time and Clark's shop facilities on a will-o'-the-wisp.

The rocket pioneer rigged up ceiling-high oval configurations of twelve-inch tubing. When Webster saw the towering apparatus, he exclaimed, "Well Robert, when you go I hope you leave all this tubing here," as Goddard wrote in his diary. Actually, Goddard borrowed a large amount of equipment from the Clark shop years later.

Goddard pumped the air out of his tubing and in the resulting near-vacuum fired small rocket chambers with various nozzles. "When the gases were fired downward, the recoil kicked the chambers upward, and the rise was registered by a scratch on a strip of smoked glass," he reported.

In some fifty trials, his rockets, set off *in vacuo*, increased their thrust by 20 per cent over those fired in the atmosphere. These tests, he wrote, would "lead in a comparatively simple way to rather startling results." He was elated by the experiments, although Webster, an expert on mathematics and other topics, was more impressed by Goddard's adroit use of the "Calculus of Variations" to explain the rocket's action than by the rocket itself.

As the months passed, Goddard grew dismayed at the rising cost of rocketry. He had spent all he could spare from his instructor's pay. His salary, increased to $1,000 a year as an assistant professor, was no match for the experiments he now had in mind. By September 1916, his meager funds were exhausted, although he had used all his Yankee ingenuity in shopping for rocket fixings, apparatus and technical counsel. Thrift had been almost as essential as genius. With the help of his father, he cajoled machinists at the L. Hardy Company into turning out machined parts according to his well-drawn diagrams. At Clark he sought out Dr. Webster's gifted instrument maker from Stockholm named Nils Riffolt, a graduate student in physics studying for his master's degree. In the tall, soft-voiced machinist, he recognized a man with great skill and respect for tools.

"The doctor seemed hesitant about asking for help," Riffolt recalled, "probably because he couldn't pay much for my services. He would come in casually, showing me one of his sketches. Pretty soon I'd be trying to work it out at my lathe. I could see he had a long-drawn-out research job. It was a lot longer than he realized." Although Goddard was not himself much of a hand at the lathe, he was a good glass-blower, a skill that was useful to him in his radio work.

In his rocket pilgrimage, the Clark university professor also called at a small Worcester industrial laboratory, specializing in studies of various fuels, whose proprietor was L. C. Leach, a graduate of Clark.

"It was almost impossible to turn him down," Leach later remembered. "Once he brought us two dozen of his gunpowder mixtures, and talked us into running thermal tests in our bomb calorimeter. We used it mostly for testing coal samples and didn't much care for testing explosives, which seemed likely to blow up our equipment and ourselves as well. But Bob lectured us on the relative forces of coal in oxygen as compared to gunpowder. As he said, coal turned out to be more explosive. So we ran off his tests, not knowing what he was up to, but feeling sure that *he* did."

Finally, on September 27, 1916, he openly solicited funds, beginning with a letter to the Smithsonian Institution, the nation's storehouse of scientific wonders in Washington, D.C., which had been established by Congress for the "increase and diffusion of knowledge among men." The Smithsonian's interests ranged from dinosaur's skeletons and archeological artifacts to famous inventions; from precious stones and fine-arts collections to a zoological park. A respected stimulator of creative science, the Institution was then one of the few agencies in the country which made grants for research.

"For a number of years," Goddard wrote, "I have been at work upon a method of raising recording apparatus to altitudes exceeding the limit for sounding balloons. . . . I have reached the limit of the work I can do single-handed; both because of the expense, and also because further work will require more than one man's time."

He described his rocket method, his calculations for mass, thrust, velocity and distance, and the results of his experiments thus far, which, he said, were "truly remarkable." He had achieved in his static rockets an efficiency of more than 63 per cent, "the highest ever obtained from a heat engine." The best reciprocating steam engine, he observed, gave only 21 per cent efficiency and the best internal combustion engine 40 per cent. His rockets reached a "velocity of ejection" of 7,000 feet per second or better.

With this velocity, he added, the rocket motor could lift a one-pound payload to 35 miles with a starting weight of only 3.6 pounds and to 232 miles with an initial weight of only 89.6 pounds. Goddard's computations were theoretically precise. They merely assumed an ideal rocket, which decades of development have not yet attained. But his theory, as such, was impressive and sound, and his optimism was irrepressible.

Concluding his comments, Goddard urged that the Insti-

ahum D. Goddard, father of Rob-
t, about 1898. [1]

Fannie Louise (Hoyt) Goddard,
mother of Robert, about 1898. [2]

ary P. (Upham) Goddard, grand-
other of Robert, about 1910. [3]

Robert H. Goddard, age five, 1887.
[4]

Four generations of Goddards at Maple Hill, about 1890. Robert's mother, grandmother, Robert, great-grandmother Elvira, and father. [5]

Robert with his mother at Maple Hill, about 190(
[6]

Robert, age 10 or 12 (1892-94), and as he appeared in the 1908 yearbook, Worcester Polytechnic Institute. [7, 8]

Goddard's photograph of the cherry tree, taken in 1900. The homemade ladder and "No Trespassing" sign are barely visible. [9]

A. Wilmer Duff, Worcester Polytechnic Institute. [10]

Arthur G. Webster, Clark University. [11]

G. Stanley Hall, Clark University. [12]

Wallace W. Atwood, Clark University. [13]

Charles T. Hawley, Goddard's patent attorney. [14]

Charles G. Abbot, Secretary, Smithsonian Institution. [15]

Nils Riffolt (left) and Clarence N. Hickman. [16]

Harold F. Stimson. [17]

GODDARD ROCKETS
World War I, 1918

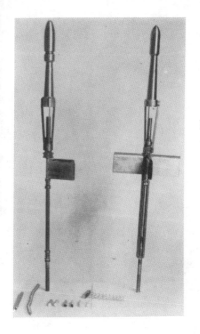

Multiple-charge rocket. [18]

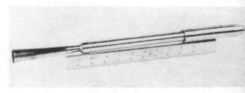

Single-charge rocket. [19

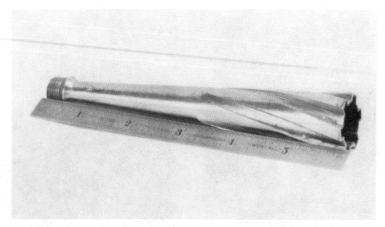

Grooved nozzle for rotating rocket. [20]

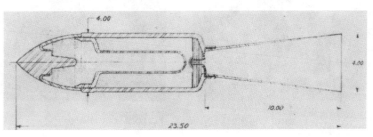

For use on planes against enemy aircraft. [21]

Goddard loading his forerunner of the "bazooka," 1918. [22]

LEFT: With tube used to demonstrate greater efficiency of rocket *in vacuo*.
RIGHT: With early rocket with steel chamber and nozzle, 1915. [23, 24]

At the blackboard, Clark University, 1924. [25]

Esther C. Kisk (later Mrs. Robert H. Goddard), 1917. [26]

tution "bring together a committee" to investigate his work and rocket calculations. Shortly, he heard from Dr. Charles D. Walcott, Secretary of the Smithsonian, requesting him to amplify his inquiry. The professor had already prepared a detailed account of his theory, and he now dispatched it to Walcott in a trim wooden box. It was an impeccable manuscript, bound in leather, with marbleized end papers, and its title embossed in gold. It bore the straightforward title: "A Method of Reaching Extreme Altitudes."

He had advised the Secretary: "It is to the Smithsonian Institution alone that I must look, now that I cannot continue the work unassisted." But he believed in the safety of numbers and also wrote, soliciting funds, to the National Geographic Society and the Aero Club of America.

The Smithsonian was interested. Fortunately for Goddard, it had a singular bequest from Thomas G. Hodgkins of Long Island, who had required that half of his gift be devoted to atmospheric research before the balance could be used for other Smithsonian purposes. Dr. Walcott, with an eye to the Hodgkins Fund, wanted to know how large a grant Dr. Goddard would need. Money was an important consideration. The professor had neglected to mention it.

V

Goddard was approaching a time of personal triumph. But as in many such moments, it came at a time of deep personal loss.

Madame Goddard, now in her eighty-third year, lay dying of old-age ills in her bedroom in the farmhouse on Maple Hill. She had seen a world of astonishing change since her birth in Northboro, Massachusetts, in August 1834. Even in her declining years, she sensed the accelerating pace of change and welcomed it.

Gram Goddard was not of the usual mold, in New England or elsewhere, her grandson reflected as he watched her life ebbing on his daily visits to Maple Hill. Out of the clan of prosperous Yankee Goddards, she had happily elected to marry one of the least provident members. She had raised their only child, Nahum, and his only child, Robert, to carry on the struggle, blessing each for his special brand of courage. To the end she was especially proud of her grandson. "You know," she often said to anyone who would listen, "Robert is really superior. The world will hear more of him."

To the frail boy she had imparted her abundance of love and pride, her firm belief in his rare qualities. None of the prevailing stodginess that passed as good manners appealed to her, he learned as he grew up under her protection. What counted was not the cast-iron deer on your front lawn, or the value of the stained glass in your staircase windows, but the strength you radiated from within. Tradition counted chiefly as a covenant through which men reached with understanding to one another.

She was alert to the end. He talked to her often as she rested, covered with quilts, while the housekeeper hovered near. He felt impelled to tell her all he believed in her fading days, how his rocket one day would offer mankind great danger but also enormous possibility. She listened gladly, accepting his hopes, helping him to dismiss his doubts, saying: "Well, Rob, we just can't stop where we are."

She died on October 17 and was buried on October 19, 1916. On that same day in 1899, seventeen years before, he had gone down through the unkempt field, past the empty barn to the brook, and climbed the cherry tree to dream of the future. Now he attended her funeral services in the farmhouse, and was last to see her before the burial.

"Went over to Gram's and saw Gram in parlor. Walked up on hill to leaning oaks, pretty, oak deep red, maples red and orange. . . . Saw cherry tree. . . ."

VI

In his letter, Secretary Walcott had asked for "some idea of the expense that would be involved in making your device" and also the time it would take. It appeared to Goddard that $10,000 might cover the cost of building and launching a high-altitude rocket, but he was sure this amount would disenchant the Smithsonian. Perhaps they would grant $2,500, which would hardly be adequate. He settled on a request for $5,000, specifying that it would pay for two mechanics and also an assistant "skilled in experimentation."

Seldom has a student of mathematics made a wider miscalculation.

". . . as to cost, I do not think that the work . . . could possibly be done within a time as short as one year for less than $5,000 . . . ," Goddard wrote Dr. Walcott. "It is difficult to make an estimate before the preliminary work is finished. I venture, however, to name $250 as perhaps a reasonable figure for one of the rockets. It might, of course, be more; especially if the altitude desired were as much as 200 miles; or it might even be less, if a number of the devices were to be made at the same time. . . ."

Although he had stressed a "sounding" rocket for atmospheric research, Goddard was soon trying to assure himself that his theoretical rocket, striking the moon, could be detected satisfactorily on earth. He undertook secret experiments with flash powders, aided by a graduate student, Henry C. Parker, and a new trusted colleague, Dr. Louis T. E. Thompson, who had succeeded Stimson as Webster's laboratory assistant. On a November evening in 1916, Goddard dispatched his friends, with various flash powders in glass vacuum tubes, to Effie Ward's farm in Auburn. Two miles distant on Maple Hill, Goddard waited with a stopwatch and a carefully timed schedule of firings to determine how far the flashes set off in Auburn would be visible.

Through computations that again proved overly sanguine, he concluded:

"It was found that one-twentieth of a grain of Victor flash powder, fired *in vacuo,* could be seen at a distance of 2¼ miles. . . .

"There is no doubt that a mass of flash powder, even of the order of a few pounds, exploding on the surface of the moon, would be visible in a telescope of one foot aperture on the earth, and even more clearly visible in a telescope of larger aperture. . . ."

Meanwhile, Goddard's "Method of Reaching" had aroused the Smithsonian. On the manuscript's arrival, Dr. Walcott turned it over to his Assistant Secretary and later successor, Dr. Charles G. Abbot, a tall, mustached astrophysicist who was engaged in exploring solar radiation. "Within an hour," Abbot said later, "I enthusiastically recommended it as 'the best presentation of a research project I had ever seen.' Dr. Walcott then asked me to get an opinion from a good man at the Bureau of Standards. I chose my friend, the mathematical physicist, Dr. Edgar Buckingham. He agreed with me and we gave our joint recommendation to the Secretary."

Dr. Abbot, considering Goddard's proposal, had advised his superior on October 2 in a memorandum written in long-hand:

"Goddard claims the possibility of reaching several hundred miles altitude!

"He proposes to do this by firing successive charges of smokeless powder in a special steel apparatus, whose recoil carries it up and up till the charges are all fired. The apparatus is to be protected in descent by a small parachute.

"I consider the method probably sound. . . .

"I believe there are several meteorological problems of great interest which might be solved by aid of the device, as:

"1. What is the composition of the highest atmosphere?

"2. How does temperature fall at great altitudes?

SMITHSONIAN MISCELLANEOUS COLLECTIONS
VOLUME 71, NUMBER 2

A METHOD OF REACHING EXTREME ALTITUDES

(WITH 10 PLATES)

BY

ROBERT H. GODDARD
Clark College, Worcester, Mass.

(PUBLICATION 2540)

CITY OF WASHINGTON
PUBLISHED BY THE SMITHSONIAN INSTITUTION
1919

"I presume such meteorological applications would involve a very considerable expense (several thousand dollars) beyond the cost of Goddard's device, and the cost of that itself may well be one or several thousand dollars."

"There is naturally some risk of failure . . .," Buckingham wrote to Walcott on December 31, "but that is a risk to which every adventure in scientific work is subject. It seems to me that a very moderate degree of success for Mr. Goddard's rocket device would bring about so great an addition to our resources for the study of the atmosphere as to be worth a considerable expenditure. . . ."

With these cautions in mind, Secretary Walcott on January 5, 1917, summed up the findings of Abbot and Buckingham in a letter to the Clark professor:

"We have verified the soundness of your theoretical work, the accuracy of the numerical data [and are] favorably impressed with the ingenuity of your mechanical and experimental dispositions, the clearness of your exposition, and . . . the value of that which is proposed. . . .

"I, therefore, have pleasure in approving a grant to you of $5,000 from the Hodgkins Fund. . . . You will report yearly, or oftener if notable progress is made, detailing results reached. . . . I am enclosing herewith a voucher and check to your order for $1,000 as the first payment . . . a list of expenditures should be submitted from time to time . . . accompanied . . . by receipted bills. . . . Should a larger payment at this time be necessary . . . so advise me . . . with best wishes. . . ."

"Read letter to Ma & Pa . . .," Goddard wrote in his diary on January 8, adding that "Pa" said: "You certainly put it to them in wonderful shape," and that "Ma" exclaimed: "Think of it! You send the govt. some typewritten sheets and some pictures, and they send you $1,000, and tell you they are going to send four more."

At Clark, news of the Goddard grant brought varied reactions. There, biologists were struggling for secrets of the roots of life; chemists for the nature and behavior of matter in reaction cycles; physicists for understanding of the mechanical, electrical, thermal and magnetic phenomena associated with matter. To these scientists, engrossed in their own projects, $5,000 seemed an astounding benefaction for rockets. A few were envious, decrying the Smithsonian for indulging in gadgetry, not genuine science. But Louis Thompson, entrusted with reading Goddard's manuscript, called it "a model example of an evaluation study" and later declared: "In those days, grants were made on far less evidence than Goddard supplied. They still are."

Nearby, at Worcester Tech, Professor Duff was delighted at the good fortune of his former student. He arranged for Goddard to use an abandoned and detached campus laboratory, originally planned for magnetic experiments, and recommended a young physics instructor at the Tech to assist him. In March 1917, Goddard began shuttling between the magnetic laboratory at the Tech and his classes at Clark.

In the spring of 1917, Worcester read a modest account in the *Evening Gazette* of Goddard's grant and his work on "a rocket . . . to make possible the study of the upper atmosphere for meteorological research." The newspaper account was headlined:

GODDARD WORKING
ON EXPERIMENT
Making Rocket to Reach an
Enormous Height

The city would shortly be hearing more sensational accounts of the professor and his experiments. Meanwhile, the rocket seemed reasonable enough. Clark often turned up new ideas and new ideas were good for Worcester. Besides, the Smithsonian Institution surely knew what it was about, paying out $5,000. Goddard, said Worcester, might be another ornament for the Heart of the Commonwealth. His activities were worth watching.

Some faculty members at this time felt these activities were drawing Goddard away from teaching to the detriment of his students. His colleagues were in error. Goddard, in his diary, recorded the reactions of his freshman classes at the conclusion of their courses in 1917:

May 31: "Class yelled afterwards."

Next day, concluding his course in mechanics, he had added:

June 1: ". . . class cheered. . . ."

His classes were an opportunity for him to teach. Devoted as he became to rocket research, he always enjoyed teaching.

A few days after he received his grant, the professor went downtown, stopped at a hardware store and bought a lock which he attached to a crate of his notes in the attic on Bishop Avenue. He kept the check from the Smithsonian for several days, admiring it, and then deposited it in the Merchant's National Bank.

The magnetic laboratory at the Tech, isolated from the rest of the campus, seemed an admirable workshop. It was a small stone building, some twenty feet square, with Gothic-style gables and a turreted second floor. He crowded the place with machine tools and drafting boards. Built a decade earlier, at the height of interest in electromagnetism, the structure had been erected without iron or steel. Even its nails were made of nonmagnetic brass. Its usefulness for magnetic studies, however, was destroyed when Worcester installed a sputtering trolley line on nearby Boynton Street. When Goddard moved in with his equipment, he covered the narrow windows with blankets. Later, suspecting possible espionage, he also installed a burglar alarm, although it was impossible for a stranger to see inside no matter how he approached the small fortress.

The inventor already bore the marks of secrecy. It was made indelible by a series of events that followed, beginning with the new assistant recommended by Professor Duff. "A humdrum man would just tie things up," Duff had declared. Goddard's new helper, whom he put in charge of the shop and two mechanics, was by no means humdrum. The assistant suffered from a back injury that required him to wear a brace and, despite his technical abilities, seemed prone to misadventures. One evening he lost a Goddard notebook filled with rocket computations. It was retrieved that night by flashlight, with the help of the distressed professor. Next, his assistant persuaded Goddard's mechanics to help him repair a car during working hours. Eventually the professor discharged him, reporting to the Institution that his assistant's work at first had been satisfactory, but that later "he shone less brilliantly."

The experience, coupled with events that followed, strengthened Goddard's inclination for privacy, his preference for carrying out his work himself. Again it aroused the curious personal duality which both handicapped and stimulated him.

After his classes at Clark, he devoted all his free hours to his new workshop and rocket experiments. When he came home to Bishop Avenue, it was late in the evening and he was often so preoccupied that he scarcely noted what he ate for dinner. Nahum abandoned his thought that his son might follow him into the L. Hardy Company and help him buy out the establishment. It was clear that Robert would somehow make his own way. At the dinner table, Nahum spoke occasionally of Robert's venture as "angel shooting," while Fannie Louise lightly inquired about his "tin gun."

The young professor had spoken with assurance of extreme altitudes to the Smithsonian, but in the months that followed, his device could not be counted on for any altitude, let alone an "extreme" one. His first major error was due to a lack of originality. He began conservatively with a breech-block, cartridge-feeding mechanism such as machine guns employ. His method, he believed, would be well served by a kind of ever-recoiling, upward-firing machine gun.

There were two principal flaws in this early approach: first, it was too complex; second, it didn't quite work. His cartridge mechanism failed, wedged and jammed, despite all efforts, as he revealed in his notes:

". . . gun bulged $\frac{1}{16}$" inside and $\frac{1}{32}$" outside. This probably means that the powder burns too slow" . . . "gun, when fired, showed ugly bulges from the pressure" . . . "breech-block jammed" . . . "to Tech. Gun blew up . . . Shopworker says, 'I no afraid of hell after that.' "

While enmeshed in this preliminary device, Goddard found that his circles of rocket theory, like the geometric circles of the ancient Archimedes, were abruptly disturbed. The disruption came from a Worcester businessman and America's involvement in the First World War.

VII

Up to the last weeks of uneasy peace, the United States hoped for neutrality, having re-elected a president who "kept us out of war." It believed in "business as usual," although business, especially in the metal trades, the machine and tool plants, the steel and related industries, was far better than usual. It believed, in event of emergency, that "a million young men would spring to arms."

The United States, entering the war in April 1917, did not suddenly spring to arms but to confusion. Confusion was by no means confined to Washington bureaucracy, but was shared democratically throughout the land. Spreading to New England, to Massachusetts, to Worcester, it reached the professor in his stubby Gothic laboratory.

With America at war, the nation's universities offered their services. At the Tech and at Clark, student-faculty meetings were held, encouraging young men to active duty and scientists to volunteer their skills. Goddard had long suspected that his rocket concept had potentialities as an antiaircraft and antitank weapon, as a mobile substitute for artillery, as a naval torpedo. But he also realized that specific and perhaps lengthy development was required.

Through the Smithsonian, he submitted a variety of proposals to the military. One to the Navy, in May 1917, suggested the possible development of a "submarine detector," an underwater sphere which would receive impulses of sound from submarines and transmit them to destroyers. There is no record of Navy interest in Goddard's pre-sonar detector.

Failing to reach the military, the professor in August that year was directed to a captain of Army Ordnance. The captain's enthusiasm greatly exceeded his authority. It was a strange encounter. The Ordnance officer exclaimed: "Can't you see there's millions in this thing for you?" He advised Goddard that he would soon receive orders to produce a quantity of five- and ten-pound rockets to replace conventional artillery, and introduced him to several officers as "the man who had invented a wonderful rocket." So Goddard recorded in his diary. "At lunch he didn't want me to talk out loud," the professor added. Aroused by this show of military interest, Goddard returned to his laboratory and waited.

After a time Goddard became embroiled in a more curious affair, which he tried, later, to dismiss as a sort of comic opera. But once more his hopes were raised, his humor frayed and his caution reinforced. He was introduced to a Worcester industrialist as "a man likely to help in the development of the rocket apparatus."

The industrialist, aware of the Goddard patents, wished the inventor to join him in manufacturing rockets for military use. Their first problem was to reach a mutual agreement. They never arrived at a second problem. The professor wanted the product to be called the "Goddard rocket," further patents to be taken out in his name, and an assurance of funds for future research. The talks broke down in a flurry of attorneys and registered letters.

The incident might have ended at this juncture, except that the more reluctant the professor grew, the more eager the manufacturer became. And the more his interest increased, the more he belittled Goddard, who heard of his off-hand remarks from a friend: "An impractical man with unworkable patents. . . . All he has is a nozzle attached to an ordinary rocket. . . . Anybody could do it."

Next, Goddard's detractor went to Washington. In the spring of 1918, the professor felt repercussions. He received an odd inquiry from the Atlas Powder Company about an order he had not placed. Suspecting foul play, he alerted the Commonwealth, which dispatched a detective, R. Nelson Molt, to investigate. Molt reported that the industrialist had ordered the powder made to Goddard's formula, obtained through a new employee, the professor's former assistant. The matter was aired in Boston before the District Attorney, who decided, finally, to stand aside.

The incident, however, grew like a toadstool in the dank woods. Shortly, a Signal Corps colonel, aligning himself with the industrialist, was in hot pursuit of the professor. He found his quarry elusive, unreachable at Clark or Worcester Tech or at home. Frustrated, the colonel threatened Nahum Goddard by telephone: "You can tell your son that if he doesn't come to see me immediately, I'll close up his laboratory, and he can put *that* in his pipe and smoke it!" Unshaken, Nahum replied: "Dr. Goddard doesn't smoke a pipe," and hung up.

By now the normally calm professor was highly alarmed. With a feeling of being followed, he boarded a train one stop beyond Worcester for Washington and the Smithsonian. His furtive departure, he would say, had thrown the blustering officer off his trail. He liked to believe Dr. Webster's report that the colonel had actually searched the train for him in Worcester. But he was never quite clear as to why he was being furtive or from what.

In Washington, Secretary Walcott and Dr. Abbot reassured the professor and acted promptly. Walcott telephoned the Army's chief signal officer, General George C. Squier, a physicist, inventor and also an officer in the Signal Corps, Aviation Section. Squier agreed to leave rocket development in Goddard's hands and offered financial support from the Signal Corps for further military applications. Abbot next discussed the affair with Professor George E. Hale, director of the Mount Wilson Solar Observatory in Pasadena, California. Hale sympathetically offered the workshops at Mount Wilson, assuring Abbot that Goddard would be safe there and undisturbed in carrying out his research.

Back in Worcester, Goddard hurriedly packed his bags, visited his dentist, and delivered one more patent application to Hawley. He unlocked his attic files and assembled his speculations on space, which he labeled: "To be opened only by an optimist." He sealed these papers in an envelope, deliberately mistitling them: "Special Formulae for Silvering Mirrors." He entrusted the packet to his friend Louis Thompson, who locked it away in a safe.

The Worcester space dreamer left by train for California, his first long journey away from home. Leaving sickness, family and New England behind, he found the trip exhilarating. In Chicago, he was amused by a porter who suddenly abandoned his baggage when Goddard lightly remarked: "Easy there, *that* suitcase is full of TNT!" In Dodge City, Iowa, an obliging stationmaster held the train briefly while his passenger observed a timely eclipse of the sun, writing in his diary: "Corona looked yellow and extended outside the diameter of the sun on one side." He arrived in Pasadena refreshed.

In the Mount Wilson workshops, Goddard set up his experiments under an allotment of $20,000 which the Signal Corps advanced to the Smithsonian Institution for his research. His assignment was broad in scope: to explore the military possibilities of rockets. It was several months before the industrialist or the colonel had the slightest notion of where he had gone.

At Mount Wilson, Goddard worked with Dr. Parker, who had assisted him with his flash powder experiments at Auburn, and with Clarence N. Hickman, a young and highly inventive graduate student from Clark, recommended by Thompson. Hickman was an amateur archer and magician, who said that his chief interest in physics was to learn new magical effects. Hickman needed his magic.

Goddard and his colleagues marked out two studies for their Signal Corps project. Parker was asked to help develop the rocket as a short-range, single-charge projectile. Hickman was given Goddard's multiple-charge machine-gun rocket system.

Hickman's task was the more perplexing. "It won't work, Dr. Goddard, because it's simply unworkable," he had declared. "Whenever a charge goes off, it leaves a gummy residue that jams your loading mechanism. On top of that, you're generating enormous pressures that freeze up your breech block."

Goddard admired Hickman's directness and asked him to mull over the problem.

"I went home and thought about the doctor's assignment, but the more I thought about it, the more impossible it seemed," his assistant recalled. "Finally I went to bed. About two o'clock, I woke up from a vivid dream and made some sketches. The solution was to do away with the breech block altogether and feed the cartridges from a magazine into the combustion chamber through the nozzle rather than the breech end. We'd do this with a piston which would be operated by the force of the discharged gases. After each firing, it would feed in the next cartridge. In the morning, I told Dr. Goddard about this gas piston idea. He was very enthusiastic and asked me to go ahead."

During this trial-and-error period, Goddard often recalled the words of Dr. Abbot: *"If you can make your rocket out of a tin can and a piece of string, you'll really have something."* Parker's project was difficult enough; Hickman's objective, despite his dream, almost defied solution. In his diary, Goddard recorded the experiments and the unpredictable results:

"July 22. Hickman fired three shots. . . .

"July 25. Parker tried firing device in am. Hickman had cartridge in magazine explode. . . . Tried black powder apparatus (broke off at joint of nozzle, and cartridge exploded up in the magazine tube). . . .

"July 26. Hickman tried 23.5 gms closely wrapped cartridges in $\frac{1}{8}$" chamber. . . . It bulged slightly where it rested. Vel. 4,600. About 27 gms split it open where it bulged previously. . . .

"July 28. Sunday, tried chamber with firing device and 70 gms, wobbled, and with fuse and 70 gms, went straight and farther, but lost it. Hunted for it. . . .

"July 29. Hickman tried two cartridges, one exploded in the magazine, jammed or detonated from shock, etc. . . .

"August 3. Hickman's magazine blew up again. Tried blasting caps on outside of nozzle . . . all blew up directly . . . showing sympathetic vibration. . . ."

These trials caused the first of three accidents in Goddard's long career of experimentation. They all happened to Hickman. He was taking apart a faulty rocket, believing he had forgotten to insert a percussion cap. "I started to tear the paper seal away. Evidently I had not forgotten to put the percussion cap in. My activity made the charge go off in my hands." He lost a part of three fingers and a thumb. An enthusiastic clarinet player, as well as magician, Hickman was now limited in both arts, although he later built a clarinet which he could play with his damaged hand.

After the bandages from the first accident were removed, Hickman was sifting phosphorus through a screen when friction ignited the chemical, burning his hands again. Within a few months, while testing a rocket for demonstration, he cradled the launcher under his arm to prove its safety and versatility, fired it and watched with satisfaction as it struck its target. He reached for his note pad in his breast pocket. The pocket had vanished. Instead of going through the launcher, the rocket had split the tube and gone through his jacket.

VIII

Far from home, the bachelor Goddard, now in his mid-thirties, emerged from his workshop with a sudden but unreciprocated interest in young ladies. According to his diary, he was noticing salesgirls, waitresses, clerks, Western Union typists. One evening, he met a telegraph operator in McCoy's Cafeteria and asked her to go with him to the theater. She declined. The next day, he recorded, he saw her with a much younger man. Another young girl, a waitress at the Hotel Marengo, seemed to regard him as an elderly man, a distinction that did not appeal to him.

One evening after dinner alone at an inn on the summit of Mount Lowe, he started off by foot for Mount Wilson Observatory. It was a splendid expedition, he wrote in his diary:

"Sunset, with purple mountains and misty half way up, pretty. Lost trail at the 'deer park.' Found it again, but went at right angles to observatory. Made fire in clearing. . . . Breeze from south in tops of pines and live oaks. Stars very clear against a dark background—like on a winter night. Saw meteors (Perseids). Heard large animal, soft tread, in eve. and near morning. In eve, before the fire was lighted, what sounded like rattlers, probably wood rats. Saw one.

"August 14. Reconnoitered at daylight. Looked south on

sea of fog, pearly white, curled up where it reached edge of mountain, distant mountain shown above. Saw sunrise, mountains purple, with yellow rim. . . . Great."

A few days after Goddard's return, Dr. Hale at the Observatory suggested a trial exhibition of the rockets. Considering its manifold problems, Hickman's gas piston device behaved unusually well. In a canyon below the Observatory, it soared nicely upward, landing 250 feet beyond the lip of the canyon, burying into the ground. One of Parker's rockets blasted across the canyon and knocked out a sizeable wedge from a granite boulder. "They all jumped at the first shot," Goddard recorded. "Then Hale shook hands and said he would send a good, strong report to Washington. Hale's assistant said: 'Prettiest thing I ever saw, to see that come flashing up over the canyon.' "

In September 1918, two skeptical Signal Corps officers came to see what their professor was up to. He quietly showed them his developments—the multiple-charge device, which needed a "little" improvement; and the single-charge projectiles which, he felt, were ready for production. One of these, employing nitroglycerin powder, could be used in trench warfare. Its charge was burned completely while the rocket passed through the tube of a thin steel launcher. It could be fired safely and without recoil by a doughboy in the field. The largest of these rockets, Goddard pointed out, was a three-inch model which could carry an eight-pound payload three-quarters of a mile. With more development, its range could be stepped up considerably.

Then he took the officers to the canyon to show them what he was talking about. That evening he wrote down their comments:

"We thought it was going to be some kind of toy."

"Don't you know that the stuff you've got there is going to revolutionize warfare?"

Yes, Dr. Goddard had said, he supposed it would.

IX

In the first week of November 1918, Goddard and his assistants came east to demonstrate their rockets at the Army's wooded proving grounds at Aberdeen, Maryland. Their audience was a select but representative one. Army Ordnance was there in its varied sections, from Aircraft Armaments to Trench Warfare. The Navy's chief of the Bureau of Ordnance sent his regrets but dispatched his next-in-command. Also present were the director of the Bureau of Standards, a professor from Dartmouth University, and Dr. Abbot of the Smithsonian Institution.

For two days they watched a display of the wartime works of America's rocket pioneer. Neither his audience nor his own assistants knew that Goddard's ultimate purpose was not a horizontal missile against an enemy, but a vertical rocket for outer space.

The program notes briefly described his offering: a 1-inch, a 2-inch and a 3-inch tube launcher, each 5.5 feet long, and designed to fire rocket projectiles of 5 pounds, 7.5 pounds and 50 pounds respectively. In practice, they would be fired by an electric mechanism, which Goddard had not yet had time to perfect, so that the demonstration projectiles would be detonated manually.

In addition, the professor would demonstrate the rocket's effectiveness when fired from a trench mortar; how it could be cut for lands and grooves to give it a stabilizing spin, similar to an artillery shell; and also a novel and still highly experimental device, a multiple-charge rocket, which would gain velocity as it traveled through the air.

Goddard left the implications of rocket propulsion to his audience and to the expert showmanship of Clarence Hickman. For Hickman, a master of insouciance and timing, there was seldom a better opportunity to display his magical effects.

"I fired the rockets in various ways," he remembered. "I

held the launchers in my hands, under my arms, in slender supports. Every rocket went farther than the Army's trench mortar. They seemed pretty impressed.

"Next, we set up two music stands about two feet apart. We had replaced their racks with wooden Y frames and to each we attached a ring. When the stands were in place, I slipped a two-inch launcher tube through the rings and then inserted the rocket. Ahead, uprange, was a revetment consisting of a sandbox and layers of sandbags behind it. I lit the fuse and the rocket roared ahead, plunging into the revetment, well into the third layer of sandbags. Meanwhile, the launchers stayed intact on the music stands. They hadn't budged an inch."

Goddard and Hickman had demonstrated the infantryman's personal artillery. Further development would put the principle to use, some twenty-five years later, as the tank-killing bazooka projector of the Second World War. Briefly, Goddard had proved the virtues of the recoilless rocket—as a weapon for the individual soldier, as prime armament for Army and Navy aircraft, and for many other applications.

Turning to artillery, the professor and his assistants showed that the rocket could gain considerable thrust with just a little recoil. Hickman, enjoying the effect on his audience, attached more constricted nozzles to the rockets, getting more thrust and added range after they left the launcher.

The demonstration was notably effective, the observers agreed. There was no question but that rockets would affect future warfare. The Army's Aircraft Armament Section urged Goddard to proceed at once to develop a six-inch, high-velocity rocket to be fired from planes. A special appropriation, he was assured, would be forthcoming.

So said the armed services on November 7, 1918. Four days later, Germany surrendered. The First World War was over. The rocket, as a weapon, was almost forgotten in the United States until the next war.

5. HOW IS YOUR MOON-GOING ROCKET?

After the Armistice, Goddard returned to Worcester and his classes at Clark. He appeared the model of a Massachusetts pedagogue. At thirty-six years, he wore clothes respectably aged and drab in color, casually well fitted, with the stiff white collar and conservative silk cravat of the period. As if to strike a balance for his baldness, he had grown a mustache which he kept close-cropped.

In lecturing his students, he was enthusiastic, with occasional interjections of whimsy. He especially enjoyed demonstrating the principles of physics with apparatus he carefully arranged. After a particularly successful classroom demonstration, he sometimes underscored his effects by stepping to the window, staring out at the campus clock tower and whistling: "It's a Long Way to Tipperary."

In all but one respect, he blended as comfortably into his surroundings as a New England cod. Neither his students nor his closest associates were aware of his aberration. None knew that attaining a vehicle for outer space was the core of his being, his central disturbance much as the central disturbance of Columbus was obtaining ships seaworthy for the Indies.

In the postwar years there was great excitement among scientists in both theoretical and applied physics. In Germany, Professor Albert Einstein released his theory of time, space and energy. Among those who grasped the significance of the new theory, Goddard consented to lecture to small faculty and other groups on Einstein's relativity and why it required a thorough re-evaluation of known physical principles.

Other research men were convinced that the venerable atom consisted of smaller particles and was subject to change, possibly violent change. Goddard, in discussing this possibility before his classes and in his private notes, underscored the idea that the atom itself might one day furnish a source of power, power for rockets, perhaps.

Meanwhile, the wireless radio had emerged from its swaddling clothes and was improving constantly. In 1923, the possibility of transmitting pictures with sound became apparent with the new iconoscope tube of Vladimir Zworykin, the Russian emigré to the United States. Goddard added some notes to his file on potential methods of rocket communication with the earth.

He raised donations of $800 from Worcester businessmen for a Clark Radio Club which fostered one of New England's pioneer radio stations. The transmitter and receiver, its parts gathered through Yankee bargaining, borrowing and makeshift, were assembled and operated by his students under his direction. Clark's station, WCUW, successfully broadcast music, crop, weather and market reports; monitored ship-to-shore calls in the Boston area, and experimented with radio advertising. In November 1920, Station WCUW received and broadcast returns in the presidential election of Harding over Cox.

Always pressed for money for his rocket work, Goddard

joined his university colleagues Thompson, Hickman and Riffolt in launching an ambitious but short-lived corporation called the Industrial Research Laboratories. They set up a small shop, bought a "company car," but were unable to arouse lasting support for their enterprise, although an electrical firm gave them some development problems and an arms manufacturer provided some funds for a year or so.

As for his own enterprise, Goddard still had no results he wished to broadcast. His preliminary efforts in the First World War might have passed without notice except for a brief, unauthorized wire service report in March 1919. The news story revealed that he had "invented and developed through its earlier stages . . . a terrible engine of war."

A reporter for the Worcester *Evening Gazette,* pursuing the news report, found Professor Goddard uneasy and guarded, but managed to piece together a somewhat prophetic account. He declared that "the Goddard rocket" would one day out-distance "the German supercannon that shelled Paris," that it would enable the foot soldier to become "the equivalent of a field cannon," that it might be useful on small boats firing against shore defenses, ships and submarines. He added optimistically:

"To illustrate the possibilities of long flight with the Goddard rocket, one weighing about 30 pounds, including 25 pounds in cartridges, aimed straight up in the air, would attain a height of 70 miles. The scientists who have figured the problem agree that this enormous altitude would be reached far, far above the last trace of the earth's atmosphere, in the vacuum of space. . . ."

Similar reports appeared in newspapers in England, France, Germany and elsewhere. Observing that Goddard's device was "the most efficient rocket ever developed," they implied that it was already capable of reaching 70 miles in altitude and 200 miles in range and declared that it was "under vigorous development by the American War Department." Actually no rocket was then under "vigorous development" and the War Department's interest was almost nonexistent.

Before his students and his colleagues, Goddard briskly dismissed the report as "newspaper talk" and discouraged further inquiry.

But the real overstatement, or understatement, was still to come.

II

Dr. Webster's views on public affairs, as in other matters, ran counter to Goddard's. As a man of strong opinions, the elder physicist was an inveterate writer of letters-to-the-editor in the Worcester press, a frequent and colorful public speaker and, in March 1920, an unsuccessful Democratic candidate for the United States House of Representatives. In addition to lecturing his students on the disciplines and fundamentals of physics, Webster had no hesitation in taking his stand on topics that aroused him. In the early 1920s, controversial topics abounded.

The troops were home, the war was over. The country craved President Harding's "return to normalcy." Americans were deep in the trenches of respectability. When Worcester citizens expressed outrage because the Austrian violinist, Fritz Kreisler, was scheduled to play in town, Webster fired off letters to the *Evening Gazette* denouncing bigotry. Later he was even more indignant over an incident at Clark.

Dr. Wallace W. Atwood, a geographer from Harvard University, was the new president of Clark when a socialist, Scott Nearing, was invited to address the students' Liberal Club in the school auditorium. Nearing was warming up to his subject, a denunciation of the control of universities by wealthy trustees, when Dr. Atwood appeared. The president twice attempted to dismiss the audience. The students remained in their seats and Nearing went on with his talk. Atwood then ordered the auditorium lights turned off and adjourned the meeting.

The incident stimulated Webster to public statements against the curtailment of academic freedom. Other Clark professors sought employment elsewhere, among them Dr. Harry Elmer Barnes, the eminent professor of history.

Goddard remained aloof throughout the controversy. When a physics student observed that other professors had discussed the Nearing affair, he replied crisply: "I am paid by the university to teach physics, not to determine university policy." He went on with his lecture.

"Lamps to Canada," he might have added, recalling his father's philosophy that the railroad should tend to the railroad's business. He had his private problem, the rocket, to handle. With his usual singlemindedness, he would have gone on handling it his own way but for Dr. Webster.

By 1919 Webster was increasingly interested in Goddard's rocket research, his support from the Smithsonian and his wartime experiments. Although he had previously discouraged the rocket researches as "unreasonable," Webster now insisted that his former student must publish his findings. The young professor, he said, was too hesitant and too secretive. He told Goddard that he must publish his results or that he, Webster, would handle the matter for him. Webster's unique encouragement propelled Goddard into print.

Aside from revealing his rocket prematurely, Goddard could imagine nothing worse than someone else revealing it for him. Troubled by the threat of Webster's intervention, he wrote to the Smithsonian about the possibility of publishing his report, "A Method of Reaching Extreme Altitudes," which he had sent to the Institution with his first appeal for funds. In reviewing his manuscript, he reflected that in specifying "extreme" altitudes, he had been most circumspect about the extremities he really had in mind. He had mentioned a lunar landing casually, as if describing a familiar laboratory test. He still wished to appear drab, having no desire to drive away potential sponsors. As he observed in his private notes:

"It was considered best . . . [not] to specify interplanetary navigation. . . . The use of solar energy in decreasing the time of transit between planets was also omitted, as was the use of the moon as a half-way station, and also the production of hydrogen and oxygen under pressure by electrolysis [on the moon]. . . ."

Dr. Abbot, also a man of caution, informed Goddard that the Smithsonian would be pleased to publish his early paper, provided its cost were covered by the remainder of his grant. Abbot hoped, he said, that publication might stimulate new financial sources to support the rocket's development.

To his original Smithsonian paper, Goddard added some footnotes on his wartime experiments and a few of his earlier concepts. One note observed that the single-charge rocket, as then developed, would have military use. Another addition to the original report dealt with the multi-stage rocket for extreme altitudes. He also discussed the merits of liquid hydrogen and oxygen as sources of power, and mentioned the probabilities of collision with meteors.

Goddard did not know at the time of publication that a pioneer physicist had preceded him—a school teacher in the small Russian town of Kaluga, named Konstantin E. Tsiolkovsky. Nor could he know that another pioneer theorist would shortly follow him, a Heidelberg student named Hermann Oberth.

On January 3, 1920, Goddard received his author's copies of the sixty-nine-page monograph, "A Method of Reaching Extreme Altitudes." Modestly bound in brown paper, the first edition of 1,750 copies was issued in the Smithsonian Miscellaneous Collections, Volume 71, Number 2, 1919. For eight days, there was no mention of Goddard's report in the press. But on Monday, January 12, 1920, the Worcester professor and his theory were front page news across the nation. The headlines all registered the same astounded note:

The Boston *American:*	MODERN JULES VERNE INVENTS ROCKET TO REACH MOON
The New York *Times:*	AIM TO REACH MOON WITH NEW ROCKET
The Milwaukee *Sentinel:*	CLAIM MOON MAY SOON BE REACHED
The San Francisco *Examiner:*	SAVANT INVENTS ROCKET WHICH WILL HIT MOON

III

While the New Year's headlines were invading the privacy of his dream, his close-knit family pattern was broken by the death of his mother, on January 29. It had been a warm, secure home on Bishop Avenue. On summer evenings, Nahum and his son put on derby hats and staged impromptu variety acts on the side porch, mimicking the broad slapstick of Weber and Fields or Laurel and Hardy. Fannie Louise, sitting in her wheelchair, was their sole audience. In her later days, she often wheeled herself into her son's study and sat contentedly reading or drowsing as he worked at his desk. While he computed escape velocities and collisions with meteors and landing speeds, he was comforted to have her near.

Frail and gentle, his mother had looked out on a world that seemed to her full of dangers. He recalled again her caution during his childhood experiments with electricity: "Be careful, Robert, or you'll go flying off and never come back." In later years, after his recovery from tuberculosis, she said: "Take care of yourself, Robert." He heard it now as a kind of prayer, remembered it as a benediction after her passing.

Nahum, like his son, inherited the durable, optimistic fiber of Madame Goddard. He was among the first residents in suburban Worcester to own an automobile, to install a telephone, to buy a crystal set and then a superheterodyne radio. He was uncommonly protective of his automobiles. He kept his Hudson sedan exclusively for touring, his Ford for work, and on rainy or muddy days, he kept both cars in his garage while he took the trolley to town.

If Robert's ideas were odd and independent, he came by them naturally, the neighbors said. The Goddards had a strong cast of mind. An Episcopalian, Nahum seldom went to church, caring little for ceremony. Although a firm Republican and Yankee, he disliked unnecessary thrift. "Genteel closeness," he called it. Money wasn't meant to be banked for eternity, he felt, but to be used sensibly.

The Goddards respected their individual privacies. If their son's work and ideas had sometimes confounded his parents, they seldom asked questions. Once, as lightning flashed during a thunderstorm, Nahum saw Robert dashing upstairs to the attic. "What's wrong?" his father inquired. "I figured I'd better bring that suitcase of TNT down to the basement, Pa," his son said coolly.

Though seldom alarmed at his rocket work, Nahum never quite trusted Robert's grasp of the automobile. His apprehension was shared by his son's colleagues at Clark. Goddard first soloed in the new black Chevrolet bought by the partners of the research corporation. He was driving down Franklin Street with Louis Thompson one afternoon when he saw his father crossing the thoroughfare. He stopped suddenly, waiting until Nahum was out of sight. As Robert put it, "He might have keeled over if he saw me driving."

On a Clark outing at Lake Quinsigamond, he set out in his car for the picnic grounds following Percy Roope, his assistant on the physics staff. Roope crossed Main Street at a policeman's signal and drove on to the lake, assuming that Goddard was right behind him. Later he learned that the professor had simultaneously stepped on the gas, engaged the clutch and snapped the gear-shift lever in half.

Shortly before his mother's death, a new sort of entry began to appear in Robert's diary. Differing from the familiar jottings—"Clark, lab in p.m.," "Calculated on H & O," "Went to see Hawley on patent"—were these annotations: "Got a good smile from Esther," " 'Babe' . . . came out to dinner," "Took kitten down to Gertrude and saw her aboard train," "Went to dancing school with Marion. . . ." "Dancing . . . with Helen . . . good time." There were mentions of "Alma" and "Grace" and "Florence" and, especially, of "Esther."

Under this altered social regimen, Goddard felt an urgent need to improve his dancing ability and to test it out at weekly dances in Worcester's Terpischorean Hall. One of his partners recalls that he was "a deliberate and persistent dancer." He sketched the patterns of dance steps on the used envelopes which he customarily kept in his pocket. "He referred to these diagrams frequently and counted the steps out loud," she said.

A year or so earlier, on his return from Aberdeen, Goddard had met a tall, blue-eyed young secretary in the president's office at Clark, Esther Christine Kisk. He found her shy, intelligent and attractive. Esther Kisk agreed to type his papers after school hours and he began to call at her home more frequently than the stenographic work required.

Miss Kisk, when Goddard met her, was seventeen years old, the forthright daughter of Swedish immigrants, saving her pay to go to college. Her father worked long hours as foreman of the woodworking shop at Crompton and Knowles, while her mother ran a luncheon stand for employees at the loom works, and strived to make college possible for her children. For a time Mrs. Kisk was cool toward the bald professor. He seemed too old and set in his ways for her young daughter, she felt. Also, he absently flecked the Kisk apartment rug with white bits of paper he punched from manuscripts so that the pages could be inserted in his notebooks.

The Kisks warmed slowly toward the professor, who became increasingly "interested" in Esther, not only because she had stood at the head of her high school class, nor because she could decipher his almost illegible scrawl. He was pleased, too, with her work. But more important, he was pleased with Miss Kisk herself.

IV

—From the Earth to the Moon
Jules Verne, 1865.

"*'Suffer me to finish,' [Barbicane] calmly continued. 'I have looked at the question in all its bearings, I have resolutely attacked it, and by incontrovertible calculations I find that a projectile endowed with an initial velocity of 12,000 yards per second, and aimed at the moon, must necessarily reach it. I have the honor, my brave colleagues, to propose a trial of this little experiment.'*

"*It is impossible to describe the effect produced . . . —the cries, the shouts, the successions of roars, hurrahs. . . . It was a scene of indescribable confusion and uproar. They shouted, they clapped, they stamped on the floor of the hall. . . .*

"*Barbicane published a manifesto full of enthusiasm, in which he made an appeal to 'all persons of good will upon the face of the earth.' This document, translated into all languages, met with immense success . . . and . . . a considerable capital. . . .*

"*United States subscriptions* $4,000,000
"*Foreign subscriptions* 1,446,675
"*Total* . . . . $5,446,675"

Shortly after the release of his Smithsonian paper, Goddard, like Barbicane of the Jules Verne fantasy, heard "the cries,

the shouts, the succession of roars." Unlike Barbicane, however, he discovered no "immense success," nor any "considerable capital." The public, and many of his peers, were
startled by his lunar ambitions which he had tried to conceal.
Then and for years to come it was Dr. Benjamin Merigold,
head of Clark's chemistry department, who often greeted
Goddard in the halls between classes with playful merriment.
"Well, Robert," he would say, "how is your moon-going
rocket?"

In fantasy, perhaps, Goddard could picture himself as a
modern Barbicane, the masterful scientist-engineer. But
fantasy and reality were now thoroughly snarled. A moon
rocket was so much more than he could accomplish, yet so
much less than his paper really implied.

The moon-rocket sensation, he learned, had come from the
Smithsonian Institution itself, which issued a press release on
January 11, 1920. It outlined his basic theory and experi-
ments and added this note:

"An interesting speculation, described in the publication,
arising from Professor Goddard's work, is on the possibility of
sending to the surface of the dark part of the new moon a
sufficient amount of the most brilliant flash powder which,
being ignited on impact, would be plainly visible in a powerful telescope. This would be the only way possible of proving
that the rocket had really left the attraction of the earth as
the apparatus would never come back, once it had escaped
that attraction. While this experiment would be of little
obvious scientific value, its successful trial would be of general interest, as the first actual contact between a planet and
a satellite. . . ."

Observing that the Institution, in fact, had made of his
paper "the first real suggestion for contact between the
planets," Goddard wrote:

"From that day, the whole thing was summed up in the
public mind in the words 'moon rocket,' and thus it hap-

pened that in trying to minimize the sensational side, I had really made more of a stir than . . . if I had discussed transportation to Mars, which would probably have been considered ridiculous and never been mentioned."

For a time, he tried to turn the press from its fixation on the "moon rocket," but he didn't recant. To one reporter, he said: "Every vision is a joke until the first man accomplishes it. Once realized, it becomes commonplace." To another, he stated that his present rocket would not shoot "more than a mile or two," although it involved "the same principle" as a rocket soaring to the moon. To a third, he pointed out: "Unfortunately, nothing can be accomplished without money. It would cost a fortune to make a rocket to hit the moon. But wouldn't it be worth a fortune?"

As the headlines continued, he tried to bring the rocket down to earth. At the same time, he saw a chance to capitalize on the public's sudden interest. Carefully and after many revisions, he released a two-pronged statement to the Associated Press:

"Since the announcement by the Smithsonian Institution a few days ago, I have been interviewed a number of times, and on each occasion have been as uncommunicative as possible. The result has consequently been a number of published articles that were not all that could be desired. . . .

"In the first place, too much attention has been concentrated on the proposed flash powder experiment, and too little on the exploration of the atmosphere. My reason for saying this is not because I believe the former is entirely unrealizable. In fact, if I were to speculate boldly instead of timidly, I would say that, based upon equally sound physical principles, there is the possibility of obtaining photographs in space by an apparatus guided by photo-sensitive cells (to guide it toward, or near, a luminous body). . . .

"The point is this: whatever interesting possibilities there may be of the method that has been proposed . . . no one of

them could be undertaken without first exploring the atmosphere. Any rocket apparatus for great elevations must first be
tested at various moderate altitudes. Also, a knowledge of
densities at high levels is essential. Hence, from any point of
view, an investigation of the atmosphere is the work that lies
ahead.

"Inasmuch as no definite action is ever obtained without a
definite proposition, I would like to propose, if the work is of
sufficient interest, the raising of from $50,000 to $100,000 by
popular subscription, to be used by the Smithsonian Institution in preparing for, and undertaking, a preliminary exploration of the atmosphere by the method in question, the
work to be begun now, or at such a time as the Institution
shall present such experimental results as will be satisfactory
to those who are subscribing."

The press published Goddard's statement, but without
enthusiasm. Some reporters thought him evasive, a few called
him "the moon-rocket man." Others demanded: "All right,
professor, when do you plan to hit the moon?" Goddard felt
he wasn't getting his message across.

Along with the flapper, the Charleston and the speakeasy,
the moon rocket temporarily took hold of the nation's fancy.
Intensively and then sporadically over the next few years, it
became a fixture on editorial pages and Sunday supplements
at home and abroad.

An inspired publicity agent at the Mary Pickford Studios
in Hollywood sent Goddard a telegram: WOULD BE GRATEFUL
FOR OPPORTUNITY TO SEND MESSAGE TO MOON FROM MARY
PICKFORD ON YOUR TORPEDO ROCKET WHEN IT STARTS.

Song writers produced novelty tunes and ballads. One was
entitled: "Oh, They're Going to Shoot a Rocket to the Moon,
Love!" Its composer offered to turn over half of his royalties
to Goddard. Unfortunately, there were no royalties.

During these years of sensation, more than a hundred volunteers announced themselves ready for lunar journeys.
Among them was Captain Claude R. Collins, a wartime pilot

and president of the Aviators' Club of Pennsylvania. Collins declared he would fly to the moon or even to Mars if the professor provided a $10,000 insurance policy on his life. A few days later, a young woman from Kansas City, Missouri, offered to accompany the intrepid captain, with or without a policy.

For Goddard, it was a nightmare. "I wish to say that I have asked for no volunteers," he announced sharply. "There is, at this moment, no rocket ship contemplated for the moon. If there were less volunteering and more solid support, I could get along much faster. . . . I am beginning to appreciate the difficulty of making oneself understood."

There were numerous misunderstandings. An editorial writer for the New York *Times,* misinformed on the reaction principle, declared caustically:

"That Professor Goddard with his 'chair' in Clark College and the countenancing of the Smithsonian Institution does not know the relation of action to reaction, and of the need to have something better than a vacuum against which to react—to say that would be absurd. Of course he only seems to lack the knowledge ladled out daily in high schools. . . ."

The London *Graphic,* in a somewhat more learned attack, stated that the velocity needed to reach the moon would cause the rocket to burn in the friction of the earth's atmosphere, that the earth and the moon were traveling at such tremendous speeds that guiding a rocket to a moon landing was incredible. Moreover, it was unlikely that a high-altitude rocket would accomplish much of scientific value. The delicate instruments needed for meteorological study could not withstand the shock of returning to earth.

It was like running furiously in order to stay in place. Goddard was more disturbed by these slurs against the spaceship than by the press reports that he was about to fly one. Feeling beset by gnats, he replied to his critics, specifically to the London *Graphic,* through the respectable pages of the *Scientific American* on February 26, 1921—"That Moon

Rocket Proposition; Refutation of Some Popular Fallacies."
He wrote:

"*First:* The extreme velocities needed to reach the moon
would not be attained until the rocket was beyond the earth's
atmosphere, in the frictionless vacuum of space.

"*Second:* A moon landing would be difficult, but by no
means impossible. Timing, of course, would be important.
Light-sensitive selenium cells fixed on the moon's light could
be useful in guidance. There were other means he was not
yet prepared to discuss.

"*Third:* Sensitive instruments could be adequately protected on the rocket's return to earth."

A parachute, Goddard went on, might open at the apex of
the rocket's flight for easy descent. Furthermore, there were
ways of transmitting data directly to the earth from the flying
rocket. He declined to elaborate this point, but in his private
files he had already described a radio transmitter signaling
from the rocket to receiving sets on earth.

Without the respect of his scientific peers, he knew there
was little prospect of raising funds. And, without funds, there
was little prospect of raising a rocket. He had been surprised
and pleased when Dr. Webster, the prolific correspondent to
the press, came to his defense in a letter printed in the
Worcester *Gazette* on January 22, 1920.

"As Dr. Goddard, once my pupil, now my colleague, came
with a bunch of manuscript which lies before me to consult
me about five or six years ago, I feel myself to be a sort of
grandfather to this rocket. I remember at the time I asked
him, 'Goddard, does it look reasonable to you?' To which he
made the Yankee reply of asking me whether I saw anything
wrong with his mathematics. I did not, nor do I now. There
are some assumptions, but it is an assumption that the sun
will rise tomorrow."

It wasn't the way Goddard recalled the incident, but he
was pleased to have so distinguished a defender. He was espe-

cially encouraged by Webster's parting shot that he had made "an extremely good rocket." Webster concluded:

"No one in the history of heat engines has ever increased the efficiency of an engine in the same degree. This is triumph enough. Never mind whether it hits the moon."

For all this public hullabaloo, Goddard's high-flying rocket had not, in truth, ascended as high as a child's balloon escaping at a New England fair. Moreover, his grants were exhausted, while rocket development was getting more costly all the time. At this glum juncture, the Smithsonian attempted to help him find additional backers.

In April 1920, Goddard addressed an audience of five hundred members of the Chicago chapter of the American Association of Engineers. It was another chance to appeal for help. Avoiding mention of the moon, planets and outer space, he spoke conservatively of his success in creating a new sort of "heat engine." He displayed films and slides of his rocket experiments, emphasizing their meteorological possibilities. The Chicago engineers felt challenged and resolved to solicit funds. What did the professor require? $50,000? $100,000? Chicago could raise any amount! The newspapers next day reported their stimulating enthusiasm. But soon these bright assurances collapsed.

Abbot next presented his protégé to Dr. Alexander Graham Bell, the venerated inventor of the telephone. Dr. Bell was then seventy-four years old and living in Washington, D.C., the *grand seigneur* of American ingenuity. On Wednesday evenings, he customarily held social seminars at his home with promising young inventors and scientists—*conversaziones,* he called these meetings. He invited Goddard to discuss his high-flying rocket and listened intently to the New Englander's discourse. Goddard grew uncommonly mellow under the aging inventor's acceptance. "Dr. Bell, while an old man, was keen-minded, and of very pleasing manner," he noted gratefully that night.

After the *conversazione,* Bell referred Goddard to Dr. Gilbert Grosvenor, president of the National Geographic Society, with the observation that "the moon certainly belongs to the earth and therefore comes within the domains of the National Geographic Society. . . ." Grosvenor heard Goddard out. How soon would the high-flying rocket be ready? What funds were needed? The professor spoke candidly, but sensed that his rocket still sounded expensive to Grosvenor. On his return to Clark, he was dismayed to read the Society's somewhat premature release to the press:

"The first test of working models of the rocket apparatus by which Prof. Robert Goddard hopes to reach altitudes above the earth's air envelope, and even the moon, will be made at Worcester, Mass., late in July or August, it is announced in a bulletin from the National Geographic Society's Washington headquarters.

" 'Should Professor Goddard's theory prove workable by his demonstration at that time,' the bulletin states, 'the event may rank in the history of the new super-aviation, as yet unnamed, along with the trial flights of the late Prof. Samuel P. Langley's flying machines.

"But while the world ridiculed Langley, and for a time regarded Bell's telephone and Morse's telegraph as mere playthings, our amazing strides in invention have created an open-minded attitude toward adventures in ingenuity so that Goddard's experiments are being awaited with keen interest. . . ."

It was a glowing tribute. But the Society, which financed terrestrial expeditions, concluded that it would be unable to supply the continuing yearly subsidies which the rocket venture obviously required.

At this low ebb, Goddard was invited to contribute a paper on rockets to the *Journal* of the Worcester Polytechnic Institute. He responded with "certain comments" which he had "kept bottled up with considerable difficulty."

"I am not a sensationalist," he wrote, "even though I realize that I am dealing with a sensational subject. I almost wish I were, for I could certainly 'start something.' To discuss details, however, before one has checked up on matters completely by experiment is unwise, for to do so merely precipitates a flood of useless argument, discussion and comment. . . . At the present time, the work that is being done is the development of a rocket of small size . . . on what remains of a $5,000 grant. Anyone who has ever had anything to do with the development of machinery—and most Tech men have—can realize what this means. It is really a greater tax on one's resourcefulness to work sufficiently economically than it is to get experimental results. And all this time I am reading articles in the newspapers about how I am receiving grants of $50,000 and $100,000!"

By the summer of 1920, the Smithsonian Institution had disbursed the remainder of Goddard's original grant, about $500. It was soon spent. In the fall, on the encouragement of President Atwood, Goddard approached the trustees of Clark University. He suggested a grant of $5,000 to complete a model of his repeating-charge rocket "to be used in high altitude investigations . . . to send recording apparatus above the highest altitudes which can ever be reached by sounding balloons."

The trustees of Clark did not anticipate a rocket to the moon. They felt that the newspapers had misrepresented the professor. They took the advice of President Atwood that Goddard would add luster to the school. Trimming the professor's request, they promised him $3,500 over the next two years to continue his research.

Their benefaction, generous at the time, seemed hardly a match for the Barbicane fantasy of $5,446,675. But it meant getting on with the work.

Like Clark, the Smithsonian was scarcely aware of Goddard's interest in space flight, except as a harmless inventor's quirk. Later, Abbot would question whether his protégé was ever serious about so outlandish a concept. Yet Abbot alone was equipped to know of Goddard's early speculations, his concepts for the future, which he had once sealed under the bogus title, "Special Formulae for Silvering Mirrors."

The Germans were beginning to discuss space travel openly. Goddard, who could hardly contain himself, responded by sending Abbot, in March 1920, a "Report on Further Developments of the Rocket Method of Investigating Space." He had not intended to bring up "these matters" until later, he explained in an accompanying letter. But he could hardly abide a German criticism that he was too unimaginative to recognize the rocket's potential. Worse than being accused as a "moon-rocket" man was to hear that he lacked the vision to see the rocket as a vehicle for reaching the planets and beyond.

The professor, however, requested the withholding of this, his "most significant" paper, as he called it. It did not seem prudent to him to publish his views on such spatial topics as "Investigations Conducted With an Operator," and "Investigations Conducted Without an Operator," in which he spelled out the use of automatic telescopic cameras to photograph the moon and planets from orbiting rockets, and of steering manned space craft by means of gyroscopes and "side-jets" to planetary landings.

Until man-carrying rockets were built, Goddard continued, various communication techniques would be useful, presupposing "the existence of intelligent beings on the other planets." One possible method, he wrote to the Smithsonian:

". . . would consist in the sending of devices to the planets that would produce a succession of colors on falling through the atmosphere: the devices containing metal sheets stamped with geometrical figures; with the constellations emphasizing the earth and the moon. . . ."

Goddard then mentioned an approach he had considered since 1907, a rocket employing liquid oxygen and liquid hydrogen. These liquids, he wrote, should provide a threefold increase in heat energy for an equivalent weight in smokeless powder; they would also be easier to regulate in combustion. Most important, they would make possible interplanetary flight. Whatever the chemical makeup of planetary bodies, some would surely contain hydrogen and oxygen, perhaps in the form of snow or water, which could be separated electrolytically.

The ultimate objective, of course, was the manned rocket, on which he speculated at length:

"The presence of an operator is desirable under many circumstances. . . . An operator is essential if investigations are made that would necessitate landing on, and departing from, planets. . . .

"Since the initial mass required for leaving the moon is much less than that required for leaving the earth, the passage to and from a planet would be made much easier if the start were made from the moon. . . .

"The time required for passage from the earth to a planet, if the path is traversed with a moderate constant velocity, can best be shown by an example. Thus if a velocity of 3,000 ft./sec. were to be maintained from the earth to the planet Mars, the time of transit would be 102.2 weeks, or nearly two years. For the sending of inanimate devices, this might not be unreasonably long, but for an operator it would, of course, be desirable to shorten the time.

"If a device that could exert a constant propelling force were to be employed, and the speed were increased during the first half of the journey [to Mars] and decreased during the other half, the time could be considerably reduced. Thus, if the average velocity were 7 miles/sec., the time would be reduced to 7.13 weeks. The limit to the reduction of time is imposed by the nature of the device used to secure this reduction. . . ."

Goddard discussed two space devices: a solar motor and one using ion propulsion. He thought enough of these ideas to take out patents. He proposed using them in space to move the rocket after its liquid fuels were expended.

His suggestion of a solar motor grew out of a blurred vision, much as had other concepts in his early thinking. His principal idea, to use the sun's rays to heat a boiler in space, did not amount to much. But his means of heating the boiler, with a so-called "solar sail," led to a far more interesting prospect. His sail, he wrote, would be a lightweight, collapsible, mirror-like contrivance of metal foil, about six hundred feet square, which would be unfurled in space.

Goddard's early report on space exploration mentioned, in passing, this inspired tangent of his thinking:

"During the initial rise of the rocket in the atmosphere, the mass is large, and the acceleration is considerable. It is thus impossible to begin employing solar energy until the parabolic velocity is approached, owing to the large size of the power plant, particularly the mirrors, that would be necessary.

"For the initial mass to be a minimum, the mirrors must be of as small weight as possible in proportion to the power plant, which, itself, must be very light. . . .

"On leaving a planet, then, when the parabolic velocity is approached (far above the atmosphere, of course), mirrors of as thin metal foil as possible, on collapsible frames, should be unfolded; the solar energy being reflected into one or more steam boilers, through one or more pyrex glass windows. . . ."

In after years, the pioneer learned how such a sail could be used to push the spaceship outward from the sun or some other star, acquiring the newly discovered light pressure from these bodies to drive the rocket outward, as an ordinary wind on earth drives sailing ships. To return toward the sun or star, Goddard's solar sail would be furled or tilted on edge, permitting gravity to draw the craft inward.

Goddard's confidential report anticipated other means of traveling in space, such as a vehicle utilizing ions to move the rocket forward. In essence, his ion rocket resembled an electric light bulb. It required a filament or foil and, for ejection, virtually any substance which could be incandesced or broken down electrically. Its theoretical advantage was in providing a maximum thrust for the least possible weight, for use in space. Ion propulsion was later to become an engineering problem of considerable importance.

Goddard refrained in his paper from further theorizing about rocket propulsion, although he was still fascinated by the possible use of atomic energy if and when man learned to crack the atom. There was no law against it. He concluded his speculations with an unaccustomed beating of drums:

"A method of carrying out planetary investigations and of communicating with planets by actual contact is outlined in the present report. It does not presuppose any new discoveries but depends upon well-established physical principles. . . .

"It is believed that the method is superior to any other so far proposed for establishing interplanetary communication. . . . The method is . . . certain to yield results of great scientific value. . . .

"In view of these facts, together with the tremendous interest and importance of the subject, it is believed that an appeal for public support is justifiable."

There is no record of an acknowledgment by Dr. Abbot of Goddard's first space report to the Smithsonian. A workable, earthly rocket already seemed overdue to the Assistant Secretary and would still seem so a few years later when Goddard sent him other suggestions on space flight. In November 1923, Abbot made his only reference to these speculations, writing to Goddard with a rare show of exasperation: ". . . They make very interesting reading. I am, however, consumed with impatience, and hope that you will be able to actually send a rocket up into the air some time soon. Interplanetary space would look much nearer to me after I had seen one of your rockets go up five or six miles in our own atmosphere."

Goddard's space papers were filed and forgotten in the Smithsonian's copious archives.

V

The professor's admiration for Esther Kisk was flourishing.

In her quiet determination, she resembled him strikingly. She had frugally saved her Clark salary to enroll in Bates College at Lewiston, Maine, where she was repeatedly elected to class offices. Goddard sent her a succession of letters and elaborate boxes of candy, called her his "golden girl" and fondly told her she was "puppy-like—enjoying everybody and everything."

On vacations and holidays, the persistent professor called at the Kisks', leaving his documents and paper punch at home, taking the fair-haired young student on countryside drives in his Oakland coupé. Occasionally, Esther was invited to dinner at Bishop Avenue. Nahum Goddard studied her quizzically, she recalled, as if wondering whether she could deal with the unpredictable problems his son presented.

VI

Inevitably the American public lost interest in the moon and space sensation. News accounts of the Clark professor grew smaller on the front pages, moved to the back pages, then out of the press altogether. In a sense, Goddard felt relieved. He put on his old, comfortable cloak of reticence, a cloak he wore for the rest of his life. For the ultimate rocket, he felt, the force of skepticism might be harder to penetrate than the force of gravity.

Following his demonstration at Aberdeen in 1918, he had tried to interest the Army Air Service in the rocket as airborne artillery. The Air Service, short on funds and imagination, suggested that he apply to Chemical Warfare.

The Chemical Warfare Service agreed that Goddard's rocket might one day replace the Stokes mortar and the Livens projector for firing gas and incendiary payloads. It might well be lighter and cheaper than any mortar. But after a lengthy exchange of letters, Chemical Warfare declared that it, too, was short of money and referred him to Ordnance.

The Army's Chief of Ordnance had been fascinated by the possibilities of the rocket as a recoilless gun, an adjunct and perhaps a replacement for conventional artillery. Writing to Goddard, he stipulated the requirements of Ordnance in detail. Goddard replied that the rocket could be developed to meet them. He would need between six and nine months and about $50,000 to produce a suitable recoilless gun. To perfect and refine a pilot model for production would require an additional three to five months and perhaps $30,000 more. On this note, his correspondence with Army Ordnance abruptly concluded.

He wondered if the United States Navy might possibly have put aside funds against President Harding's era of "normalcy." After a year of negotiations, the Navy's Bureau of Ordnance submitted, in the spring of 1920, a frugal rocket development contract which offered a retainer of $100 monthly, plus travel expenses and $15 per diem "when working for the Bureau in a designated place." Goddard signed at once.

The designated place was the Indian Head Powder Factory in southern Maryland, about thirty miles south of Washington. A bleak and dreary flatland of tobacco fields near an isolated bend of the Potomac River, the Indian Head area had been staked out in 1890 for the manufacture of gunpowder and as a proving ground for heavy artillery. After the First World War, the proving ground was transferred across the river to Dahlgren, Virginia. The deserted firing range, in a valley beside the Potomac, seemed remote enough to conceal a professor and his promissory rockets.

Between July 1920 and March 1923, Goddard reported to Indian Head on weekends, holidays and summer vacations. He needed no reminder from the Navy that his work was confidential. He considered it top secret. His scrupulous regard for security, however, was somewhat wasted. Living at the modest Powder Factory Hotel in Indian Head town, he was promptly recognized by local citizens as "the moon-rocket man."

In the morning, the bald professor, swathed in scarves and equipped with an umbrella and overshoes against inclement weather, pedaled his bicycle a mile and a half from the hotel down a wooded path to the abandoned valley. There he entered an empty powder magazine, built against a substantial hill. Engineers, metallurgists and machinists up at the Powder Factory were available when he needed them. Usually he chose to work alone.

He had three neighbors in the valley: a retired petty officer named Francis C. Torrens and two Negro workmen who were dismantling range equipment for shipment down the river. Lieutenant Commander L. P. Johnson, the range officer who was also in charge of research, had already moved to Dahlgren. One day Johnson received an agitated telephone call from the usually placid Torrens. "Mr. Johnson," Torrens shouted, "please come as quick as you can! Dr. Goddard is going to blow himself up—and the rest of us too!"

Years later Johnson recalled the incident. "It was a cold winter day during Christmas week and Indian Head was drearier than usual," he said. "When I got there, I hurried down to the valley and found the doctor in his makeshift workshop. He was sitting at a small table, lost in his thoughts, pressing black smokeless powder into discs. Beside him was an open twenty-five-pound can of powder and he was dusted all over with the stuff. Near him was a red-hot potbellied stove."

Johnson suggested that sitting in smokeless powder beside a blazing fire did not conform to the Navy's safety standards.

Goddard left Indian Head after a series of successful shoots on the deserted firing range, the sounds of his rockets roaring up from the valley. By March 1923, when his funds once more ran out, he had developed a depth-charge rocket for use against submarines and a rocket for propelling an armor-penetrating warhead. He sent his final report to the Navy, urging further development. The report was acknowledged, officially stamped and filed away. It marked Goddard's last effort with the United States' armed forces until the Second World War.

The Navy's investment in Goddard was a thrifty one. It cost about $2,000, strikingly less than the $20,000,000 the Navy spent two decades later to perfect rockets for use from landing craft. In the Second World War, the Navy also revived his Indian Head rockets for depth charges in combat and adapted them for use with deck-penetrating weapons.

But few of the Navy's ordnancemen realized what the New England professor was offering—the prospect of scrapping many a cherished weapon as obsolete.

VII

By 1920, at the start of his excursions to Indian Head, Goddard was facing up to the unpleasant conclusion that his vision had far outreached his achievement. His multiple-charge, machine-gun approach to space flight was overcomplicated and undependable. He had spent four years on Smithsonian grants, but had achieved no rocket for reaching extreme or even moderate altitudes.

Between weekends at Indian Head, he used what free time he had in a last effort to make the multiple-charge rocket work. With Nils Riffolt, he labored in Clark's basement machine shop and in the sheet-metal shack they constructed just outside the shop. "We figured that if anything went wrong, we would merely blow up the outbuilding and not the whole department of physics," Riffolt recalled.

Riffolt worked with Goddard sporadically on the multiple-charge rocket and then intensively on the liquid-fuel rocket but, like all his later crew members, his assistant never realized the thrust of Goddard's space vision until after the scientist's death.

The final trials of the multiple-charge rocket were dismal, Riffolt observed, impressed by Goddard's gift of resilience. "One thing would go wrong after another. He'd come in with pencil sketches on the backs of envelopes and we'd talk over ways to handle the problems. After a while, we knew we were running down rabbit trails, that a workable cartridge rocket was at least a long way off."

In his diary, Goddard recorded the results of each try:

"June 23: got apparatus set up. . . . June 26: tried it . . . nozzle split. . . .

"July 14: chamber cracked. . . . July 17: cartridge jammed. . . .

"August 7: tried multiple, fired four shots. . . . August 8: tried multiple with parachute. . . . It fell and magazine blew up."

Reporting to the Smithsonian Institution on September 29, 1922, he outlined his problems in more detail:

"It was found . . . that the bases of the cartridges, which were made firm by glue, were frequently broken by the force of the impact. . . . A means of producing greater toughness of the bases of the cartridges was found, July 2, 1920, by dipping the bottom of the cartridges in a solution of nitro-glycerin powder dissolved in acetone. . . .

"Closely associated with the problem of cartridge design is that of the form and material of the firing pin. . . . It was found that, on repeated firing, the steel of the screw peeled away from the piano wire, thus leaving the latter exposed. . . .

"A difficulty which developed on continued firing was the occasional rotation of the magazine. . . ."

Goddard and Riffolt made several last attempts to send up an improved multiple-charge device at the Effie Ward farm in Auburn. He described one of these tests late in August 1920:

"An attempt was made . . . to start the rocket from an initial height . . . sufficient to cause the large parachute to open . . . the rocket was raised by two ropes extending between trees . . . until it was about 50 feet above the ground. Before the rocket could be fired . . . the firing strings leading up to the rocket became entangled, and in an effort to loosen them, the rocket became dislodged and fell, naturally exploding the magazine, which contained nine cartridges."

They gathered up the pieces and a few days later tried again. On this test Goddard decided that it was "more desirable to start the rocket from the ground, where all the parts would be within easy reach." The rocket was supported in a vertical position by three threads fastened to posts just outside the launching frame. On firing, four of the cartridges successfully entered the combustion chamber, exploded and carried the rocket to its highest altitude—60 feet off the ground. When the fifth cartridge failed to fire, the rocket crashed beyond repair.

Goddard's commentary was as bland as ever. "The fifth tappet had broken away from the corresponding feeding springs," he wrote. The parachute had also failed to open. Characteristically, he pointed out improvements to be considered. But after January 1921, he made no further attempts with the cartridge rocket.

VIII

After years of relentless experiment, Goddard had come down to earth as resoundingly as his ill-starred rocket. Though hard to convince, he finally realized that he must abandon conventional ways to reach his unconventional goal. His new approach, after so many failures, led to the first flight of a liquid-fuel rocket in 1926.

One advantage of using smokeless powder was that the fuel contained its own source of oxygen, indispensable in the emptiness of space. But there were notable disadvantages. The system's intermittent and explosive thrust made the rocket almost impossible to control. Ideally, he needed a smooth, continuous thrust of power; a combustion, rather than a jarring explosion, of the fuels; and a very high velocity of the escaping gases. It would be decades before solid fuels were developed to meet such requirements.

Goddard returned to his theorizing. The primary source of fuels was hydrogen; of oxidizers, oxygen. His calculations showed that a tremendous thrust was possible by combusting the two elements.

Liquid hydrogen was still unmanageable and unobtainable in the 1920s, but there were possible substitute fuels such as propane, ether, alcohol, gasoline: a whole series of hydrocarbons. Goddard experimented with most of these fuels before settling on gasoline as cheap, easily obtainable and dependable.

For his oxidizer he chose a perfectionist's substitute. "Oxygen," he wrote, "is the most obvious liquid to use with a liquid fuel because it gives complete combustion." He added dryly that there were "difficult problems involved in using the very cold liquid oxygen." It boiled at 298 degrees below zero Fahrenheit, had to be kept below this temperature, and was subject to other severe difficulties of handling.

Goddard's venture with liquid oxygen was a step of faith into a wilderness. Liquid oxygen was a key to future rocket development, an indispensable substance for the German V-2 and subsequent high-altitude missiles. One day rocket men would refer familiarly to "lox," but in 1920 there was nothing familiar about it.

G. Edward Pendray, one of the founders of the American Rocket Society, said of the early use of liquid oxygen:

"Even in the 1930s, engineers told us of frightful things that would happen if we used the stuff. They said if it got on our clothes and we happened to light a cigarette, we'd go off like a torch. Mixing and igniting lox with an inflammable substance like gasoline seemed a guarantee of catastrophe. Goddard's first test was a tremendously courageous thing."

Pendray's recollection is supported by a letter from the Linde Air Products Company to Goddard in 1926, presenting many reservations about the use of "High Purity Liquid Oxygen (commonly termed Liquid Air)." Obviously, Linde had little conception of the astonishing use to which Goddard was putting their product, but warned him, generally, of the perils of handling the liquid:

" (1) No organic material (including oil or greases) or inflammable substance of any nature should be allowed to come in contact with it.

"(2) Flames of all types should be kept away from it and from the vapors resulting from its evaporation. . . ."

Goddard doubtless recognized the personal hazards of his perfect oxidizer, although he never troubled to say so. He simply respected its properties and executed the necessary precautions in its use. In the midst of his pioneering tests, he was living a busy and highly compartmented life, teaching his classes at Clark, making periodic trips to Indian Head for the Navy, seeking new funds for his work and continuing his determined courtship of Miss Kisk.

In his diary of January 28, 1921, the professor first spoke of his new oxidizer:

"Clark, took cylinder to Linde Air Products." Next day, he added: "Clark, got oxygen . . . corrected exams in p.m. and eve." It sounded as casual as calling at the neighborhood store for a bucket of nails.

The Linde Air Products Company, which became a subsidiary of the Union Carbide Corporation, maintained a sizable plant in Worcester. It supplied New England manufacturers with gases and equipment for oxyacetylene welding. In one phase of Linde's production, gaseous oxygen was reduced to a liquid. It was this modest supply that Goddard coveted for his work. Over the next few years, the professor and Riffolt repeatedly visited Linde with their vacuum containers to haggle for the oxidizer.

Using liquid fuels, Goddard envisioned a flawless motor. But before it could fly, it had to be made to work. With Riffolt's assistance, he devoted the next few years to the testing of fuels, the design of light but durable chambers, and a means of feeding combustible liquids into them. While probing these matters, he opened up a new field of engineering.

Lacking funds for his increasingly expensive research, Goddard was forced to acquire a maximum of information for a minimum of time and money. "Before we started to machine a new component," Riffolt said, "we tried to consider its potential use as well as its immediate application, and whether it would hold up under testing.

"Whatever Dr. Goddard had at stake, he tried to keep it to himself," Riffolt went on. "Most of our tests ended with something jamming, or sticking, or the chamber burning through. Yet I never saw him discouraged. These were not failures, he usually said, but what he called valuable negative information."

The early liquid-fuel tests were conducted secretly in the sheet-iron extension outside the basement physics shop at Clark. There Goddard and Riffolt securely anchored their static rocket chambers and measured the thrust of the expanding gases.

Toward the end of 1921, Goddard's diary was a staccato recital of error:

"September 10: Went to Linde Air Products Co. about

O. Drew on pump and engine design in p.m., and worked setting up apparatus with Riffolt in eve.

"September 12: . . . Tried O expt. with Riffolt in eve. Lost part of it, used up all rest without getting it to reach chamber. Planned new apparatus.

"October 15, Clark. Planned on pumping apparatus. . . .

"October 18, Got model started. . . .

"November 7 . . . got book on centrifugal pumps. . . .

"November 11, Planned on rotary pump in p.m.

"November 12, Drew on rotary engine in p.m.

"November 28 . . . Took piston pump and motor down and tested it for RPM and HP in p.m.

"December 11, Sunday, drew on high speed multi-vane pump. . . .

"December 13, Got pump outfit ready in a.m. . . . and tried pump in p.m. It jammed. . . .

"December 15, Tried pump . . . It bound. . . .

"December 28, Tested pumps in a.m. and p.m. Had chamber and pipes welded in p.m.

"December 29, Tested 3-vane pump in a.m. It gave no pressure. . . ."

Despite this repeated "negative information," Goddard had proved to his own satisfaction that happier results were possible. Early in 1922, he recorded the beginnings of success:

"February 22 . . . Went down to Clark and tried intermittent feeding in p.m. 'Coughed' once a little and then ether caught fire.

"February 25, Tried gravity feed from two small tubes, with Riffolt in a.m. Fair pop—OK . . .

"March 25 . . . Went with Riffolt to farm in p.m. Tried starting apparatus in p.m. Got 4 lbs. for a short time. . . ."

In the spring of 1922, Goddard and Riffolt moved their testing base to the Auburn farm, the site of earlier trials with powder rockets. They had found it increasingly difficult to explain the pops, roars and minor explosions in the shed outside the Clark physics building. Neighbors were saying that if the professor was aiming at the moon, they'd prefer that he do so elsewhere.

The Ward farm in Auburn, locally known for its fine strawberries, was owned by Miss Effie Ward, a spinster and distant relative of Goddard's, who ran it with the help of a hired man. Tall, spare and chipper, "Aunt" Effie wore her iron gray hair drawn back in a bun and kept a large family of cats in her kitchen. She accepted her unusual kinsman without hindrance or questions, allowed him to put up his testing tower in the back acres and offered him an unused henhouse to store his equipment. She heard the occasional blasts from the field with equanimity. On sighting Goddard, she would say proudly: "Here comes the rocket man!"

He reported in some detail on his liquid-fuel research to Riffolt and to the trustees of Clark, and continued to report on his earlier work with the cartridge rocket. Until 1923, in discussing a new device with Riffolt, he customarily added: "Let's keep this under our hat." One day he asked his bemused assistant to sign a pledge of secrecy, with Riffolt's signature notarized.

While the Clark grant was expiring, Goddard sought to entice Abbot with the promise of liquid fuels. America's rocket development, he said in a letter, was in danger of being surpassed abroad. (By American development, he meant his own.) Liquid oxygen, vital to his new work, was expensive, he added. "There is a concern in town which charges $10 for two liters, and will not sell under this amount." The remainder of Clark's grant, he wrote, "will suffice for machine-work . . . [but] will hardly hold out with the above rate for liquid oxygen."

Abbot hesitantly asked for an estimate. Goddard, raising his sights, replied that "an exploration of the atmosphere to its outermost limits would be an undertaking costing between $25,000 and $50,000. . . ."

IX

In the early 1920s, there were two important distinctions between Goddard and the European rocket buffs. First, the Yankee underplayed the prospect for ultimate journeys. Second, he was actually building a rocket.

The small band of Europeans showed no such fondness for self-restraint. At the time, they had neither funds nor experience for rocket construction. But on theory alone, they proclaimed the dawn of both interplanetary and interstellar flight. The rocket age had begun for them with a whoop and a holler.

Shortly after Goddard's Smithsonian report was published, he received numerous requests from abroad for information. An astronomer at the Vatican observatory wanted to know if and when he would send his rocket to the moon. The Vatican wished to observe its flight through telescopes. An Italian general inquired for Goddard's plans for a spaceship. The German Consulate General in New York asked for copies of all of his writings. The Japanese requested blueprints and photostats.

A knowledgeable letter came from Robert Esnault-Pelterie of France, a pioneer aviator, engineer and aircraft manufacturer. Esnault-Pelterie said he had "proved" that space flight could take place only through radioactive energy, that chemical energy was inadequate. He invited Goddard's comments.

Goddard sent the Frenchman his Smithsonian paper, underscoring the use of a multi-stage rocket "by which empty casings were discarded, thereby maintaining a preponderant ratio of propellant to casing or rocket proper." The multi-stage principle, he added firmly, was conceived in 1909 and covered by his United States patent No. 1,102,653, dated

1914. Years later, in 1930, Esnault-Pelterie sent Goddard a first edition of his book which gave the new field of engineering a name. It was titled *L'Astronautique*—astronautics, or navigation among the stars.

Goddard accepted the Frenchman's interest in space craft. The Gallic spirit, he believed, was attuned to beneficial goals. The French had been first to welcome the peaceful possibilities of the balloon and the airplane. He felt less cordial toward the Germans, however, suspecting their tendency to turn inventions into weapons of war. He was uneasy on receiving a letter from that country, dated May 3, 1922, as translated by a friend of the writer into quaintly worded English. It read:

Dear Sir,

already many years I work at the problem to pass over the atmosphere of our earth by means of a rocket. When I was now publishing the result of my examinations and calculations, I learned by the newspaper, that I am not alone in my inquiries and that you, dear Sir, have already done much important works at this sphere. In spite of my efforts, I did not succeed in getting your books about this object.

Therefore I beg you, dear Sir, to let them have me.—At once after coming out of my work I will be honoured to send it to you, for I think that only by the common work of scholars of all nations can be solved this great problem.

> Yours very truly
> Hermann Oberth
> stud. math.
> Heidelberg.
> Kaiserstr. 48^1
> Germany.

With his dogged preference for working alone, Goddard felt threatened by young Oberth's suggestion that "only by the common work of scholars of all nations can be solved this great problem." Moreover, he had no wish for "common work" with a possibly bellicose Germany. With proper courtesy, however, he mailed his 1919 publication to the Heidelberg student and wished him well. He received in time a well-printed, well-reasoned, ninety-two page treatise, published in Munich in 1923 and entitled *Die Rakete zu den Planetenräumen.*

Goddard was disturbed on reading Oberth's treatise and remained so for years. Although Oberth had been born a Transylvanian and did not become a German citizen until the Second World War, Goddard referred to him from the beginning as "that German Oberth." He studied the work of his rocket rival uneasily, translating into English the more difficult German phrases. Goddard never recovered completely from the idea that Oberth had borrowed heavily from him.

Oberth knew his mathematics. He understood, much as had Goddard before him, how a rocket would operate in ultimate flight. What dismayed the Yankee most was possibly Oberth's boldness, but more likely his brilliance. Oberth was not content with a mere moon-striking rocket, but carried his calculations, beyond Goddard's, to the mathematics of spatial trajectories. He declared his intentions in his title: *The Rocket into Interplanetary Space.*

If Goddard was pained, Oberth was also troubled. Knowing of Goddard's priorities, he registered his discomfort in a brief appendix to his 1923 monograph:

"Just at the time of printing this paper, the work of an American scholar, Prof. Robert H. Goddard of Clark University in Worcester, Massachusetts, became known to me. The work was published in 1919 by the well-known Smithsonian Institution. It is called 'A Method of Reaching Extreme Altitudes' and is concerned with rockets.

"Prof. Goddard could experiment with considerable means, while I had to attempt a theoretical handling of the problem. On this basis, both works supplement one another."

Oberth set a style for his German followers. Later, he implied that Goddard was rather pedestrian, interested essentially in atmospheric flight. The Clark professor, he admitted, had mentioned a hydrogen-and-oxygen rocket and other spaceworthy devices. But he was too conservative for a broad understanding of ultimate rocketry.

Goddard brooded about Oberth's treatise for weeks. He neglected so long to acknowledge the monograph that its author sent him a second copy, assuming that the first had been lost in the mails. Goddard tried to be passive. For a time he corresponded briefly with the student, who questioned him on various rocket problems. But Riffolt, who kept hearing grumblings about "that German Oberth," and Dr. Abbot, who received a new rash of papers on space flight, sensed Goddard's distress.

Following Oberth's monograph, the battle for priorities began. The British Interplanetary Society rediscovered Congreve; Germany declared that Oberth was the "true father of rocketry," but Goddard, at home, remained uncelebrated. In 1924, an Austrian ex-pilot named Max Valier published a popular volume called *Der Vorstoss in den Weltenraum,* or "A Dash into Space."

Valier's book set the pattern for Germans seeking to elevate Oberth over Goddard. Valier's view, which infected others, held that the American Goddard was a tinkerer and not really a rocket pioneer while Oberth was a bona fide visionary.

In his efforts to dismiss Goddard, Valier also suggested that the American was "afraid to handle" liquid fuels, unlike Professor Oberth who "has not permitted himself to be frightened away." Then he summoned all true Germans to the launching pad:

"There is no doubt: the moment is here, the hour has come, in which we may dare to undertake the attack on the stars with real prospects of results. It is clear that the armor of the earth's gravity will not lightly be pierced, and it is to be expected that it will cost, to break through it, much sacrifice of time, money and perhaps also human life."

On January 9, 1926, Russia's Nikolai Rynin, "Professor of Aerial Transport," wrote to Goddard from Leningrad requesting a copy of his 1919 paper. After reviewing it, he wrote again on April 11:

"I have read very attentively your remarkable book 'A Method of Reaching Extreme Altitudes' edited in 1919 and I have found in it quite all the ideas which the German professor H. Oberth published in 1924 as new about flying in 'infinite' altitude."

In Europe the flights of fancy far outdistanced the flights of fact. Writers, technicians and theorists accused one another of misrepresentation and foul play. One result of the uproar was the rediscovery by the Soviet Union of their own Konstantin E. Tsiolkovsky (1857–1935), now considered to be the "father" of present-day Russia's achievements in rocketry. Stalin's Russia frequently made elaborate and reckless claims to technical firsts in innumerable sciences, but with Tsiolkovsky they restored a true pioneer. The school teacher's article on rockets, "Investigation of Space by Means of Rockets," published in 1903, had suggested liquid fuels, multiple stages, and the attainment of outer space by rocket power. Previously ignored, he was now hailed by the Kremlin as the first of the space men, which indeed he proved to be. Celebrated at last in his own country, Tsiolkovsky issued a revised edition of his rocket theory in 1926 in which he cited the works of Goddard and Oberth as appearing "many years" after his own. Oberth eventually admitted, in a letter to Tsiolkovsky, that "I would certainly be much further in my own work today . . . had I taken into account your superior work."

(In 1928 Rynin published a nine-volume work on "Interplanetary Travel," based on the considerable investigations of early Russian scientists and technicians. According to

Colonel G. A. Tokaty of the Moscow Military Air Academy, who defected to the British in 1948, rocket projects and theories in Russia dated back to 1881, before Tsiolkovsky. The Russian rocket scientist's report was delivered before the British Interplanetary Society in London on September 22, 1961.)

At the vortex of his own difficult experiments, Goddard wondered how soon the European theorists would catch up with him. As in *Alice in Wonderland,* when the whiting warned the snail to "walk a little faster," Goddard sensed that there was, indeed, "a porpoise close behind us and he's treading on my tail."

He had summed up such sentiments in 1923, in a memorandum to the Smithsonian Institution:

"I am not surprised that Germany has awakened to the importance and the development possibilities of the work, and I would not be surprised if it were only a matter of time before the research would become something in the nature of a race."

x

On a bright May morning in 1923, Dr. Webster reported to his cluttered and comfortable office in the physics building at Clark. His white hair and flamboyant mustache were combed, his collar immaculate behind a black four-in-hand tie, his rimless pince-nez magnifying the intensity of his outlook. In his sixtieth year, he was a master of fundamental theory, a pioneer in dynamics, an expert in ballistics. He lifted a pistol, pulled its trigger and killed himself.

Goddard heard of the event late in the afternoon when he returned to the university. It was a tragic end to a dreary day he had spent at the Viscoloid Company in nearby Leominster. His rocket components had been having an unpredictable series of breakdowns. When one part worked, another part failed. He had been exploring new possibilities for his piston pumps. These subjects were on his mind when he heard the news and also learned that he was being considered as Webster's successor.

After the funeral, Webster's colleagues and former students paid tribute to the great physicist's genius and tried to account for his suicide. Some said that Webster had sought to encompass the whole field of physics, but that modern discovery had made it impossible for him, or indeed for anyone, to keep up in all areas. Others declared that he had hoped to be called to a larger university. A few, trained in modern psychology, suggested that the reasons lay deeper.

Goddard's tribute to his dean and teacher was measured:

"As I think of the late Dr. Webster, two things come strongest to my mind. The first of these is Dr. Webster as a lecturer; for as a lecturer and teacher in mathematical physics I cannot imagine an equal in the clearness and elegance of presentation of his subject. He was an inspiration even to those who were not natural mathematicians.

"The second thought is the tremendous loss to physics in America occasioned by Dr. Webster's death, for I can think of no man in America today who is more active and stimulating, or who could inspire such high enthusiasm over the fundamental conceptions of physics.

"As time passes, Dr. Webster grows more and more to be an ideal and an incentive. . . ."

XI

Shortly after Webster's death, Goddard was appointed head of the university's department of physics. Meanwhile, his life had taken a radical turn. He proposed to Esther Kisk, persuading her to leave college to marry him.

Her parents had all along been dubious about her marrying a man so much her senior and apparently in frail health. He assured them that his tuberculosis was under control, submitting himself to the Kisk family doctor, who said that he and his bride might expect a reasonably lengthy life together if he took care of himself.

They were married in a small, quiet ceremony at St. John's Episcopal Church on Saturday morning, June 21, 1924, and left in a new blue coupé for a week's honeymoon in the White Mountains of New Hampshire. Goddard's colleagues at Clark, considering him a permanent bachelor, were surprised at the match. His former nurse, Miss Doyle, upon noting a resemblance, exclaimed: "Heavens preserve us, Robert! You've married your own mother!"

"I had expected a placid academic life with Bob," Mrs. Goddard recalled. "I'd heard of his rockets, but they really hadn't made much impression. As for space flight, I was sure it was just a newspaper sensation. He seemed so sound and sure of himself that I was thrilled to go along."

His young bride's estimate of the professor's conservatism was soon altered. A few months before their marriage, he had undertaken some editorial work for Watson Davis at Science Service, a Washington news agency. Davis planned to reissue and serialize the novels of Jules Verne, and asked Goddard to correct Verne's technical errors.

Shortly after arriving at their honeymoon inn, Esther was surprised to see her new husband laboring over a mound of manuscript he had brought along.

"What are you doing, Bob?" she asked.

"Oh, just puttering around with an old book," he replied.

"What old book?"

"A novel by Jules Verne," said the professor, "called *From the Earth to the Moon.* . . ."

Verne had transported his space travelers to the moon in an artillery shell fired from a huge cannon. Goddard deftly transferred them to a multi-stage rocket. The new version, however, was never published. Perhaps it was too advanced, even for Jules Verne.

6. LITTLE DOG WITH A GREAT BIG BONE

Shortly after his honeymoon, Goddard put the Jules Verne fantasy aside. He spent the next two years bringing his own vision more clearly into focus. The liquid-fuel method, he was sure, was workable—"a satisfactory lifting force could be obtained." But his new model was undergoing a protracted adolescence.

He tried to develop a miniature, high-pressure piston pump to send the fluids coursing into the rocket's combustion chamber. He packed the small pump with asbestos and devised a water jacket to cool the walls of the chamber, but the rocket rejected his ingenuity by freezing up, burning out, exploding its valves.

On February 11, 1925, he confided the problem to Dr. William J. Humphreys, the meteorological physicist.

"My hardest job is to make things operate on a scale sufficiently small to avoid the use of much liquid oxygen," Goddard wrote. "I spent two months last summer trying to make one feature operate when made small, and had to give it up at last, and do it another way (which took another month). It is proving most conclusively to be a case of 'the bigger the better.' It is the same old story of no support until results are had, and no results unless sufficient support is had. . . . I confess it would be much more exciting to work on a larger scale, but it is not possible to think of that now."

Handicapped by uncertain support, Goddard concluded the costly pump experiments, simplified his rocket and hoped for a modest flight. By eliminating the balky pumps, he kept the device at a weight of only 4¾ pounds when empty. It was an unavoidable compromise. For great rocket flights, he knew, self-contained pumps were essential. But they would have to wait for a while.

By December 1925, Goddard was testing a new rocket engine in the static rack attached to the physics building. Instead of pumps to force-feed the fuels, he now employed the back pressure from an inert gas, stored in a nearby stationary tank. The engine, under its own power, lifted itself for 27 seconds in the static testing rack. For the first time, the liquid-fuel rocket behaved as Goddard had planned.

The professor was elated. He reported the news that evening to his bride: "The rocket lifted today. It lifted its own weight." She looked at him uncomprehendingly. "That's nice," she said. Dr. Abbot was also unmoved by the news. He wanted an actual flight, not merely a demonstration. A few months later, the Goddard rocket flew.

March 16, 1926, was a clear cold day in Worcester with snow on the ground and no promise of spring in the sharp morning air. It was a Tuesday, the professor's free day, with no classes scheduled when he met Henry Sachs, his new machinist, in the Clark physics shop. For a time Goddard had missed Riffolt, who left Clark to go with Louis Thompson to the Naval Proving Ground at Dahlgren, Virginia. But Henry Sachs was working out well. The son of a German blacksmith, he had accepted Goddard's offer of "six months' work, maybe longer."

The physicist carefully locked the door of the shop and climbed into his coupé beside Sachs. Goddard always preferred coupés— "You don't have to take an excess of people." Between them were two fresh liters of liquid oxygen. There was no guarantee of more from Linde Air Products for several weeks. If their March flight failed, it would be April, at least, before they could try again.

The professor was bundled against the Massachusetts chill, thanks to Esther's concern for his health. In cold months, he now wore high-buckled galoshes, a greatcoat buttoned up to his neck, a muffler and a warm woolen cap. In this costume, he left the Clark campus, driving along Freeland and Cambridge streets to Southbridge, then up Pakachoag Hill to Auburn and Aunt Effie's farm.

Parking at a ravine some distance from the farmhouse, Goddard and Sachs carried, slid and eased the wooden crates containing tools and the rocket's motor, tanks and piping to a secluded spot near a cabbage patch. They erected a pipe launching frame and hopefully placed the fragile rocket inside it.

The two men worked through the cold morning hours, rigging their gear. The rocket consisted of tubing, ten feet long, framing a two-foot motor and nozzle. The inventor, in a futile try for stability, had positioned the motor and nozzle ahead of the rocket's fuel and oxygen tanks, rather than behind them. He believed at first that the engine would travel more truly if it preceded, rather than followed, its source of power, much as a wagon follows the tug of a child. But it was a mistake to burden the new device with old analogies and, shortly, Goddard would locate the motor at the rear of his rocket, where it remained.

His invention, Goddard was finding, demanded novelty throughout—in its design, its fuels, its components. At Waite's

Hardware Store he might shop for routine items such as nuts and bolts, files and drills, or lengths of steel piping. But for other parts, he learned to put things together, using a discarded coffee tin when it served or sending to the William Jessup Steel Company in England for sheet steel when the local product failed him. Sachs, at first, had thought him unduly finicky. But Jessup's steel, he learned, withstood twice as many bends, without snapping, as the American variety.

Shortly after noon the rocket was ready. Percy Roope, Clark's assistant professor of physics, arrived at the Ward farm with Mrs. Goddard. She had her husband's latest purchase slung over her shoulder, a French "Sept" motion picture camera, so named because it ran for seven seconds without rewinding. On many occasions she had chatted briefly with Aunt Effie in her warm, commodious kitchen, with its familiar windowbox of bright geraniums. Miss Ward, never quite sure about rockets, once again offered Esther and her fellow adventurers a cup of hot malted milk as her specific against the chills.

There was no intricate electrical system to ignite the rocket motor. When black smoke issued from the igniter, Sachs turned a valve and lighted an alcohol stove beneath the motor. Goddard waited for ninety seconds, then released the rocket. He and Roope edged behind a sheet-iron barricade; Sachs ran toward them; the rocket roared off as oxygen and gasoline combusted.

Esther's camera, unfortunately, ran down in the preliminaries of launching. There is no motion picture of the actual flight which began with a sharp, popping sound and then a whitish blast from the nozzle. The sire of spaceships left its frame, flew 41 feet high and 184 feet away, as Roope recorded it on his theodolite. It traveled this distance in $2\frac{1}{2}$ seconds; then it crumpled to earth.

The maiden flight of the liquid-propelled rocket received brief notice in Goddard's diary:

"March 16. Went to Auburn with S in am. E and Mr. Roope came out at 1 p.m. Tried rocket at 2.30. It rose 41 feet & went 184 feet, in 2.5 secs., after the lower half of the nozzle had burned off. Brought materials to lab. . . ."

Goddard permitted himself more excitement in his experimental notes one day later:

"March 17, 1926. The first flight with a rocket using liquid propellants was made yesterday at Aunt Effie's farm in Auburn.

"The day was clear and comparatively quiet. The anemometer in the Physics lab was turning leisurely when Mr. Sachs and I left in the morning, and was turning as leisurely when we returned at 5:30 p.m.

"Even though the release was pulled, the rocket did not rise at first, but the flame came out, and there was a steady roar. After a number of seconds it rose, slowly until it cleared the frame, and then at express train speed, curving over to the left, and striking the ice and snow, still going at a rapid rate.

"It looked almost magical as it rose, without any appreciably greater noise or flame, as if it said: 'I've been here long enough; I think I'll be going somewhere else, if you don't mind.'*

"Esther said that it looked like a fairy or an esthetic dancer as it started off.

"The sky was clear, for the most part, with large shadowy white clouds, but by late in the afternoon there was a large pink cloud in the west, over which the sun shone.

"One of the surprising things was the absence of smoke, the lack of a very loud roar, and the smallness of the flame."

Shortly after the flight, Goddard wrote glowingly to Abbot that the test "proved conclusively the practicality of the

---

* What Goddard actually said for his rocket, Mrs. Goddard recalled, was: "I think I'll get the hell out of here!"

liquid-propelled rocket," adding that he needed more funds "if great heights are intended." He attached a still photograph showing the launching frame after his rocket's departure. "I might entitle this 'The Empty Frame,' inasmuch as I have been working to make a liquid-propelled rocket leave a frame since 1920."

If Goddard regarded the flight as historic, he soon learned that the modest lift fell short of impressing his Washington sponsor. In his "Material for an Autobiography," the professor, with some dismay, recorded Abbot's reaction:

"This flight, to be sure, was small, and was not considered by the Smithsonian Institution as a flight that would convince the public of the possibilities of the method. As a first flight, it compared favorably with the Wrights' first airplane flight, however, and the event, as demonstrating the first liquid-propelled rocket, was just as significant."

Of the few who knew of the pioneer flight, each responded in his own way. While Goddard was jubilant, Abbot seemed disappointed. After a nine-year promise of "extreme altitudes," his protégé's rocket had "soared" a mere 41 feet.

Asa Ward, Aunt Effie's nephew, called Goddard's try an example of New England cussedness. He said: "Bob Goddard was the most stubborn fellow I ever knew. Once I asked him about his moon rocket. 'Asa,' he told me, 'all I'm trying to do is to get this thing off the ground.' "

In Esther, the flight aroused an enduring enthusiasm for her husband's quest.

"He was in love with a will-o'-the-wisp, more glamorous than I could ever be," she said. "But it took this flight before I could share his excitement.

"Looking back, it was the most beautiful sight in the world seeing the rocket take off. We slogged jubilantly through the mud of Aunt Effie's cabbage patch toward the broken and twisted wreckage. . . ."

II

When Robert Goddard married, he became the head of his own household, bringing Esther to the old home on Maple Hill which he had inherited from Madame Goddard. He was forty-two years old. If his grandmother's house was shabby and rundown, Esther told him, she could soon put it in order. She explored it thoroughly, planning an ample fireplace in the living room; a commodious porch; a modern kitchen; tidier grounds. Then she went downtown to open a savings account.

The professor's wife quickly went to work. She covered old furniture with new slipcovers, draped windows with fresh chintz, had dreary walls repainted. She took Robert to an office supply store where he bought a large old desk for his study. Then she attacked the attic, a mausoleum of files, cartons, outworn clothes and bric-a-brac. The Goddards, apparently, had never thrown anything away.

The young bride tried to adjust to her husband's middle-aged ways, including his odd preoccupation with rockets. She liked to think of him in terms of the popular ballad, *"Just Plain Bill. . . .* You'd pass him on the street and never notice him. . . ." Most faculty wives were free to bob their hair and wear lipstick, but not Dr. Goddard's wife. Her blonde hair, usually worn in a figure eight at her neck, looked right to him.

For relaxation her husband enjoyed painting landscapes which, according to an artist friend, showed more enthusiasm than talent, or playing the piano by ear. He rendered with cheerful abandon selections from *Die Meistersinger, No, No, Nanette,* and various popular songs he had heard on the radio. He was fond of movies, particularly such fare as Buster Keaton, Harold Lloyd, and Laurel and Hardy comedies. He heartily disliked bridge. At faculty bridge parties, he often sat in an easy chair, smoking a cigar and daydreaming. "Just doping," he explained these reveries.

Esther, however, succeeded in drawing him into the convivial society of the young professors whom President Atwood was recruiting. Together, they attended picnics, parties at one another's homes and shared a genial good humor. Behind Goddard's façade of reticence, his younger colleagues found a man eager for friendship, except when it concerned his work. One of Goddard's new companions was especially flattered when he was invited into the workshop to meet Sachs and the latest rocket model. "The younger faculty people were casual and Bob liked them," said Esther. "He began to mix more easily."

She had few of the usual bride's prospects of changing her husband, either before or after their mission to Auburn. If he was one of a rare, obsidian breed, New England had recently sent to Washington another example in the person of Vermont's Calvin Coolidge. When asked about unemployment, the new President tersely declared that unemployment existed when people were out of work. The Goddards, father and son, had much the same granitic humor.

In August 1928, while Coolidge was still in office, Nahum Goddard came home from the L. Hardy Company for the last time. In spite of his reticence, Esther felt a warm kinship with her father-in-law, then in his seventieth year. Under Nahum's Yankee reserve, she sensed and shared his concern for his unfathomable offspring.

On September 15, 1928, Nahum lay in bed, dying from cancer of the throat. He attempted to speak to his son, then asked if Esther were in the room. She came to his bedside, knowing that Nahum once more was entrusting to her, in Robert, an uncertain life poised at the edge of achievement. She felt profoundly committed. By morning Nahum was dead.

Robert turned back to his work, with the comfort of a newly dedicated wife.

After his appointment as Dr. Webster's successor, Esther had helped Goddard move into his former teacher's office. They had refurbished it, hanging a large portrait of Webster behind the desk and, in the nearby hall, a gallery of noted physicists, wearing laboratory aprons.

Esther was now a rocket buff and defender of inventors' ways. When Clark, Worcester and his colleagues occasionally criticized Goddard for his secrecy, she stubbornly defended his trait as "proper Yankee pride." "Robert isn't secretive," she would explain. "He just doesn't like to talk too much."

Once she mentioned to Goddard the difficulty of pursuing an objective so beset with problems. "If it were easy," he told her, "somebody would have done it long ago." When she was caustic about the lack of public support, he spoke as the unruffled physicist: "The greatest of all forces is inertia. Most folks lack the ability to move."

The rocket was now taking most of his free time. It meant postponing dinners and weekend holidays, and spending summers in the laboratory. The summer was "the golden time," he said. He could devote his full energies to research. After his father's death, he turned more to Esther. Since the 1926 flight, she too was immersed in the rocket's progress—as secretary, photographer, stomper-out of brush fires and seamstress of parachutes which rarely functioned as they were expected to do. When his optimism lagged, she stepped in to buttress it. But it seldom needed buttressing.

If Worcester and even his faculty brethren failed to esteem his rocket, Goddard felt that some day they would. He liked to recall to Esther his father's story of the astonishment in a small Ohio town during the Civil War when it heard that Ulysses Grant, a well-starred general, was leading all the Union forces. A citizen exclaimed, "Lead an *army!* My God, he comes from the same town I do!"

If Goddard was little known at home, he would soon attract attention abroad. When his mail began to report a rush of rocket activity in France, Italy, Japan, Russia and, especially, in Germany, he would say wistfully to his wife:

"I'm just a little dog—with a great big bone."

III

At the Smithsonian, Abbot pressed on for higher altitudes. In 1924, Goddard's sponsor had obtained $2,500 through a private foundation, the Research Corporation of New York, established on patent royalties issued to Dr. Frederick G. Cottrell, an inventive chemist. Abbot administered the Cottrell Fund proceeds in $500 doses. It was like feeding peanuts to a hippopotamus.

In July 1926, after the historic rocket flight, Abbot offered a second Cottrell grant of $2,500, to be given in similar allotments. Goddard was expected, within a year, to produce a spectacular rocket. Once again, the funds diminished with alarming speed.

Abbot sent Goddard the customary $500 in January 1927, advising him that the Institution's work would soon be reviewed by President Coolidge and other distinguished visitors. Then Abbot added plaintively: ". . . if it should happen that a successful flight was made before February 11, it would be a grand thing for the Smithsonian." At the end of his letter, Abbot wrote in longhand: "I hope you will not fail to let me have the scoop on the story of the first [sic] flight." The $500 allotment was soon expended. There was no scoop.

A year later, when Abbot succeeded Walcott as Secretary of the Smithsonian, Goddard sent his sponsor a note of congratulations: "A better choice for Secretary could not have been made." Abbot's reply was unusually crusty. "May I ask how the work is coming on?" he inquired.

It was an unfortunate question. The work was coming along slowly. After flying his liquid-fuel rocket a second time on April 3, 1926, Goddard had tried to increase its dimensions and its potential altitude. In 1928, he had made it 10½ feet long with a combustion chamber 8 inches in diameter, more than 20 times the size of his 1926 model. But it presented unexpected problems when it was positioned in the new 60-foot launching tower at Aunt Effie's farm.

Goddard labored for solutions. He devised ignition and launching systems, and created a method he called "curtain" or "film" cooling. This cooling technique, intended to withstand the heat of combustion, spiraled the gasoline fuel or liquid oxygen along the inside wall of the fiery chamber. It was like wetting your finger for insulation before touching a hot stove. When the interior walls of the chamber were completely covered by fuel, the method worked. But if the liquid film exposed the walls, even momentarily, to the cauldron of combustion, they burned through at once. One of Goddard's most ingenious inventions, "curtain cooling" would take years beyond the pioneer's time to perfect.

The larger rocket was not merely an expanded version of the earlier model. Its innovations posed a new set of problems, which sometimes included carting it through the mud or snow between the farmhouse and the launching tower.

The professor's diary was a bleak recital of human and mechanical errors: "There was no appreciable lift" . . . "Ran test. Nozzle burned off" . . . "Tried valve" . . . "worked with Sachs on valve" . . . "S forgot the alcohol stove."

Goddard thought about new means of feeding fuels into the chamber, of a rotating platform to give his rocket spin and stability, of a new ignition system. But beyond these devices was the unremitting fact that the large rocket, burning, smoking and splitting, simply refused to move.

Pushing for altitude, the professor had tried for too much, too fast, too soon.

Test after test with his oversized rocket, recalled Esther, "found us holding our breaths during long, brilliant runs, only to see the jet die out, never attaining enough push for flight. Bob lay awake nights, planning one modification after another. But instead of a little flier, he had built a big sitter." In September 1927 Goddard stopped work on his large rocket.

He had no thought of abandoning his soaring quest. In the same month he decided to return to a more modest model, 9 feet and 7 inches long, and 10 inches in diameter between the outer piping, but with a much smaller motor. It was a strategic retreat. Dr. Abbot made one of his rare inspection trips to Worcester and, as Goddard said, "seemed pleased by the simplicity of the design."

When Goddard's graduate students lacked topics for their theses, he was always ready to supply them with his. In an unpublished paper, "The Ultimate in Jet Propulsion," he explained his method:

"With a problem as fascinating as the navigation of inter-planetary space as a hobby, it has been natural to assign Master of Arts thesis topics in the field, when the student did not already have a problem upon which he desired to work. The results of these theses, in affording a check upon the theoretical conclusions, have been interesting, although unknown to the students carrying out the investigations."

Perhaps the closest he came to confiding his scheme to a student was to Albert E. Erickson, who helped him devise a so-called "resonance chamber" in 1932, for which Goddard had scrupulously applied for a patent a year earlier. Compared to his more ambitious rockets, the chamber was a modest device, designed to fly within the earth's atmosphere.

It was an air breather, equipped with louvered shutters at each end to gulp in air, and used gasoline as its fuel. Erickson was one of Goddard's few students who witnessed a rocket test. He died before the Germans converted a "resonance chamber" into the better-known V-1, or "buzz bomb," of the Second World War.

Other students, unknowingly, became involved in Goddard's distant aspirations. Even Nils Riffolt, his dependable assistant and instrument maker, was not aware that he was advancing space flight through his master's thesis, "A Study in the Absorption of Radiant Energy." Riffolt's thoughtful paper helped prove that a solar motor could operate in space beyond the earth's atmosphere.

In 1925, Goddard assigned his 1906 vision of an ion-propelled rocket to Russell B. Hastings under the academic title, "The Emission of Electricity from Substances on Incandescent Carbon." The results were inconclusive, although the experimenters heated carbon in the physics laboratory up to 2,500 degrees centigrade. In 1926, Goddard passed on the problem to another graduate scholar, Lewis M. Sleeper, who called his thesis: "The Emission of Positive Electricity from Potassium, Heated on a Platinum Filament in a Vacuum." Sleeper provided the proof his professor wanted.

None of his students suspected Goddard's intentions. Years later, when Hastings was head of the physics department at Macalester College in Minnesota, he remembered only one occasion when the professor showed inner stress. Goddard was making his way to the laboratory on a rainy day, neglecting to close his umbrella. It caught in a doorway and turned inside out. "I'll be damned," said Goddard, abandoning his usual equanimity.

"Unlike most research physicists, who were usually poor teachers," Hastings said, "Goddard was the best I ever had. But I never suspected that he was planning to use my work to prove ion repulsion for rockets."

Although the operation of such concepts lay far in the future, the doctor began to set down in an array of red notebooks a flood of new ideas. When his notions seemed workable, he had them notarized and took them to Charles Hawley to apply for patents. Among them were Goddard's plans for "curtain cooling," a turbine-operated rocket, a turbojet system and the employment of gyroscopes in steering rockets.

He visited the attorney whenever he could affort to invest in more patents. Although Hawley's charges were moderate, they were a drain on Goddard's modest salary. Once, short of funds, he tried to process his own application for a vaporizer to be used with a solar boiler. The patent office, disallowing the application, wrote bluntly: "As the value of patents depends largely on the care with which the disclosure and claims are drawn, applicant is advised to secure the services of a regular patent attorney in the further prosecution of this application." Sheepishly, Goddard took his vaporizer plan to Hawley, who prepared the application and secured the patent.

The lawyer knew he had an unusual client. "Most professors are glad to tell you everything they know," he said later. "Bob was superb at explaining general principles, but he was always careful to protect his ideas. I don't believe he expected his patents to make money. He knew they were basic devices and it could take years before they were commercially useful. What he really wanted was to protect his priorities."

IV

The model Goddard would fly in the summer of 1929, and which brought him unwanted notoriety, was proved through an arduous series of tests. As flaws in design and function were resolved, the rocket's jet became shorter, whiter, more pointed, its lift steadier and of longer duration.

By May 1929, he had a model 11½ feet long, 26 inches wide at the guiding vanes, weighing 35 pounds when empty. After running some promising static tests, he installed recording instruments. The rocket's first payload for meteorology included a small aneroid barometer, a thermometer and a camera. The camera was intended to be triggered automatically as the rocket's parachute was released at the zenith of its flight. It would photograph the readings of the barometer and thermometer, giving the top altitude, the temperature and a view of the receding ground.

On May 17, Goddard's first flight with an instrumented rocket failed when a fuel pipe blew off its fastening and the nozzle burned through. After repairs were made, another flight was scheduled for July 17, 1929.

The rocket needed more assistants. In addition to Sachs, Goddard in 1928 employed Albert Kisk, his brother-in-law, and a machinist, and Lawrence Mansur, a Clark graduate student.

The morning of July 17 was spent in preparations for flight. Goddard made a final check of the rocket's components, then rehearsed his crew in their duties. His physics assistant, Percy Roope, and Esther, also attended the performance. They all took their places shortly before two o'clock. Goddard wrote in his experimental notes:

"Dr. Roope was well in the rear of the shelter with his theodolite and stop watch. Mrs. Goddard stood just outside the right end of the shelter, holding the Cine-Kodak camera in her hands. Beside her was Mr. Kisk, who was asked to watch the cord to the cotter pin, to make certain that it was pulled off. I came next, and to my left was Mr. Sachs, who operated the pressure-generating tank, using the two cords for that purpose. At the extreme left end of the shelter, Mr. Mansur was stationed, and asked to watch the behavior of the rocket as closely as possible. . . ."

After these preliminaries, Goddard ordered the test to proceed. Sachs ignited the alcohol stove, then retired to the shelter:

"Thirty seconds after the alcohol stove was lighted, the igniter was fired, and the next three controls were operated. Mr. Sachs then gave the rocket 125 lbs. pressure. . . . I waited until the rocket had risen three inches, as indicated by the aluminum vanes on the rocket rising up to the white marks, 3 inches long, on the vertical $\frac{3}{8}$ inch pipe guides. I then pulled the two releasing cords in succession.

"The noise did not appear to change, and I kept pulling the $\frac{1}{4}$ inch rope, thinking that the rocket had not been released, until I heard someone shout 'Look out!' When I looked out of the right end of the shelter I saw the rocket just before it hit the ground. . . ."

Goddard was visibly pleased. His rocket, Dr. Roope reported, went 20 feet above the 60 foot launching tower, turned right, rose another 10 feet. Before striking the ground 171 feet away, it had climbed to twice the altitude of the 1926 flight.

First to reach the fallen rocket, Goddard began evaluating its virtues and flaws. It had failed to reach enough height to trigger its parachute, landing with a jarring impact. From his inspection, it was clear that the gases had left the nozzle in an irregular fashion, caused by "occasional rushes of gas or gasoline, on one side or the other, or to 'sloshing' of the liquids in the tanks from side to side. . . ." He decided to improve the release mechanism, "to have a single lever operate all the releases in the proper order."

An examination of the rocket showed that the camera, although scorched, was still operating and that the barometer was functioning. The thermometer was broken, evidently from the rocket's soaring heat.

It was a hot, quiet afternoon. Sounds traveled far from Pakachoag Hill and attracted attention.

"We should have been packed and back to the laboratory before they found us," Goddard wrote later, "had it not been for the lever device on the top of the cap for the gasoline tank, to open as a vent in an emergency. This could not be found, and as it represented considerable work, we stayed and hunted for it."

While the Goddard crew was thriftily hunting for the lever, they heard the shriek of a siren. They looked up to see a police patrol car, two ambulances and a convoy of automobiles stopping in Aunt Effie's farmyard. Two policemen, perhaps expecting catastrophe, inspected the rural scene, saw the steel tower and asked questions. The professor had been causing quite a stir, one policeman said. Neighbors were saying that an airplane had crashed and exploded.

The crew, noncommittal, referred all questions to Goddard, who tried for nonchalance. Nothing had crashed, he reassured the patrolmen. He was engaged in a little experiment with a rocket. He was Professor Goddard, over at Clark University. It would help if the police would keep things quiet.

"Not likely, Professor," they told him. "Those two men there are reporters for the *Gazette* and the *Post*."

The reporters were already inspecting the charred field, especially the boulders beneath the tower which were blackened and partly disintegrated from previous tests. They asked questions which Goddard deflected, still attempting to guard his once secret retreat. But they knew him by reputation. "The moon-rocket man," a reporter mused. "How close did you get this time?"

For several days, Goddard denied he was trying to reach the moon and had somehow missed it by more than 200,000 miles. Nothing extraordinary had happened in Auburn, he said. Nothing had exploded. He was conducting "one of a series of experiments in rockets." "The rocket," he explained, "is normally noisy, possibly enough to attract attention, but the test was thoroughly satisfactory."

Again Goddard was adrift in a sea of publicity. He wanted to tell the public that, yes, the rocket would be man's great prime mover. Yes, it would eventually reach the moon. But the public kept asking the same old question. When would it happen? When will your rocket do what you say it can do?

The headlines and front-page stories were all that he feared. They made him out as a reckless moon seeker, a public amusement. It was the next morning, that Larry Mansur, entering the Clark laboratories, had spoken of the newspaper sensation with annoyance, adding the cliché from the old melodrama: "They ain't done right by our Nell."

Thereafter, the Goddard rocket had a name.

v

In Worcester and Auburn, Nell caused uneasiness, eventually alerting the Massachusetts fire marshal, George Neal. Once alerted, it was impossible to unalert him.

Goddard tried to "clarify" matters to a state fire inspector representing the marshal. His rocket tower, he said, was at least a half mile from the nearest dwelling, except for that of his willing Aunt Effie. There was no danger of an uncontrollable explosion. The model was small. It had almost no chance of flying beyond its testing field.

The inspector passed along to the marshal the professor's bland reassurances, trying to put out the brush fires of concern:

"Professor Goddard's experiments are of real value to mankind and, at the same time, are conducted under absolutely safe conditions. He is conducting them under a certain amount of secrecy which cannot be avoided if the type of explosive he is using is not to become public."

But neither the fire marshal nor the townspeople of Auburn were so easily placated. Aroused, Auburn declared that the moon rocket be outlawed as a public menace. Fire Marshal Neal demanded that the professor remove his menacing tests from the Commonwealth.

In a letter to Dr. Abbot, Goddard summed up his predicament:

"Since the recent tests, the Auburn farm has been besieged by newspapermen and sightseers, who have photographed and measured the tower and gathered souvenirs. . . .

"It seems to me that it will hardly be possible to continue the work unless the tests can be carried out in a location from which trespassers can be barred, and where there is no chance of danger to private property. . . .

"With this situation in mind, I took a trip recently to Camp Devens, a federal property, which was a training camp during the war, part of which is now used as a camp, and other parts of which are used occasionally for rifle and artillery ranges. I located a place which looks promising. . . . It is not visible from outside the reservation. . . .

"If you could arrange with the authorities in Washington so that we could have this spot and have government no trespassing signs posted at the two ends of the old road . . . I think it would be as near an ideal arrangement as we could have. . . ."

Like Dr. Pangloss in Voltaire's *Candide,* Goddard soon learned that this was by no means an ideal world, although possibly the best of likely ones. Through Abbot's intercession, he received permission from the War Department to use the Camp Devens property. There were several limitations, however. The commanding officer there would determine where his launching tower might be erected, where

NO TRESPASSING signs could be placed. Flight tests were permissible only after rains or when the ground was covered by snow. Also, Goddard would have to maintain properly approved fire extinguishers.

In October, he shifted his testing to the Devens military base, twenty-five miles from Worcester, where he was assigned to the bleak extremity of an artillery range, at the end of a jolting country road.

An empty henhouse near an abandoned farm building, riddled with shellholes, served as headquarters. There Goddard installed an old stove on which Mansur, or Esther on her visits, warmed up soup for lunch. The tower at Aunt Effie's was dismantled, hauled to the new site and erected at the bottom of a sloping hillside which gave some shelter from the wind. Nearby was a stagnant, unshaded pool called Hell Pond. It was no misnomer.

At Hell Pond, Goddard improved his motor's combustion, but the place was impractical for flight tests. Even though Goddard, Sachs and Kisk left the Clark shop before dawn, to allow time for setting up the apparatus, the rutted roads into the reservation usually jarred the rocket components, putting them out of order. Whenever that happened, the repairs lost them several hours of the day.

If Goddard despaired, however, he never revealed it. The road to Camp Devens brought him past a statue of an Indian warrior, bow bent, arrow cocked at the heavens. The Indian was named Pumunangwet, meaning "he who shoots the stars." But there was no star-shooting that dreary winter.

On a gray afternoon in November 1929, Goddard dismissed his last class for the day. He was sitting at his desk, planning the next morning's odyssey to Devens, when he received an unlikely telephone call. It was Charles A. Lindbergh, the world-famous flier, announcing that he was interested in the rocket and wished to drive to Worcester the next morning to visit with Goddard. The professor listened, incredulous. He would be available at the colonel's pleasure, he said.

"Esther," Goddard began, unfolding his napkin at supper that evening. "I had an interesting call from Charles Lindbergh."

"Of course, Bob," his wife replied airily. "And I had tea with Marie, the Queen of Rumania."

VI

Only twenty-six years before, in 1903, the Wright brothers had flown the first successful motorized airplane over the sand near Kitty Hawk, North Carolina. Man's flight seemed then so improbable that even in Dayton, home town of Orville and Wilbur, streetcar riders watching them in flight over nearby fields were still debating whether flight was possible. But for all their astigmatism, the air age had come.

Within a quarter of a century, young eagles were attempting to vault the Atlantic Ocean between the United States and Europe. In 1919, the U.S. Navy's NC-4 accomplished the first of these flights. Eight years later, in 1927, Charles Lindbergh, flying solo, succeeded in the first non-stop airplane flight between the two continents. He thought it extraordinary when France, the United States and the rest of the world were so aroused by his solitary flight and landing in Paris.

VII

Of all Americans, Lindbergh was perhaps most closely attuned to the orbits of Dr. Goddard. At their first meeting in Goddard's office at Clark, the pilot and the professor were mutually impressed. Both were essentially soli-taries. Goddard was excited by the young flier's lively, in-tuitive sense of what the rocket might accomplish. Lindbergh was delighted, in turn, to hear what the professor had al-ready accomplished. The development required additional financial support. Of course, said the flier. That was always a problem. He had faced it himself in attracting St. Louis businessmen to underwrite his monoplane.

It was two and a half years before, that the son of the Minnesota congressman had flown the Atlantic. He was still celebrated for ushering in the age of air travel and heralded as America's great flight pioneer. But with all his fame, young Lindbergh approached Goddard with admiration. He had some questions to ask that troubled him. Since his re-turn to the United States, he had had a persistent daydream.

"I was trying to look far into the future of flight, and this took me into space," Lindbergh said. "I realized the limita-tions of the propeller, and this led me into the field of rockets and jet propulsion which I decided to investigate. I became very interested in the idea of spatial travel and the possibility of using rockets on airplanes as a preliminary step."

A few weeks before visiting Goddard at Worcester, Lind-bergh had taken the rocket problem to the Du Pont Corpora-tion in Wilmington, Delaware. "I felt that such a great organization, with more than a century's experience in mak-ing chemicals and explosives, might be able to answer my questions," he said.

No door was closed to him. The Du Pont executives ar-ranged a conference of their chief scientists and engineers to discuss his ideas. By the end of the first quarter of the twentieth century, man had successfully conquered the earth, sea and air, Lindbergh observed. Would it be possible in the next quarter century to travel through space, using a rocket for propulsion? The boyish colonel at once sensed the skepticism of the Du Pont experts. He promptly limited his questions to the use of rockets within the earth's atmosphere for added thrust to conventional aircraft.

The Du Pont engineers had little regard for either proposal. A rocket to propel piloted aircraft would consume incomparably more fuel than a reciprocating engine with a dependable propeller. The idea was rather impractical, they told him. A rocket, however used, would generate such enormous heat and pressure that its combustion chamber would require a heavy lining of fire brick. And to elevate a load of fire brick into the atmosphere—this seemed most unreasonable.

It was after the Du Pont session that the brief but noisy uproar over Goddard's 1929 flight attracted Lindbergh's attention. The colonel read an account in the New York *Times* of Goddard's rocket and his difficulties with the Massachusetts authorities.

When they met and talked at Clark, the professor explained the difference between the true rocket, which carried both fuel and oxygen, and the air-breathing rocket, which needed only fuel. With either type of jet engine, he told Lindbergh, no fire-brick chamber was necessary if proper cooling methods were designed. With some pride, he showed Lindbergh movies of his early tests.

What fascinated Goddard was the promise of soaring through the earth's atmosphere and into the voids above. For this outward reach, a combustion chamber could be built of light, almost paper-thin Duralumin. Means for cooling the chamber and controlling its flight were essential but these, too, could be developed. His rocket, the physicist said quietly, was being designed for really high altitudes, 100 miles or more above the earth.

If a start could be made toward these altitudes, then why not greater ones? Goddard explained to Lindbergh the operation of a multi-stage rocket. If this could be developed, then, theoretically, a rocket to reach the moon might also be built.

He had never revealed so much to anyone on so brief an acquaintance. Perhaps it was risky. But Goddard was taken by the young man's evident integrity. He brought the colonel back to Maple Hill, where Esther served them chocolate cake and coffee.

Lindbergh asked, "What would help you most in carrying out your experiments?"

Later, he recalled the professor's careful answer:

"He replied that, more than anything else, he wanted to be free of the classroom duties which took so much of his time. Then, he would look for a place where he could set up a laboratory and launching tower and test his rockets without worrying his neighbors or being restricted by the police.

"How much money would be required? Well, if he could obtain a grant of $25,000 a year for four years, he thought that would cover all expenses—his own salary, one or two assistants, transportation, material, rent and equipment. Under such circumstances, he felt he could accomplish within forty-eight months what might otherwise take a lifetime. He spoke as though such an amount was part of a dream beyond realization."

It was no dream that Goddard needed money and needed it soon. His latest grant from the Smithsonian was almost exhausted and Dr. Abbot was no longer speaking of "spectacular flights." Instead, he was saying that the rocket needed more support than the Smithsonian could muster. To Goddard, it now seemed that a lifetime's work would terminate in the pitted artillery range at Hell Pond.

After listening intently, Lindbergh observed that substantial help might not be impossible. In the weeks that followed, Goddard remembered their visit with hope. Meanwhile, he continued the unrewarding trips to Camp Devens.

VIII

Shortly after their meeting, Goddard was invited by Lindbergh to discuss aircraft and rockets in Wilmington with Henry Du Pont and his staff. There, he spoke of the rocket method in general terms, but when the Du Pont engineers began asking specifically about his rocket design and started taking notes, he backed off cautiously. Later, he wrote of his suspicions to Dr. Abbot:

"I realized soon that the object of this questioning was not so much to determine what could be done on airplanes, as to find every last detail of the rocket I had developed. . . . I assumed that they were questioning me to determine whether or not the performance I had made would warrant support of my research work. But nothing was said about this. . . . I hardly know whether it is a desirable [event] or not. . . ."

Nothing came of the conference, except that Lindbergh piloted the rocket professor in his own plane from Wilmington to New York, where Goddard took a train back to Worcester. The professor had seemed strangely distracted on their flight, Lindbergh recalled. It was his first airplane trip, Goddard admitted, but he appeared so taciturn that Lindbergh gave him a brisk, professional demonstration of the capabilities of propeller craft. Goddard was not quite so casual as he appeared. In his diary that night, he confided:

". . . up to 8,000 feet and down to within 50 feet of the tops of pine trees, the latter proving a good test of my nerves. . . ."

Lindbergh next arranged a conference with the Advisory

Committee of the Carnegie Institution of Washington. Goddard had met Carnegie scientists before. Earlier, two Carnegie men had come to see him at Dr. Abbot's behest, unannounced and impeccably garbed. They had found him at Clark, after an aborted test in Auburn, dressed in a worn shirt and old trousers hitched up with twine. He must have appeared to need a handout more than a grant, he had told Esther that evening.

This time, however, the professor was flawlessly groomed. The Washington conference of December 10, 1929, was held in the home of Dr. John C. Merriam, the Carnegie president. It included, in addition to Lindbergh, Goddard and Abbot, Dr. C. F. Marvin, chief of the United States Weather Bureau; Dr. John A. Fleming of Carnegie; and Drs. W. S. Adams and Harold D. Babcock of the Mount Wilson Observatory.

Goddard felt unusually at ease, if not downright expansive. Dr. Adams later spoke of the "high enthusiasm" of the scientists and said that he wanted "to give this investigation my strongest support." The value of Goddard's research, he said, was "so extraordinarily great that I should favor the support of the work even if the prospect of success were much less favorable."

The meeting, as the Clark professor recorded, began with Colonel Lindbergh's enthusiastic introduction. "The limit of speed has very nearly been reached with the present airplane, making a new method—the rocket—necessary," he said. The rocket should be developed first for study of the earth's atmosphere and then be given greater objectives, Lindbergh added.

Goddard offered a familiar outline of his high-altitude rocket and a review of previous experiments. If he were given time and support, the results could be "interesting." On this note, Dr. Merriam asked his scientific colleagues what Goddard's rocket might accomplish.

Adams declared that if the rocket went more than 50 miles high, above the ozone layer, it would "settle the nature of cosmic rays." Fleming said it would provide electrical data about the atmosphere and "throw important light on the nature of the Kennelly-Heaviside Layer." Babcock thought it might make photographs of the sun's corona without the delay of waiting for a solar eclipse.

The Carnegie meeting ended with questions. Marvin asked what heights Goddard expected to reach; Merriam asked how much his rocket would cost. "I replied," said Goddard to his confidant Dr. Abbot, who was now relieved of supporting his research, "that judging from the expense and time so far, $100,000 would not be too much to speed the work along."

Marvin of the Weather Bureau interjected a harsh but realistic note. He thought that $100,000 might possibly carry the rocket 10 miles high but that 100 miles would take a half million dollars or more.

President Merriam, before closing the meeting, said he considered Dr. Goddard's work among the most interesting research projects of the day. No one else in America had the Clark professor's experience, but he felt that Goddard might do better by enlisting other professional help. Rocket development, he felt, required massive support. Unhappily, the Carnegie Institution lacked a massive budget.

But Merriam, warmed by Lindbergh's enthusiasm, said he would recommend that his directors grant $5,000 for Goddard's research. He wished they might offer more. When he asked Goddard how such a grant should be disbursed, the professor, from old habit, replied: "$500 at a time, and when that's used up, I'll send you the vouchers." The professor was thrifty, Merriam recognized. Perhaps he could go farther on $5,000 than Dr. Marvin believed was possible.

After the Carnegie conference, Goddard could see that

scientists were beginning to accept his work. It was a happy change from earlier skepticism. At Princeton University, Dr. C. S. Stewart was openly speculating on speeds needed to escape the earth's gravitational pull. At Harvard, Dr. Harlow Shapley asked Goddard to address his astronomers and meteorologists. Afterward, Shapley told him everyone was "fascinated." Across the country, institutes of technology wanted Goddard to address their classes. But prestige was a poor substitute for tangible aid.

Their best hope for a research grant, said Lindbergh, was to find a financier, an unusual sort of financier, one with enough vision to risk good capital on a wild rocket venture which might not, for quite a while, pay even the smallest dividends.

There were few such financiers. Most sensible businessmen approached by Lindbergh had an apparently sensible refrain. Their funds were tied up in a stock market which was daily reaching higher altitudes than any college professor could achieve.

IX

Goddard had no reason to doubt the phrase he had passed on to Esther. He was "a little dog with a great big bone." He couldn't hide it, or protect it, or use it himself.

Alone in the United States, he was following a course which one day would require a score of new scientific and technical specialties: aerodynamics, thermodynamics, metallurgy, and hydraulic, mechanical and structural engineering. But he had no desire to recruit a team of emerging artisans, even if someone offered to finance the team.

His letters from Germany, meanwhile, were growing in volume, frequency and insistence. He felt that the publications he received from that country were claiming rockets and space flight as if they were purely German concepts. When German scientists mentioned Goddard, finding him unavoidable, they often disparaged him as overly secretive and uncooperative.

As for rocket research in the Soviet Union, which was by then appreciable, neither Goddard nor anyone in the Western world could know of these developments.

Goddard, at the time, also had no way of knowing that Germany's Army Ordnance was specifically interested in the rocket's belligerent possibilities. The dictators of the Treaty of Versailles, remembering Big Bertha, had ruled out Germany's manufacture of aircraft. But the peace-makers had neglected to outlaw the rocket. In 1930, Germany set aside an initial $50,000 for new rocket weapons.

Germany's interest in rocketry had developed fast, beginning in 1927 with the formation of the *Verein für Raumschiffahrt,* the society for space travel. Johannes Winkler, a rocket theorist, was the society's first president; and Max Valier, the Austrian flier, and Hermann Oberth were charter members. They embraced the same Verne fantasy which had privately captivated Goddard. But unlike the reticent Yankee, they courted public sensation.

Valier prompted the German automobile manufacturer, Fritz von Opel, to attach a cluster of powder rockets to a racing car, which Valier rigged up to run on railroad tracks. The flamboyant racer zoomed up to 125 miles per hour. A newsreel, which Goddard witnessed unhappily, was shown in a Worcester movie house. Later, Valier tried unsuccessfully to propel an Opel with a liquid-fuel rocket. In 1930, he was killed when one of his models exploded.

Oberth, in 1929, was also lured into the publicity quest as technical adviser for a motion picture, *"Die Frau im Mond,"* or "The Lady in the Moon," with Fritz Lang as director. Oberth was promised funds to build a spaceship.

Its launching was to herald the film's release. Oberth's quickly contrived rocket failed to reach space or even completion.

While Goddard was seeking a new sponsor, the German society was pursuing theory. Its theory turned out to be uncomfortably sound. Soon the Germans began to build workable rockets. Characteristically, Goddard replied to German inquiries only that his own work was still in progress, that there was nothing new to report.

Shortly after his 1929 flight, Goddard allowed an unusually frank interview with the New York *Times* correspondent R. L. Duffus, who reported that Goddard had flown "the first rocket, so far as is known, to make successful use of liquid fuel" and that he had employed some "liquefied mixture of oxygen and hydrogen, the exact formula of which he has not yet made public."

The professor's uneasiness increased with each bit of news from Germany. By 1930, the German interplanetary group claimed eight hundred members. It had staked out the *Raketenflugplatz*—its rocket flying field—in Berlin. Its experiments led to the society's first liquid-fuel rocket, the "Repulsor," which was designed by one of its members, Walter Riedel, and flown in May 1931.

In this complex field of engineering, the German approach to the rocket took a different turn from Goddard's. Aside from publicizing new developments, the Germans worked in teams, writing cheerfully of interplanetary space, as if one could soon buy a round-trip ticket to Mars.

After two decades of rocket pioneering, Goddard was now hemmed in both by his fondness for privacy and by the complacency of his countrymen. The United States had emerged from the First World War as a prospering first-rate power. In this euphoric state, few Americans wanted to get out of this world and into another.

While Lindbergh was opening new vistas, Goddard was seeking other avenues of support. In July 1929, he had received a letter from Hugo Gernsback, a struggling proprietor of science-fiction magazines, who wrote that he had an "interesting proposition." The professor was sufficiently entranced to go to New York, where he met the publisher in an old office building on Park Place.

In explaining his proposition, Gernsback said that his magazine, *Wonder Stories,* would open thresholds in all the sciences, particularly in space flight. He invited Goddard to contribute "editorial services" in that field, in exchange for stock in Gernsback's publications. David Lasser, Gernsback's editor-in-chief, also expounded on the possibilities of *Wonder Stories.* Goddard left New York without committing himself. But he was dubious about whether a block of space-fiction stock would appreciably advance his rocket research.

Later, after his meeting with Lindbergh, Goddard received an invitation from David Lasser to become a member of the new American Interplanetary Society and to address the interplanetarians on his next visit to New York. He was also asked for his decision about Mr. Gernsback's proposal. He declined both offers.

Among contributors to Gernsback's magazines and to the *Journal of the American Interplanetary Society,* was G. Edward Pendray, one of the society's founders. A knowledgeable science reporter for the New York *Herald Tribune,* he turned out space fiction after hours. Following Lasser, Pendray chided Goddard for his failure to give out information or join forces with his compatriots. In the spring of 1931, after a visit to the *Raketenflugplatz* in Berlin, Pendray again urged Goddard to take the fledgling American society into his confidence:

"It is impossible to get the facts anywhere in a way which makes them appear to be based on definite knowledge or intelligent observation. . . . The newspaper reports . . . are all obviously erroneous or garbled. You are reported to have used everything from dynamite to liquid hydrogen.

"I think you may be sure that neither myself nor the members of the American Interplanetary Society wish to detract from or belittle your work in any way. Nevertheless your apparently distrustful attitude has continually placed the Interplanetary Society and its leaders in an embarrassing position. They are besieged by students of rockets, would-be students and writers for information of a definite nature on what you are doing and what you have done. . . . The Society is forced to reply to all inquiries that it has no information. . . .

"While I sympathize with you in the undoubted fact that your ideas were lifted abroad and used without acknowledgment, I am nevertheless forced to the conclusion that your long silence is causing more harm to your reputation and to the development of rockets than any amount of idea-piracy that might occur as a result of greater frankness. . . ."

Goddard was unmoved. Through his patents, his few publications and his careful interviews, he had said all he intended to say. He had no desire to publicize his work furthur. "It happens," he wrote to Pendray, ". . . that so many of my ideas and suggestions have been copied abroad without acknowledgment usual in scientific circles that I have been forced to take this attitude. Further, I do not think it desirable to publish results of the long series of experiments I have undertaken until I feel I have made a significant further contribution to the problem."

But Goddard read with high interest Pendray's account to the American society of his visit to Berlin. The son of Wyoming homesteaders, Pendray wore an impressive Van Dyke beard and carried himself with aristocratic bearing. Perhaps the Germans had mistaken him for an American millionaire. They showed him precisely how their liquid-fuel rocket worked and allowed him to witness a static test. "It was while standing on an embankment above the German test stand and seeing and hearing the indescribable roar of a rocket motor that we found an important mission in life," Pendray recalled later.

Back home, the fiction writer became a practical rocket buff, telling his colleagues that the American society must now build and fly rockets, not merely write about them. Rockets, said Pendray, were undergoing serious development abroad; foreign scientists were taking them seriously. With or without Goddard, they must get on with the work.

The society's space-fiction writers turned to other interests. One, the president of a nursery company, withdrew from extraterrestrial affairs. President David Lasser left space flight to become a union organizer and, in 1933, led a march of the unemployed in Albany, New York. When young engineers joined the "interplanetary" society, they changed its name, for respectability, to the American Rocket Society. Pendray, alone of the founding fathers, remained.

"We couldn't get Dr. Goddard to throw in his lot and come along," he said years later. "But I guess we had more to gain from him than he had from us. I still wonder, though, if he might have gone even further if he hadn't insisted on going alone."

x

In the spring of 1930, Goddard was using the last of his Smithsonian funds for experiments at Hell Pond, but there was scarcely enough time between classes or enough help to develop his new rocket components. Meanwhile, unknown to the professor, Lindbergh had approached a close friend, Harry Guggenheim, on his behalf.

Before the notable flight to Paris, Lindbergh had met Harry Guggenheim briefly. Young Guggenheim, a naval aviator in the First World War, had encouraged his father,

Daniel, to become a strong advocate of air travel. The family fortune, amassed in finance, mining and smelting, permitted a wide choice of philanthropies. But aviation became a prominent Guggenheim cause. With his son as administrator, Daniel established the Daniel Guggenheim Fund for the Promotion of Aeronautics, which endowed various universities for research and education in aeronautics. In days when aircraft were used only for stunting, barnstorming and carrying the mail, the Fund was influential in promoting passenger aircraft and scheduled airlines, in popularizing flight, developing instrument flying and improving aircraft safety.

"The Guggenheim Fund was timely, well directed, and of extraordinary benefit to aeronautical progress," Lindbergh once said.

After the First World War, Harry Guggenheim successfully managed his family's mining interests in Chile and otherwise demonstrated his business acumen. But he also remained much interested in aviation, where he found a camaraderie among pilots and aeronautical engineers that could not be matched in Manhattan board rooms. He had opened his Long Island estate during the war for the training of Navy sea pilots, and later he was in close touch with the preparations being made by fliers and flying teams planning to span the Atlantic.

While Lindbergh was at Curtiss Field, Long Island, in 1927, preparing to take off in his *Spirit of St. Louis* for Paris, Harry Guggenheim was awaiting the expected departure for Europe of Richard E. Byrd, a fellow wartime flier. Shortly before, two French pilots, Pierre Coli and Charles Nungesser, attempting to span the Atlantic from Europe, had apparently been lost at sea; they were never heard from after leaving for the United States. Two Americans also had crashed in a swamp during a test flight.

Byrd was equipped with a tri-motored Fokker plane called

the *America* and seemed likeliest to make the crossing. Although there was considerable newspaper interest in the trials of these pilots, experts thought little of the chances of Lindbergh, the slim young mid-Westerner with a small monoplane. "Look me up when you get back," Harry Guggenheim told him, with a deliberate effort at cheerfulness.

On his return from Paris, Lindbergh had looked up Guggenheim, who invited him to the sanctuary of his Long Island home. Under the aegis of Harry, who shortly became Ambassador to Cuba, Lindbergh was presented to America's men of status and influence. When the flier became enthusiastic about Goddard's work, he thought of approaching Daniel Guggenheim for help. But for months Lindbergh hesitated to use his friendship.

After a series of delays and disappointments, however, Lindbergh called on Daniel. He had developed a warm respect for the short, heavy-set financier who called him "Slim" and, on one occasion, outlined his criterion on the proper use of wealth. "He who gives when well gives gold, when ill gives silver, when dead gives lead," Daniel had said, recasting an old Hebrew saying. He was seventy-three years old then and hearty.

On this precept of philanthropy, Daniel Guggenheim had become an active promoter of the Air Age. Most of his financial peers felt he was rather excessive in his interest in air travel. Railroads, steamships, possibly automobiles—these were the means of transport that would pay off some day. But soon Guggenheim would be thinking of transport even more fantastic.

Lindbergh called on Daniel Guggenheim at Hempstead House on Long Island, a gray stone castle of a home. Without preliminaries, he told the keen old man about Goddard's work, his plans, his requirements.

Daniel Guggenheim's questions were crisp.

"You believe these rockets have a real future?"

"Probably," Lindbergh replied. "Of course one is never certain."

"But you think so," Guggenheim said, pinning down the point. "And this professor of yours, he seems capable?"

"As far as I can tell, he knows more about rockets than anybody else in this country."

"How much money does he need?"

"For a four-year project, he would need $25,000 a year."

"Do you think it's worth my investing $100,000?" Guggenheim put the question flatly.

"Well, of course it's taking a chance," the colonel said. "But if we're ever going beyond airplanes and propellers, we'll probably have to go to rockets." The young man paused, stared at the fire in the great hearth, looked at Daniel. "Yes," he said, "I think it's worth it."

Guggenheim put the money aside: $50,000 for the first two years; $50,000 for the next two if Slim and Harry and his advisory committee, reviewing this professor's work, still agreed.

Lindbergh telephoned Goddard at home. He said he had found a supporter for the rocket work, willing to accept the professor's estimate of the necessary funds. He would write in a few days, confirming the details.

Goddard put down the telephone slowly. It wasn't entirely set, he told Esther, but it looked promising. They might now be able to get the time and equipment needed. They would be able to establish themselves wherever it suited them. It would mean leaving New England.

Esther was preparing dinner, but it could wait for another day, she said. They ought to go out and celebrate.

Her husband agreed. But not too much celebrating just yet. There was still no contract. Nothing was really firm.

They dedicated their tentative celebration to Nell's future at Hong Fong's Chinese restaurant, ordering egg roll as well as won ton soup and chicken chow mein.

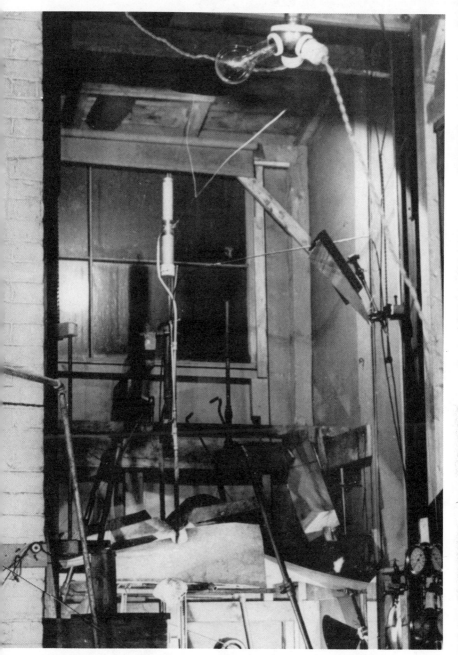

Static test in structure adjoining physics laboratory, Clark University, December 6, 1925. Goddard: "This was the first test in which a liquid-propelled rocket operated satisfactorily and lifted its own weight." [27]

Before the world's first flight of a liquid-propellant rocket,
Auburn, Mass., March 16, 1926. [28]

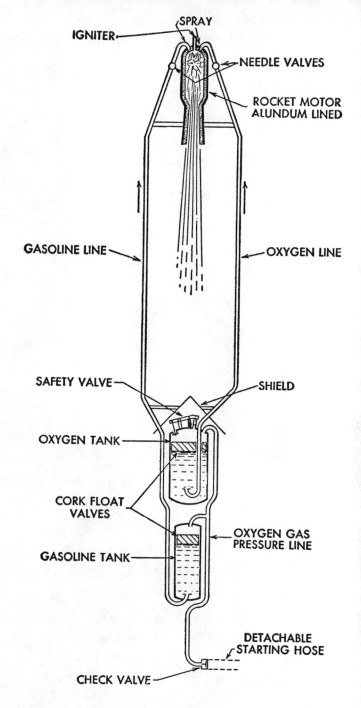

Cross section of the 1926 liquid-fuel rocket. Drawn by Goddard for
The Coming Age of Rocket Power by G. Edward Pendray. [29]

Before flight at the Ward farm, July 17, 1929. No casing was put on this model. [31]

LEFT: Rocket motor twenty times larger than in first liquid-fuel rocket, showing piping system and tanks, December 1926. [30]

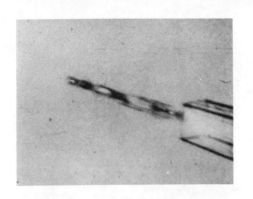
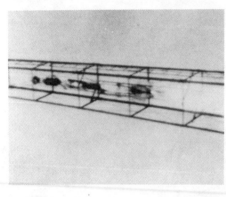

LEFT TO RIGHT: The July 1929 flight. From motion pictures taken by Esther C. Goddard. [32]

ABOVE: Fallen rocket after July 1929 flight. From left: L. Mansur, Goddard, Sachs, Kisk, Roope. [33]

Near "Hell Pond," Fort Devens, Mass., winter, 1929-1930. [34]

Hermann Oberth, Transylvanian-born rocket theorist. Photographed in 1929. [35]

Konstantin Tsiolkovsky (1857-1935), Russian rocket theorist. Photographed a year before his death. [36]

7. HIGH LONESOME

At Lindbergh's suggestion, Goddard had summed up his expected expenditures for two years of rocket research. It was more than he dared hope for; as much as he dared ask. In the past, he had drawn up similar estimates to no avail:

Machinists and experienced assistants	$20,000
Travel and transportation, including train fares, freight and trucking	6,000
Shop expenses, including new machinery and equipment, power, materials and incidental supplies ..	10,000
Manufacture of parts in outside shops	4,000
Amount to meet salary of Dr. Goddard	10,000
	$50,000

In approving these round numbers, Daniel Guggenheim set no restriction on the professor's two-year activity. Goddard could select his own staff, choose any site he wished, carry out his experiments as he saw fit. The funds would be channeled through a newly formed Clark University Research Corporation as a special "Daniel Guggenheim Fund for the Measurement and Investigation of High Altitudes." The arrangement was a legal safeguard to protect the donor from liability if the professor's pioneering produced a catastrophe instead of a high-flying rocket.

Goddard concluded his work at Camp Devens, saving much of the $5,000 grant from the Carnegie Institution to build a machine shop in his new location. President Atwood gave him an extended leave of absence from his classes and loaned him equipment from the Clark shop.

In later years, considering the soaring cost of rockets, the Guggenheim bequest appeared modest; at the time, it was a rare endowment for a private scientist, and Goddard was delighted at the chance to spend all his time in his consuming research. His sponsor's chief requirement was that the professor advance the art of rocketry and report to a new advisory committee. The committee included Abbot, Atwood, Lindbergh, Marvin and Merriam, who was chairman, Dr. Walter S. Adams, director of the Mount Wilson Observatory; Colonel Henry Breckinridge, Guggenheim's attorney; Dr. John A. Fleming, director of the department of terrestrial magnetism of the Carnegie Institution; and Dr. Robert A. Millikan, president of the California Institute of Technology.

Goddard's experience with the Smithsonian had been educational. Now he avoided lofty promises. He had learned that even lavish assistance was no guarantee of high altitudes, 25 or 50 miles above the earth. He planned to employ his new funds thriftily to make his rocket go as high as it could, while keeping his loftier purposes to himself.

Methodically, he set about finding a location for his rocket launchings. He wanted optimum weather, flat terrain and open, unencumbered space. He presented his problem to

Dr. Charles F. Brooks, then a meteorologist at Clark, who had made climate charts of most of North America. The professors spent several days examining weather and climate maps of the country. In an unpublished article for the *National Geographic Magazine*, Goddard said:

"We wanted a relatively high region with a minimum of rain and snowfall, a minimum of cloudiness, and freedom from fog. We looked, too, for a place without extremes of heat and cold where we could count on considerable periods without wind. In other words, we wanted good outdoor working weather the year round, and good visibility on every score. With these conditions overhead and surrounding us, our final need was for good, level ground underfoot, and a great deal of it. Above all, we wanted ground with a minimum of people and houses on it, where rockets could rise, or crash, or even explode without wear and tear on neighbors' nerves."

While seeking a place for his rocket trials, Goddard also found an optimum environment for his presumably arrested tuberculosis, the warm, arid prairies of the southwest. In his discussions with Professor Brooks, however, he did not mention the tubercle bacillus, only the requirements of Nell. "Not too hot, not too cold, not too wet, not too windy— that's what he wanted," Brooks later remembered.

The meteorologist had drawn a large red circle on his map around a high central plateau in the southeast corner of New Mexico. "You might try somewhere around this town of Roswell," he said. "It has a Weather Bureau station. They can probably help you. Of course you can tell the area better after you see it yourself."

Goddard, deciding to head for Roswell and "look around a bit," invited his crew to come: Henry Sachs; Albert Kisk; Larry Mansur and his brother, Charles. "We're going west and I'd like to have you along," said Goddard. "We'll be away for two years, maybe more. Think it over." Few explorers had less trouble assembling a crew. None of his men declined.

Their first task was to dismantle the launching tower at Hell Pond and crate it for shipment, together with rocket parts accumulated there and at Clark. They also packed up most of the university's physics shop equipment. Goddard's inventory to President Atwood listed lathes, milling machines, wrenches, drills, grinders, welders, clippers, calipers, hammers. They were returned in a dozen years. Clark's loss was New Mexico's gain, creating, as the "Land of Enchantment" would boast, "the finest machine shop in all the southwest."

The equipment filled two-thirds of a freight car; personal belongings of the Goddards and crew filled the rest. The physicist and his wife would go ahead, traveling light, with the men and their families to follow. They were to meet at the Weather Bureau in Roswell and then move on to their new location.

Goddard approached the westbound trip enthusiastically. A year had passed since his last flight tests in July 1929. His frustrations at Devens had built up a storehouse of ideas for improving the rocket. He was eager to get on.

Before heading west, the Goddards had their old Dodge checked out for the 2,500-mile trip. A mechanic advised its prompt replacement. Goddard accepted the verdict, although the car, to his way of thinking, was merely five years old.

It was Esther Goddard's first journey west, as they traveled out of New England in their newly acquired second-hand red Packard coupé. En route, she and her husband stayed in tourist homes, whose merits and demerits she described in letters to her family. She wrote of creeping along congested highways in the east; of reaching the open, fertile farmland of the midwest; of arriving in the dry, bleak prairie of the southwest, with its scrubby trees, stretches of desert and haunting solitude.

At a crossroads village in New Mexico, she saw a symbol of their rocket adventure. A sign creaked on rusted hooks near an abandoned filling station. She looked up and read its name: HIGH LONESOME.

Then they went on down the road through the Staked Plains, to Roswell.

11

Roswell, New Mexico, had precisely the qualifications Goddard wanted. It was a small but well-appointed town, surrounded by open prairies, clear skies and an elevation that invited flight. He had no feeling of loss in leaving New England, although the land contrasted sharply with the one he had left behind. He had come to conquer stranger lands beyond. The first of a new breed of explorers to invade these desolate plains, he would be followed to New Mexico within a decade by atomic scientists headed for Los Alamos and, later, by teams of technicians, come to establish the Army's rocket proving grounds near White Sands, less than a hundred miles from Roswell.

With a local meteorologist, Goddard discussed mean temperature, wind velocities, climate and other features of the Roswell area. The town, perched 3,600 feet above sea level, had 11,000 inhabitants. It was a busy cattle and sheep center, with daily railroad connections on the Santa Fe line, a ready access for supplies. He could see no reason to look elsewhere.

Roswell had also an atmosphere of pioneering that appealed to him. During his lifetime, in 1912, New Mexico had become the forty-seventh state of the Union. Pioneer trails ran through the town to the border of Mexico. The Pecos River lay just to the east, and the old-timers still referred to "the law west of the Pecos," an idiom for rough-hewn justice rendered lawbreakers. The natives recalled accounts of Billy the Kid and other desperadoes who had made their names notorious here. They spoke of the days when no one was called a "rugged individual" because an individual who managed to survive was necessarily rugged.

The town had originated as a small trading post and thrived because of its underground supply of water for grazing land. But when drought, in 1916, affected Roswell's artesian wells and war began to draw off its younger residents, the Roswell Gas and Electric Company announced that the community's major utility was near bankruptcy.

The town, financially sick, then turned to an untapped resource in sickness itself. It discovered that Roswell's climate could be promoted as beneficial for ailments of the lungs. After consulting with local doctors and with the Gas and Electric Company, the Chamber of Commerce advertised in the *Journal* of the American Medical Association under the slogan: ROSWELL—THE BEST PRESCRIPTION FOR YOUR PATIENT. The gas company circulated the same idea among lung specialists around the country.

In a letter to her parents, Esther Goddard referred to Roswell's colony of tuberculars: ". . . a large percentage here are health-seekers. The high altitude and warm, dry air, together with certain ingredients in the water, are said to be very favorable to the arresting of respiratory diseases."

Roswell, like other towns across the country, had its familiar five-and-ten-cent store, its well-stocked hardware emporium, grocers, dry-goods outlet, its movie theater on Main Street with the standard fare to be found on any Main Street. The professor's wife wrote home about the wide-paved streets shaded by cottonwood trees and willows:

"The first thing we noticed about Roswell was its fine dry air, so clear and pure one was glad to breathe. . . . Most of the time, Roswell lies serenely in the sunshine, one day much like the others. Day after day, the sun wheels through a cloudless azure sky, and seasons come and go almost imperceptibly. In March alone the fine weather passes—and then the winds and sands blow. . . ."

Westerners, she said in another letter to Worcester, were naturally polite, without the formal politeness of New England. They were friendly and casual, believing that every one had a right to bury whatever secrets he chose, wherever he came from. When the men came to town from the prairie, even to the bank, they wore blue jeans, high-heeled boots and broad-brimmed hats. "In the East, it is customary to look one's best in a bank on business," Esther said. "Here ranchers and farmers come in from the range and field as they are. This has broken down my awe of banks considerably."

The immediate task was to find quarters, preferably a place with outbuildings for the machine shop and quarters for his crew. Transportation and living expenses could seriously erode his rocket funds.

Early in August, before his men reached town, Goddard rented a commodious, furnished, pueblo-style ranchhouse, three miles northeast of town. Mescalero Ranch and its eight acres of land belonged to Miss Effie Olds, a spinster member of the Oldsmobile family. Although there were no outbuildings and the place, untenanted for several years, needed repair, it had the advantage of lying at the dead end of a dirt road. No casual visitor could happen by, unexpected. The professor signed the lease at once.

When his men arrived, they were given Goddard's rough sketch for a new machine shop. While they were helping a contractor build it, the professor looked for a site for the flight tower, the dismantled 60-foot apparatus he had used at Auburn and later at Hell Pond. To the secretary of the Roswell Chamber of Commerce, Claude Simpson, he explained that he wanted a site "reasonably near the Olds place, away from main highways, unobstructed by buildings and fences, on sufficiently poor grazing land so that few cattle are

likely to be present, and level for at least a three-mile radius."
He inspected a thirty-mile area and was then sent to Oscar
White, a rancher and cowhand. White owned some range
land called Eden Valley about ten miles from the Olds ranch.
Its name appealed to him. From Hell Pond to Eden Valley.

In talking to White, Goddard led up cautiously to the
fact that he needed a place to shoot off rockets. The rancher
studied him carefully, apparently liking what he saw. No explanations were needed. "Glad to have you use the field,
doctor," he said. Goddard wondered aloud whether the
"field" was quite big enough. He wanted no trouble with
neighbors. "Oh, it's a nice little field," said White. "About
16,000 acres, I reckon."

The professor then inquired about the rent. White
breezily dismissed this question. His only requirement was
that Goddard follow the "law of the range." The "law"
seemed simple enough: "Leave the gates like you find them.
If they're open, leave them open. If they're closed, close them
after you go through."

Protect your cattle, safeguard your property. It was a
familiar struggle with nature. If you accepted nature's pattern, no place was strange. Unlike other easterners, who
found the prairie a barren waste, Goddard saw that it teemed
with life, hard, durable, appropriate to the land. In New
Mexico's mesquite and cactus were creatures accustomed to
protecting themselves—tarantulas, vinegarroons, rattlesnakes.
They reminded him of his need for strength.

Before beginning his new rocket tests, he applied for accident and liability insurance. He was a researcher, he reported, but was somewhat vague about the nature of his
research. He admitted that it had to do with rockets. The
local insurance agent, understandably curious, asked for
more details. Goddard's reply was circumspect:

"As to the nature of the work, I can say that it is no more
hazardous than any research involving machine shop work

and experimentation, such as an airplane or motorboat development. In the shop, and in such tests as we perform, all the usual safeguards are maintained.

"I may say, also, that the materials we use are non-explosive, in themselves. This point is worth emphasizing as accidents have occurred abroad in rocket researches, where propellants of an explosive nature have been employed. The work in many college chemical laboratories is far more hazardous than the present research. . . ."

The insurance company was now thoroughly alerted, sending the unusual application to its branch and main offices. On specific inquiry, the professor insisted that, while he was employing combustible liquid oxygen and hydrocarbons, both ingredients were being used with scrupulous care.

The actuaries were not persuaded. "We appreciate your inquiry, but we do not wish to undertake this sort of risk," they advised the professor. It was no better when a company doctor examined Goddard for life insurance. "He ought to be in bed in Switzerland," he said after listening to Goddard's chest with his stethoscope.

III

In most respects, the first rocket-testing center in the United States was crude when compared with a modern missile base, where thousands of specialists spend millions of dollars in one day on preliminary models, where control shelters and observation posts are a complex of electrical and electronic systems in concrete "blockhouses" as sturdy as bomb shelters. But with all the elaboration of million-pound thrusting and multi-thousand-mile trajectory rockets, the essentials are much the same as at Goddard's small pioneer establishment. There the struggle with the machine and its demand for perfection would go on: the repeated trials, the testing and retesting. Whether the rocket was as long as two arms extended or as tall as a building, the smallest of flaws would ground the balky space striver.

The hub of Goddard's enterprise was the frame machine shop erected near the ranchhouse. On a slab outside the door, the builder had scrawled with a nail in the soft concrete: "R. H. Goddard." When the machinery was properly installed along one wall, the professor's old writing desk was moved in and, next to it, his lathe and a work bench, which he outfitted with a pair of tin snips, soldering iron and a number of tin cans. There he sketched out ideas on scraps of paper, and sometimes worked up in metal crude replicas to show his machinists.

Years later, Charles Mansur looked back on these early days from his post at White Sands Proving Grounds, where he was chief of components, liquid propellant branch, of the electromechanical laboratory. "We've come a long way from the doctor's optical tracking system—a pair of binoculars and an old alarm clock to drive a recording drum. Modern tracking systems are as complex as the missile itself. At White Sands we work on one rocket component, or a fraction of a component. In Goddard's day, we did everything from scratch. We were each personally involved in whether Nell flew or not."

Once a model was built, assembled and approved at Mescalero Ranch, it was tested in the small static frame about 100 feet from the machine shop. There the rocket's fuel was ignited and its thrust held down by water-filled oil drums weighing up to 2,000 pounds. This weight was supported by strong steel springs connected to a measuring apparatus which recorded the engine's lifting force on a revolving drum. A concrete trough, called "the bathtub," withstood the scorching blasts under the frame. After repeated static tests, Goddard would try his rockets in flight, carting them out to his launching site in Eden Valley.

In Roswell, he was free at last to pursue his rocket dream, step by step. First he would try to perfect a lightweight, more powerful motor, able to withstand the heat of combustion. Next, he would review the problems of steering the rocket to assure its vertical flight, and of recovering it by parachute. Finally, he would return to building miniature pumps to feed the combustion chamber. If he succeeded in each of these tasks, he would have, in a small model, the rocket he had planned on for twenty years.

The first static test at Roswell, on October 29, 1930, was one more in a series of trial and error. When it was over, he said, as he had said so often: "Let's haul in the pieces and see what happened." A gas tank had exploded. Possibly the cork float in the fuel line got stuck, or wedged, or jammed.

The static tests blasted on through 1930. Flaws in the motor were explored. Some were faults in the pressure-regulating valve, a minor contrivance with frequently major flaws. Tests were postponed while the crew worked on the regulator valve. Meanwhile, Goddard was designing a set of large vanes to add to the rear of the rocket for stability. He was learning that time itself was a restriction, persuading him that even a pioneer could proceed only so fast.

Goddard's motor now gave reasonable power for its size, with reasonable dependability. It was 5¾ inches in diameter, weighed 5 pounds, and rather consistently developed a thrust up to 289 pounds for some 20 seconds, about 200 times the horsepower of then current airplane engines, per pound of weight.

He was eager for at least one rocket launching before the year ended. With his men, Goddard carted the rocket out to Eden Valley early on the morning of December 22, 1930. Nell was blanketed and trussed down in the trailer hauled by the covered black Ford truck which they called "the hearse."

There were the usual painstaking preliminaries before

Goddard ordered the test to begin. On ignition, the rocket seemed to behave well, giving a deep, satisfying roar, straining to lift from the tower. On his instrument panel he watched the pressure rise, then ordered the rocket's release. There was only one trouble this time: ". . . the rocket was accidentally pulled from between the two pipe guides and was thus prevented from leaving the tower."

The rocket was undamaged. With a few improvements in the launching arrangements, Goddard prepared again for a flight. To this end, he had Lawrence Mansur devise a small scale model of both the rocket and the flight tower, "just to be sure that everything fitted together." Meanwhile, he waited for a new shipment of liquid oxygen from the Linde Air Products branch in Amarillo, Texas.

The oxygen arrived in time for a flight before the year was over. This test of December 30, 1930, as described in Chapter I, came off with astonishing success. Compared with his earlier launchings at Aunt Effie's, it was spectacular. Nell rose from the tower and then soared 2,000 feet above it and 1,000 feet away. She achieved a maximum speed of 500 miles per hour, perhaps the greatest obtained by a man-made contrivance up to that time.

Goddard and his men brought the rocket back to the machine shop, where they salvaged all that was usable. After the customary examination, he wrote in his experimental notes that the gasoline tank and some of the piping had been crushed on impact. The parachute mechanism had failed, but he already had a better design in mind. He allowed himself to record his elation:

"The flight was very impressive. It seemed more like the operation of a vehicle than the flight of a rocket. The sustained and effortless qualities of the flight were the most striking. . . ."

There had been a "marked absence of smoke and a very small flame," he wrote, with a "continued increase of speed second after second." The rocket had heeled over toward the horizon too fast, "with a loud whistling sound heard easily a half mile away," he added.

"It is believed that the present flight proved two things: first, that a light, very high speed rocket can be made for obtaining records, and for other uses, at a few thousand feet, without the employment of gyroscopic stabilizers; secondly, that the attainment of great heights cannot be made without the use of automatic stabilization.

"It seems desirable, therefore, to proceed at once with automatically stabilized flight. . . ."

More was gained from the flight of December 30 than the recordings of theodolite and camera, the analytic lessons learned from crashed machinery. It was a promise of future flights. The professor was invigorated. But he had the outward capacity, as his wife once commented, "to reduce the essentially dramatic into the humdrum." While he and his crew were toasting the triumph of Nell with ginger ale, he was already "doping out" plans for her future.

Although his early reports to the Guggenheim committee were optimistic, he was troubled by the chamber's cooling system. He could never be sure when the holocaust of combustion would burn out his motors. He had to stay with this problem or go on to another that also tantalized him, the rocket's stability in flight. The two tasks would later occupy teams of engineers.

The problem of "tangential" or "curtain" cooling of the combustion chamber remained a continuing concern. Early in 1931, Goddard injected sprays of gasoline and liquid oxygen to cool the inner side of the chamber wall. The chamber burned through. He modified the size of the orifices, the angles at which the liquids were fed, the ratio of gasoline to liquid oxygen. With any imperfection in the spiraling liquid, the heat still knifed into the thin metal walls.

He persisted in his experiments with curtain cooling. Theoretically, it was an ideal technique, permitting almost limitless combustion temperatures in very light motors. The problem of how to contain the rocket's temperatures perplexed all the early experimenters, in the years before new alloys and ceramics were developed. In 1938, a more foolproof but heavier method of cooling than Goddard's was made practical by a young rocketeer named James Wyld, of the American Rocket Society. Wyld's "regenerative cooling" method called for the addition of an outer jacket to the combustion chamber. The gasoline swirled through fixed conduits in this jacket, cooling the motor before being injected into it as fuel. Meanwhile, Goddard continued his efforts to perfect his ideal but undependable system.

IV

New Mexico was a marked change from the restraints of New England and Goddard enjoyed it thoroughly. He happily stored away his high-starched collars, his four-in-hand ties, his blue serge suits. A well-worn pair of slacks or shorts and an open-necked shirt were all he needed for coming and going between the ranchhouse and the shop. His wife objected to his favored pair of disreputable crepesoled shoes, saying they left bits of rubber about the house. One night she committed them to the backyard garbage trench. Goddard fished them out the next morning, complaining that "somebody" was always throwing away perfectly good things.

A cloud of secrecy now settled over the Goddard establishment. He briefly addressed the Roswell Rotary Club, hoping that an explanation of the principles of jet propulsion might foster the town's indulgence. He endeavored to scotch wild rumors. "I do not consider that the time has arrived for any attempt to communicate between the planets," he said. "The

Wright brothers did not try a trans-Atlantic flight first, nor shall I try to reach the planets."

Roswell newspapermen, requesting interviews, met Goddard's genial but firm resistance. They promised to respect his privacy on condition that he advise them of newsworthy developments. He agreed. The working arrangement lasted throughout his residence at Mescalero Ranch.

For his young wife, these early years in Roswell were lonely. Dedicating her energies to her husband, she became as zealous as he was. She attended to his bookkeeping, transcribed his reports and managed his household, a chore that sometimes included the routing out of centipedes, black widow spiders and vinegarroons, the last of the three distinguished by an odor resembling vinegar.

Esther became Goddard's chief emissary to town, picking up equipment at the Mabie-Lowrey hardware store, running errands for the shop and house, collecting the mail. There were frequently foreign inquiries, which increased as interest in rocketry developed abroad. After their usual Sunday morning steak, they answered the week's accumulation of mail.

The Goddards made few friends during their first years in Roswell. They met their nearest neighbor, attorney Herman Crile, through the professor's search for dependable legal services. The Criles, who lived within earshot, were already keenly aware of the newcomers through the alarming roars and eruptions during static tests at Mescalero Ranch.

Goddard got in touch with Crile to see about his rocket affidavits. "He wanted some papers notarized without being read and was happy when I said this was possible," Crile later observed. "After that, he came by often, bringing his papers on which he had covered up everything except a space at the bottom where my notary could put her seal and her signature."

The professor, absorbed in research, was only vaguely aware that his young wife needed more than Nell for companionship. Esther began making tentative ventures toward the community. She joined the Roswell Women's Club and the League of Women Voters. She entered the Goddards in the annual Cotton Carnival parade, representing Massachusetts, with a picture of a beanpot on one side of their coupé and a codfish on the other.

People in Roswell then saw little of Goddard himself, who seldom left Mescalero Ranch. His dedication had already persuaded his wife that she was sharing the adventure of an extraordinary man. Her husband had little patience with personal sickness, behaving as if it were a needless interruption of his work. Although he was periodically sent to bed by a local doctor for chest colds and recurring eye trouble, he continued on these occasions to sketch out plans for rocket components and summoned his crew to his bedside for conferences and assignments. A few years later, Esther learned that his ailments were symptoms of a recurrence of his long-dormant tuberculosis.

It was easier to dismiss these problems of health than to devise new rocket valves and stabilizers, and keep his crew intact. After a few months, his chief machinist, Henry Sachs, spoke reluctantly of resigning. Goddard tried to tempt him with the promise of a new lathe, but Sachs still declined. His wife, the machinist said, had developed a strong dislike for the southwest and he had no choice but to return east.

The dreary news of Sachs' departure came at a time when Goddard was having considerable difficulty in getting his gyroscopic stabilizer to work. In the midst of these perplexities, which he kept manfully to himself, Esther discovered another clue to her husband's nature. Before Christmas, their Spanish-American maid Deeka invited the Goddards to attend an evening Yuletide program at the small Berrendo School.

The Goddards stood quietly at the side of the schoolroom, warmed by the performance of the Spanish-American children in their homemade, ill-fitting clothes as they dramatized the Nativity, looking anxiously at their teacher whenever they forgot their lines. Their play was followed by a string trio, woefully off key, as the class sang familiar carols. At this point, Esther noticed that Robert had left her side. She found him in the back of the room, sitting knees to chin at a school desk, chiming in with gusto with the singing children. She remembered the old verse:

> "Backward, turn backward, O Time, in your flight,
> Make me a child again just for tonight!"

v

In February 1931, the professor went to Washington, D.C., to review his work before the advisory committee, show them Esther's current motion pictures of Nell, and find a machinist to replace Mr. Sachs.

But the rocket man was never to meet his sponsor. Daniel Guggenheim had died of a heart attack in September 1930, at the age of seventy-four.

At the meeting of the Guggenheim committee in a conference room at the Smithsonian, Goddard concluded his report with an intended disclaimer:

"Just . . . when we can expect a really high flight, I cannot say. I feel certain, however, that it will be a number of months."

Dr. Merriam doubtless realized the monumental proportions of the assignment Goddard had given himself. He suggested that rocket research might benefit by "group thinking," rather than by a purely "lone wolf" approach. He neglected, however, to specify what group would do the thinking, who would finance it, who would manage it. It was a casual but potent thrust.

Goddard again felt threatened. In the early years of his space dream, he had tried to persuade his countrymen of the rocket's possibility. Now, virtually singlehanded, he had established a sound, scientific basis for the work, but his project was already subject to question. He masked his distress, and Merriam did not press the point. As he told Esther afterwards, it was "hurrays and damns, but mostly hurrays."

Before returning to Roswell, Goddard looked in vain for a new machinist. Finally, he chose Nils Thure Ljungquist, known as "Oley," who was recommended by Al Kisk. Oley Ljungquist's family had settled in Worcester, where he had trained in the shops of the Tech. A skilled mechanic, he was working in an automotive service department in California when Goddard wrote to him. He came to Mescalero Ranch in May 1931, and in time took over the duties of Henry Sachs. Oley had one aberration. He was a devoted reader of science fiction, a secret he kept strictly to himself.

VI

Goddard's new experiments to achieve high velocities were rather quickly resolved. They proved what he had suspected: that a principal factor was the size of the combustion chamber and the quantity of fuel and oxidizer combusted. It became increasingly evident that there was no easy, magical route to high altitudes. It was a case of a little bigger and a little better each time—provided all the components worked. And until they worked, no rocket would go soaring into space.

Before building a larger model, Goddard urgently needed to improve his technique for maintaining pressure in his gasoline and liquid oxygen tanks in order to force these liquids into the combustion chamber. The solution, he felt, would be a small, light and powerful pump, but there was no such pump on the market and he had neither funds nor time to develop one now.

The method he chose was a makeshift. It employed an auxiliary tank of compressed nitrogen with an automatic regulator to control the pressure—enough pressure to force the liquids into the chamber but not so much as to blow the lightweight rocket apart. He spent weeks in his shop on this regulating device—testing it, redesigning it, improving it —until it gave a successful demonstration in the static test frame.

In September 1931, Goddard was ready for another flight test with new devices he had developed that spring and summer. In addition to the improved pressure regulator, he was trying out a modified combustion chamber, a parachute-releasing timer, a streamlined casing of thin Duralumin, and his first remote-controlled releasing method.

Early on September 29, his crew, anticipating the flight, reported for the usual preliminaries. After nine months of work since the last flight, they were festive as they wrapped Nell for her trip to the valley. Inside the ranchhouse, Esther finished the breakfast dishes. In a few minutes she joined the others and the caravan set off for the prairie.

Nell flew that afternoon. She rose rapidly from the tower but, after reaching a height of some 200 feet, she lost interest in the proceedings, turned into the wind, roared toward the ground, then raced along some 500 feet like one of Fritz von Opel's rocket cars. She ended in a loud explosion. "The explosion was found to be the gasoline tank bursting, the remainder of the rocket being comparatively undamaged . . . ," Goddard recorded.

The pressure regulator, after performing properly in static tests, had supplied too little pressure, "either due to lack of heat or lack of liquid oxygen supply, or perhaps due to too small a pressure-generating jacket. . . ." Each test presented another series of ifs, ands or buts.

The new parachute release also had failed to operate. The parachute was to be released "by a timer, consisting of a 'Tip-top' wrist watch, with the side cut open so that the balance wheel could be held by a piece of rubber on a screw in a lever." But the "powder exploder, for releasing the parachute, did not explode."

In October, Goddard's experimental notes recorded two modest flights, up to 1,700 feet high. They employed his improved pressure regulator. But when the regulator worked, weak spots appeared elsewhere. The jet in one test showed an excess flow of gasoline; in the second, the gasoline tank again exploded.

Meanwhile, he devoted all the time he could spare to his gyroscopic stabilizer. It was among his most ambitious technical accomplishments. When finally perfected, the sophisticated and sensitive contrivance weighed only nineteen ounces. He wrote:

"It was decided to attack this problem of stabilization by developing a system of movable steering vanes that could be pushed by the controlling action of a gyroscope, into the blast of hot gases that rushes out of the end of the rocket. Acting on the vane, the powerful blast would shove the rocket's nose back toward the vertical.

"It had to be a complicated device—a veritable mechanical brain directing mechanical muscles. The problem was similar to that presented by the construction of an automatic pilot for an airplane, but as with all other rocket features, weight was a vital factor."

The key to the gyroscopic stabilizer was its capacity, once set in motion, to resist any change in its position. Goddard's stabilizer, on which he was later granted a patent, steered the rocket by controlling four tail vanes moving into the blast of the ejected gases. Before launching, the gyroscope was set in motion, spinning on an axis parallel to the axis of the rocket as it stood upright in the launcher. If the rocket veered from its vertical course, the gyroscope opened a valve which worked a piston which, in turn, forced the pair of vanes into the rocket blast, causing the device to correct any deviation.

The effort was ingenious and, even in its earliest flight tests, showed signs of working.

On April 19, 1932, Goddard's first gyroscopically controlled rocket rose slowly from the tower, then, following its short ascent, crashed heavily. The professor, however, after studying the wreckage, declared the flight a success:

". . . we had the cheering experience of learning from some quick detective work . . . that we were making progress in solving our important problem. The flight was somewhat straighter than the preceding ones. . . . I rushed to the rocket and felt the four vanes. The one that should have been forced into the blast was warm—the others cold! Thus I knew that our idea was sound, and concluded that we merely needed larger vanes. . . ."

He tried another flight a month later, having enlarged and modified the blast vanes of his rocket. It failed to get off the ground. His unreliable combustion chamber burned through; the gyroscope tilted; the parachute, suddenly released, hung grotesquely over the smoking rocket. With this aborted test, the Roswell research program came, for the time being, to an end.

VII

In the spring of 1932, there was the tragic news of the kidnapping of Colonel Lindbergh's son. Newspaper headlines were also growing black with news of the Great Depression.

Factories closed down in the east and men without work lined up at soup kitchens. In the midwest, drought was drying up farmland, scorching once fertile fields into dust bowls.

Mortgages were foreclosed and people were on the move, hunting for jobs. Soon the "Okies" headed westward in decrepit jalopies. Some stopped overnight in Roswell, where city fathers saw they had food. At Mescalero Ranch, where Goddard was seeking stability in reaching other worlds, his own unstable world was ending an era.

In May 1932, the professor again set off for Washington. In the uneasy national capital, President Hoover, campaigning for re-election, was pleading for a return of public confidence and pledging that prosperity was "just around the corner." It was an impossible prophecy, as disturbing events brought closer the victory of his Democratic rival, New York's Governor Franklin D. Roosevelt.

Goddard had come to Washington to ask the Guggenheim advisory committee for the promised support of two more years of research if they approved of his work.

The scientists listened gravely to his report, cautiously endorsed his program, pointedly mentioned the effect of the depression on future financing, and sent him to see the Guggenheim attorney. Goddard seemed to them like an intelligent traveler who had recently returned from Mars, in urgent need of a worldly briefing.

The facts were brought home in short order. Henry Breckinridge explained regretfully that the recent stock market crash had badly shrunk the Guggenheim estate. For the time being, it would be necessary to suspend the grants.

Goddard was "a good sport to take such a disappointment with so much courage and philosophy," Breckinridge wrote to him. Years later, in recalling his impression of the professor, the attorney said:

"You couldn't possibly stop him. He was indomitable. He had restraint, self-respect and a faith that would move mountains. He behaved as if he had all the time he needed to carry out his work."

VIII

Goddard returned to Roswell. He told his men the bad news. They would have to close down the shop.

Most of the shop equipment was crated and stored in the warehouse of Mabie-Lowrey, the hardware store they patronized. Miscellaneous pieces from discarded rockets were hammered into a flat, indistinguishable mass and buried in a trench on the ranch grounds. The shop was swept clean and boarded up.

The men left one by one, with Goddard's letters of recommendation for other jobs. He said he hoped to call on them in a year, perhaps two, if his grant were resumed.

The Goddards were the last to leave. After the men had gone, the professor walked into the shop. The place was still. He took off his dusty, sweat-stained hat, and laid it down on an empty bench. A few flies buzzed forlornly.

"I wonder if I'll ever pick it up again," he said, walking quickly to the door.

8. A MATTER OF TIME

In the summer of 1932 he was home, settled in the old house on Maple Hill, preparing to resume his teaching at Clark. Esther noticed her husband's ability to return to old patterns as if nothing had changed. His crew, his testing grounds were gone, his experiments ended, perhaps at the edge of success. But she found no despair in him. For a week he scarcely mentioned the rocket. Perhaps he was planning to relinquish his arduous trials for a simpler academic life. Then, one evening, she saw him sketching out a centrifugal pump.

At her urging, Goddard went to see Dr. Edgar A. Fisher, their family physician. Fisher examined him closely, X-rayed his lungs, warned him gloomily against too much exertion. He might still recover fully if he took advantage of his opportunity to live in the southwest. In his diary, Goddard remarked sardonically that Dr. Fisher "apparently thought" the grant was made "to go West for a rest cure."

Dr. Fisher was not alone in failing to find the wellspring of Goddard's stamina. A few colleagues at Clark University were also aware of his unusual staying power. His sponsors could never account for his capacity to endure repeated and arduous trials and errors.

Once again, troubled by the instability of human nature, Goddard found comfort in nature itself and wrote of the familiar sound of cicadas and spring peepers, the purple lilacs, the elm trees in foliage.

In October, he celebrated his fiftieth birthday without a note in his diary, but on October 19 he wrote: "Anniversary Day . . . Went to cherry tree." Before Christmas he observed another ritual. Again he reread *The War of the Worlds*.

Then he wrote two letters, one, already noted, to H. G. Wells, the science dreamer, on May 3, 1932; another, on June 20, 1932, to Lincoln Ellsworth, explorer and man of action.

Lincoln Ellsworth was about to leave for the South Pole. Goddard had read of his exploits. In his letter, Goddard identified himself with the fraternity of explorers and wished Ellsworth success on his polar mission:

"Your desire . . . parallels closely my own early dreams to fly to the moon by airship. These led me, about twenty-five years ago, to the study of rockets as a means of exploration in the upward direction. . . .

"To my mind, the investigation by high-efficiency rockets of the region above the earth's surface is the last great exploration, and is in a field practically untouched, so far."

II

Before school that fall, Goddard was again in the Clark machine shop, working on his rocket pump with Al Kisk. Although not too handy at the lathe or with welding equipment, the professor was a good machinist. They had produced a crude but not quite workable model. Secretary Abbot once more rallied with a grant of $250 to pay for emergency supplies and a part-time machinist.

By mid-September, Goddard was back with his classes as professor of physics. With the best of efforts, he knew that some of his freshmen would be openly bored with the subject; that some would stifle their boredom and get by; that only a few would share his own sense of excitement.

In teaching freshmen, Goddard usually began with a lecture on "The World As It Appears to a Physicist," telling why he was drawn to the field himself:

"Physics is the science of matter and energy. It is the study of every material thing in the universe and of the motions of every material thing. The study which engrosses the mind of the physicist is, therefore, a very fundamental one. It is not amiss to term physics the fundamental science."

Physics, he held, was the capstone of all the sciences:

"Mathematics, although fundamental to be sure, does not necessarily deal with the universe as it is, but with the premises, whatever they may be, that are granted by the mathematician, and with the logical consequences derived from these premises."

In Goddard's view, all the sciences depended on man's understanding of matter and energy:

"Chemistry, the science of the transformations of matter, requires physics in order to explain the ultimate nature of chemical forces. . . . The other and more restricted sciences, such as astronomy, geology, meteorology, biology and psychology, must needs have basic explanations expressed in terms of the laws of physics. All of them, sooner or later, return to physics for their answers. Even the little understood psychic phenomena that are just beginning to be investigated can only be explained in terms of physical laws. . . ."

This was how it seemed to him. Nature, the world, the universe, could all be explained in terms of physical concepts. Then he would speak of the masters of physics and the continuity of their work: Sir Isaac Newton and his three laws of motion; Sir Ernest Rutherford and his electron theory; Nils Bohr and his concept of the atom; Clerk Maxwell, Michelson and Morley, and their experiments; Albert Einstein and his theory of relativity. It was all a continuum, a search for knowledge, he told his new students. There was never an end of searching. And now, he would say softly, looking out the classroom window at the old clock tower, they, too, had come to the beginning.

III

Goddard's next two years at Clark were a time for reflection, for reviewing his particular quest—"to do as much as time and funds would allow . . . to develop new methods and new techniques in as many lines as possible . . . to find what lines of development, and what methods, would appear most desirable in accelerating further progress. . . ."

His mind was restless with ideas. His notebooks of affidavits bulged with plans for pumps, igniters and fuel injection devices; for solar motors, ion motors and nose cones; for glide patterns to protect a spaceman from cremation as he re-entered the earth's atmosphere.

He repeatedly visited Hawley's law office. The attorney helped him to patent a better means of gyroscope steering; a more ingenious centrifugal pump; other improved components. He would have avalanched Hawley with applications if he had had the necessary funds.

By the end of 1934, Goddard had twenty-six patents, among them concepts which would bear closely on German V-weapons of the Second World War. Two patents, issued to him on September 27, 1932, would prove almost identical in design to components of the later V-2. One of these, "Apparatus for Igniting Liquid Fuel," No. 1,879,186, dealt with Goddard's "curtain cooling"—his means of protecting the thin rocket chamber from the intense heat of combustion with an interior spray of liquid fuel. The paper was in great demand at home and abroad and became one of the rare "best-sellers" of the patent office, which reprinted it several times.

The second patent, "Mechanism for Directing Flight," No. 1,879,187, described Goddard's method of gyroscopic steering. It disclosed the complexities of his gyroscope-valve-piston-and-vane arrangement which enabled the rocket to correct its deviations in flight.

The professor enjoyed his visits with Mr. Hawley. The attorney, according to his secretary, Mrs. Inez W. Powers, was "a true New Englander, a sort of second Calvin Coolidge." After working with Goddard and his patents for twenty years, Hawley had grown attached to the professor. He found him a happy diversion from the usual Worcester inventor who was salaried by manufacturing firms which owned the resulting patent rights.

Hawley's firm recognized the professor as a client who created devices of considerable intricacy. The attorney's patent draftsman, a withdrawn and talented artist named C. Forrest Wesson, had been helping since 1913 to decipher Goddard's sketches and ideas. Frequently he had to submit drawings to Goddard for explanation and approval.

On one occasion, Mrs. Powers told the inventor that she found his gyroscopic steering idea beyond her grasp. Goddard, waiting to see Mr. Hawley, amiably showed her how the gyroscope works.

He borrowed the draftsman's revolving stool and asked the secretary to sit on it. Then he fashioned a cardboard disc and made a hole in its center. "You will kindly place the forefingers of each hand through this hole so that your fingertips touch," he instructed her. Then, to the secretary's surprise, he spun the stool, twirling her around. As he did so, the disc also started to turn, but in an opposite direction.

"Now this, Mrs. Powers, is the general principle," she recalled his saying. She was never quite sure what the principle was, but she was flattered by his attempt to explain it.

Lectures and shop experiments were not enough. He was increasingly eager for full-time research. With the encouragement of Abbot and Lindbergh, he offered his rocket again to the military. The Germans had disbanded their *Verein für Raumschiffahrt* and the military was secretly taking over its work. The United States Army was still disinterested in rocket development; and the Navy's Bureau of Ordnance also turned him down. Of course, the Navy would inspect his device—*after* he had it perfected.

Most rocket work in the United States was now falling behind the German secret developments, although the budding American Rocket Society, pooling its modest resources, was firing small liquid-fuel rockets in Lambertville, New Jersey. The professor still declined the Society's invitation to "cooperate actively." He recalled a typical family saying, concerning cooperation, "getting you to do something to help me." He responded to the invitation as if through layers of New England flannel:

"I regret that it is necessary to make so unsatisfactory a reply . . ." (the Society's rocket, he gathered, was roughly equivalent to his own model of 1926) ". . . but the present uncertain state of affairs makes definite planning impossible."

At this "uncertain state," Lindbergh once more became his champion. Through Lindbergh's intercession, the Daniel and Florence Guggenheim Foundation in the fall of 1933 granted $2,500 for Goddard's research at Clark. In August

1934, the Foundation renewed its full support, enabling him to return to New Mexico.

IV

In 1934, Adolf Hitler in Germany, combining the offices of president and chancellor, became Führer on the death of Von Hindenburg. . . . A year later Premier Benito Mussolini in Italy was exhorting his troops to invade Ethiopia. . . . And the United States was still hopeful that the changing balance of power in Europe would not trigger an explosion . . . and ratifying, after a nine-year delay, the optimistic Geneva convention on the control of armaments. Meanwhile, the Germans were building rocket weapons.

In September 1934, the Goddards, traveling west in their red coupé, stopped in Chicago to see the Century of Progress Exposition. They spent most of an afternoon at the science exhibition. The professor then took Esther to a sideshow of science fiction, an enactment of the comic strip "Buck Rogers." They were less struck by the swashbuckling space pilot than by his colleague, "Dr. Huer," the rocket ship inventor.

Dr. Huer was an amiable caricature of Goddard—bald-headed, mustached, confident. "He wore a smooth cap of some sort to make him as bald as he looked in the funnies," Esther wrote to her parents. "He walked and talked like Groucho Marx and whenever Buck and his companions got into difficulties, he would say: 'Now don't you worry, the old doctor will take care of that!' "

In the months ahead, whenever Nell's quixotic behavior verged on the insupportable, Dr. Huer's words were a tension-breaker. "Now don't you worry," Esther would declare. "The old doctor will take care of that!" There was a lot to take care of.

When they arrived at Mescalero Ranch, Goddard opened

the dusty shop, replaced a wall calendar dated June 1932, and retrieved his old hat from the workbench where he had left it. His crew, again including Al Kisk, Charles Mansur and Oley Ljungquist, installed his shop equipment while he drove out to Eden Valley to inspect the tower. This symbol of present and future hopes was in need of repair:

"When we shut up shop and went to Massachusetts, we left the tower intact, trusting that it would be protected by its lonely situation. But it was far from intact when we came back two years later. Everything that could be removed had been stripped away up to the twenty-foot level: all of the sheet steel shield, braces, cross pieces, wires, ladder, concrete weights, guy-wire posts—everything except the four main supports of the tower itself. . . ."

There were signs, in the upper reaches of the tower, of other predators. Crows had nested among the cross-hatching, weaving tough, heavy homes from bits of wire the Goddards had left behind. Wire cutters were needed to remove these habitations. The professor put one nest on his scales. It weighed almost ten pounds.

He had ample reminders of the need for success. The Foundation, granting him $18,000 for a year of research, had made it clear that further support would depend on his progress. A letter from the Smithsonian's Dr. Abbot also awaited his arrival in Roswell. It contained the same familiar theme:

"May I urge you to bend every effort to a directed high flight? That alone will convince those interested that this project is worth supporting. Let no side lines, however promising, divert you from this indispensable aim which I hope you can accomplish with the grant you now have."

Shortly after the Goddards' return to Roswell, Colonel Lindbergh and his wife Anne flew into town en route to the West Coast. The community buzzed with reports of their visit to Mescalero Ranch. Next day, the Roswell *Morning Dispatch* gave its front page to the news:

FAMOUS LINDBERGHS PAY VISIT TO CITY

With a bustle of civic pride, the newspaper stated that Roswell was accustomed to famous visitors, among them "Will Rogers and Admiral Richard E. Byrd, whose names appear on the city's guest book."

The colonel, wearing "a blue business suit," had declined to discuss his present plans, saying that "he could work much better if he were left alone," the *Dispatch* reported.

Goddard thoroughly agreed with these sentiments. He showed Lindbergh about his shop, introduced him to the rocket crew, and accompanied him on a brief flight to Eden Valley to inspect the tower and the launching area. On landing in the prairie, a tire on the colonel's plane was punctured by a cactus needle. Lindbergh cheerfully waved off Goddard's apologies and repaired the damage.

"We had no beds and scarcely chairs to offer them, since we had just moved back," Esther Goddard said later, "but we were not permitted to feel embarrassed. Their visit was a field day for the town and an inspiration to us."

For all Lindbergh's warmth and encouragement, his visit was a further reminder of the need for a high-flying Nell. Goddard reviewed his program with the colonel, emphasizing the importance of a deliberate, orderly approach. A freak high flight might be possible; more likely, he said, a try would end in no flight at all and the expenditure of all his funds.

His first task was to improve the stabilizer, test it and then develop a small, lightweight pump to replace the heavy nitrogen pressure tank. When the pumps were ready, he would redesign the rocket for minimum weight, maximum fuel, greater altitudes.

After Lindbergh's visit, Goddard began his A series of tests. The plain letter "A" seemed adequately descriptive for

LEFT: Charles A. Lindbergh, in a photo taken November 14, 1931. [37]

Daniel Guggenheim, receiving the "Spirit of St. Louis" medal, June 1929. From left: Elmer A. Sperry, Harry F. Guggenheim, Daniel Guggenheim, Emory S. Land. [38]

Harry Guggenheim, Goddard, and Lindbergh at the New Mexico launching site, September 1935. [39]

Before flight, September 29, 1931. From left: Ljungquist, L. Mansur, Goddard, Kisk, C. Mansur. [40]

Mescalero Ranch, near Roswell, New Mexico. [41]

Machine shop at Mescalero Ranch. [42]

LEFT: Twenty-foot static test tower. [43]

Flight tower and shelter, Eden Valley, New Mexico. [44]

Charles Mansur and Albert Kisk transferring liquid oxygen before rocket test, 1930. [45]

Kisk in dugout near launching tower. [46]

ABOVE: Before first New Mexico flight. [47]

First New Mexico flight, December 30, 1930. Altitude about 2000 feet; speed about 500 m.p.h. [48]

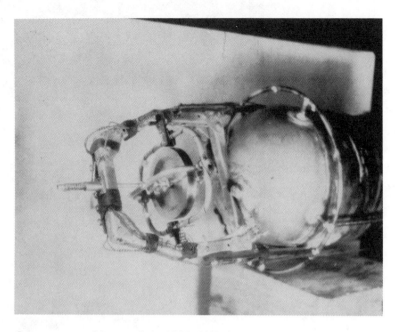

Gyroscope and mounting, 1932. [49]

Vane system and jacket, 1931-32. [50]

Goddard with 12-inch
diameter motor,
1932. [51]

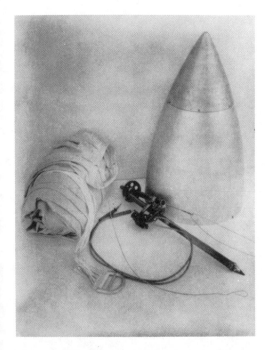

Parachute, releasing
device, and nose cone,
1935. [52]

the trials. Then and afterward, he disparaged the tendency of foreign enthusiasts to attach high-flying names to their experimental models. These much-publicized devices could be seen crashing or blowing up in newsreels throughout the country. They gave rocketry a bad name, he believed.

Goddard's A series led to the first successful flights of a self-stabilizing rocket. A major technical accomplishment, it was by no means managed overnight. His intricate stabilizer and the rocket to house it slowly took shape in his machine shop. Its lightweight gyroscope was obtained from an aircraft turn-and-bank indicator manufactured by the Pioneer Instrument Company. Goddard was thankful for the rare assist from private industry with a workable component he did not have to manufacture himself. But developing the entire stabilizing system, complete with tubes, pistons, valves and vanes, occupied the Goddard crew until the end of 1934.

They also spent months on the parachute release, designed to protect the rocket and its hand-tooled components on landing. Success depended on the proper instant of release, at the zenith of ascent, when the ten-foot pongee parachute was intended to open and slow Nell's descent. A "pilot parachute" was also folded into the rocket's nose cone. It was more than a year before these contrivances worked.

The first flight tests of the new A series began in January 1935, while Roswell was being visited by the most severe dust storms in the history of the region. "The days were yellow with dust," Esther wrote, "and when the sun shone, it was an unearthly blue. Then came the rains and a plague of insects—black 'beet bugs' and moths. At night, while Bob puzzled over Nell and her problems, we lay awake, each fearing to speak lest he drive away sleep for the other."

Beginning in March, Nell behaved better. The new models were bigger than any others Goddard had flown, ranging up to 15 feet in length and weighing up to 85 pounds without fuel and oxidizer aboard. The complex gyroscope stabilizer, which had been damaged in a February flight, was in the shop for repairs on March 8, when the rocket was tried with a simpler pendulum device.

The professor regarded the substitute as an imperfect compromise, although adequate for the testing of other components. Whether Nell sat and broiled in the tower or flew and crashed, the makeshift stabilizer was expendable. On March 8 the rocket, Goddard reported to his sponsor, "rose from the tower, heeled into the wind at 1,000 feet, snapping off the parachute, and roared in a powerful descent across the prairie, at close to, or at, the speed of sound."

After this satisfying demonstration of power, Nell's remnants were once more returned to the shop. On March 28, Goddard's crew was ready for another try, this time with gyroscope controls. They left the shop at 4:30 A.M. and had Nell rigged in the tower by 7:00 o'clock. This time the rocket proved its stability as well as its power.

Nell lifted out of the tower. Gathering speed, she soared to 4,800 feet. Then, with her fuel almost expended, she veered off to the horizon and raced 13,000 feet before striking the prairie floor. What excited Goddard, however, was how the gyroscope stabilizer took hold, correcting the rocket's deviations from the vertical.

"It was like a fish swimming upward through water," Esther exclaimed. Moderating his own enthusiasm, Goddard wrote to his sponsors:

"Inasmuch as control by a small gyroscope is the best as well as the lightest means of operating the directing vanes . . . a gyroscope having the necessary characteristics was developed after numerous tests.

"The gyroscope was set to apply controlling force when the axis of the rocket deviated 10 degrees or more from the vertical. . . . On March 28, 1935, the rocket, as viewed from the 1,000-foot shelter, traveled first to the left, and then to the right, thereafter describing a smooth and rather flat trajectory. The result was encouraging as it indicated the presence of an actual stabilizing force of sufficient magnitude to turn the rocket back to a vertical course."

In subsequent tests that spring and summer, the professor found it more difficult to restrain his elation. On May 31, 1935, Nell climbed to 7,500 feet, almost a mile and a half, under gyroscopic control. Moreover, the deviation from the vertical had been decreased from 10 degrees to about 2 degrees and the velocities were building up. Describing the flight to the Guggenheim Foundation, he wrote that the rocket emitted "a small, intensely white flame from the nozzle, which occasionally disappeared with no decrease in roar or propelling force." There were "occasional white flashes below the rocket," caused by explosions of gasoline vapor in the air. "The continually increasing speed of the rockets, with the accompanying steady roar, make the flights very impressive," he added.

This flight at the end of May was Goddard's highest up to that time. To the experimenter, it was a major achievement, but he sensed, correctly enough, that others might not be overwhelmed by a flight of a mile and a half. To achieve altitudes of 10, 20, 40 miles above the earth required essentially only a few more steps: the perfection of pumps . . . a more powerful motor . . . a rocket of giant dimensions. A giant Nell, he thought. It was still a question of patience and support, of funds beyond the capacity of private benefactors and perhaps more time than he had to command.

v

Goddard's years of trial and development were now bringing results. After Nell's flight of 7,500 feet, he felt it was time to invite Harry Guggenheim and Lindbergh, the Foundation's technical adviser, to come to Roswell to see for themselves.

The flier and the Foundation president flew into Roswell in a two-seat plane on September 22, 1935. For their visit Goddard had built two flight models as a precaution against a misfire. He and his crew checked and rechecked every component.

On September 23, the professor and his guests drove out at sunrise to the launching tower. They were followed by the truck and its trailer, bearing the cloth-covered rocket. The weather had turned out just right. In the dawn stillness, the crew went about preparations for the flight. Nell waited, trussed in the prairie tower, pointed upward, gleaming from tip to tail. The tension rose as Goddard, standing with his distinguished observers, pressed the telegraph key for ignition. But the rocket sat and cooked.

The professor's notes give no hint of dismay under "A-11: Attempted Flight Test":

"On making the test, a flame showing excess gasoline appeared in the concrete gas deflector, occasionally rising up toward the nozzle but not reaching it. This flame lasted during the entire run of 10 to 15 sec.

"Apparently the oxygen gas, which during the filling of the oxygen tank passed down through the chamber, had caused premature burning of the string holding the igniter in the chamber before the run. After ignition, the propelling charge burned entirely outside the rocket."

Goddard made his inspection, quietly pointing out what had gone wrong. Guggenheim and Lindbergh politely assured him they understood the foibles of experiment, that early aircraft were also unpredictable. Goddard nodded to his men, directed them to take the rocket back to the shop, and to bring out its replacement.

Before his crew returned to the valley, the sky became overcast with a flash rainstorm. It was hopeless for that day.

The second rocket was rain-soaked; it was senseless to risk another test.

Before heading back to the ranch, the professor diverted Harry Guggenheim with a demonstration of the properties of liquid oxygen. He showed how it could turn rubber tubing brittle in an instant, how it could incandesce a tumbleweed bush. Lindbergh meanwhile was exploring the area. He restlessly turned up a hawk in the launching tower and, nearby, a sidewinder snake. With a blast of his Colt revolver, he disposed of a large tarantula, confessing he had seldom seen so many venomous creatures in one place.

It rained the next day. The day after that, on September 25, Goddard and his guests went down to the valley with the second model of Nell. He had sent his men ahead to prepare for the flight. Now immersed in the professor's problem, Guggenheim had spent a restless night at the ranchhouse. At the first sounds of waking, he went into the kitchen and helped Esther prepare breakfast for the party.

The test was no better than the previous one: ". . . a gasoline flame appeared near the top of the chamber, followed by a large bright flame. The flame during the short lift period was whiter and noisier than usual, indicating an excess of oxygen.

"The chamber was found to have burned through under one of the gasoline orifices, the burning evidently occurring under pressure, since the edges of the hole were found to be bulged. . . .

"The rocket did not rise."

Lindbergh said later: "He was as mortified as a parent whose child misbehaves in front of company."

Guggenheim observed: "Goddard's faith in the ultimate success of his work was contagious. I promised I would come back."

Guggenheim did return to Mescalero. But, ironically, one

of the few Americans who backed rocket development in its early days would never see the professor's rocket in flight.

Following the second attempted launching, Goddard put down in his diary:

"Mr. Guggenheim and Col. Lindbergh left soon afterwards, after having a hurried lunch at the ranch house. At lunch, Col. Lindbergh said that the work was just about where aviation was in 1912. The writer drove them to the airport, where they took off at about 11 a.m. The colonel flew to the tower, circled it twice and dipped his wings in salute. . . . Had nap."

Goddard and his men dismantled the aborted rockets. They unbolted the sleek aluminum sheaths, set them to one side, laid out the components on the shop benches for a searching examination. His usual reassurances, that out of failure one finds the answer, sounded somehow less convincing to his crew. And to himself.

VI

How much longer could he maintain his isolation, how much time was left to carry out his private vision to a culminating success?

He was disturbingly aware of a widespread and growing interest in rocketry. His mail from Germany continued to be knowledgeable and disquieting. There was now a suggestion from a German technician named Eugen Sänger for pumping liquids into rocket chambers. The idea was all too similar to Goddard's work in progress. In the United States, the American Rocket Society was now using its collaborative energies for essential experiments. Perhaps, as some members said, Goddard was too isolated to see that he was no longer a single colossus. Still he was ahead of the pack. But how far ahead? And for how long?

Among scientists and the public as well, his rocket method was earning respectability. Two nights after Lindbergh and Guggenheim left, the Goddards sat in their living room, beside the fireplace blazing with cottonwood logs, and tuned in a radio station in Dallas, Texas, broadcasting a network radio program, "The March of Time."

At Harry Guggenheim's earlier suggestion, Goddard had hesitantly agreed to a dramatization of his work. Now, from New York City, he heard an actor speaking his prophecy of 1919: ". . . I believe that a rocket can be made that will reach the moon or the planets. . . . But first we must send up small rockets to explore the atmosphere. . . ."

As the actor's voice faded, Esther said: "He makes you sound like an unctuous clergyman." Perhaps. But the broadcast had presented his theory in all seriousness. The sound effects, the sonorous roar of a rocket at launching, its intensifying noise as it rises from the ground, all this was certainly authentic. Almost too authentic, he may have reflected.

Although the Foundation had pledged to support the research for another year, external pressures were becoming more intense. Much development was still ahead. He felt encouraged by a letter from Lindbergh, written when the flier had returned from Roswell:

"I want you to know that I consider our visit with you very much worth while, even though we did not have the personal satisfaction of seeing a rocket flight. In fact, I do not feel that our seeing a flight would have been of material importance aside from our own interest and the satisfaction I know it would have given you to have everything go perfectly while we were there. . . ."

Lindbergh went on to say that the "important part" of their visit was seeing the manner in which Goddard carried out his research, and observed that he and Guggenheim "came back with the feeling that the project is being managed with unusual efficiency and intelligence, and that success was a matter of time rather than possibility."

VII

A matter of time. This was precisely the problem. From his experience with the patient Dr. Abbot, Goddard was aware that his sponsors would eventually want more than promises of things to come. Lindbergh was kind, "exquisitely kind," as Esther said. Yet even he was beginning to tap at the cocoon which the professor had woven about himself. For six months, Lindbergh had been urging Goddard to emerge, to establish himself more firmly in the scientific community. The flier had several suggestions.

At Falaise, Harry Guggenheim's estate on Long Island, Lindbergh in the spring of 1935 had asked Goddard about his plans for publication. When had he last informed the scientific fraternity of his progress?

"Oh, not so long ago," Goddard answered uneasily. "I guess it was 1919."

Lindbergh laughed. Goddard managed to laugh with him and agreed that perhaps it was time to publish his results with the liquid-propellant rocket.

In Roswell, the colonel had offered several other ideas. He presented them with such warmth and sincerity that the professor could muster no defenses against them. He encouraged Goddard to accept an invitation to address the American Association for the Advancement of Science at its annual convention in St. Louis, Missouri, at the end of the year.

His next proposal was more troubling. He wanted Goddard to send a complete liquid-fuel rocket to the Smithsonian Institution.

The inventor was anxious about shipping off his fledgling engine, exhibiting it in the nation's museum of science and engineering. It was scarcely ready for public inspection, he said. It still needed development.

Lindbergh quietly, dispassionately heard him out. The rocket, he said, need not be exhibited until Goddard gave his permission. But if it were kept at the Smithsonian, the priority of his work would be established beyond question.

Goddard balked, agreed, balked and reluctantly agreed again. He would send a suitable rocket to Dr. Abbot and arrange the details for its future display.

Now, with his visitors gone, he had to find out what had ailed his latest version of Nell. After a month of testing and probing, he discovered the flaw. It was "rather obscure," as he reported to Guggenheim in a letter of October 28, 1935:

". . . a number of tests have been required to clear up the matter satisfactorily. It has been found . . . that the streams of gasoline which entered the combustion chamber were not of the proper amount nor of the proper form, owing to variations in the edges of the orifices. The test you saw was, incidentally, the first one in which the orifices have given trouble. The knowledge gained in this series of tests will be valuable in connection with the large model, with which we shall begin static tests shortly. I have not yet, however, forgiven fate for bringing the matter of the gasoline orifices to my attention just at the time you and Colonel Lindbergh were here. . . ."

Goddard did not specify that one of his mechanics had unfortunately drilled the holes too small. He reported simply that a slight decrease in the size of the orifices had prevented sufficient gasoline from entering the chamber. The flaw was now corrected. Winds and rain had delayed flight testing, but he eventually got the model to fly. As he wrote further:

"It seemed desirable, in order to make certain that matters were under control, to have an actual flight with a rocket provided with the improved orifices. This flight was obtained today, after a delay of over two weeks, due to bad weather. The rocket fired well, and also corrected itself well, notwithstanding the fact that some wind was blowing at the time. . . . It rose for about three-quarters of a mile, and then turned sharply downward at an angle, before the parachute could be released. The chamber, after the test, was found to be in perfect condition. . . ."

Guggenheim replied:

"[I] have rather expected to get such a letter from you. . . . I think you can well forgive fate which was so hard on you while we were visiting with you because, as I told you, I was so well impressed with your organization and your approach to your problems that the failure of a complete demonstration seemed incidental rather than fundamental to me. . . ."

The three-quarter mile launching of October 29, 1935, was recorded in Goddard's journals as Test A-14. It was a satisfactory if not sensational culmination to the A series of tests, designed for the dependable control of flight.

VIII

He began to assemble a complete A series rocket for the Smithsonian Institution, after cautioning Dr. Abbot on handling it:

"It is not desirable to have it on exhibition for a time, in order to give me the opportunity of completing the work to the extent of reaching an important height before details of construction are made public."

The venerable Smithsonian found Goddard among its most circumspect donors. The rocket pioneer prepared Nell for posterity as devotedly as an Egyptian mortician arranging Tutankhamen for the ages. In his diary and journal Goddard mentioned that all "sooted parts" of the rocket components were scrupulously cleaned before assembly, that every piece was oiled, wiped clean, oiled again, and then given a protective coating of grease "inside and out, and the nozzle plugged with a shellacked cork." After assembly the rocket, wrapped in old comforters, was anchored in place in a well-made wooden box, its lid firmly nailed shut.

In his diary of November 2, 1935, Goddard recorded the departure of this space age sarcophagus from Roswell to Washington, the longest journey his rocket had taken:

"E and I watched train at 1 P.M. as 'Nellie' went. . . . Oley says—'Old Nellie, she's going for a ride. . . .' "

At the Smithsonian, the arrangements for storing Goddard's donation were no less precise. Paul Edward Garber, later curator of the Institution's National Air Museum where the rocket was eventually displayed, recalled the disposition of the long, coffin-like box from Roswell: "The box was placed against a wall in a remote part of the Institution and carpenters and plasterers were called in to build a false wall in front of it up to the ceiling."

There Goddard's liquid-fuel rocket would remain until after his death and the end of the Second World War. Garber, remembering the rocket's interment, found among Goddard's correspondence his request that it be placed on exhibition only after "authorization from me, or, in the event of my death in the meantime, from [Colonel Lindbergh] and Mr. Guggenheim."

While his rocket was on its way to Washington, Goddard responded to another Lindbergh nudge. On December 31, 1935, he spoke before the American Association for the Advancement of Science at its annual convention in St. Louis. This rare appearance was arranged through his friend Dr. Brooks, who had once helped him on climate studies at Clark and was then meteorologist in charge of Harvard's Blue Hill Observatory. Brooks had written to him:

"Since you alone of many American investigators are engaged in developing a direct means of making observations in the high atmosphere, it would be very appropriate, as well as exceptionally interesting, if you could take part in the program."

Goddard cautiously titled his address: "Progress on the Atmospheric Sounding Rocket." For the first time, he publicly showed motion pictures of the rocket's earliest flights. Shyly but pleased, he received the warm approval of his peers. "You know, Esther," he said to his wife, "they seem to *admire* what I'm doing!"

Dr. Abbot, who spoke to the conference about his own work on solar motors, also took time for a lavish endorsement of Goddard's experiments, observing that "a few hundred thousand dollars invested in the development of the rocket now would pay the nation dividends amounting to millions of dollars in the next two decades."

Goddard was grateful for Abbot's praise. "A few hundred thousand dollars"—with this he could dream of reaching extreme altitudes. But who would pay for such dreams?

IX

He could no longer object to Lindbergh's other suggestion, that he publish a scientific account of his labors with the liquid-fuel rocket. It was brought out by the Smithsonian Institution as part of its "Miscellaneous Collections," in the same manner as his monograph of 1919. The report, titled "Liquid-Propellant Rocket Development," was issued on March 16, 1936. It consisted of ten pages of text and twelve additional pages of plates illustrating his experiments.

Goddard, however, did not release a comprehensive record of his latest rocket designs. He did not wish to bring up to date his experiments with curtain cooling and other still-pending devices. But with these important exceptions, he reported on the major steps of his liquid-fuel research since 1920.

Unlike the 1919 paper, which proved the theory of the rocket method, the new monograph dealt with specific progress. It described his first experiments with liquid oxygen and various hydrocarbons and his finding that liquid oxygen and gasoline were apparently the "most practical" combination. He firmly established his priority to the world's first liquid-fuel flight, in Auburn in March 1926, a fact which he felt had been treated vaguely or ignored abroad. He spoke of "other short flights . . . that of July 17, 1929, happening to attract public attention." He referred to his early work in New Mexico, his gyroscope stabilizer, and finally, in summing up, made this comment: "The next step . . . is the reduction of weight to a minimum. . . ."

For all its blandness, Goddard's 1936 paper excited the new generation of rocket technicians in the United States and abroad. As his 1919 paper had done, it presented a responsible physicist suggesting that space flight was not so wild a dream, a scientist who was working independently on its probability.

One commentary on Goddard's 1936 report echoed the past, but was also a firm underscoring of his achievement. It was written by Pendray and appeared in the American Rocket Society's *Astronautics* in July 1937. Titled "Rocketry's Number One Man," Pendray's article stated flatly that Goddard had made "notable strides," and then proceeded to list them:

"He had (1) demonstrated that rockets could be useful, (2) that dry fuels [then available] were inadequate, (3) developed a suitable fuel combination, (4) developed the method of forcing fuels into the chamber with inert gas pressure, (5) produced a workable liquid-fuel motor, (6) shot the first liquid-fuel rocket, (7) shot the first instrument-carrying rocket, (8) determined the 'best location' for the motor; and (9) brought the rocket forcibly to the attention of reputable scientists and engineers as a possible instrument for reaching altitudes. . . ."

Another commentary, written by Goddard himself, was sent early in 1936 to the alumni secretary of the Worcester Polytechnic Institute:

"The question of greatest interest which this paper raises is, perhaps, 'What heights can be reached?' I am rather reluctant to specify what heights I believe possible. . . .

"The work will eventually open a new field of engineering; a fact which is only beginning to be recognized. . . . The liquid-propellant rockets are . . . about as complicated as automobiles, and consist of a similar variety of substances, and of many individual parts. Like the automobile, also, every part must function perfectly if the machine as a whole is to operate satisfactorily.

"The inquiry is sometimes made as to when the research will be completed. The answer is that it will probably be the same year the automobile and airplane are completed. It has not the finality of building an individual machine, but is a new method of transportation, which I feel certain will have many more applications than the sending of recording instruments into the high atmosphere. . . ."

Despite his enthusiasm for this "new method of transportation," there was one application of the rocket that disturbed him—its potential wartime use by Germany. His suspicion was growing into a major distrust. The Germans might be studying his work far more closely than they would willingly admit. Esther Goddard reflected this thought in a letter to her mother in Worcester:

". . . one package of mss. has mysteriously disappeared in the mails—and another has been opened before Bob got it. With all this activity on the part of those . . . Germans, it looks suspicious. . . . Be sure to tell our tenants not to let anyone into the back store rooms at the house. . . ."

With his Smithsonian paper out of the way, Goddard became absorbed in his plans for a new and larger rocket. Two questions remained. They were, in effect, the same question:

How long would his Guggenheim grant continue . . . and how long would his patron be satisfied with his step-by-step development?

A few months later, he had a partial answer in a calm, almost casual letter from Lindbergh, who wondered how long it would take the professor to have "a really successful flight." A spectacular high-altitude flight, the pilot observed, "would be splendid for everyone's morale."

9. GALLANT EMPRISE

Few places in Roswell permitted a more isolated life than Mescalero Ranch. The adobe-walled Goddard residence, near the end of the dirt country road, was now screened against outsiders by a tier of cottonwood trees, buttressed by arbor vitae, planted abundantly by the professor and his wife.

Behind the ranchhouse, the machine shop was closed to everyone, including the professor's wife and wives of the crew, and stoutly locked after working hours. The rocket launching tower, some ten miles across the prairie from town, could be reached only over an unmarked trail, barred by ranchers' gates. By the mid-1930s, Goddard was firmly guarding the privacy of his machine and himself. But it was becoming a losing struggle.

In Roswell, where "no questions asked" was a civic virtue, he might have remained comfortably inconspicuous were it not for the rocket's tendency to draw attention. It was hard to ignore the sudden blasts behind the ranchhouse; the headlines accompanying the visits of Lindbergh, Guggenheim and their fellow aviator, James H. Doolittle; the numerous letters bearing foreign stamps, particularly German and Russian, which were noted by the local postmistress before she wedged them into the Goddards' mailbox.

The small cattle town relished the aura of mystery and importance which the scientist inevitably brought. During his early years in New Mexico, curious townspeople fancied him as their moon-rocket man with solitary Yankee ways, an impression which Goddard did nothing to dissipate. When knowledgeable science writers sought him out, such as Herbert Nichols of the *Christian Science Monitor* and Howard Blakeslee of the Associated Press, he spoke of his work more freely. To non-scientific reporters, however, he rarely granted personal interviews. Ernie Pyle, a roving columnist at home before he became a correspondent in the Second World War, could reach him only by telephone. In his nationally syndicated column, Pyle observed that "Prof. Goddard . . . says the work goes so slowly that he doesn't know whether he's accomplished anything anyhow. I was able to gather, however, through adroit questioning and double-talk, that Prof. Goddard has not yet been to the moon."

Although Goddard made private notes on space flight when he had time, he remained conservative in his few public statements.

"The aspect of the rocket which undoubtedly appeals to the imagination," he wrote in an article, "Some Aspects of Rocket Engineering," for *The Tech Engineering News,* of the Massachusetts Institute of Technology, April 1938, "is its possible use for flights outside the earth's atmosphere. . . . As in many radically new developments, so much emphasis has been placed in the early stages on the ultimate possible achievements that the public comes to believe these must be within easy reach. Actually . . . progress must be made one step at a time. . . ."

The professor, absorbed by his experiments, stayed happily aloof from Roswell society. Esther's trips into the town, however, were now leading to friendships with a small coterie of wives whose husbands taught at the nearby New Mexico Military Institute. Although these ladies at first thought Goddard's wife "shy and rather stiff," they soon learned that Esther was expert at contract bridge and also an eager worker in civic organizations.

After a few years in New Mexico, she had become active in the Roswell Music Association; the Women's Club; and the Shakespeare Club, Roswell's exclusive intellectual society. She founded a book club that is still in existence. She also won a town-wide writing contest; read *Enoch Arden* to the Women's Club with a musical accompaniment; and won a duplicate bridge tournament.

Gradually Esther began to lead her husband into social activities. "He needed to relax," she recalled. "But he was also ready to come out a little. Otherwise, you couldn't have moved him any more than you could have moved El Capitan."

Doubtless Esther was correct. But Goddard, emerging, seemed at first like an owl found large-eyed and blinking in daylight.

The scientist occasionally accompanied his wife to a bridge foursome, although he thoroughly disliked the game. While the players gathered at the card table, he would find himself a comfortable chair and settle down with a book, a mystery story or perhaps a scientific treatise. On one occasion, he almost upset a bridge lamp and considerably upset the card players by hurling a German history of rocketry across the room. "I never saw such nonsense—the book, I mean," Goddard sheepishly explained to his host.

His next venture into town affairs was at the invitation of Reverend Theodore Howden, the young rector of St. Andrews Episcopal Church. An occasional rather than constant churchgoer, Goddard arrived in his Sunday best to address Howden's young people's group.

"He was a little anxious about it, but it was good for him to get his mind off Nell and try to lecture again," Esther wrote to her mother.

In an age increasingly confused about the relationship of science and religion, the professor drew a deft distinction for the class. There was no conflict between science and faith, he said. "Science is knowledge, essentially. Religion is right living and acting, essentially. To keep the world going, we need both of these forces, going hand in hand. But the passive state is not enough. Evil and crime are active and aggressive," he declared, emphasizing his abiding sense of morality. "What we must have is militant decency throughout the world."

What had seemed to Roswell a rather exotic bird began to resemble, outwardly, a more conventional rooster. Goddard was heartened to discover his acceptance as a reasonable member of the community. Even Esther, who took the faintly dramatic position that she was caring for a "great man," as Roswell friends observed, liked to point out that Bob was "just as plain as blueberry pie." This judgment was confirmed by a clubwoman who called one evening, tapping hesitantly at the Goddards' door. "Come in, come in," the scientist greeted her. "But let's be quiet for a few moments. We're listening to the Charlie McCarthy program on the radio." The visitor, charmed, reported her encounter with the professor to her friends.

He found himself comfortable among people who accepted him easily, while respecting the privacy of his work. Among the cluster of young scientists and scholars gathered around the Military Institute, he made such close friends as Barry Duffield, dean of the school; Samuel H. Marshall, an oil geologist; Paul Horgan, who became a notable writer of the southwest; and Peter Hurd, a distinguished young artist of the area.

With these genial companions, the Goddards were Bob and Esther. Together they celebrated holidays and birthdays, met for outdoor picnics, shared lighthearted family pleasures. "Every Fourth of July," Sam Marshall later recalled, "Bob came to our backyard, his arms full of Roman candles and skyrockets for our three young sons. He became a kind of godfather to them. As far as I know, they were the only ones in town who were ever invited inside his machine shop."

On Christmas eve, the Goddards and their friends would gather at one another's homes. When they met at Mescalero Ranch, Esther was ready with a time-honored bowl of Swedish *glögg*. Bob, as master of ceremonies, read small, whimsical verses he had written about each of their guests, and led the singing of Christmas carols.

Whenever travels interrupted their holiday festivities, the Goddards continued the camaraderie by exchanging bizarre gifts with those at home. "They were fine little atrocities," Paul Horgan recalled, "an ornate velvet pillow case inscribed 'To Mother with Love,' an outlandish bit of crockery, a thermometer imbedded in a ceramic key to the city, a small trout confected of marzipan."

Although the scientist joined in these japeries, his obvious pleasure appeared as protective coloring to two of his Roswell friends. Horgan, the writer, struck by what he described as Bob's "overwhelming averageness, an almost Boy Scout conventionality," recalled his instantaneous response to "the slightest sort" of humor.

"At the most modest of jokes, he would rock back and forth in his metal porch chair, engulfed in laughter," Horgan said. "It took so little to amuse him, maybe just the feeling that he was among people who liked him as he was.

"But beneath this ordinariness you recognized some hidden and extraordinary sense of purpose. You felt there was a physical frailty about him, although there was never a word about his health or that he was a tubercular. Bob's voice had a suspiciously husky tone and he coughed rather often, but he dismissed your suspicions with his cigars. I never knew anybody who enjoyed a cigar so much, smoking them down to the last pinch.

"What drove him, you came to understand, was some kind of vision into the future. He told us, and we believed him, that his secrecy was a matter of government orders. When a newcomer asked too many questions, Esther and Bob quickly derailed the subject—gently, tactfully, but quite firmly if necessary. None of us saw his shop while they were here, or his rockets, or his tower, or expected to. When he showed us films of his early flights, Esther assured us we were distinctly privileged."

Peter Hurd, the artist, was no less fascinated by Goddard who was many years his senior. Hurd's view was that "Bob was so wrapped up in his work, no amount of abandonment by his fellow humans could bother him." When they went on painting expeditions together, Hurd felt that the professor "approached the outrageous contrasts of New Mexican color with considerable gusto. He was always generous with his oil paints." For his older companion, painting became a communion with nature, said Hurd.

"We never painted side by side. Bob would go off to choose his own location, his own point of view. What mattered most to him was not what he drew, but what happened inside him —that deep, almost religious feeling that touches every artist. You confront a landscape. You lose yourself in fleeting moments of light and shadow. And when you've done spilling pigment on canvas, if you've done anything, you feel a keen sense of belonging to what you've seen and tried to set down."

Hurd, remembering these hours with Goddard, recalled one incident more. He was standing with the quiet, reflective scientist one night on his father's front lawn in Roswell. The

New Mexican skies that evening were astonishingly clear. Goddard suddenly pulled a flashlight from his pocket and began to point out planets in the skies, lecturing his younger friend on the ways of the sun's satellites.

"Years later, after his death," Hurd recalled, "I realized what he was doing there. He was pointing out landing fields in the solar system."

II

A dependably controlled high flight, Goddard knew, required more fuel, more thrust, more power, more rocket altogether. His completed A series was powered by a combustion chamber 5¾ inches in diameter. With its limited size, it had performed perhaps as well as could be expected.

His new experimental series, which he designated with the letter K, tested a much larger chamber, ten inches in diameter. The rocket's ambitious motor also compounded the factors for error: the intricate problems of feeding in fuel and oxidizer, the difficulties of cooling the combustion chamber against intensive temperature. But without a larger rocket, there was little prospect of great altitudes. Goddard began the K series to deal with these problems. His store of optimism was still his calling card on the universe.

The K series, consisting of ten proving-stand tests, was carried out between November 22, 1935, and February 12, 1936. It was an imperative gamble. Despite the usual winds, Goddard hoped to perfect and prove the components of a soaring rocket by spring, in time to assure the renewal of his grant.

But how high was high?—5 miles? . . . 10 miles? . . . above the reach of airplanes? . . . 20 miles? . . . above the reach of sounding balloons, of man's highest recorded altitudes? Eventually, he knew, rockets would soar far above such heights, and man would look down on his earth as on a relief map. But now it would be fine if he could conquer the foothills toward space.

For his static trials of the new motor, Goddard prudently shifted his tests from the twenty-foot stand beside his shop to his launching site in the valley. There he felt more secure than in his backyard, where even tests of small rockets aroused comment. His next-door neighbor, Herman Crile, recalled later how the roar of Goddard's rockets had upset his cook and his hens, and the owner of a nearby dairy complained of blasts that made his milk cows uneasy.

In the valley, Goddard and his men excavated a waist-deep, static-test shelter, fifty feet from the test tower, with a heavy metal-shielded lid capable of being slanted, or lowered entirely, for protection. Inside the shelter Goddard installed an elaborate set of controls to start and stop his static firings; to measure their lift, temperature and time; and to photograph results automatically at precise intervals. The professor devised and admired his new and makeshift arrangement, with all its multi-colored wire stretching across the prairie floor.

The new model Nell could generate as much horsepower as a steam locomotive, although it weighed only 1/500 as much. Too frequently, however, the fierce heat inside the combustion chamber still sliced through thin metal walls, spilling a dense gasoline flame that enveloped the rocket and the static tower. On such evenings, the professor turned to his experimental journals, patiently recording aberrations, brooding over ways to improve the powerful engine.

Although the K rocket motors were barely out of the shop, Goddard, eager for a flight, concluded his static tests in February 1936. In adding up the results of the series, he wrote to Lindbergh in England, where the flier had moved for his own privacy's sake:

". . . we are already two months behind the schedule of the year's work which I had submitted to Mr. Guggenheim, but the efficiency [is] not as great as I had expected. We tried varying a number of conditions, including pressures and modes of spraying. The greatest lift in these static tests was about 800 lbs.

"Two encouraging results were obtained. In all the tests the lift rose from zero to full lift in between one and two seconds. It was also found that the excess of gasoline could be reduced considerably over that for small chambers, without serious heating. It became clear that maximum efficiency can be obtained only by the use of high-pressure pumps. . . ."

The pumps, Goddard added, must wait on the satisfactory flight of rockets big enough to house them. These he now planned to build in his L series. The high-pressure pumps would constitute a major last stage of his rocket development. Thereafter, he said, the perfected rocket could be increased in size for very high altitudes.

Despite the scientist's flat, formal style, Lindbergh was aware that Goddard felt under acute pressure, that he was depending heavily upon him to advance the rocket cause with Guggenheim. The professor's letter concluded:

"It seems desirable if it can possibly be arranged that another year be had on the development. I am writing to Mr. Guggenheim, asking what prospect there is for this, although I realize the Foundation has already done more than was anticipated. . . ."

Lindbergh wrote to Harry Guggenheim in April 1936 that "Goddard would have no feeling but one of gratitude if the Foundation decides that it is unable to finance him further." The Foundation had fully met any obligation incurred by Daniel Guggenheim, he wrote reassuringly. But after admitting that the professor's "results, to date, have not been very spectacular," he ended his letter with an irresistible challenge:

". . . if you intend to continue an active interest in anything which goes under the general heading of aviation and science, I feel quite sure that you can find no more interesting project, or one that holds more future possibilities. I am thoroughly convinced that rockets will be sent to altitudes measured in the hundreds of miles in the fairly near future. I believe also that Goddard will probably be the first man to make flights of really high altitudes and to make observations of definite scientific value if he is financially able to continue his work. . . ."

Harry Guggenheim was then hearing counter-arguments on the use of the Foundation's money. Among these voices was that of Dr. Robert A. Millikan, president of the California Institute of Technology, for which the Foundation was already supplying research funds. Millikan favored an institutional approach to aeronautical research. Cal. Tech, moreover, was already forming a new rocket research group. But Guggenheim was his own administrator and still sided with Lindbergh for Goddard. He replied to the flier:

"Personally, I am in favor of the Foundation continuing the work for another year. . . . I have enough confidence in Goddard to be willing to recommend this. . . . I am personally deeply interested in this development and feel, as you do, that it offers unusual possibilities in the development of a new means of transportation. . . ."

The Foundation appropriated another $20,000 for one more year, Guggenheim agreeing with Lindbergh who wrote to him in May 1936:

"I would much prefer to have Goddard interested in real scientific development than to have him primarily interested in more spectacular achievements which are of less real value. From a practical standpoint I would like to see him attempt high altitude flights, as soon as he feels his model is really capable of making them. Of course I am not in favor of attempting to push a man of Goddard's type and intelligence into anything which he feels is definitely inadvisable. . . ."

III

In the spring of 1936, Goddard started on a new flight model that would occupy him for more than two years, until the summer of 1938, when he turned to pumps. As Goddard answered a letter from Isabel Hornibrook, a New England novelist who had written a space-travel story for children: "I sometimes envy you writers—you can drink so deeply of imagination. In my own case, I can uncork only just enough to help me solve the problem that lies immediately ahead."

The new L series model offered an abundance of interesting problems. More sophisticated than the rockets he had tried during Guggenheim's earlier visit, his flying model was now 13 feet, 1 inch long and weighed up to 200 pounds when empty of fuel. In his journal, he listed the major ingredients of the new rocket: the assemblies of stabilizers, valves, tanks, cooling devices, pressurizers, controls. There were seventeen components, all told. Later, he would add to this complex his intricate lightweight pump-turbine assembly to feed the rocket in flight. Meanwhile, he continued to use his old ally, a pressure tank of inert nitrogen to force-feed the liquids. The nitrogen and its tanks, carried aboard the rocket, added undesirable weight. But, until he could get to the pump's development, they would have to serve.

The first of Goddard's L series tests, a static run, was conducted on May 11, 1936. The blast was impressive enough to terrify prairie dogs, but otherwise unpromising. The nitrogen tank failed to supply enough pressure; a regulator valve failed; the rocket split and, drenched in its own gasoline, produced a blazing eddy of flame. Esther managed to see the test as encouraging. She declared that "we found the ground behind the jet green and glazed in spots, indicating higher jet temperatures than ever before."

In the prairie heat in 1936, Esther watched her husband closely for signs of fatigue, coaxed him to put aside his evening's "doping" to relax at dinner in town and a motion picture at Roswell's air-cooled Yucca Theater. His diary mentions visits to the Yucca, twice, three times a week, sometimes as often as the feature attraction was changed.

Subsequent flight tests that year proceeded in spurts and sputters. None of the larger models came close to Nell's highest altitudes. A principal difficulty was that Goddard's curtain cooling, again being tried experimentally, was subject to flaws which the professor managed to say were "understandable." Esther's letters to her mother that summer were less cheerful:

June 14, 1936: "We were out to the tower Friday and Saturday hoping for a test. Friday too much wind, and Saturday a valve leaked, so we must try again next week. . . ."

June 21, 1936: "We've had the blues the past week. . . . Nell did not behave nicely . . . and that evening came your news about the O'Gradys (tenants on Maple Hill) moving. . . . Up at 3 a.m. Thursday to see Nell sit and sputter. I wish I could cry . . . we had so hoped Nell would do well. . . ."

July 5, 1936: "Went to the country Thursday, not very good test. . . . Today Bob's 'doping' hard to discover what ails Nell, so I don't even dare run water to wash up. . . . The days in the country are long and hot, and Bob is pretty well shot after them. Thursday night he woke with pounding heart and pulse, as he has done many nights after a test. He told me about it next morning, so we went right down to the doctor to check . . . the doctor said his nerves were bad and he simply must relax. . . ."

IV

By mid-August, neither Goddard's nerves nor the performance of his rocket were vastly improved. For years, he had successfully resisted his physician's talk of a vacation. "After all, we were accustomed to take poor tests in stride,"

Esther said years later, "and Bob learned something from each of them." But he was looking frayed in Roswell's oven-like heat, and she urged a holiday trip to California. His crew was due for their annual vacation. Everyone would benefit.

In California, as suggested by Harry Guggenheim, Goddard took time from his holiday to visit Dr. Millikan at Pasadena. He knew of President Millikan's desire to make the California Institute a center of the aeronautical sciences; of his interest in "teamwork"; of his employment of Dr. Theodor von Kármán, the gifted aerodynamicist from Hungary.

Goddard dreaded the encounter with Millikan, and with reason. It brought one more reminder that the rocket might not remain his exclusive preserve.

Millikan's view was familiar. Many engineering skills and many new techniques could help to perfect the rocket. Quite true, Goddard agreed, but one had to work with what one had. The Institute might supply these skills, Millikan said. That would be fine, said Goddard. He would be happy to have such assistance in Roswell.

There was no such suggestion from Millikan. With the preliminaries aside, the president got to his point. The real way to proceed, he said, was through open collaboration, a complete interchange of ideas.

To reject this idea, Goddard knew, might confirm what some scientists were saying—that he was possessive, secretive, uncooperative. Well, it was true that he suspected this sort of "teamwork." But as an inventor, he could not bring himself to "turn over to others," as his wife later put it, the work of three decades.

Goddard thanked President Millikan for his suggestions, said he would give them careful attention, added all the pleasantries he could think of and left town.

The Californian was not so easily sidetracked. The Goddards had no sooner returned to Mescalero Ranch at the end of August than they found one of Cal. Tech's graduate students waiting to see the professor. The same day Goddard received a note from Millikan asking him to extend "all possible courtesies" to the young student, Frank J. Malina.

If the professor was relaxed by his western vacation, his relaxation vanished with Malina's visit. To Goddard the student seemed too inquisitive and brash. To the young rocket buff, the professor was too reticent and guarded. It was not a happy encounter, Esther Goddard remembered. Malina, who later became a founder with Dr. von Kármán and others of Aerojet, a West Coast missile enterprise, asked penetrating questions, trying to learn the basic developments that concerned Goddard most. The professor parried questions until Esther, feeling the tension, hurriedly announced that lunch was ready.

After lunch, Malina suggested he might like to "look over" the shop. Goddard successfully distracted him for several hours with a trip to the empty tower in Eden Valley. On their return, the student was still asking to see specific rocket components on which Goddard's men were working. Finally, he was admitted into the machine shop where the latest version of Nell lay completely covered under her canvas sheeting. And there she stayed.

Goddard was more receptive to John W. Sessums, Jr., an Army Air Corps lieutenant who in October flew in without warning from Wright Field. Sessums, who is now an executive of a corporation doing space work, had read of Goddard's work in an aviation magazine. "I was enough of an engineer to realize that he was working on sound principles mechanically," Sessums has written, "and I put on my best personality for the visit. His guarded attitude was immediately apparent. I could almost see his mind working, deciding what he could afford to let me see and hear about his scientific endeavors. There was much in his passion that reminded me of Orville Wright. The big difference was that Dr. Goddard had a charming wife who was a great aid to him in his work."

The Goddards invited Sessums to lunch and afterward the professor, talking about rockets, drove the pilot to the launch site. "Dr. Goddard became so interested in the technical discussion that he was literally jumping. I asked him if he had considered catapulting the rocket to give it a flying start so that all the fuel would be used to better advantage. That did it! I could not get another word in edgewise. We perfunctorily got back into his car. Dr. Goddard not missing a breath, talking, consumed with ideas, really in another world. I did not hear much of what was said as I became completely engrossed in the fact that he had forgotten to shift out of first gear. The engine was running away. He never gave it a thought. We returned the eight or ten miles in the new car in low gear. I didn't have the heart to interrupt him and remind him to shift gears."

v

By Thanksgiving Day, 1936, there were no high flights of the L series to celebrate. In three launching efforts, the large-motored rocket reached a maximum altitude of 300 feet. Usually, the combustion chambers burned through in a cascade of smoke and fire. One modified rocket, equipped with a cluster of four small motors, successfully cleared the tower in early November. But then it toppled, erupting in flame. There was one source for thanksgiving. His sponsors had not seen the performance.

Goddard's current grant still had six months to go, into the summer of 1937. With sufficient time, he felt he could perfect the 10-inch chamber, or the clustered motor, for high flight. But it might take more than six months to perfect that most demanding device, his curtain-cooling system. He decided to return again to his smaller, more dependable model, improve it for all the thrust and altitude it could possibly produce. Writing again to Lindbergh, he proposed this course:

"Regarding future work, the plan is to use a small chamber model in flights, adding successively the features already worked out for the large model. These are the following: higher pressure to increase the lift and range; reduction in weight of tanks by the use of high strength materials without loss of strength in fabrication, as developed by shop tests; liquid nitrogen pressure generation, as already used on large models; and, finally, pumps with very low pressure tanks. . . ."

Then he made his familiar bid:

"The question I am now faced with is whether or not the above plan, including pumps and low pressure tanks, can be carried through by the middle of next August. Frankly, it does not appear so, and to reach the heights that have been planned, it seems very desirable, if it can be arranged, to have the work continued for another year or more. . . ."

Now Lindbergh's reply was kindly but noncommittal. Goddard, however, proceeded at once with his plan. From December 1936 through February 1937, he tried three flights with an improved small-chamber rocket. The tests were moderately successful, the rockets rising as high as 1,870 feet. His crew was exhilarated to be flying rockets that at least blasted off in the right direction. When Nell reached the apex of her ascent, the doctor joined them in the cry of: "Parachute! Parachute!" Once the parachute did open, its shrouds holding, and Nell made a dignified descent.

In March, Goddard redesigned the flight model again, lightening all of its parts to a minimum. The new rocket was 16 feet 5 inches long, but weighed, when empty, only 100 pounds. He and his crew rigged it up in the launching tower on a windy morning of March 26. At noon the rocket was ready, but the prairie wind was still strong. With the doctor, his men sat in the shade of their truck, chatting idly, their eyes watching the telltale wind sock, fluttering at the top of the tower.

As the afternoon passed, the crew's impatience mounted. But the professor still sat calmly, waiting. Shortly after four o'clock, the wind sock was motionless. Goddard told his men to fuel the rocket and then take their assigned positions. He quickly took his own place at the control panel, saw that all was in order. He pressed the control key for ignition. A pointed, bluish flame darted from the rocket nozzle. He watched the pressure indicator closely, then pushed the release key.

The gods of space flight smiled. Or perhaps they were merely tired of frowning. Nell rose from the tower, gaining speed fast, heading directly upward through the 22-second period of propulsion. After the fuel was expended, the rocket continued its upward course, then started down.

At this point, the parachute was intended to take over, but something delayed its opening until the rocket was halfway down. The parachute lines snapped, tore the parachute loose and the rocket plummeted to earth. But this was of little immediate moment. Goddard's rocket had reached its highest altitude.

As the professor cheerfully remarked in his report to Guggenheim, the rocket "rose higher and more nearly vertical than in any previous flight . . . between 8,000 and 9,000 feet. The height is somewhat uncertain as there was a slight haze in the air from a dust storm of the previous day, and the observer at the distant station lost sight of the rocket when propulsion ceased."

Whether the haze resulted from the dust storm or from the observers' astonishment, Nell's flight unquestionably improved morale.

On April 14, 1937, Lindbergh wrote:

"Research of the type you are doing is bound to require a great deal of time and to hold many unexpected setbacks,

Goddard with centrifugal pump and turbine, 1934. [53]

Esther Goddard at ranch, 1937. [54]

Paul Horgan. [55]

Peter Hurd. [56]

Goddard painting at
Mescalero Ranch,
1936. [57]

HT: Goddard examining
np mounted in machine
shop, 1938. [58]

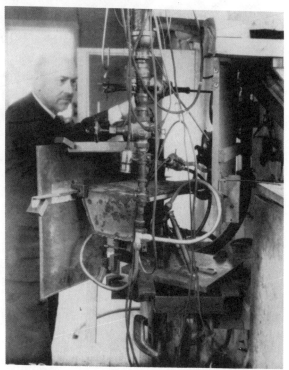

On one of his visits to the Goddards, Lindbergh
photographed the launching tower and rocket
from top (ABOVE) and ground (RIGHT). [59, 60]

LEFT: Four-chamber rocke
mounted in tower, 1936.
[61]

RIGHT: Catapult-launched
rocket, using gimbaled
steering, 1937. From a mo
tion picture by Esther God
dard. [63]

Tail piece of 1937 rocket showing movable air and blast vanes. [62]

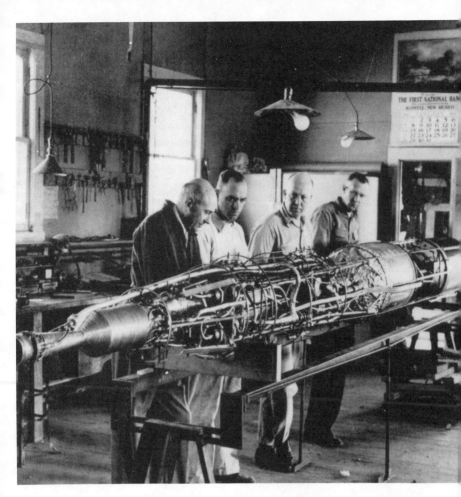

Rocket on its assembly frame, without casing. Combustion chamber at left, oxygen and gasoline tanks at right. Beyond Goddard: Ljungquist, Kisk, C. Mansur. 1940. [64]

but I believe you are very close to the successful conclusion of what I consider the first stage of the project—that is, the development of a rocket which can attain higher altitudes than those reached by sounding balloons. . . ."

Goddard replied in mid-May:

"A letter from Mr. Harry Guggenheim states that a grant has been made by the Daniel and Florence Guggenheim Foundation for another year on the rocket research. . . ."

VI

Robert and Esther Goddard sat on folding chairs, among other guests, on President Atwood's lawn in Worcester. It was a June morning in 1937, the fiftieth anniversary of the founding of Clark University. The physics professor-on-leave, his face tanned to parchment by the southwestern sun, was slightly more venerable than the school itself. Fifty-four years old, he would be almost fifty-five when the new academic season began in September. Atwood and Clark had given him indispensable aid, keeping his professorship open in event his grants concluded. But Nell was flying and his work would go on, Goddard could reflect, recalling events of the past few days.

On their way to Worcester and the Clark ceremonies, the professor and his wife had made two stops. The first was in Washington, D.C., where, at Guggenheim's behest, he had tried again to arouse the United States military to the rocket's potential. He was cordially received by Major General A. H. Sunderland, chief of the Army's Coast Artillery Corps, and showed him motion pictures of flights above Eden Valley. The general seemed fascinated, listening attentively while Goddard explained once more the remarkable military applications of his novel engine.

The United States was always trying to fight the next war

with the last war's weapons, the artilleryman observed. Precisely, said the professor.

The rocket at least offered a method of towing targets for air gunnery practice although, of course, it had more important capabilities, said Sunderland. Of course, Goddard agreed.

The general said he would have to "blast the Air Corps people out of their position," Goddard wrote later in his diary. That would be fine, the professor replied. But he was skeptical that much would come of the meeting. Sunderland suggested that they "keep in touch." He would be available at any time, Goddard told him, making way for the next appointment on Sunderland's busy schedule.

At the second stop, the Goddards had been house guests at Falaise, the Guggenheim estate in Port Washington, Long Island. There the professor was warmly congratulated for his recent high flier. Esther was enchanted by the manorial house which she described to her mother as: ". . . a French chateau effect, with peacocks, espaliered fruit trees, horses, dogs, a terrace overlooking the Sound . . . a fairyland." Guggenheim, she recalled, was received with yelps of joy by his pedigreed spaniels when they had visited the kennels. "A man like that just *has* to be nice!" she announced.

Esther prodded Goddard out of his revery, bringing him back to Atwood's lawn and the Clark celebration. The president was now expanding on the rôle of the American university in an era of change, speaking of pioneers who had "squarely put Clark on the map." With a smile at the Goddards, he began reading a statement on "The Significance of the Rocket." He said it had just been received from "a notable American now living in France." Goddard roused himself to listen:

"Clark University is taking part in a project which may

have far-reaching effects on the future of civilization . . . the early experiments of Professor Goddard. . . ."

For science, the rocket would ultimately outreach the sounding balloon, President Atwood was reading. For commerce, it would create enormous speeds of transport. For war, it would "carry explosives faster than the airplane and farther than the projectile."

It was an unexpected public tribute from Lindbergh, put in unexpected ways. Obviously, the flier had suspected, all along, the dreamer in Goddard, who had tried so scrupulously to conceal his dream from others. Skillfully, Lindbergh spoke for Goddard as the professor had seldom dared to speak for himself. Referring to a "mythical rocket enthusiast," Lindbergh concluded his message, as read by Atwood:

"In an unguarded moment, he might prophesy that we will eventually travel at speeds governed only by the acceleration which the human body can stand, and that in rocketing between America and Europe, we will accelerate half way across the ocean, and decelerate during the other half. Or, he might even point his rocket toward another planet and, without regard to fuel supply, landing facilities, or Professor Goddard, lose himself in interplanetary space."

Even among the older faculty, Lindbergh's spectacular greeting was pleasing. Goddard received a standing ovation. A few days later he wrote to thank the pilot for his "excellent" treatise, neglecting to add that it had stimulated the local press, once again, to ask when he planned to hit the moon.

After the Clark reunion, the professor made several calls. He visited at length with Charles Hawley at the attorney's office overlooking the Worcester common, where they discussed his patent application on a movable tailpiece, or gimbaled steering. Then, at Esther's urging, he kept an appointment on Pleasant Street with Dr. Fisher, the aging family physician.

Fisher made and studied a new set of X-ray plates of Goddard's chest, issued another stern warning and was decidedly glum. His patient had apparently paid little attention to Fisher's earlier advice. After leaving the doctor's office, Goddard lightly told his wife that he was in fine shape, better than ever, and that it was time to get back to work.

She had been watching her husband's growing fatigue with concern. In letters from Roswell she had recently mentioned: ". . . a cold, raw day with searching wind, which made Bob shiver, and is probably responsible for his tight chest. . . ." ". . . We went to the country Wednesday, fine in the morning, but it blew like mad toward noon. . . . Bob ill. . . ." She had encouraged him to take trips on balmy weekends, describing "a short ride up into the mountains, lovely in the sun. . . ." That day, she wrote, they drove until they came to a dead end road, prominently marked: FORT STANTON, U.S. MARINE CORPS TUBERCULOSIS HOSPITAL. There he spent several hours visiting patients, speaking to them as one who had recovered from the disease.

Esther remained skeptical about Goddard's report of Dr. Fisher's supposed findings. After their return to New Mexico, she wrote confidentially to the Worcester doctor. He replied promptly:

"The X-ray taken on June 10th shows very little change from the one taken in March 1933. There is considerable increase in the fibrosis in the upper portion of the left lung, and below the fibrosis the disease in the lung seems to be rather more active. There is no considerable change in the size of the cavity.

"He persistently overdoes and it is surprising that he does not suffer more as a result of it. I should think that the increase in the quantity of the sputum suggests an increase in the activity of the disease, probably due to his fatigue. He certainly ought to cut down on his work until the thing quiets down again. He ought to spend larger proportions of his time lying down, and little or no physical work until he is back again where he was before his trip east.

"I think it would help you to determine the necessary period of this enforced quiet, if you took his temperature three or four times a day, and if you found some rise in it, make that the guide."

Then, before signing the letter, Dr. Fisher wrote out in longhand:

"A little while now may be his salvation and he ought not to treat the thing lightly."

A day later, Esther Goddard wrote again to her mother:

"Had a letter from Dr. Fisher on result of X-ray in Worcester, saying I must take [Bob's] temperature three or four times a day.

". . . as if I could even *catch* him that often!"

VII

By July 28, 1937, Goddard had added a few more improvements to Nell: a movable tail section designed to steer the rocket upward in powered flight and later, during its coasting period, after the burn-out of fuels; a stronger pressure tank; a newly designed nozzle and parachute release.

The rocket, once more improved, reached an altitude of 2,055 feet on its first flight test. Esther described it:

"Nell went very straight, used up all her fuel nicely, commenced to fall, fall, fall, without parachute, until we were all groaning at the coming smash, when lo, the parachute opened just in time to break the fall. We were all lifted up spiritually, though she must get up higher before we shall really be content. . . ."

But the rocket would not go higher that year. In late August, Goddard tried again for altitude, this time using a catapult launcher to boost the rocket out of the tower. Esther mentioned the test in another letter:

". . . no luck. Nell broke in two, a new stunt, part smashed and part floated serenely down on the parachute as though nothing was wrong."

Adopting her husband's optimism, she then added: "The parachute problem commences to show signs of being solved, good operation three times now. . . ." The doctor happily recorded that his rocket's stabilizing system had corrected itself seven successive times in flight.

Beginning on October 17, Goddard stepped up his static tests, calling for overtime in the shop for necessary modifications and overhauling. Of one of these tests Esther wrote:

". . . out at the tower, with the lovely broad prairie all around, and a brilliant blue sky overhead. But, alas, a high wind . . . Bob is asleep on the seat beside me, and the rest have gone back to town, to return at 4 p.m. if the wind dies down. . . ."

The wind subsided, but the improved rocket turned up a variety of flaws. On October 19, Goddard increased the fuel load by 50 per cent. Unfortunately, "the dash pot weight stuck . . . near the top of the stroke." Several days later, "the chamber opened along the seam." On November 24, he tried again for a flight, according to his journal:

"It seems probable that the rocket would have traveled straight if it had left the tower at a substantial speed. The small excess of lift over weight prevented this, and as soon as the rocket became inclined, the action of the blast vanes reduced the vertical component of the thrust and allowed the rocket to fall . . . about 100 feet from the tower. . . ."

As Esther came to share her husband's purpose, she relished their camaraderie, riding across the prairie beside him, their legs dangling against the tailgate of the old Ford truck. She remembered mornings when birds nested in the launching tower; stillness and wide skies; sudden movements of prairie creatures such as coyotes and antelopes; Robert's un-spoken ability to withstand failures—"not really failures but lessons to learn, a scientist's way of learning"; times "when everything that can go wrong did go wrong, when igniters didn't ignite, valves leaked, controls failed to operate, when liquid oxygen was too impure to function properly and Na-ture itself seemed to conspire against the ascent of Nell."

She also wrote home of her personal victories over rattle-snakes, tarantulas and vinegarroons, which occasionally en-tered the ranchhouse through its French doors; of the "dust devils" common to the southwest, when "the wind picks up dust to form whirling funnels of varying diameters and speeds . . . as many as twenty at one time scattered over the prairie . . . forming on highways, dancing across and off the fields, rather pretty if they are small enough to be harmless. . . ."

The "dust devils," however, were lyrical hazards com-pared with the new anxiety of a national recession, coupled with a year of indifferent rocket results. Again, finances were discussed in Esther's letters to Worcester.

On January 9, 1938: "We are in our annual jitters about next year." Two weeks later: "We are both nervous about next year, but can do nothing yet, of course." On January 30: "Test only fair, another due this week. . . . With this de-pression and punk tests, I don't think our chances are good of staying here longer." On April 17: ". . . But all is up in the air, for we can't tell a bit what the Foundation will do. As I told you, Lindbergh has cabled and written the results are most satisfactory, but the depression is on, and there just may not be money, regardless of the merits of the job here."

In February, Goddard had sent a hopefully strong report to New York: ". . . the development has now reached a cross-roads." He added:

"The work on high pressure rockets, with more powerful chambers, may be continued. . . . On the other hand, I feel there is no short cut to high flights and that work should be continued on pumps until a satisfactory pumping system has been made. . . .

"In view of the present state of world affairs, it seems desirable to continue the work along the most advantageous lines, especially since the problem has been brought to a point where definite applications appear to be within reach. . . ."

His report stirred Lindbergh, in northern France, to commend him genially on his stepped-up testing and to encourage more of the same. "I do not think it is necessary to make an extremely high flight," Lindbergh now wrote. "A reasonably high one would accomplish all the objects I have in mind." Observing that Guggenheim was "thoroughly acquainted with the early years of aviation" and understood "the problems and difficulties connected with developmental work," Lindbergh maintained that a "good" rocket flight would make it "much easier" to obtain further financing. By "good," Lindbergh later said, he was thinking of a 10,000 to 15,000 foot flight.

Lindbergh also wrote to Goddard and Guggenheim of "a growing interest in rockets from both a military and scientific standpoint . . . throughout the world" and of "a rumor that the Germans are devoting a great deal of attention to the development of rocket projectiles for war." Therefore, he held, "it is very desirable" for Goddard "to consolidate his position by obtaining the first high altitude flight . . . verified by . . . the N.A.A. . . ." to establish his lead.

Goddard agreed at once. ". . . the matter of heights reached by rockets is uncertain, and I am not sure a well-recognized record exists. It seems quite possible that even the modest heights we have obtained have exceeded the record for powder rockets. Regarding liquid propellant rockets . . . I have not been able to find records of more than a few hundred feet . . . [it] appears to be virgin territory."

In the spring, while arranging for the "authenticated flight" suggested by Lindbergh, Goddard frequently wondered how much longer his idyllic research center would continue. The official flight, he told Esther calmly, would probably assure next year's grant. Esther recalled other times when Bob, showing less calm, had made well-timed trips to Guggenheim's door. He planned these visits so casually that Guggenheim was only vaguely aware of the tensions aroused by delays in the annual grants.

In advance of one pilgrimage, the inventor drew up an economical telegram code to signal Esther from New York:

1. GREETINGS—"We stay another year but say nothing."
2. GREETINGS TO THE BOYS—"We stay another year. Tell all the boys."
3. RETURN DELAYED—"Decision delayed."
4. STOPPED AT UNIVERSITY—"We return to Worcester in September."

Although he was never obliged to use the last message, the fund-raising trips were physically wearing. On his eastbound missions, the man who pioneered space travel always preferred to travel by train, then a slow, rattling journey without benefit of air conditioners. He came home exhausted. Esther, meeting him at the Roswell train station, would greet him with what passed for family humor: "Here I am with the wheelbarrow to pick up the pieces."

But in 1938, the testing of Nell for the public record made such a trip impossible. The National Aeronautic Association soon supplied a height-measuring barograph and assigned three men on the staff of Roswell's New Mexico Military Institute to serve as official witnesses: Colonel D. C. Pearson, superintendent of the Institute; Major John E. Smith, physicist; and Captain Howard E. Alden, mathematician. A local group, as Goddard explained to Harry Guggenheim, would avoid "the inconvenience to which an observer living at a distance might be subjected, if one or more postponements should be necessary. . . ."

Before proceeding, he cautioned his sponsor not to expect too much. "The height that will be reached with the present rocket will probably not exceed 5,000 feet, and the speed will probably not exceed 300 miles per hour," he said.

After flying two modest rockets in March, he planned to begin his barograph tests as soon as the seasonal winds permitted. The Goddard crew prepared Nell fastidiously for her official launching. By mid-April, the professor was showing concern. The barograph was designed for airplanes, not for lightweight rockets, he told his wife. "Bob is afraid the barograph is too heavy, or not accurate, or will be smashed, or not mounted properly, or a million other things to keep us awake nights," Esther reported in a letter home.

The winds died down. Early on the morning of April 20, Goddard and crew were ready at the tower in Eden Valley. The official observers, with Esther, arrived around eight o'clock. They carefully inspected the N.A.A. barograph, wound its clockworks, sealed it and placed it inside the rocket. Then they took their places behind the professor at the sandbagged shelter with its plank-boarded walls and roof, 1,000 feet from the tower.

It was Nell's first flight to be witnessed by outsiders. In his official report, Major Smith commented:

"At the words 'Ready-Go!' Dr. Goddard evidently released the fuel and fired the same for there was seen a great burst of flame and smoke at the base of the tower and a roar as of a hundred safety valves on boilers all let loose at once. When the doctor so willed, the rocket was released from its moorings and it began to move upward. At first the speed was not so great, but one could easily note a rapid acceleration. . . . The rocket did not go straight up but veered slowly to one side or the other—apparently responding to the controls of the gyroscope stabilizer."

The flight, Smith observed, ". . . was easy to follow because of the dark smoke trail and the bright portions of the rocket. After the fuel seemed to diminish the rocket began to follow a path like a very rapid ball thrown high into the air but with the object of attaining great distance as well.

"During these few seconds, the observers were 'begging' the parachute to open, but it did not and presently the rocket headed straight to earth, and the crash came. The sound reached us a little later—as of a rather heavy charge of dynamite. . . ."

The rocket enthralled the witnesses. Colonel Pearson, the most restrained, reported to Washington that it "landed about one and one-third miles to the northwest of the tower and was completely wrecked. We very carefully examined the wreckage and found the barograph a shapeless mass and no record available."

Moved by the spectacle, Major Smith reported:

"We all went across the country to see the wreckage. I arrived first but no one touched any of the body of the rocket until Dr. Goddard came. He directed that the remnants of the barograph be found. They were found but were utterly ruined along with the entire rocket. The rocket landed nose first and made a cavity in the ground some 14 inches deep and perhaps 18 inches across at the top. Dr. Goddard and his assistants took charge of the wreckage."

Years later, Captain Alden recalled that "there was no tearing of hair, cursing or alibi-making, but we could feel something of the bitter disappointment which must have flooded his whole being . . . and we realized that the morning's experience was one of many such, when so many things can go wrong. . . ."

In a brief memorandum to Harry Guggenheim, Goddard reported that the rocket had flown to "a height of 4,215 feet as indicated by the average for the theodolite and recording telescope, but to a height of a mile and a half in the opinions of the committee."

Goddard advised the committee that he would need a new barograph and would try again. Meanwhile, he had a little "fixing" to do on the rocket.

It was more than a month later, on May 26, 1938, when Nell, the barograph, a fresh supply of liquid oxygen and the observers were all assembled again. For this test, Goddard's experimental notes suffice:

"About 3 seconds after pressing the first key, a flame was seen, and about a second after this became large, the lift indicator light showed. The rocket was immediately released, and rose through the tower at about its usual speed.

"As soon as it emerged from the tower, however, it immediately veered to the right, and showed no sign of correcting, curved over and struck the ground 500 or 600 feet away from the tower. The greatest rise was perhaps to 140 feet. The parachute was not released, as the rocket continued to fire until it struck the ground. . . ."

Whatever the reason, Nell had failed on her second command performance. It was after this test that Colonel Pearson observed, with feeling: "I wouldn't build rockets for one million dollars."

The Goddards had seemed remarkably philosophic to their observers. But while Nell was undergoing her trials, the scientist and his wife were eagerly examining each day's mail. When May ended, Esther said in a letter to Worcester: "Not a word yet regarding next year, so we are nervous as cats still, but hoping."

They were still hoping while Goddard and his crew prepared for another test in June. As Esther wrote:

"We have had no word yet. . . . We have got so numb that we don't even know what we'll do if we do get the grant. . . . Sometimes I wish we'd stop all this striving and be content with a teaching job, summer travel, etc. [like our friends]. . . ."

On Wednesday morning, June 14, 1938, Esther drove to the postoffice in town. Her husband and his men once more were rigging up Nell in the tower hopefully. There was a tantalizing envelope from New York. Esther put it carefully aside. That evening, Goddard read the opening lines out loud: "I take pleasure in informing you that the Directors of the Daniel and Florence Guggenheim Foundation have approved . . ."

The grant was made, she wrote to her mother. "A letter came yesterday, before a test. I didn't dare show it to Bob until afterwards, for fear he'd be nervous. . . . Mr. G. is a prince if there ever was one."

Next morning the early winds were once again too strong for the finicky rocket. Goddard postponed the test until later that day. Esther was in the kitchen at the ranchhouse, shelling peas for dinner, when a small localized tornado struck Eden Valley. She recalled later:

"Al burst in . . . with tears in his eyes, and the dreadful news that at 3:15 a 'twister' had hit the tower, reducing it to a mass of wreckage—and the rocket in it! . . . We hastily shut up the house and tore back to the tower. What a sickening feeling to drive from Marley's ranch and search the horizon in vain for the lovely shaft against the distant blue mesas, around which all our hopes clustered and our lives focussed!

"When we finally came in sight of our wounded equipment, I had to swallow hard to keep from being sick. . . . The tower lay sprawled to the northeast . . . the heavy concrete foundations were torn up . . . the heavy guy wires had been snapped like twine—and lovely Nell lay on her side, protected somewhat by her launching establishment . . . and to cap the climax a small desert bird perched on a piece of grotesquely projecting angle iron, singing his head off!"

At the tower wreckage, Esther found the crew and her husband "stunned in discouragement." Charles Mansur had been in the tower, busily covering Nell with canvas, when he heard "an ominous roar from the southwest, saw a cloud of dust approaching, and ran. He evidently was knocked out for a few minutes, for it was all over when he came to, with only a scratched arm. . . ."

That evening Colonel Pearson was informed that all tests were temporarily cancelled.

"These major catastrophes, unlike the minor ones, have the effect of making me angry and stubborn and determined that we *shall* have a success," Esther reflected. ". . . [Only] the little things . . . make me wonder if it's all worth while. But when I do, I need only look at Bob's face and eyes, despite the sagging shoulders, to know that this is The Adventure, the supreme experience and to ask the cost is unworthy. . . .

"I shall not forget how Bob looked. . . . Fatigue showed in every line of him especially his shoulders, bent forward, as they always are, to protect the weakness of his lungs. A man who 'should be in bed in Switzerland' coming in at 7:30 at night after a day that began at 3 in the morning. And yet when I remonstrate, he looks as though I had insulted him.

"In the broiling heat, in discouragement and defeat, there is never a hint that he should be spared on his health's account.

"And as he came in last night, almost staggering, the undefeatable was still in his eyes, and made me ashamed."

VIII

A few days after the twister, Goddard and his men were rebuilding the launching tower, using new structural steel purchased from Mabie-Lowrey, the hardware store which supplied such steel for windmills in the Roswell area. To his sponsor, the scientist had reported the disaster as "an

unfortunate event," an understatement that required generations of New England to produce. His crew, like "the boss,"
as they sometimes referred affectionately to Goddard, showed
little more emotion as they repaired the wreckage. "I'm surrounded by Swedes," Goddard once said amiably to his wife.

Near the end of July, the tower, 20 feet higher, was ready,
hopefully, for concluding the N.A.A. barograph tests. He
would be glad to be done with official observers who usually
looked upon his efforts as an ordeal, whether in kindness or
dismay.

The recent troubles, more than the mere "failures" of
tests, had strengthened his determination. What did one expect of experimental work but trial and error, flaws followed
by the occasional redeeming success? After their years together, Esther could understand that he was following the
disciplines of science, that his was a joyful course.

Along the way, his wife had found clues to his powerful
stamina, lying beneath the frail and remarkably humdrum
surface. Later, after his death, she found confirming notes in
the strangely impersonal diaries her husband kept for almost
half a century. Among thousands of cramped, workaday
entries, jokes for speeches, cryptic notes on his work, he had
copied, with a sense of discovery, excerpts from his reading,
maxims such as a schoolboy might be required to set down.

Through these borrowed or adapted expressions of thought
and emotions, Goddard revealed a self-portrait he could never
paint for himself, the portrait of the man apart, pursued by
a nagging destiny, the explorer, soldier, uninvited adventurer
come to reshape a world.

In May 1933, he copied: "Happiness comes from struggling,
and overcoming difficulties. . . ." In February 1937, he ad-
justed a thought of George Santayana to the surrounding
prairie: "Morning in the desert, when the impossible not
only seems possible, but easy." In *Westward Ho!* by the Eng-

lish clergyman Charles Kingsley, he found a parallel to his own adventure:

"Battles (as soldiers know, and newspaper editors do not) are usually fought, not as they ought to be fought, but as they can be fought; and while the literary man is laying down the law at his desk as to how many troops should be moved here, and what rivers should be crossed there, and where the cavalry should have been brought up, and when the flank should have been turned, the wretched man who has to do the work finds the matter settled for him by pestilence, want of shoes, empty stomachs, bad roads, heavy rains, hot suns, and a thousand other stern warriors who never show on paper."

And in Sir Walter Scott's *Ivanhoe,* he had come across a line he sometimes recited to Esther, old-fashioned words that made up a legend under which he chose to march:

". . . there . . . is no yielding up of a gallant emprise, since the difficulties which render it arduous also render it glorious. . . ."

Gallant emprise. . . . He had not yet tested the limits of his endurance.

IX

By the end of July 1938, the N.A.A. flight test was being scheduled, postponed and rescheduled, due to high winds in the valley. Meanwhile Goddard, at Lindbergh's request, was preparing a broad prognosis of the rocket's future. The flier, back in France from an inspection of air power in Germany and Russia, was taking a long view of Goddard's work.

"When you can take the time to do so," he had written, "I believe it would be worthwhile and very helpful if you could let me have a general idea of what you would like to accomplish with the rocket development during, let us say, the next ten years."

In the small, condensed script which Esther always managed to decipher, Goddard wrote a paper for Lindbergh: "Outline of a Ten-Year Program on Rocket Development." Projecting the rocket's future was no problem. He felt sure where his work should lead. He reviewed his progress, declaring that ". . . a ten-year program would be, to a large extent, a continuation of the work so far undertaken." He emphasized his hope of expanding the project in New Mexico, and concluded with a recommendation of the sort of teamwork he would encourage:

"In carrying out any of the extended programs such as outlined in this statement, it would be desirable for the writer to have at least one trained physicist as an assistant, to aid in planning the work, supervising the shop, and constructing special control parts. With the assurance of a number of years of development work, it would also be of advantage to have from time to time a number of enthusiastic young men from technical schools who are interested in rocket problems. Further, work on some of the problems that do not require making actual flights might be carried on in other laboratories and institutions. The present location in New Mexico, however, still appears to be best for flight tests, both because of climatic conditions and lack of curiosity regarding the work."

After the wind lifted in August, there was another slight delay while Goddard waited for a shipment of liquid oxygen from El Paso. But at six o'clock on the morning of August 9, 1938, he would be ready for a flight and so advised his N.A.A. observers. Colonel Pearson and Major Smith, he heard, would not be available for the sunrise launching. At the tower, the Goddards met Captain Alden and his wife, also a mathematician at the Institute, who were delegated to represent the N.A.A.

Alden wound and sealed the barograph, scaled the tower, mounted the instrument in the 18-foot rocket, and then rejoined his wife and the Goddards at the 1,000-foot shelter. This time, the rocket, including its pongee parachute, worked to perfection. In her official report, Marjorie Alden observed:

"At about 6:30, Dr. Goddard threw the switch, there was a metallic click followed in a moment by an explosion, and then a steady roar. The flame, at first yellow, became white, and in about three seconds after the contact Dr. Goddard released the anchoring weights and the rocket began to rise. Its rise from the tower was slow, and after clearing the tower, it turned into the wind. Its great acceleration was easily apparent, and after a moment its direction corrected to vertical, altered into the wind and corrected at least once again, and then remained almost vertical. The rocket continued to move with increasing speed and left a slight trail of bluish white smoke. Its size diminished so rapidly that by the time the fuel was exhausted it was almost invisible. It continued to rise almost vertically, then turned horizontally and the cap came off releasing the parachute. The flight, with the parachute release, was the most thrilling sight I have ever witnessed."

When the rocket, swaying lightly on its shrouds, reached the ground, Alden carefully removed the barograph. Before mailing it with their reports to Washington, the Aldens observed that the barograph stylus showed an altitude of 3,294 feet, while Goddard's recording telescope and theodolites gave an estimated height of some 5,000 feet. There was a brief discussion about the accuracy of the barograph. The Aldens accepted Goddard's calculations. All agreed with Marjorie Alden that it was a "wonderful flight." She said that her knees shook from the moment of the rocket's first roar until its remarkably gentle descent.

X

Ever since the twister, Esther had insisted that her husband take a rest after the rocket trials. She had tried to order steamer tickets for Hawaii, as far from Eden Valley as she could imagine, but the El Paso travel agency advised her that trips to Hawaii were fully booked. As a substitute, they reserved two round-trip tickets, tourist class, on the French liner *Normandie* for a month in Europe.

Goddard had agreed to the European trip at once. First of all, he might discuss his work with Lindbergh and personally deliver his "ten-year program." Second, as he said to Esther, "It might be best to see Europe now before it blows up."

Esther handled the details for their trip with dispatch. She drove her husband in his work clothes to Roswell for passport photographs. Before his picture was taken, she borrowed a pair of shears from the photographer to trim his frayed shirt collar. A few weeks later, the Goddards, laden with travel folders, left for Europe from the Roswell train station.

When they boarded the *Normandie* in New York in August 1938, Europe was boiling into the Second World War. Within six weeks, Sir Neville Chamberlain would meet with Adolf Hitler in Munich and declare that he had achieved "peace in our time." Earlier in the summer, Colonel Lindbergh had found the Soviet Union's air power relatively unimpressive, while German air strength appeared greater to him than that of all other European nations combined.

Goddard missed Lindbergh in France and mailed his rocket prognosis to him, glad to have it out of his suitcase. Then as plain Mr. and Mrs. Goddard, Americans, they began their vacation. At the American Express office in Paris, Mr.

Goddard inquired about his mail, cashed a few traveller's checks, bought tickets for several tours. On one of these, Goddard gained a moving and enduring impression of the stained-glass windows of Chartres Cathedral.

At a sidewalk café in Montmartre, the professor and his wife cheerfully made ice cream sodas with Vichy water and watched the passing crowds. They sat self-consciously through the Folies Bergère among equally self-conscious American tourists. After attending several French plays, the professor entered Esther's comment in his diary: "Most of these situations could be cleared up with a little common sense in the first act."

Esther Goddard had saved $150 from her household expenses for a gift to her husband. Seeing his fascination with a Swiss travel poster in a tourist-agency window, she presented him gaily with two round-trip, all-expense bus tours. Switzerland was quite as far into Europe as he wished to go. He had no intention of going nearer to Germany.

X I

After the *Normandie* docked in New York, the professor had no sooner cleared customs than he notified Guggenheim's office of his arrival. Then he took Esther to a Schrafft's restaurant, where they ordered "chicken patties and *real coffee*."

When they read Goddard's "Outline of a Ten-Year Program," both Guggenheim and Lindbergh were discouraged. Obviously, the professor was thinking of long-term and independent research, an approach far more costly and time-consuming than either had expected. From France, where he read Goddard's report, Lindbergh wrote to Guggenheim this analysis of their protégé and his methods:

"It seems to me that he has a tendency to underemphasize the importance of actual rocket flights. Even if he is correct in his judgment of the relative importance of laboratory and flight tests, he is not a very good judge of the psychological effects of too much laboratory work on the other people who are connected with his project. This is a difficulty frequently encountered in scientific work. On the one hand, the scientist feels that the people who are behind him financially do not recognize the importance of detailed and comprehensive laboratory experiments. On the other, no one but a specialist is in a position to judge the value of highly specialized work, unless it can be demonstrated by its effect on more easily understood accomplishments. . . ."

The Goddards were invited again to Falaise, a visit that now seemed less idyllic. For the first time, Guggenheim proposed to "speed up" the rocket work, to "farm out" some of its problems, to move the venture from "pioneering" to what he called the "engineering" phase. He spoke of a more "businesslike" approach, then mentioned the "fine work" the Foundation was sponsoring at New York University and at the California Institute of Technology. Although considerably disquieted, Goddard took what comfort he could from their talk, writing that night in his diary: "One thing Mr. G. said was pleasant: 'You have done all the things you said you would do.' "

Replying to Guggenheim, Goddard did not object to farming out components of Nell, although he still held it might be "unwise" to release the rocket's development until his work was further along. He would welcome skilled assistants, he said. He had written to Dr. Hickman, who had collaborated with him during his earlier work on solid fuels and was now a chief researcher at the Bell Telephone Laboratories. He had offered Hickman $5,000 a year to join him in Roswell, a salary identical to his own. Hickman rejected the offer. He was research director of Bell's telephone switching machinery and couldn't afford to leave.

At the same time, Guggenheim also had problems with the

singular project. His family had invested a total of $148,000 in Goddard and based on the scientist's ten-year prognosis, there was still no evident end to the road. "For Harry, it was a tremendous shot in the dark," Lindbergh said years later. "He never lost interest, but, by 1938, he simply wished he had more to show."

Guggenheim, listening to the professor, spoke again of co-operation. He had arranged meetings at Falaise between Goddard and the directors of two Guggenheim aeronautical research centers, Dr. Alexander Klemin of New York University, and Dr. von Kármán and Dr. Clark Millikan of the California Institute of Technology. Dr. Jerome C. Hunsaker of the Massachusetts Institute of Technology and the National Advisory Committee on Aeronautics (NACA) would also be on hand.

At the conferences each of these men, in his own way, encouraged Goddard to become less secretive, to deal more openly with his colleagues, to turn loose his researches.

Dr. Klemin showed interest in having some of his younger physicists explore the possibilities of a power plant for rockets, but said that it would be helpful to know more about Goddard's over-all design. Dr. Hunsaker said he would delegate some of his assistants to explore rocket-chamber efficiencies. They would be better prepared, however, if they could inspect his rocket.

The most difficult discussion was with Dr. von Kármán, not because of his somewhat fractured English, but because of his point of view. Years later, von Kármán recalled the meeting: "Goddard thought he would sub-contract to Cal. Tech the design and calculation of the thrust chamber. We were interested only in cooperation which covered the whole project. I said this was the only way we could cooperate intelligently. So we did not come together, although Harry Guggenheim recommended that we both think it over."

After her husband's death, Esther Goddard declared that

"perhaps we were wrong, perhaps we should have joined some team, but it didn't seem so to us at the time. I'm not sure Bob knew how to give up control of his rocket."

In reply to Lindbergh's recent letter, Guggenheim shortly wrote: ". . . It is quite hard, as you know, to get the prima donnas of science working together. . . ."

Goddard, he said, was "one of those lone wolves who didn't want to hunt with the pack."

XII

During the years he had been in New Mexico, Eden Valley was a proving ground for both the professor and his flying rocket. To get to his secluded tower on Oscar White's ranch, Goddard and his crew customarily passed through Marley's pastures, where May Corn Marley, an unschooled ranch woman, and Cort, her husband, kept twelve hundred head of cattle and a few hundred sheep on their scrubby acres. Neither May nor Cort, who gave the professor a right of way, thought it necessary to ask if they might watch his rocket trials. When the Goddard caravan appeared, Cort simply saddled up his horse, rode to a rise in the pastureland and watched.

The professor felt at ease with the Marleys. At times he stopped to exchange small talk with Cort. Once, to the rancher's wife, he told his childhood dream in the cherry tree.

"We first met the doctor in the early 1930s," May Marley recalled. "They sent him out to see us and he told us what he wanted—a place where nobody would interfere with his work. Mr. Marley showed him our pastures and then took him over to Oscar White's valley, next to ours, where it was very private.

"Through the years, people would ask us where the Goddard tower was and we'd tell them stories. I told so many lies, I guess I'll never get to Heaven. We'd send them south of

Roswell, usually. If anybody heard a rocket shoot and asked about the noise, we'd say it was the Indians up in the Capitan mountains, shooting cowboys, or we'd tell them it was the cowboys shooting the coyotes, or we'd say, if it was cloudy, that the noise was thunder—anything that popped into our heads.

"Right at the start, we liked Dr. Goddard. My father came up here from Texas, and he taught me not to make fun of people or laugh at things they did. I remember the doctor talking about this, how people had once made fun of his rocket, figuring, maybe, that he was one of those crazy inventors, a sort of crackpot.

"One day, waiting for the wind to die down, I told Dr. Goddard that I really believed what he said about the rocket and asked him to tell me more about it. He looked up quietly for a while and then he said: 'That's quite a big question, Mrs. Marley, but since you've asked me, I'll try to tell you.' "

Goddard spoke openly of the rocket, how high it might go, how difficult it was to say what any particular model might do, but that if it didn't get enough height, he might not get enough funds to go on with his work.

He told May Marley that "some day the rocket would be so powerful that probably only the government could build it. When that day came, why then the rocket might orbit the earth like a moon or leave the earth altogether and go off into space."

After a long pause, she inquired: "Doctor, where did you ever think of such a thing? How did you ever get this rocket idea?"

Goddard looked thoughtfully at Mrs. Marley, she said, and then he spoke easily of that October afternoon, long ago, when he had climbed the cherry tree in his backyard, when he, Mrs. Marley remembered, had "a most peculiar feeling, a sort of vision, a kind of presentiment."

"I said, 'How wonderful it is!' " May Marley recalled.

" 'Yes,' the doctor told me, 'it is wonderful. But I'll never finish it. Others will work on it, a long time from now.' "

XIII

In 1938's season of uncertainty, another storm touched the rocket professor. It began that fall south of Portugal's Cape Verde Islands in the east Atlantic. It headed toward Florida, veered back to sea, turned north and then reached up the east coast of the United States. The storm tore into New England, leaving in its wake uprooted summer resorts, damaged homes and trees—an assortment of destruction which insurance actuaries calculated at $40,000,000.

Climatologists regarded it as a major storm. When the nameless destroyer—hurricanes were then unnamed—found New England, it worked its way through Worcester, passing over the Goddard house on Maple Hill. There it ripped out an ash tree on the front lawn. On the side of the house, it destroyed a catalpa. And in the backyard, down near the creek, it felled a gnarled cherry tree.

Goddard first learned of the loss from his tenant, who wrote to him in Roswell. It was a year before Goddard could inspect the damages for himself, but he knew which cherry tree had been struck down.

On the following October 19, in 1939, he wrote in his diary: "Anniversary Day—40th."

Now, in 1938, the comment in his private papers was:

"Cherry tree down. Have to carry on alone."

10. THE HOPE OF TODAY

In the years preceding the Second World War, it was clear to Goddard that a new age was coming, that his time as a solitary rocket scientist was passing swiftly. At home and abroad, from Cleveland to Berlin to Moscow, young engineers were widening the trail he had marked out. The once-ridiculed American Rocket Society was becoming a national order, its official journals filled with technical discourse and mathematical formulae. In the east, students were learning the fundamentals of rocketry at New York University and at the Massachusetts Institute of Technology. On the west coast, they were enrolling in Dr. von Kármán's advanced courses in aerodynamics at the California Institute of Technology.

Goddard's private dream and reality were once more in conflict. Now he felt a divided kinship with these well-grounded students. As a professor, he wished to encourage their efforts, possibly to enlist their assistance; as an inventor, he still wanted to be left alone, to proceed at his own pace.

There was no easy compromise. When the inventor was ascendant, Goddard would reflect on how his lifelong preserve was being invaded, and wonder how long he could keep ahead of the pack. But to the professor, considering American apathy, they were also his colleagues in arms. At these moments, public derision that touched them touched him too.

Through these years, the spaceship was still to most Americans a sideshow distraction, a match for sword swallowers and the two-headed calf. At the New York World's Fair in 1939, a model of a "futuristic" launching port was portrayed, with an accompaniment of recorded rocket roars and blasts while tourists lined up at the entrance. At the Golden Gate Exposition in San Francisco during the same year, an "illusionary planetarium" was also crowded. In this exhibition, passengers strapped themselves into a fanciful spaceship, its bullet-shaped nose poking into artificial clouds 60 feet above the fair grounds, while a soundtrack played jet noises and a disembodied voice extolled, among others, Goddard and his early rocket tests.

Through this blurred period of fantasy and physics, Goddard continued to state, in public, that his rocket was a meteorological instrument. But, in private, he went back again to his source, rereading Wells's old novel, *The War of the Worlds*.

During his early days in New Mexico, Goddard's mechanics had heard such comments as: "How's Buck Rogers? How are things up there on the moon?" But after the town and the scientist became better acquainted, the wisecracks ended. Roswell, protecting its local hero, now insisted that Goddard had been grossly misrepresented, doubtless by "sensational reporters from the east." Goddard was pleased to find himself cordially invited to join the local chapter of Rotary, International.

To the Rotarians' surprise, he promptly accepted their invitation. Thereafter, he faithfully attended weekly luncheons in town at the Nickson Hotel, wearing his Rotary badge—"Bob Goddard—Aeronautical Research." Occasionally he gave talks on his rocket method. He was pleased when Roswell's business and professional men and retired tuberculars greeted him as "Bob." No one since high school had called him by his first name on so brief an acquaintance.

His new Rotarian brothers were glad the reclusive professor—was he, as some said, a genius?—had turned out to be easy to meet, a cheerful and comfortable companion. They were not alone in relishing his seeming conventionality. His associates and patrons had long been reassured by the same ordinary façade.

Goddard's extraordinary objective, however, was being tested during these last few years in Roswell. Then, if ever, he had to bring Nell to impressive altitudes. In this long quest, he had come to depend on three men.

II

In the late 1930s, the Goddards played host in Roswell to their three patrons and comforters—Abbot, Guggenheim and Lindbergh.

The Secretary came in the summer of 1938 on his only visit to the New Mexico laboratory. As he had notified the professor, he was traveling east from California by bus and believed it would be instructive to see how the meteorological rocket was making out. The professor and his wife welcomed and prepared for his visit. Before his trip was over, Abbot, a Yankee himself, was finally sure of Goddard's New England conventionality.

In Roswell, Abbot saw a demonstration of the properly dedicated scientist. When the bus stopped at the prairie town, just before dawn, he was greeted by the well-groomed inventor, who proposed, as they drove out to Mescalero

Ranch, that the Secretary might like "a little nap." It was a well-recommended rest. After breakfast, they began with a tour of the machine shop, where the inventor gave a lecture on pump design. Next, he took his sedate visitor on a thumping ride over the prairies to the launching tower, where he described in detail his techniques for testing rocket motors.

At the ranchhouse, there was a modest noonday lunch of cold cuts and potato salad. Goddard then invited the Secretary to make himself comfortable for an almost interminable succession of home movies of Nell, accompanied by a lengthy commentary. After this matinee, the professor brought out cartons of experimental notes for Abbot's inspection. His guest, somewhat glassy-eyed, managed to sidetrack this offer by suggesting that he had recently taken up dancing lessons for relaxation. Esther Goddard graciously accepted his invitation to dance on the porch while her husband, putting his papers aside, plinked out Viennese waltzes on the living room piano.

Dr. Abbot expressed his thanks to the Goddards with a New Englander's highest accolade. "It was like being back home," he said before boarding his bus for the east.

The second comforter was Abbot's successor, Harry Guggenheim, who arrived in the summer of 1939.

In business circles, the Guggenheims' contributions to aviation were frequently regarded as risky, their involvement in rocketry as foolhardy. Harry had grown accustomed to such carping. Shortly after Lindbergh's trans-Atlantic crossing, a prominent New York lawyer had taken Guggenheim aside and inquired: "Do you think in our lives man will be flying across the ocean?"

One might make allowances for conservative bankers and lawyers. But Guggenheim had expected more understanding from academic leaders. Presumably they were spokesmen for bold and independent ideas, the "unregimented, unconforming spark," as Esther Goddard once put it. Yet none of these scholastic heads, who readily accepted Guggenheim funds, approved of the Goddard project. They appeared increasingly irked by the inventor's lone-wolf approach, advising that available funds should be invested in sound academic institutions—their own, for example, rather than in maverick individuals.

Guggenheim had come to Roswell to resolve this problem, to encourage Goddard again to join them, to persuade him that the time of lone rocket pioneering was passing.

Years later, Guggenheim analyzed his responsibility as president of the Foundation:

"My job as an administrator was to promote the flight sciences by every means available. Engineers, scientists, educators, manufacturers and pilots were the tools with which I worked. We had limited resources that had to be carefully expended over a wide field.

"My associates and I had simply come to the conclusion that other abilities, building on the genius of Goddard, would assure quicker success and hasten the day of space flight. The scientific team or task force had not then been developed, but that is what I had in mind. Goddard had done his work. A vast amount of metallurgical, engineering and flight skills were needed and still are to strengthen and mature his brain-child."

It was a sound conclusion. But Guggenheim's judgment, which had seemed so logical in a Manhattan office, was now exposed to a different setting.

Goddard's patron arrived in his own plane with his new bride, Alicia Patterson Guggenheim, at the Roswell airport, where the Goddards awaited them. To the professor, the visit possibly appeared as a last, clear chance to continue the research. Without Guggenheim's help, he knew, the rocket experiments in New Mexico would terminate like a tumble-weed caught by a rancher's barbed-wire fence.

Whatever his apprehensions, Goddard seemed as imperturbable as a New England pond. If it had been Guggenheim's intention to part with the professor now, it was obviously an error to visit him in New Mexico.

Before dinner, Goddard and his guests exchanged small talk. Bob was at his best, Esther saw: cheerful, entertaining, detached. Between trips into the kitchen, where she was ministering to a roast leg of lamb, she wished she could radiate the same becoming ease. Harry Guggenheim, however, sensed her uneasiness, her unstated question: "Would there be funds for another year?"

He had no immediate answer. Instead, he set about warming the Goddards with his own specially potent tranquilizer—a supremely dry martini. Proposing a toast to the future of Nell, he overrode Esther's protest that she had dinner to serve. The tranquilizer was effective. The professor's wife, thoroughly thawed, raised no objection when their patron urged: "Have another!" She wondered what her forebears would make of her abandon—perhaps that Guggenheim martinis were more treacherous than Swedish *glögg*. Somewhat irrelevantly, she found herself announcing:

"I think people are wonderful! But I *know* they can't be as wonderful as I think they are!"

Less than a week after his return to New York, Harry Guggenheim assembled his trustees. His faith in the Roswell project was restored. Before the meeting adjourned, he dispatched a telegram:

HAPPY TO INFORM YOU THAT APPROPRIATION FOR PERIOD SEPT. 19, 1939 TO SEPT. 19, 1940 HAS BEEN AUTHORIZED. WARM REGARDS TO YOU BOTH.

Like Abbot before him, Guggenheim had found that his rocket scientist, once seized, was almost impossible to unseize.

Goddard's third comforter, Charles Lindbergh, also flew to Roswell in 1939, landing in an Army P-36 pursuit plane, alone and unexpected. It was ten years since he had first called on the physics professor at Clark, four years since his visit to New Mexico.

Of Goddard's comforters, Lindbergh had been, perhaps, the most perceptive. "He never spoke to me of space flight and of course I didn't pry," the pilot said years later. "But I never doubted that this was precisely what he had on his mind. I felt we had a lot in common."

The professor hastily left his shop to meet Lindbergh at the airport, scarcely hearing Esther's entreaty that he change into more presentable clothes. Once he may have pictured the flier as a colleague—Goddard as creator of the spaceship, Lindbergh as its able pilot. But such a fantasy would long since have evaporated like prairie dew during the prolonged experiments and the flier's lengthy absences in Europe.

Time had altered their trajectories since the first meeting in 1929 when the flying hero was twenty-seven years old, the professor forty-seven. Now, as they drove along the country road to the ranchhouse, Goddard saw that the pilot's hair had thinned, that he had fleshed out somewhat, that he seemed preoccupied with other projects in other places.

Although Lindbergh was as considerate as always, Goddard could sense his distraction. In Europe, he had found a variety of interests to absorb him. For a time he had assisted Dr. Alexis Carrel, the French surgeon and mystic, in his cellular studies, devising for him a perfusion pump to maintain life in organs after their removal from the body. In aviation, he was charting international air routes and improving safety factors for America's emerging airlines. For United States embassies abroad, he had been an inspector of Europe's military aviation. His visit to Roswell in 1939 was a side trip in a hedgehopping survey of American air power, made on assignment from General Henry H. Arnold of the Army Air Force.

As the two men talked—the flier quick and crisp in speech, the inventor speaking slowly and methodically—Goddard drew the aviator back into the web of his rocket experiments: his new, lightweight pumps; his tube-wound combustion chambers; his gyroscopic controls and movable vanes.

Lindbergh stayed longer than he had expected, as he wrote to Guggenheim a few days later:

"I flew up from El Paso and had planned on spending only an hour or so with Goddard before going on East, as I had to be in Washington. . . . However, Goddard had so much to talk about, and had apparently carried on so many developments since I last saw him, that I decided to spend the night. . . .

"I have the impression that he accomplished more this year than during any similar period in the past. Possibly it is because the results of his less obvious works are beginning to show up. . . .

"Goddard now seems to feel that he can accomplish a much higher rocket flight than at any time in the past. He seems to have much more positive control over the flights and functioning of the rocket."

In the quiet prairie evening, as twilight settled in the cottonwood trees, the pilot and the inventor sat on the veranda of Mescalero Ranch. The inventor's mood changed and grew uneasy. He wondered whether outer space would command much attention in the world Lindbergh had seen, a world in which Europe stood helpless against overwhelming German might. The Germans were already occupying terrestrial space in the Sudetenland, in Czechoslovakia, in Poland.

As for rocket development, he told Lindbergh, he was increasingly alarmed by the Germans and their use of science for warfare. The knowledgeable inquiries he had received from German experimenters had now abruptly ceased. Lindbergh's observations left him more uneasy. In 1936, on a mission suggested by Colonel Truman Smith, the United States military attaché in Berlin, the flier had managed to ingratiate himself with German air authorities. The Nazis repeatedly showed him their Luftwaffe factories and were outspoken about their air strength, as though to impress Lindbergh with their might and, through him, the United States government. On the subject of rockets, however, they were extremely reticent.

It wasn't much to go on but it was something, Lindbergh said that evening. He remembered a luncheon with Adolf Boemker, Hitler's chief of aeronautical research and development.

"We were at DVL, an experimental station near Berlin," he said. "Boemker was unusually responsive until, in passing, I asked about rockets. Then he turned the discussion quickly, so deftly that I felt I'd been cut off."

Goddard listened quietly. "Yes," he said, "they must have plans for the rocket. When will our own people in Washington listen to reason?"

Lindbergh went on to talk of other things. A powerful Germany would eventually organize and dominate Europe; that the Asiatic hordes of Stalin's Russia were, in his opinion, a greater danger to civilization; that the United States, with disastrous consequences, might try once again to pull Europe's hot chestnuts out of the fire.

Goddard nodded with interest, but without commitment. He wasn't sure whether the United States could, let alone should, remain apart from the emerging conflict. But he shared Lindbergh's respect for German technology and his skepticism that science necessarily meant the advance of civilization. The rocket, he knew, could be turned from service as a vehicle to the stars into a destroyer, carrying death at almost incalculable speeds.

Unknown to the two Americans at Mescalero Ranch, Europe's rocket experimenters had already entered a new phase of research. In the Soviet Union, a liquid-fuel rocket had been successfully tested in 1934. In his brief visit to Russia in 1938, Lindbergh had been unable to learn the extent of Soviet technology. What little he had been able to see of their aviation production persuaded him that the ultimate danger to the West would come not from their technological progress, but from Soviet ideology.

Later, historians would record that in December 1934 the German Wehrmacht had fired over the North Sea liquid-fuel rockets which they called A-2, achieving an altitude of 1.4 miles. By April 1936 the Germans had built a rocket experimental station in an obscure village at the mouth of the Peene River. Even as Goddard and Lindbergh met, engineers and money were finding their way to Peenemünde and to Russia's research centers.

Within the space of a few years, the rocket that Goddard was designing in the United States was to receive its greatest impetus behind the armed sentry posts of Hitler's Third Reich.

The flier left Roswell the next morning. The storm of war, then rising in Europe, was soon to end Lindbergh's own cherished privacy. In his zeal to keep America out of the war, he would become a dedicated voice for the dissident, political movement known as "America First."

Lindbergh flew out to the launching tower in Eden Valley and then circled back over the airport where, in the tradition of aviation's early barnstormers, he once again dipped his wings in salute. It was his farewell to the rocket professor.

That night Goddard wrote in his diary of the pilot "zooming down to about 20 feet above the fence and then going upward at about 45 degrees." After his visitor's departure, he drove back to his shop. His diary entry closed:

"Worked on dented strips for sprays (n.g. not deep enough) and finished conical dents with a No. 80 hole—edges too strong. Worked on apparatus."

III

Twice a day in Eden Valley, at sunrise and shortly before sunset, the winds crossing the flat prairies subsided. During these hours of calm, the last flying models of Nell underwent tests for the newest component, the small, high-speed pump-and-turbine assemblies to force-feed gasoline and liquid oxygen into the combustion chamber.

The pump tests, ranging from 1939 to 1942, were, as Esther described them, "the most trying and disheartening phase of the research."

Even his colleagues could supply no ready answer for the professor's stamina. Some suggested that Goddard, unlike the rocket theorists Tsiolkovsky of Russia and Oberth in Germany, was driven to demonstrate, rather than merely to expound, his principles. Their idea had merit. As a professor at Clark, he had always enjoyed proving physical theories to his students. Perhaps he still expected a sunrise in Eden Valley when Nell would take off from the tower, her parts functioning perfectly, routing the skeptics in a great conclusive proof of his "Method of Reaching Extreme Altitudes."

The professor himself gave this answer to one correspondent:

"It is not a simple matter to differentiate unsuccessful from successful experiments. . . . [Most] work that is finally successful is the result of a series of unsuccessful tests in which difficulties are gradually eliminated."

If the new self-contained pumps worked, the rocket engine

could shed the weight of extra tanks, carry more fuel and, theoretically, head for limitless altitude. In his late fifties, Goddard now undertook a major new model. His enthusiasm baffled even Esther. "We were back at the grim beginnings," she said.

IV

Guggenheim had urged Goddard to get "outside help." The professor had applied to America's leading pump manufacturers. All declined. The cost of developing such a powerful, miniature pump was excessive and there was no ready commercial market. So said the Ingersoll-Rand Company and the Worthington Pump and Machine Corporation. Goddard thanked them for their analysis. Then, like the little red hen of the nursery story, he set out to design and build the pump himself.

"Both theory and common sense," he said in the unpublished article prepared for the *National Geographic Magazine*, "dictate that the total rocket weight be made up chiefly of fuel, and that the structure be as light as possible. This situation can best be met when the fuels are carried in light tanks at low pressure and are fed into the chamber at high pressure, by pumps."

Guggenheim did not question the need for pumps. What still concerned him was whether any foundation could afford the time and cost of such one-man development. Years later, after the rocket method was thoroughly proved, government engineers would still be awed when they inspected Goddard's early pumps. Accustomed to working with federal funds that matched in a week what Goddard spent in a lifetime, they declared that the Yankee professor had stretched the dollar to a new degree of elasticity.

Goddard was now also stretching himself. On one hand, he wanted to turn his rocket to wartime service; on the other, he was driven to complete his pump model with a great demonstration. In his workshop and in the valley, in day-dreams and in night dreams, his mind wrestled with ideas. One morning, when he got up from bed, he recorded:

"Dreamed last night of having drops of gasoline in liquid gas, ignited, and passing to the place of ignition coated with liquid of low vapor pressure and non-inflammable, so that there was almost instantaneous generation of heat, but no danger of flare-back, if the mixture passed forward rapidly enough (and passed through a copper grid or grill, to keep it cool, back of the flame). . . ."

In these trying days, dreaming and wakefulness were all the same, all part of his remaining thrust and purpose. But few who knew him detected his internal pressures. As the new pumps were built, tried, discarded and rebuilt, probably Esther alone noticed the deeper slope to his shoulders, and detected the weariness in his voice when he came home evenings to the ranchhouse. Again she put the question: "How did it go today, Bob?" "It went," he said, but his familiar fire was banked.

At length he produced five pump models which seemed worthy of further testing. As the weeks passed, he narrowed these to two centrifugal pumps. Their hand-crafted assembly was a tribute to his ingenuity and his machinists' skill. About twice the size of a human heart, Goddard's new aluminum pump consisted of 20 machined parts weighing less than 4 pounds. It could achieve 46,000 revolutions per minute and produce pressures sufficient to raise water one-third of a mile. He had accomplished more than the basic requirements he had put to the reluctant pump manufacturers.

To complete Nell's circulatory system, Goddard's pumps needed one more ingredient, a gas generator to run their turbines—"a light source of power to drive them, originating on the rocket itself," as Goddard explained. "The means which we adopted was to boil liquid oxygen so as to produce a supply of expanding gas which drove our little turbines on the pumps just as steam drives large turbines in power stations."

The pump rockets, painstakingly put to static tests in Eden Valley, presented a galaxy of difficulties. The pressure of the pumps on the liquid fuel and oxidizer tanks led to explosions of the delicately curtain-cooled combustion chamber. When the cooling system held, the gas generator often gave way or one of the pumps would suddenly stop.

The new pump models also presented a distressing problem in starting. The pumps usually took hold with a violent shudder. "Such a shaking was all too likely to dislocate various control devices," said Esther. "The opening 'grab' of the pumps was gradually eliminated, but it was a long, hard task." From late spring of 1939 to the end of the year, Goddard's notebooks recorded gradual improvement in duration and lift, and also many breakdowns:

"May 18: Chamber opened up longitudinally. The main oxygen valve broke. . . .

"June 3: The gas generator did not fire. . . .

"June 14: The chamber blew up, and there was also an explosion higher up. . . .

"June 23: Temperature of the gas from the gas generator was uncertain, and also the behavior of the liquid oxygen. . . . Gas velocity may be calculated from the lift, time of the run, and fuel used. . . . Total lift was 693 lbs . . . gas velocity 4,020 ft/sec . . . average horsepower 2,560. . . .

"July 5: Started off all right, but the gas generator pipe burned off. . . .

"July 11: No great force at any time, and the gas generator finally burned through. . . . Fresh nitrogen cylinders, at 2,000 lbs. pressure, should be used. . . .

"July 17: Rim of oxygen turbine . . . broke off, and was found about 20 feet from dugout. . . . Inside of cement gas deflector showed evidence of much heating. The stones used in the concrete were broken off in planes parallel to inside surface of deflector, these stones evidently having started grass fires up to 100 feet from the tower. . . .

"August 4: Loud explosion at first, then a noisy flame, rather broad, and yellowish white. . . .

"November 18: Igniter worked but there was no pressure, and the run was stopped. . . .

"December 2: Turbine gas tube . . . became red hot and then burned through. The emergency gasoline shutoff key was then pressed. . . . Maximum lift, near start 785 lbs. . . ."

V

Throughout these months, the men borrowed heavily from Goddard's seemingly inexhaustible spirit. "We'd go out to the valley day after day and the rocket would misfire, or fizzle on the stand with one trouble or another," said Oley Ljungquist, chief machinist. "The doctor would be out by five o'clock in the morning and put in a full day. It was enough to wear down a coyote. The only time he sounded off was after a terrible test, when everything was twisted or blown apart. I remember him walking slowly away from the tower once, saying, 'Well, there goes $10,000 up in smoke!' "

The professor rarely discussed with his crew the theories that had brought them out to the prairie, keeping his distance. But his men, moved by his grace under pressure, became increasingly protective. Without formalities, the most closely knit of teams took shape, growing close to the doctor and his mysterious works.

When his handyman, Calistro Sanchez, was dispatched in the Fork truck to the office of the truck line from El Paso and returned with two large vacuum containers of liquid oxygen, he knew he was carrying a precious cargo. If a test was delayed a few days, some of the oxidizer would evaporate.

"The professor would anxiously put a rod in the containers to see how much was lost," one of the crewmen recalled. "He believed he would lose less oxygen if he kept one thermos filled to the brim. We'd keep transferring lox from one container to another, hoping we could run a good test before too much was gone."

Albert Campbell, the son of a grade school teacher and a free-lance blacksmith for southwestern ranchers, spoke of Goddard's liking for secrecy. "When I was hired, the professor asked me to sign the same kind of paper that all of his crew had signed," said Campbell. "The paper certified that I would not reveal anything I knew about his rocket." The pledge may temporarily have puzzled Campbell. But it also persuaded him that he had joined a project of significance.

One of Goddard's last recruits was Sidney "Tiny" Squire, a Roswell radio repairman and a former weightlifter from York, Pennsylvania. His immediate attention was drawn to the growing proliferation of wires between the 1,000-foot control shelter and the rocket in the launching tower. His electrical skills, as well as his remarkable ability to hand-carry a rocket, were welcomed by Goddard's mechanics.

"When I first saw the wiring setup in the valley, it seemed as complicated as a three-family Christmas tree," Squire recalled. "There were wires of every color running across the prairie, hitched with Fahnstock clips to the rocket at one end and to the makeshift instrument panel at the other.

"I suggested that we simplify things a bit. The doctor thought it was a fine idea. So I rigged up an arrangement of plugs and sockets, the sort of thing any electrician would do. Instead of taking the professor a couple hours to get his wires in order, he could now manage the job in about fifteen minutes."

Throughout this long series of static tests, Calistro Sanchez at times stayed overnight on the prairie. When bad weather or unexpected defects postponed a run, he would help the mechanics wrap the rocket in tarpaulin and watch the lean doctor lead his caravan back toward town. Then, in the quiet valley, he would settle down for the evening. The doctor always promised they would be back early next morning to try again.

Calistro could not readily understand Goddard's wondrous machine but he believed in it emphatically. Clearly one could not leave such a motor alone and unprotected. Before falling asleep at the control shelter, a blanket pulled up to his chin, Calistro would look out at the shrouded rocket, poised in the tower.

In May 1939, after a shattering test run which again split the new model's chamber, Calistro scraped off the soot from the launching tower and repainted it with red lead. In the midst of his work on the hot prairie, there was a sudden explosion. Its cause proved harmless enough. A threadbare tire on the old Goddard touring car had blown out. For a moment it seemed to Calistro as if Nell had taken off on a great flight. It may have been a sort of omen, a sign, of what the doctor's engine would accomplish one day.

Wherever they came from, whatever alchemy had brought Goddard's crew together, they shared the same expectation of things to come. In the most trying of static tests, after the shabbiest misbehavior of the new pump rocket, they sensed with the Goddards the growing power of Nell and were reassured.

As the pump model neared the time for her first launching trial, the professor's wife wrote:

"I have always been fascinated by the power of machinery —the slow grind of steam, the busy hum of the dynamo, the hiss and bite of acetylene, and finally the roar of the airplane engine. But now I saw Power. The new preliminary menacing whine of the pumps prickled my scalp, and the rip of the starting roar shook me from head to foot, but even my accustomed ears were unprepared for the inferno that followed. Such furious sounds were streaming from the nozzles that the earth seemed to writhe beneath them. My mind would not grasp that this could be anything but a terrific explosion and 'it can't last' was formed again and again through tense lips.

"But it did last, with the fear that something must give way in such a blast, growing until my chest ached. And still that incredible stream of fire and sound with the jubilant pump whine continued second after second. It stopped suddenly, fuel exhausted, and the silence was terrific. We knew we had seen one of the most powerful things in the world."

V I

After New Year's Day in 1940, the professor assigned his men to assemble the first flying model of the new pump rocket. Supported on sawhorses, the flying machine's internal structure soon occupied the stage, front and center, of the sixty-foot shop. Then they shaped an aluminum sheath to cover the assembled rocket.

As the new model took form, Goddard knew it was risky to try it in flight. But it was a chance he could no longer avoid. The newest components were far from foolproof. There had been a few successful tests with the pump and generator. On several occasions, they built up pressure well, producing enough sustained lift to carry the rocket aloft. Too often, however, there had been the slight flaw, the small error, the minor difficulty that postponed flight. Unlike the automobile, steamship or other means of locomotion, the rocket could not be repaired in mid-course. In all details, it would have to work from its initial upward thrust, or sit in the tower, another aborted try.

On one score the professor had no doubts. After years of experiment, he had produced at last the space striver in miniature, the model of the creature of his dream. With enough time, it would prove itself. Was it now too much to hope for its perfect functioning, for a dramatically soaring flight?

While his men completed the assembly, Goddard, in early January 1940, sent his annual report to the Foundation. In a covering letter to Harry Guggenheim, he also issued an invitation:

"I have set forth the work we have done in preparing the flight model for performance tests . . . and have discussed what can reasonably be expected through further work with the present type of rocket.

"I hope to be able to give you a definite date for the flight test within 10 days or so. . . ."

In mid-January, while unseasonably chill winds blew over the prairie, he set a flight date with Guggenheim and hoped for a break in the weather. With his principal concern a successful launching for his sponsor, he also invited a few select guests to witness the trial.

Some months before, at Lindbergh's urging, Goddard had reluctantly agreed to collaborate with the *National Geographic Magazine* in a popular account of his experiments. Now he advised the magazine that he was about as ready as he was likely to be. The *National Geographic* promptly dispatched McFall Kerbey, a staff writer, and B. Anthony Stewart, a photographer, to Roswell. They arrived on January 29 ready to see Nell fly.

Next the professor alerted Colonel Pearson of the New Mexico Military Institute and his committee. Again, Pearson was asked to install an official N.A.A. barograph to chart Nell's hoped-for ascent. Having experienced earlier flight attempts,

Pearson accepted Goddard's new invitation more out of duty than gusto.

At the end of January, during Nell's installation in the launching tower, unusual weather assaulted the valley. During Goddard's years in New Mexico, only light snow had touched the flatland; usually it contained itself on the peak of El Capitan and the higher surrounding mountains. But now the prairie was gripped by protracted cold; snow laced steadily down; the tower was coated with ice.

In the dark hours one early morning, the frail professor, bundled in his greatcoat, headed with his men for the valley, checked the rocket and knocked ice from the tower's steel girders. In these weeks, Esther was far more concerned about her husband's durability than the durability of Nell. He would come home exhausted and chilled but, when she expressed her concern, he airily waved off discussion. He was "perfectly all right," he told her. It would be easier to change the weather, she knew, than to deflect him now from his course.

The rocket in early February seemed reasonably ready, if only the weather would improve. The Guggenheims were in Roswell, radiating geniality and high spirits, while the weather continued bad. For another week Calistro Sanchez and Charles Mansur took turns on the chill night watch, hoping like the rest of the crew for a break in the weather. Goddard's diary notes were drained of dramatics:

"Feb. 4: Went out with the men at 6 a.m., filled gasoline tank for a test, but the wind started at noon. . . . Talked and showed movie of static pump tests, eve.

"Feb. 5: The men went out to the tower at about 8.30, and took off the canvas to warm the model while the sun was out, about 15 min. Weather: showers, cool. Went to 'Destry Rides Again' at Yucca, with E and the Guggenheims in p.m. Sat in living room in eve.

"Feb. 6: Went out with the men at 6 a.m., to the tower.

Mr. and Mrs. G, Col. Pearson, the Committee and the Nat. Geog. men came at about 7.45. Filled up, N tank having to be blown out twice, and tried to run a test at about 10.15 a.m. The lever of the 2nd dash pot stuck—due to rust. Stayed at the tower with Al and Charles, after taking Mr. G. to the Nickson Hotel, in p.m., and Oley and Maurio took truck and got a motor-blowing outfit.

"Feb. 7: Worked in shop, and went out with Al to the tower; Oley and Charles going out first. Weather: fair, windy. Checked exploders, dried out tanks etc. with a compressed air outfit and a copper tube coil, heated by a gasoline blow torch. Came back at 5.30. Had supper, and Mr. and Mrs. Guggenheim came at 8 p.m. Talked in living room.

"Feb. 8: Worked in the shop, and went down town in a.m. Weather rainy, showers, a.m., snow p.m., clear in eve. Started Al on saw-cut O orifice and Oley on liquid O bearing, in p.m. Sat in living room in eve. . . ."

Although Guggenheim assured him there was plenty of time, the professor discovered that his sponsor was quietly calling New York to rearrange his schedule. On February 8, Goddard resolved to try for a flight if there was any possible chance of success.

In the early morning of February 9, the weather showed signs of clearing. Instead of an impossible day for rocket flying, it was merely a wretched one. Before starting for the valley, he left word with Esther to notify his sponsor and other guests. He would attempt a launching later that day.

At 6:00 A.M., as the sun rose over the cold prairie, the small caravan arrived in Eden Valley. It was not too encouraging. Morning dew and moisture from the night had turned again to ice, glistening on the tower's crosshatching. Adjusting his greatcoat against the cold, Goddard instructed his crew to knock the ice from the tower and unswaddle the rocket. He examined Nell closely, talked briefly with Oley, gave orders to begin linking up the control cables.

About two hours later, his guests arrived in a moderately festive manner: Harry and Alicia Guggenheim, with Esther; Colonel Pearson and two junior officers from the Military Institute; Kerbey and Stewart from the *National Geographic Magazine*. At noon the weather seemed about as good as it was likely to be. Without further delay, he assigned his company to their observation posts, distracted momentarily by Stewart's absorption in rigging up his tripod, poising his camera at the rocket, squeezing off a few preliminary shots and then settling back to wait.

The new Nell looked admirably ready for flight. Her sheathing was painted glossy black except for one aluminum quadrant which glinted in the sun. At her tail, below the nozzle, were four fixed and four movable air and blast vanes, to correct her course aloft. From these vanes to the tip of her nose cone, she measured 21 feet 11⅜ inches, and 18 inches in diameter. She was the most imposing of all Goddard's rockets. Without fuel and oxidizer, her weight had been kept down to 236 pounds, 10 ounces; with gasoline and liquid oxygen aboard, she weighed 480–500 pounds. To rise above the prairie floor, she would need an initial lift of almost 600 pounds. In his brief, offhand remarks, the professor made the crucial lift seem as simple as raising an elevator in an office building.

Of all his guests, Guggenheim was most aware of the magnitude of Goddard's gamble. Inside the sleek sheath of Nell were the ingenious products of thirty years of research, theoretically perfect, sometimes perfect in action, but all too often subject to flaws—the gyroscopic stabilizer, responsive to the external vanes; the curtain-cooled combustion chamber, pocked with small holes to receive a swirling curtain of gasoline, protecting the thin walls from the inferno of combustion within; the parachutes and their automatic release mechanism in the nose of the rocket, intended to assure Nell a dignified descent; the new pump-and-turbine assemblies on which he had labored for more than a year.

Later rocket engineers, who subjected new components to thousands of static tests, would marvel that Goddard's rockets ever rose from the tower. They would describe his approach as a sort of "trust-in-the-Lord" engineering, in which one barely-proved-but-not-quite-foolproof component was combined with another in the hope that the combination would somehow work infallibly. What astonished them was not that Goddard's pioneer models often failed to fly but that they occasionally succeeded. In the privacy of research, he had anticipated virtually every major component of the modern rocket.

If the star of space flight had shone at times on Eden Valley, its light turned dim that cold February afternoon in 1940. At his control panel, Goddard undoubtedly wondered how the rocket's mechanisms had fared in the week's delay, how they had been affected by the freezing, thawing and refreezing temperatures. What he showed, however, was his usual self-assurance as he set in motion the final sequence for firing, his deliberate but unspoken countdown.

His journal that day revealed the scientist's massive composure:

"On February 9, preparations for a test began at the tower at 6 a.m. The canvas covering of the rocket, as well as the entire tower, was coated with ice. It was necessary to knock the ice off the tower in two operations. Before the sun warmed the tower, the worst of the ice was knocked off, and later the remainder was scraped off. Preparations and checks were made for a test, although water continued to drop from parts of the tower.

"The test was carried out about 12:15 p.m. The flame at the start seemed more yellowish than usual, and the noise somewhat less. After about 2 sec. a flash appeared at the level of the pumps, the casing at this place being blown off, and the white vapor produced by a stream of liquid oxygen was visible thereafter.

"An examination showed that the bolts holding the casings of the oxygen pump had given way, causing the pump to break in two. The flame that appeared was forced back through the oxygen line by the chamber pressure. The oxygen starting valve came off with the oxygen filter and outer section of the pump casing, and was considerably damaged. The oxygen turbine was broken off around the hub and was not recovered. The chamber was undamaged. The tower guides were bent owing to the force with which the pump casing was blown off. . . .

"Conclusions: The breaking of the oxygen pump may best be explained by the supposition that ice particles occurred in the oxygen line and that these started clogging the oxygen orifice in the top of the chamber from the start. This explanation would account for a yellowish rather than a whitish flame at the start and for the less than usually intense noise."

With an embolism of ice in her fuel system, Goddard's pump-driven Nell had failed before her distinguished observers. Although his guests were pained, Goddard still seemed unshaken. At the launching tower he studied the now shattered rocket, seeking the cause of its failure. After brief instructions to his crew, he explained to Guggenheim that the rocket would need study and repairs. In a few weeks, no doubt, she would be ready for another flight. Meanwhile, there was no purpose in detaining his sponsor in Roswell. He would notify Mr. Guggenheim as soon as the rocket was ready.

Guggenheim, deeply distressed, was magnanimous. The rocket's failure was completely understandable, he said. This sort of thing often happened in pioneering research, he repeated. Whenever the professor was ready, he would of course return. To Esther Goddard, he repeated the same assurances, declaring that he and his wife Alicia had thoroughly enjoyed their visit.

That evening Goddard wrote succinctly in his diary, leaving poignancy to those who might one day read between his lines:

"Took the Guggenheims to the airport at 2 p.m. Stayed in bed until 6 p.m., when the men came back. Went to the Nickson and had dinner, with E, and Mr. K. and S. Sat in lobby, and had a smoke, afterward. Weather: fair, cool, snow flurry in p.m."

It was, as it turned out, Harry Guggenheim's last visit to Eden Valley. He returned to New York and less disturbing affairs. Except in Esther's motion pictures, he was never to see the successful launching of a Goddard rocket.

VII

After the Guggenheims' departure, Colonel Pearson and his men went back to work at the Military Institute. Shortly, Kerbey and Stewart returned to their duties at the *National Geographic Magazine* in Washington, D.C. The professor had spent several days with Kerbey, giving him material for his interview, and with Stewart who took photographs of Goddard, his rocket and the space age tower with the anachronism of a ruminative cow in the foreground.

The next flight attempt was postponed until 8:35 A.M. on March 21, 1940. Nell had been thoroughly overhauled and the weather, though blustery, had improved. Goddard informed his patron but advised him that there was no need for him to return to Roswell. If the flight succeeded, he would report the results in detail. Colonel Pearson and his assistants were again on hand to install the barograph and witness the test. Anthony Stewart, summoned from Washington, came back with more photographic gear than exuberance. In his diary, Goddard wrote:

"Tried a test. . . . There was the sound of gas escaping, and the pressure was low and pulsating. Finally, apparently, the 2 manifolds exploded, they being very cold and brittle. The 2,000 lb. reducing valve (safety valve) was hissing after the test, and the reduced pressure was 180 lbs. Came back at 2 p.m., and stopped work 20 mins. early."

In his experimental notes he added:

". . . there were 2 successive explosions, one halfway up the rocket, and the other over the chamber. The emergency gasoline valve-key was pressed to stop the run. . . ."

As frustrated as the exploding rocket, photographer Stewart took the next plane for Washington with his film of the second aborted launching. Goddard's article for the *National Geographic Magazine,* which Stewart had come to illustrate and on which the professor had worked with Kerbey, was never published. The magazine, lacking their photographs of his rocket in flight, filed the article away.

Five months later, in August 1940, Goddard was ready again to try for flight. He had subjected Nell's components to repeated static tests with a few encouraging results.

The flight attempt on August 1 was another abort, with Nell transfixed and blazing when a gasoline control circuit broke down. A week later, after dawn, the doctor and his men again headed for the tower but his car, as he wrote, "got stuck in the mud near the Pine Lodge Road, for an hour and a half. . . ." When he eventually reached the tower, the wind was too lively to attempt a flight.

Next morning Goddard managed to avoid the mud and reached the tower at dawn. Colonel Pearson sent his mathematicians, Dr. and Mrs. Howard Alden, to represent him and the N.A.A. The Aldens picked up Esther on their way to the valley. Goddard wrote in his journal:

"The usual loud initial explosion took place after the usual delay. The white lift light soon showed, and after a second or so the red lift light showed. The main release key was pressed about a second afterward.

"The rocket rose, seemed to hesitate for an instant after it had risen a short distance, and a yellow flame spread out. It then rose slowly, but apparently no more slowly than in a number of tests with the 9-in. model. It left the tower straight, but soon tilted toward the left for no apparent reason, and showed no evidence of stabilizing vane action. It continued to rise and turn, then plunged straight downward, still turning, and struck the ground about 400 ft. from the observers. It exploded and a strong concussion was felt soon afterward. A dense black cloud of smoke arose.

"The rocket appeared to leave the tower at about 10 to 15 m.p.h., and rose 200 to 300 ft. The flame was rather long and yellowish, and the lower end was fuzzy. There did not appear to be much smoke. Apparently the explosion did not occur inside the rocket, since the parts were not greatly torn or scattered. It seems likely that the two tanks burst simultaneously, and that the two liquids mixed violently, igniting immediately afterward."

The report was complete except that Marjorie Alden, as Esther recalled, said: "Oh" and "Oh" again when the powerful pumps shuddered, grabbed and took hold. Before his overjoyed wife, his crew and his observers, the professor was barely able to contain his delight that the pump model, the sophisticated grand dame of all his efforts toward space, had at last cleared the launching tower.

He planned to try for higher altitudes in the months ahead. But in this initial flight, however short, the pump-driven motor had performed successfully. It would take time to repair or construct a new rocket. The first and hardest problem, however, was solved. Next morning, Goddard wrote to Guggenheim and Lindbergh that the pump model had flown.

Then, almost at once, the doctor was involved in other applications, other goals for his rocket.

VIII

From all points of the compass, dusty trains pulled slowly into the capital's Union Station in the spring of 1940. Converging on Washington, they disgorged a humid assortment of salesmen, bureaucrats, business executives, men of influence and influence men, all hoping to use their talents or arrange a deal with a democracy preparing itself for an unwanted war.

Among this purposeful crowd was the shy, slender professor from the New Mexico prairies, wearing a freshly laundered shirt and accompanied by his wife. In his right hand he carried a well-worn, well-strapped briefcase.

For Dr. Goddard, it was the second time around. At Guggenheim's behest, he had come again to the capital to arouse the armed services to the potential use of rockets as weapons.

From the Roswell *Daily Record* to the New York *Times,* newspapers were tracing the quickening pace of the war in Europe, giving Americans a sense of its immediacy and momentum. Neville Chamberlain's vision had evaporated. After the breakup of the Republic of Czechoslovakia, Soviet Russia and Nazi Germany signed a nonaggression pact. It was quickly followed by Adolf Hitler's invasion of Poland, Great Britain's declaration of war on Germany and the brutal sweep of the lowlands.

Before May 1940, when the Goddards arrived in Washington, Hitler was bringing down the governments of Norway, Denmark, Belgium, Luxembourg and Holland, deploying as his principal striking force battalions of Panzer tanks. Against these mobile tons of artillery, the defending forces west of the Maginot Line were soft-shelled and helpless.

France was doomed. The invasion of Soviet Russia was to come later. Meanwhile, Hitler was training his Luftwaffe to pound England, softening the island empire for surrender.

The Goddards walked through the crowded, high-domed rotunda of Union Station, past waiting rooms, telephone booths and popcorn machines to join others waiting for taxis. A few blocks away, members of the United States Congress, in late session, were trying to determine America's relationship to the spreading war in confounding and vociferous debate. Their arguments reflected the views and confusions of constituents, still undecided, back home.

Some heard the voice of Lindbergh, the earlier hero, whose experience and conviction had turned him from pilot to polemicist. The United States, he was saying, must stand aside from the war, which he characterized as one of Europe's "eternal quarrels." He made several independent radio addresses before he joined the America First Committee.

A few nights before his trip to Washington, Goddard had noted in his diary: "Heard Lindy's talk on the radio." He offered no further comment. Perhaps he remembered Nahum's watchwords: "Let the railroad tend to the railroad's business." But Goddard doubted that his country could remain apart from Europe or that he, himself, could stand aside.

A second voice in the land, deeper and more dominant than Lindbergh's, came from the White House whose tenant would be elected later that year to an unprecedented third term. President Roosevelt declared the country in "a state of limited national emergency." Soon he would arouse noisier debate in Congress by asking for lend-lease aid to Great Britain in its struggle against Nazi Germany. In the President's mind, there seemed little question that the United States was already involved. On May 14, Goering's Luftwaffe bombed Rotterdam, and three days later Roosevelt called for the unprecedented production of 50,000 military airplanes. The "Phony War" was over in Europe. After a time, even the thought of American neutrality was academic.

The Goddards spent the night of May 27, 1940 in Washington's Mayflower Hotel, while an ocean away British armed forces began the evacuation of Dunkirk. In the hotel lobby, on previous trips to the city, the professor had leisurely seated himself in an overstuffed chair after dinner, smoked his cherished cigar to the stub, happily noting and unnoticed by chattering young ladies in mink wraps and evening gowns. That evening, when her husband lighted his cigar, Esther excused herself. She had things to straighten up, letters and postcards to write. The professor sat down and thoughtfully began blowing smoke rings.

The next morning, he and Guggenheim were to meet top officials of the Army and Navy. His sponsor planned to offer the professor's services and the New Mexico establishment to the military services. Goddard had accepted the proposal. Obviously, the rocket's further development needed more than private funds.

Still Goddard wished that his pump model, his miniature space striver, had flown successfully during his patron's last visit to Roswell. It might have made a difference at the Foundation. Well, it was too late for regrets.

He snubbed out his cigar and took the elevator up to his room. Esther had arranged their belongings familiarly. She asked if he'd enjoyed his cigar. He had, he said, as he unbuckled his briefcase and removed a folder prepared for his conference the next morning.

At the top of the pile was a memorandum which Esther had neatly copied, adding a few modifications of her own. Principal points were underscored; words and phrases to be emphasized were typed in capital letters.

He studied the typescript briefly, then put it back in his folder. He would refer to it again in the morning, he said.

Briefly he thumbed through another paper, prepared for Colonel Lindbergh in 1939, in which he had summed up three kinds of military rockets. It still sounded apt, if anyone would listen:

"1. *Long-Range Projectile.* Probably the best line of attack on the long-range projectile application is the line we are now following here, using high-pressure pumps and a gas generator.

"2. *Rocket-Turbine for Aircraft.* If jet propulsion is to be applied to aircraft without adding extensive equipment and liquid oxygen, the atmospheric type rocket . . . would seem to be the best plan.

"3. *Simple Short-Range Projectile.* Powder rockets, as relatively short-range artillery, have the advantage of simplicity of construction, even when they are given an initial spin, as I was able to demonstrate in 1918. They also permit the use of a very light firing tube, much lighter than a gun or a modern trench mortar."

The next morning the Goddards had early breakfast before the professor left for his appointment at the War Department. He had not forgotten his papers, he told his wife. He would refer to them during the day. He recalled an earlier memorandum she had prepared for another trip he made to the city—*Have haircut, shoe shine . . . at lunch, order whatever* THEY *would like . . . be expansive . . . pick up the check yourself.*

It was comforting to have Esther at his side. Somewhat to her surprise, he firmly pressed her hand as they entered the lobby.

IX

Promptly at 8:30 A.M., the professor presented his credentials to a military guard at the War Department. He was directed to the office of General Henry H. Arnold, Chief of the Army Air Corps. A uniformed aide explained that General Arnold would be unavailable, but had designated his Chief of Matériel, Brigadier General George H. Brett, to represent him. General Brett would see Dr. Goddard after Mr. Guggenheim arrived. Mr. Guggenheim's flight from New York, the aide reported, was unfortunately delayed by bad weather.

The professor found another cigar in his vest pocket. He had intended to save it for dinner. He bit off its end, lighted it and then unstrapped his briefcase. Arnold's aide was engrossed in his own affairs amid a battery of telephones and intercommunications buzzers. Goddard turned to his memorandum and silently reread the familiar lines:

"This is now a formidable weapon; pumps have been developed since 1938 and the point has NOW been reached where intensive development in several directions, esp. military, would make great strides. These pumps are a major step in the development and are the key to great heights and LONG ranges.

"Goddard doesn't come with a military invention to peddle; he is NOT an unemployed inventor. His purely scientific work under the Guggenheim Foundation for the past few years in secluded New Mexico can, HOWEVER, so easily become of value in a military way that he feels he should call it to the attention of the authorities. He is active on it NOW, backed by the Guggenheim Foundation, and is not trying to promote something because of the threat of war.

"What RHG has done on the problem.

"What the problem is; also that this aspect in N.M. is *vertical,* the *hardest* way, for lightness and precise stability required. War rockets for horizontal ranges could be heavier, more rugged. The fundamental rocket principles are simple; these refinements are not so simple. A rocket for long horizontal ranges much easier to develop. Mathematical theory has proved correct for many years. . . .

"Reasons for coming:

"1. It is important that proper authorities should know about this work and its possibilities, from the one who has personally done the work. . . ."

The aide was asking the professor to come with him. Goddard hastily bundled up his papers and followed his guide down a corridor, past bustling young officers exchanging brisk hand salutes. In General Brett's office, he was presented to several men in uniform. The Navy's Bureau of Aeronautics had sent Commander J. W. Pennoyer, Commander W. S. Diehl and Lt. Commander R. S. Hatcher. Army Ordnance had dispatched Lieutenant Colonel K. F. Adamson. Captain C. A. Ross was on hand to assist General Brett for the Army Air Corps. Together, around a large conference table, they waited for Brett and Guggenheim.

There were no full minutes of the meeting, but from Goddard's notes and correspondence the discussion can be adequately pieced together. For the United States, it was an early opportunity to take on the rocket in all its varied forms, to use it as one of the most novel carriers of destruction since the catapults of the Roman phalanxes.

While awaiting their superior, the field officers exchanged pleasantries with the scientist. Goddard was then asked about his work in Roswell, of which they had heard little; about his rocket experiments, what he had done, what he hoped to achieve. Without hesitation or reference to his notes, he explained the reaction principle and how a rocket could carry a payload to great distances. As he warmed up to his subject, he spoke as he might have addressed a class of graduate students at Clark. There were "several interesting military possibilities," he began, employing his usual understatement.

The military was already aware of jet propulsion, one of the officers interrupted. . . . Of course we're interested in useful hardware, said another. . . . Perhaps you have sketches of what you propose? a third officer inquired. . . . Between us, another interjected, there is a feeling, Doctor, that you haven't talked openly about your work.

Then Guggenheim was ushered in. An erect, forthright personality, commanding in appearance, the executive greeted the junior officers with the air of one accustomed to getting down to business. Without waiting for Brett to appear, he announced, as Goddard later recorded, that the Guggenheim Foundation "would be glad to turn over the [Roswell] shop for war work for the duration."

Turning to his protégé, Guggenheim invited the professor to discuss the military possibilities of his research. While Goddard was carefully outlining the rocket's potential, General Brett arrived, apologized, sat down and listened.

Goddard mistook the sudden concentration of the younger officers as evidence of genuine interest. He reached for his briefcase. He happened to have a few movies of his rocket in flight, he said, if the gentlemen were inclined to take the time. General Brett consulted his watch. He was already due at another meeting, he said.

In the remaining few minutes, the general proposed that the professor work up a report on a possible liquid-fuel rocket to assist pursuit planes in their take-off and climb. It might be worthwhile. But as for broad-based research, the prospect was bleak. The military establishment, Brett said, was in a terrible bind, caught between the need for new weapons and the lack of emergency appropriations.

The Navy representatives agreed. Although funds were hard to come by, the Navy might be willing to invest in a liquid-fuel take-off device and possibly in a rocket motor for planes for "extreme speeds."

Before the meeting adjourned, Goddard tried once more to arouse interest. He said his rocket could readily be converted to a mobile, lightweight, recoilless gun. It could be carried and fired by a single soldier. It was, in essence, a tank killer. He had demonstrated the principle of such a weapon more than two decades earlier, at Aberdeen Proving Grounds, shortly before the end of the First World War.

One of the officers was aloof. He had been ordered to work with a group of professors in preparing a report for the White House on a fantastic new kind of super-bomb. Possibly he shared the prevalent attitude that if the military wasn't careful, these scientists might take over the whole establishment. They were like the Arab's camel—let them get their nose in your tent and soon they were inside and you were outside. Called on for comment, the officer made a retort that neither Goddard nor Guggenheim easily forgot.

The new war, like the old war, he said, would not be won by super-rockets or super-bombs. It would be won by improving the venerable trench mortar.

With a cheerful wave of his hand, General Brett left. The conference table was strewn with pads of paper, crumpled sheets of doodles, ashtrays filled with cigarette butts, some still smoldering.

On his long train trip back to Roswell, Goddard wondered if there was any way to encourage a flowering of the rocket in his own country while it was finding a better planting season and a more fertile soil abroad.

11. I WAS WONDERING
WHEN YOU'D ASK ME

Goddard rarely yielded to self-display in any of its varied forms. In concealing emotion, there was scarcely an Oxford don who could match him in understatement. On days in the prairie when his rocket performed outrageously, he would describe the result of the test as "fair." When he referred to Nell's dazzling prospects as a space vehicle, he spoke obliquely of "interesting possibilities." Later, when his own health failed disastrously, he told Esther: "You know, I just don't feel well."

After his experience in Washington, however, the taciturn professor was in no mood for Yankee reticence. He had gone to the nation's military establishment to offer his rocket development and returned, frustrated, to Roswell. In addition, he heard that the California Institute of Technology had already obtained a military contract for some sort of rocket work.

For several weeks a flurry of protests and appeals went out from Mescalero Ranch.

To Smithsonian Secretary Abbot:

"I feel that every effort should be made to put my work, turned to national defense lines, on as powerful a footing as possible. . . . Apparently my experience and years of work . . . [were] given no consideration. . . .

"I would appreciate it very deeply if you would make inquiries among the National Research Council members as to just why I was not even considered on the grant for rocket propulsion."

To Senator David I. Walsh of Massachusetts, then chairman of the Committee on Naval Affairs:

"I have been working on rocket and jet propulsion for a number of years. . . . I believe that I have had more experience with the problem than anyone else in the country, and so far as I know, have obtained the only authenticated flights of a liquid fuel rocket. . . .

"Both the Foundation and I are convinced that this research has much to offer. . . . The work has already been carried to such a point that it may easily lead to valuable military applications, and we feel that it is our duty to offer what we have. . . .

"It would be most important if you could help in any way in putting this work quietly upon a rather large scale. . . ."

And again to Senator Walsh:

"I would appreciate it very greatly if you would make inquiries to learn if the committee [National Defense Research Committee] which the President is forming for the mobilization of the research workers of the country will be in a position to take an active interest in the matter. . . .

"I might add that time is a factor, for if the Army or Navy do not have a specific problem to be worked upon, and if the Guggenheim Foundation does not feel in a position to finance next year's work here, it will be necessary for me to return to teaching at Clark University, and continue this work on a greatly reduced scale. I believe this would be unfortunate, for I feel that my many years of experience in this line should be made available to the government to the fullest possible extent."

To Lindbergh:

"I cannot help feeling that with rockets as a possible factor in light artillery equipment, and jet propulsion as an almost certain factor in future high-speed aircraft, it would be extremely desirable for the government to back this work on a large scale. I imagine it is a little too much to hope for this, at the present time."

To General Henry H. Arnold, Chief, U.S. Army Air Corps:

"I was sorry not to see you at the meeting in Washington on May 28 arranged by Mr. Harry F. Guggenheim to consider the possible military applications of the rocket and jet propulsion work in which I have been engaged. . . . As a result of this conference it was decided that I estimate on a rocket chamber to be used in the take-off and climb of a P-36 pursuit plane. The Navy representative spoke also of their interest in work which might lead to a motor useful at extreme speeds.

"While this is very encouraging, I cannot help feeling that twenty-odd years of experience on rocket problems, the flight results which we have obtained to date, and the general acceptance of jet propulsion as of real engineering importance warrant having this project undertaken on a much more extensive scale."

To Dr. Hickman, his colleague during the First World War and now the Bell Telephone Laboratories' magician inventor:

"Frankly, I have been filled with disgust at the fact that no intensive fundamental work appears possible, and I suspect that I have been hard to live with since my return. . . ."

In Washington, General Brett had lightly suggested that

Goddard submit a "complete report" on a liquid-fuel pump
rocket for aircraft. Reports were presumably easier to file
away than professors on one's doorstep. Neither Goddard's letters nor his report to Brett produced incandescent
sparks.

The general reviewed Goddard's report, asked for "a more
concrete proposal," and then for "an estimate of the cost."

After a thrifty analysis of his pump rocket, the professor
replied that "a program covering two or three years, with
$93,500 the first year, and $71,000 each year thereafter,
would produce results." For fear of undue optimism, he
wrote: "The above recommendations should not be considered as implying that the application of jet propulsion to aircraft is an engineering problem of no special difficulty." He
added, almost as an afterthought, his concepts of a turbojet
plane and an antiaircraft missile.

Weeks passed. There was still no reply from General
Brett. But there were two other notes. One came from
Guggenheim:

"For your peace of mind and that of the others on the
staff, I can assure you that if we are not able to make
some plan with the Government, the Foundation will carry
on the work for another year."

Goddard had almost forgotten that his grant was again due
to expire.

The other bright note came from Hickman, who wrote:

Dear Dr. Goddard:

As a patriotic American, I feel that it is my duty to call the
attention of our government to the possibilities of your rocket
for defensive purposes. Before doing so I thought I should write
to you to see if any work was being done on the single charge.

I am firmly convinced that if the French and English had
rockets fully developed along the lines we worked out that the
situation today would be quite different. In looking over the

computations that I made when I was with you, the possibilities seem more definite than at the time I made the computations. You must remember that our experimental shells were machined and were rough on the inside. We only had nickel steel at that time. The great advances that have been made in metals have completely changed the possibilities. Methods of fabrication have been so improved that I am sure we can increase the gas velocity by a large margin.

. . . I think that Heaven and Earth should be pushed to get this work started. Every precaution should be made to keep it a complete secret. If nothing is being done and you will give me permission to do so, I will bring the matter before our government in a way that will insure complete secrecy and will insure that the possibilities be given serious attention.

It is unbelievable that the matter would not be given immediate consideration. Since I have no axe to grind and can present the matter as an enthusiastic American trying to help in our national defense program, my presentation might have considerable weight. . . .

If you are in agreement with my plan, will you write by return mail giving me permission to bring the matter before the proper government officials?

If ever the rocket needed a magician's touch, it was now. Goddard's answer was prompt and direct:

"My reply, in brief, is 'Go ahead, and God bless you!' "

He complimented Hickman on his enthusiasm, invited him to come west to Roswell to work on the rocket, offered to come east himself "to help out if I can." Goddard concluded: "If you can sell the idea of any part of the work, you would have my everlasting gratitude, for I have never had a talent for any kind of sales talk."

With his salesmanship and Goddard's "God-bless-you" letter, Hickman urged the armed services to consider a solid-fuel rocket as an antitank weapon, a submarine torpedo against destroyers, a missile to be launched by small boats against enemy shipping and coastal defenses.

Hickman's tenacity finally obtained a few results. The Navy asked him to develop a solid-propellant rocket accelerator for armor-piercing bombs, designed to penetrate decks of enemy ships. He was also appointed chairman of a new rocket section of the National Defense Research Committee. From this point of leverage, he finally prodded Army Ordnance into accepting a weapon which would stop the Nazi tanks as they lumbered across the deserts of North Africa.

Years later, Hickman informally recounted the affair:

"Our antitank weapon combined Goddard's powder rocket and an old principle, the shaped charge or the 'Monroe effect.'

"At the close of World War I, the Navy was studying the destructiveness of depth charges, which were nothing more than ash cans into which molten TNT had been poured, with a detonator to set them off. When the TNT solidified, it hardened first next to the can surface, and then sank, leaving a conical void at the top. It was suspected that this cone, shaped by nature, increased the destructiveness. It was an example of the well-known Monroe effect.

"By World War II, it was proposed that antitank missiles could make use of this principle. The gas velocities in the jet of the cone would literally wash away armor plate much like a garden hose can do to the earth. The shaped charge eventually cut through metal up to 14 inches thick.

"Someone proposed to hurl these shaped-charge missiles at tanks with rifles, much like the rifle grenades of World War I. A strong tube with the missile attached was fitted over the rifle barrel and a heavy blank cartridge was fired to give the missile a velocity of about 75 feet per second.

"Army Ordnance got so enthusiastic that they ordered about one million of these rifle missiles for use in World

War II. When the missiles were delivered, Ordnance found that the gunners could not stand the recoil. It would knock them down or break their shoulders. They tried putting the butt of the gun against the ground, but that ruined the rifle. Then they let out a contract to develop a mortar to fire the missiles.

"Finally someone in Ordnance got to thinking about rocket launching and sent Colonel Leslie Skinner to consult me. I told him about the recoilless gun I had worked on with Goddard in 1918 and of my unsuccessful efforts to sell it now.

"I never had an official request to develop the gun, but we started investigating it down at Indian Head, Maryland. All we had to do was provide a nozzle, powder trap and suitable powder for the shaped-charged missile and a simple launching tube. Except for the powder trap, the development went very fast. We got much higher velocities than they did with the rifle, and without recoil, and we found that by bore-sighting we could hit the target within plus or minus one mill probable error.

"Colonel Skinner and I soon had a formidable weapon, but General Barnes, the chief of Army Ordnance, wanted no part of it. He didn't want the soldier to have to carry another gun —and he wouldn't be budged.

"Meanwhile, the new mortar for shaped charges was being demonstrated at Aberdeen. Lt. Edward Uhl, a young officer assigned to me at the time, went to see it. Fortunately, he took along our new recoilless gun. The trench mortars all collapsed on firing.

"Somehow, Uhl got permission to show our gun. We hadn't taken time to put sights on it, but Uhl was a clever boy and he understood physics. He improvised sights with some wires and a nail. He shot at a moving tank and hit it nine times out of ten.

"A visiting major couldn't get over it. 'What is that damn

thing?' he asked. 'It looks like Bob Burns's bazooka!' Well, the name stuck. Right then and there, the Ordnance chief was overruled and the American army had a bazooka to meet the German tanks in Tunisia."

II

As the architect of great rockets for space, Goddard was possibly ill fitted for the requirements of the military before the Second World War; when its demands were for immediate, practical and hopefully inexpensive weapons. He had repeatedly argued for the merits of liquid-fuel propellants as against solid fuels. Liquid-propelled devices might require somewhat more work in development, but the resulting rockets would be far more powerful, he held. After his trip to Washington in May 1940, it was clear that he was not quite getting his message across.

He had turned to another colleague from Clark University, Dr. Louis T. E. Thompson, then chief of research at the Naval Proving Ground at Dahlgren, Virginia. They had corresponded while Goddard awaited the Navy's delayed decision on his various proposals, observing to Thompson: "I am wondering if this is a case of the slow motion of large bodies. . . ."

Increasingly, the rocket professor felt drawn to Washington, hoping to speed up the motion of large bodies, ready to leave his desert sanctuary like a bear emerging into the spring sunlight.

In August 1940, after stirring as much interest as possible by mail, he made his second trip to the capital city. Hickman had written: "We are anxious to have you come . . . to discuss various phases of this work with us . . . as soon as it is convenient for you to do so."

Goddard didn't hesitate. It was of course convenient. After

arranging other appointments, he took an early morning airplane on August 27 heading from Amarillo, Texas, for the east.

One day his liquid-fuel rocket would soar miles beyond the stratosphere. But he himself had flown only briefly before, with Charles Lindbergh. That evening, he wrote to Esther from Washington:

"FULL ACCOUNT OF MY FIRST TRANSCONTINENTAL FLIGHT. READ ALL ABOUT IT!

"It was dark when I went aboard the plane. The sunrise was not spectacular, as there were no clouds, except some far off in the east. Later, however, we passed over some white clouds that looked like blocks of ice on end, as far as the eye could reach. . . . It was worth pushing your nose against the window to see.

"We made Kansas City in three hours, and I will have to admit three hours is less than seventeen. . . . We passed into a dense fog, and the plane slowed down. I would have felt better if the captain had come to me and said he knew what he was doing."

Aside from minor misadventures which he detailed to Esther—the plane's buffeting in a brilliant electrical storm; the mistaken shipment of his luggage to Pittsburgh—Goddard's second expedition to Washington seemed more promising than his first. On this mission he felt less on the outside looking in. Through Dr. Thompson, he met Admiral W. R. Furlong, chief of the Navy Bureau of Ordnance. The admiral received him warmly and presented him to several leading scientists who were already at work for the government.

"Admiral Furlong introduced me as the country's foremost authority on rockets," Goddard wrote at once to Esther. "He . . . seems to think a lot of me, which makes it mutual." When Furlong invited him to outline a comprehensive program for rocket development, he spent a day in his hotel room drafting the requested memorandum.

In this hopeful mood, Goddard was able to absorb, for a time, a new series of disappointments. He accepted the news that the Navy preferred a solid-fuel rocket accelerator, rather than his own liquid-fuel system. But after all, he had long since abandoned his work on powder rockets and Hickman was equipped to handle the task. When Hickman asked him to serve as a consultant to the new solid-fuel rocket section, Goddard said that of course he would help, but would continue to work with liquid fuels.

Goddard still had not heard from General Brett of the Army Air Corps about his rocket proposals. Hoping to learn the status of his report, the professor found his way back to the War Department office where he had sat around the conference table with Brett and his junior officers.

It was a stage setting with the players vanished. General Brett was gone. So was his aide, Captain Ross. No one could say for sure where they were. An unfamiliar Air Corps major greeted the professor, consulted filing cabinets and declared that he could find nothing on Dr. Goddard's report. Undoubtedly, the Experimental Station at Wright Field was exploring the matter. The professor ought to go to Dayton, Ohio, to follow up the matter. Meanwhile, the major would inform Wright Field, saying that Goddard was coming.

Before leaving for Dayton, Goddard visited Harry Guggenheim in New York. He found his sponsor at the election headquarters of Wendell Willkie, who was then Franklin Roosevelt's Republican opponent for President. After lunch at the nearby Yale Club, Guggenheim gave Goddard one of his private-brand Havana cigars, which the doctor enjoyed leisurely in the lounge. When Guggenheim asked him if the cigar was satisfactory, "I told him," the physicist wrote, "that 'The world is full of flowers and birds of paradise!'"

After hearing of Goddard's experiences with the military, Guggenheim prepared a crisp letter to General Brett, requesting either an acceptance or rejection of the professor's unanswered proposals. Goddard then went on to Dayton.

The visits to Wright Field "served to harden Bob's misgivings as to politics and 'influence' in the granting of contracts," his wife recalled. He confided the Dayton trip to her in a letter:

"Well, here is the record . . . without profane or obscene comments.

"I arrived at the Field at about 9 a.m., and wrote on the card they give you that I wished to see Major Kemmer. (Major Chidlaw in Washington had said he would write Major Kemmer that I was coming.) I waited about an hour and a half, and then was shown to a Mr. LeTour. I told him what we [could do] and he seemed to think it was more than adequate, as it stands, for the take-off problem.

"I then saw a Lieutenant (I will get his name) who said he believed that jet propulsion was in the shadow just now because of the difficulties they had encountered. He said, when I told him about my July 27 recommendations, that they had never received them at Wright Field. I asked to see one of the ships they wanted to have taken off, and he said none were here, because they had no way of taking them off. . . .

"They then had me see a Mr. Loeding [Alfred C. Loedding] a young fellow, who is their man in charge of the rocket work they are doing at Wright Field. He said that the powders they had were OK, and that there was no erosion, either with their rockets at Wright Field, or with the Cal. Tech rockets. . . .

"I am going to send a night letter to General Brett, asking him to tell me who to see here who has authority to report to Washington, and also telling him that the recommendation was never received here. . . ." Then he concluded, unable to resist a shade of profanity:

"P.S. Jesus Christ! How many homely women there are in Ohio!"

During the remaining period before the shock of Pearl Harbor, events great and small were shaping the marriage of United States science and the military establishment. The military mind and the scientific mentality often found the courtship difficult. Yet their marriage, sometimes strained, thrived during World War II. However, at the time, the adventures of a professor from a small New England school seemed unimportant to a nation learning to flex its scientific muscles.

On his return to Roswell, Goddard soon learned that his various efforts in Washington were still missing fire. In September, there was a letter from General Brett:

"The proposals as outlined in your letter . . . have been carefully reviewed. . . . While the Air Corps is deeply interested in the research work being carried out by your organization . . . it does not, at this time, feel justified in obligating further funds for basic jet propulsion research and experimentation. . . ."

Admiral Furlong of the Navy took a little longer to apply a similar *coup de grâce*. Rocket devices would be more effective and practical, he believed, if fueled by powder, rather than by liquids, inasmuch as liquid oxygen and gasoline created both problems of design and logistics. Powder rocket research, he said, was being carried out effectively by the research team at the California Institute of Technology. Besides, Cal. Tech was also experimenting with liquids.

A third communication, from Dr. Vannevar Bush, confirmed a Goddard appointment recommended by Hickman. Dr. Bush, formerly of the Massachusetts Institute of Technology and president of the Carnegie Institution of Washington, was then chairman of the National Defense Research Committee and the National Advisory Committee for Aeronautics, and was President Roosevelt's chief link to the scientific community. In his letter, he invited Goddard to serve as a consultant to Dr. Hickman's section on powder rockets. Although Goddard accepted this modest role, the invitation aroused the usually placid Dr. Abbot of the Smithsonian.

"I remonstrated with Dr. Bush," Abbot recalled years later. "I stated that it was unconscionable to put Goddard in a minor role instead of on the main committee dealing with jet propulsion. 'Surely,' I said, 'a committee on jets without Dr. Goddard would be like a committee on solar rotation without Dr. W. S. Adams.' "

But the pattern was set. Dr. Bush's deputy on rocket propulsion was Dr. Richard C. Tolman of the California Institute of Technology. Dr. Tolman was a firm believer in scientific teamwork. Years before, according to Goddard's diary, Tolman had observed pointedly during a meeting that Goddard's work was already "too big for a one-man approach," that rocket development "obviously required a team."

Through the Second World War, the American military and scientific partnership would demonstrate remarkable strength in producing weapons. The function of the N.D.R.C. was to explore and recommend research for immediate military application. Its policy left little opportunity to encourage long-range developments.

Years later, Louis Thompson candidly summed up the matter:

"If there was a fault, perhaps it would go to an assumption that Goddard was inclined to take more time than the fellow who likes to run things through fast and get out a piece of hardware. In time of war, this could possibly be a problem.

"But he could and should have been handled far better—not for his sake, but for the country's sake. Anyone with imagination and authority might have gone to him and said: 'Now you're doing fundamental work here in Roswell and we want you to keep going in this area. We'd like to give you all the facilities we can, but we want to set up another group to product-engineer the work and get out the devices in production. We'd like you to give these young men the benefit of your counsel, but let them have the responsibility for carrying out the work.'

"I believe he would have been enormously pleased by such an opportunity, coming at that time. And there is no doubt in my mind that if we had followed this approach, we would have gone much farther and faster in the whole field of jet engineering that Goddard opened up for us—particularly in his fundamental exploration. We were unimaginative. I don't know of any branch of engineering in which any one individual has contributed more."

But Goddard's persistence in seeking a place with the military was by no means finished. Among America's young rocket engineers, a few visited him in Roswell, sat on his veranda, asked questions that showed they had done their homework in physics and mathematics, and understood his work. They, in turn, recognized Goddard as a man of the future rather than of the past. They would soon help to lead him out of his prairie sanctuary.

IV

The once-splendid isolation of Roswell was no longer satisfying. After his two trips to Washington in 1940, Goddard still heard the echoing words of his colleagues. "If you want to stir up the military, you've got to *sell* them and *sell them hard!*" Dr. Hickman had declared. Dr. Thompson, more gently, had advised him: "You might get along faster,

Bob, by giving out more. People feel that you're somewhat secretive."

The more Goddard tried to dismiss these unpleasant thoughts, the more they nettled him. On weekdays, he resumed his experiments in the machine shop and out at the testing tower, devising ingenious improvements for his pump-driven rockets. On Sundays, after his usual steak breakfast and cigar, he dealt with the week's accumulation of mail, scrawling in pencil for Esther's typing his familiar clam-like refrain: "The work is still in progress . . . there is nothing new to report."

But now he began to question this ritualistic response, fearing that others might be passing him by. More and more, he felt like the member of a New England gentleman's club who had sat for years in an overstuffed chair, his privacy respected, until he discovered himself to be out of touch. He then began edging his chair out from the wall, plucking at the sleeves of his fellow members and saying softly: "You may speak to me when I'm in the line of traffic."

In his changing mood, Goddard found two young enthusiasts in his own line of traffic. One was the Navy pilot, Lieutenant Charles Fink Fischer, who had first passed through Roswell in 1939 on his way to the California Institute of Technology, met the professor and asked his advice on studies suitable for rocket engineering. Fischer would return later. A second visitor was an Army Air Corps pilot, Lieutenant Homer A. Boushey, who called on the Goddards in the summer of 1940. His visit led to an astonishing talk at Mescalero Ranch.

Homer Boushey was not the first of the professor's would-be disciples, but to Goddard he was the most appealing. In many respects, he resembled Goddard himself. A graduate engineer from Stanford University, the lieutenant's mild manner masked a zealot. He was an accomplished flier, a student of aeronautical science, a hopeful inventor and a private reader of Jules Verne, H. G. Wells and space-fiction magazines. He had discovered a copy of Goddard's early and classic Smithsonian treatise, which he regarded with the awe usually reserved for the Pentateuch. He wrote to his hero from an Army Air Corps base. At Goddard's apparently offhand invitation, Boushey flew to Roswell in a pursuit plane, arriving like a pilgrim racing to Mecca.

Probably only such a winning disciple coming at such an opportune time could have penetrated Goddard's reserve. In age they were more than a generation apart—Boushey, thirty-one years old; Goddard, almost fifty-eight. By the summer of 1940, the childless professor was troubled by the growing pains of Nell, his mechanical offspring. There was a new note in his thinking after Boushey's initial visit. "That young fellow seems to know what he's talking about," he told Esther and then added: "Maybe we're not alone any more."

A few weeks later, when the pilot returned, Esther firmly reassured her husband. "After all, Bob," she said, "we have to trust *someone!*"

Afterward, Boushey remembered his second trip to Roswell in sharp detail:

"When I got to the ranchhouse, the doctor invited me to follow him into his machine shop. It was a Sunday afternoon and the place was empty. The rocket they called 'Nell' was propped up on sawhorses, extending almost the length of the shop and covered by a white cloth. I gathered it was unusual for any outsider to be in the shop.

"Then he pulled back the cloth and let me inspect the rocket, giving me a detailed description of how it worked— the pumps and turbines, the gas generators and gyroscopes— all those exquisite hand-tooled parts. It was a tremendous experience. At a later meeting, he told me how he managed to cool his combustion chamber with a swirl of gasoline—his method of curtain-cooling, perhaps his most important single invention."

After supper, Goddard and his young friend sat on the veranda. It was a warm New Mexico evening, a summer night admirably equipped with a lightning storm on the horizon, as if it had been designed and staged for the discussion that followed. Homer Boushey recalled:

"It was the sort of night when you felt you could look out and almost touch the stars. It seemed an ideal place to talk of interplanetary flight, and we finally got to that subject. I'm sure I wouldn't have started on this topic if I hadn't sensed it was on his mind too. We rather drifted into it. I felt more and more that I was in the presence of a great and humble man and that I was highly privileged to be hearing what he was saying to me.

"There had been something of a legend about Esther Goddard being a tigress, fierce to protect her husband's secrecy, but I didn't find her this way. The secrecy seemed to be his idea as much as hers, although I recall that in answer to some of my questions, there would be a little pause, the doctor would look at her, and then he would go on to answer.

"What did we talk about? Well, the conversation moved along easily, often seasoned with the professor's wry humor. He spoke first, I think, of what he had done with his liquid fuel devices, then of his efforts to get supersonic flights, and how Nell was still rather unpredictable.

"I remember how hesitant I was about mentioning interplanetary flight. The doctor exchanged glances with Esther and then went on to speak not just of travel to the planets, but of interstellar flight as well. He spoke as if it were merely a matter of work and experiments, and a little patience and understanding by the public generally. He wasn't sure how long it would take for people to understand and support his work, but he felt they would do so in time. He reminded me of the man who plants the seed of a tree, so that others might one day sit in its shade.

"I was curious about the eventual possibility of atomic

energy for rocket flight, without dreaming that we were so close to this source of power. I remember Goddard saying: 'But why try to generate this power on the earth, when we have such an ideal source in the sun?' At first, I didn't quite grasp his idea, but then he began to explain.

"Speaking very quietly, he compared early interstellar ships to the sailing ships of Columbus. Future space craft, he said, might be equipped with a very light, mirror-like sail. It would be opened up in the vacuum of space like a parasol, and there would be nothing to damage it. It would lock on to the sun's rays, and the energy it received might operate a small boiler which would emit a jet of steam, perhaps, and the ship would sail on and on.

"I was astonished to hear this from him, but when I looked over at Esther Goddard, she just nodded pleasantly. If I had read these ideas in a science-fiction magazine, I might have been entertained but skeptical. Instead, I was hearing them from a great physicist as if they were the most natural topics for conversation. At that moment, there were lightning flashes across the sky and the professor turned his discussion to that phenomenon.

"By this time, I had run out of caution completely. I asked the doctor to tell me why he thought mankind ought to explore other planets, or solar systems, or other parts of the universe. Obviously, he had given attention to such questions and seemed rather pleased when I brought them up.

"He allowed that *this* was a speculative field—as if everything he had said before was demonstrable fact. He suggested that one day, far in the future, the sun and its planets might grow cold, or lack sufficient oxygen, or water—and that mankind might need a better soil for survival. Man's survival seemed especially on his mind.

"He declared that man, no matter what system of beliefs might govern him, was at his best as a curious, exploring creature. He thought that man would inevitably benefit by learning the ways of the universe, that he would be better governed by scientific laws rather than by emotional dogmas. The greatest force against man, he said, was the force of human inertia.

"And then he went on to talk of some far-off day when earth people would conquer their inertia and become universal explorers. They would travel like the Pilgrims did in their early voyages to New England, carrying something of human nature to other solar systems, seeking hospitable grounds where they might again propagate the human race.

"He allowed that these voyages would entail enormous self-discipline. The pioneers who set off on such expeditions might find their greatest personal adversary in time itself. They might marry, give birth, grow old and die long before their journey was over; their sons might follow the same course and their grandsons and great-grandsons. Unless man could find a way of postponing death—perhaps by freezing human protoplasm—these original explorers would never reach their ultimate destination, but perhaps the fifth or sixth generation of their descendants would make a successful landing."

It was several nights after his experience before Homer Boushey could spend a full eight hours in sleep. When he flew east the next morning, he remembered the professor calmly discussing an incredible future and his wife Esther nodding quietly in agreement. He had successfully pried open a long-guarded sanctum and released more phantoms than he had planned on. A privileged and also a troubled young man, he wasn't quite sure whether he had heard fantasy or reality on the veranda of Mescalero Ranch.

But a few days later, when he received a brief note from the rocket pioneer, he knew it was reality and that he would do all in his power to advance the endeavors of Goddard. The professor's note concluded with a substantial New England greeting:

"We will be happy to see you whenever you come this way. The latchstring is out."

V

For Goddard, the remarkable meeting with Homer Boushey had come rather late, perhaps too late. But at last he had spoken openly, without distrust, and his immediate feeling was one of relief. Now he would talk to Esther of a time after the war when Boushey, and other bright young men, would join him in rocket research, creating larger Nells for the missions that lay ahead.

Meanwhile, there was work to do. Goddard renewed his efforts to arouse the military to his rocket's potential, while Boushey became his ardent missionary to the Army Air Corps. For more than a year, until the fall of 1941, Boushey made frequent trips to Roswell and labored in Goddard's behalf.

One of Boushey's early letters merely confirmed what the professor already knew, that the armed forces might be interested in specific rocket devices, but were not prepared to sponsor broad-based rocket research. In August 1940, his young friend wrote:

"I . . . gathered the idea that money for any radically new development, or pure research grants, would be most difficult to obtain at this time. This seems to me a very short-sighted policy, but the consideration of augmenting production and greatly increasing present equipment is so acute that I believe Wright Field intends to devote all their efforts along these lines. . . ."

By early October, Boushey was promoted to a captaincy and put in charge of a modest jet propulsion project at the Wright Field Experimental Engineering Station in Dayton. "To me this is the very best news in the world," he wrote enthusiastically. "Perhaps now I shall be in a position to do something more substantial than 'missionary' work."

Boushey was delighted to find that "interest in jet propulsion is developing all around" and urged the professor to take heart. For the Air Corps, at least, "the door is not closed." Unfortunately, they learned, the door was open somewhat wider to the team workers of Cal. Tech than to the scientist-inventor from Roswell.

By the end of 1940, Goddard's proposal of a liquid-fuel, jet-assisted, take-off device for the Air Corps seemed thoroughly rejected. "The matter . . . is closed, unless it is opened up again by General Brett's office," Goddard advised Boushey. "I hope to continue the present research here, as I believe it is the most fundamental approach. We have both exerted ourselves to the utmost this summer, only to arrive at a dead end."

But Boushey was merely spurred on by such dismal declarations. He was convinced that if someone in authority knew the professor's work as he did, the Air Corps would surely support him. After making arrangements with the professor, he flew into Roswell on July 11, 1941, with two Wright Field engineers, Captain Frank Moyers and Alfred Loedding, a civilian Goddard had met at Wright Field.

After cautioning his guests not to expect too much, Goddard said he would show them a static test. But even these experiments were subject to flaws. Once again, Nell balked before strangers, this time because the windblown dust made a lever stick. In his journal Goddard filled in familiar details:

"Test of July 11, 1941: Just before filling, a thunder shower was observed in the east. It appeared to be travelling south, however, increasing in intensity and remaining stationary, and filling was accordingly started.

"There were three spectators from Wright Field: Capts. Boushey and Moyer[s], and Mr. Loed[d]ing. They planned to leave as early as possible in the afternoon, as their plane was too large for the Roswell hangar. The rocket setup in the tower was explained to them, in the morning.

"At about the time the oxygen tank was filled, the gale before the shower arrived, and the air was filled with sand and dust. . . .

"When the igniter key was pressed, the igniter fired after the usual time interval. Gasoline then came from the nozzle, and the high pitch from the motors could be heard, but no flame was visible. A large cloud of white vapor then appeared from the cotter pin safety valve, and also from below the oxygen tank, and the yellow and green keys were pressed, to stop the run. . . .

"It was not possible to examine the rocket, as [they] required immediate transport to the airport. . . . On returning, it was found that the oxygen fused wire release had operated, but that the levers thus released had stuck, being clogged with sand that had blown into them during a sudden squall just before the test."

A week later, Boushey was back in Eden Valley, deputized by Moyers and Loedding to witness another run. Nell and the winds were better behaved and Boushey, attending his first successful firing, was overwhelmed at the sight and sound of the "big" rocket in action.

"I had been out to the tower before," Boushey recalled later, when he was a brigadier general for the Air Force and its first director of Advanced Technology. "I had seen where the blast of the rocket had fused the prairie sands, even melting the cement in the gas deflector they called the 'bathtub.' I had heard Esther and the doctor talk casually of the rocket as 'Nell'—'the girl that ain't been done right by.' But I was hardly prepared for what I saw.

"The static test in the valley began with a mild explosion," he went on. "Then there was a roar, a yellow flame, and the ground started to shake. Smoke and dust swirled up as the rocket motor took hold. I had never seen anything like it before. Next to me, the professor was solemnly reading his dials. I glanced at his wife. Esther was standing quietly, her motion picture camera pointed at the blasting rocket."

When the motor grabbed and took hold, Boushey jumped out of the barricaded dugout and started toward the tower— "to get a better look," he said. The professor quickly pulled him back to the shelter. There was no whimsical reference to "Nell." The rocket was unsafe until the run was finished, Goddard said sharply. He had managed his volatile experiments for two decades without accident and had no intention of inviting hazard now.

On earlier visits, Boushey sat fascinated through Esther Goddard's "home movies"—her 16 mm. films of Nell's development, her trials and rare, occasional flights. After witnessing a static test, however, Boushey needed no further proof.

Back at Wright Field, the lieutenant prepared and submitted a glowing report to his superiors on Goddard's rocket. He recommended its immediate modification for jet-assisted take-offs. Small, solid-fuel JATO devices, then being produced at the Jet Propulsion Laboratories of Cal. Tech, were delivering a 50-pound thrust. In Eden Valley, Boushey had just seen a rocket produce a thrust of 825 pounds.

Privately, Homer Boushey shared Goddard's conviction that liquid-fuel rocket research deserved broad government support, that it offered far more than modest military hardware. But he confined his recommendation to JATO, his service's limited interest at that time. If the Army Air Corps accepted a little Goddard now, he reasoned, perhaps it would later accept a great deal more.

While Boushey's report was being shuttled among the in-baskets and out-baskets of the Army Air Corps, the Navy sent Lieutenant Fischer back to the Goddard establishment. Since his first meeting with Goddard in 1939, two years before, Fischer had immersed himself in the study of jet propulsion. To the professor, the return call must have seemed as overwhelming as Fischer's earlier long-distance call on Cal. Tech's aerodynamicist, Dr. von Kármán. "Nobody had ever asked me before for a fellowship by telephone," von Kármán said later. "I was so impressed, I gave it to him."

Goddard was also impressed by Fischer's directness. Speaking for the Navy, the flier extracted the professor's views on a variety of topics: on rocket engines to replace propeller-driven aircraft; on the fueling and feeding of combustion chambers; on velocities needed to escape the earth's atmosphere.

Under Fischer's questioning, Goddard listened, responded, hedged, responded again. "I decided not to ask him about space flight," Fischer recalled. "I just assumed he wasn't spending his life on a mere 'meteorological rocket,' but had the wisdom to know he was ahead of his time."

Fischer and Goddard quickly disposed of lesser questions. The Navy was prepared to offer the professor the rank of captain, together with the appropriate pay and perquisites. Goddard said he was "flattered," but doubted that either the rank or the honor would improve the quality of his research, or necessarily benefit the Navy. He turned his attention to more substantial problems.

The Navy's Bureau of Aeronautics was not yet sold on the potential of rocket power for long-range projectiles or as the driving force for manned aircraft, Fischer admitted. He planned, much like Boushey, to educate the service and then to open the door for Goddard. Meanwhile he had a Navy contract to offer for a liquid-fuel JATO.

A firm Navy contract seemed promising, as Fischer described it. His immediate senior officer was Commander Calvin M. Bolster, chief of the Ships Installations Division of the Bureau of Aeronautics. Bolster, too, had studied aerodynamics at Cal. Tech and had a good background in rocket technology. He had already assigned some development work in solid-fuel JATOs to two industrial firms: an enterprising west coast organization called "Aerojet," led by von Kármán and his former students; and an east coast corporation named "Reaction Motors," established by members of the American Rocket Society. Bolster now wished to "round out" the Navy's effort, said Fischer, by enlisting the dean of jet propulsion, Dr. Goddard, and his liquid-fuel rocket.

The professor thanked Fischer for his interest. He would be happy to come to Washington to discuss the matter at the Navy's convenience. At the Roswell airport, he and Esther watched the lieutenant's plane as it taxied off, lifted in the sky and turned toward the east. As he helped Esther into the front seat of their car and started home, Goddard thought of the young flier's vigor and of a sudden felt old.

VI

That summer Esther saw signs of a change in her husband. Among their close friends and at Rotary luncheons in Roswell, Goddard still displayed his gentle humor. With his crew, he proceeded patiently, in apparent good spirits about his pump-system rocket. There were no outward complaints. But when they were alone, Esther was aware of some inner distress. Their old whimsical exchanges—"Here I am with the wheelbarrow to pick up the pieces"—no longer stirred his amusement. One Saturday evening they sat outside, listening to the festivities of a family of Spanish-American laborers who occupied an adobe outbuilding behind the ranchhouse. They watched several battered jalopies rattle up to the hut and disgorge celebrants bearing jugs of wine, guitars and accordions. The singing and dancing went on lustily for hours. Esther recalled his wistful comment that night: "I wish we could let ourselves go like that."

Toward the end of the summer, however, they felt lifted and reassured. The promised letter from Fischer arrived, officially inviting Goddard to Washington for a conference. Meanwhile, Guggenheim again renewed his support.

The problems of Nell continued. On May 8, 1941, she had made a short flight, which would be her last. In August, Goddard tried twice more to fly his pump-driven engine. On the first attempt, a sparkplug collapsed:

"Test of August 10, 1941 (P–34):

"Flight Test . . .

"The rocket started with a mild explosion. Immediately afterward, the whiteness left the flame, which became large and sooty. The run was then stopped.

"The porcelain on the sparkplug was found to have been broken off back to about $1/4$ in. from the end of the core. Chips off the oxygen turbine vanes indicated that the broken piece or pieces had passed through this turbine . . . and resulted in little or no flow through the oxygen line."

A week later, after repairs, he tried again:

"Test of August 17, 1941 (P–35):

"Repeat Flight Test . . .

"Up to the initial explosion, the start was the same as usual. Just after this, and before the hoses had been pulled off, the oxygen flow apparently stopped, and a large gasoline flame appeared. The two shutoff keys were not pressed immediately, in the hope that the run would start up again. In the meantime a sharp explosion was heard, and the casings were blown off, probably from the mixture from the gas generator or from the pump seals. The stop keys were pressed. . . .

"Examination of the rocket at the shop disclosed faulty functioning of the shutoff part of the main oxygen valve, which probably was the cause of failure of the two preceding tests. . . ."

During these weeks, the professor was unusually solemn. At first, Esther believed that the grueling rocket trials alone were testing the limit of his endurance. Then she considered another possibility, her new lessons in flying.

For ten years, Esther had seen able pilots landing in Roswell to call on the professor: the Lindberghs and the Guggenheims, flying in to see a test; James Doolittle, to discuss the possibility of better fuels; private and military fliers, to talk about jet propulsion. Inevitably, her imagination was captured by a chance to get her own pilot's license.

When she enrolled for evening preflight courses in 1940 at the Roswell High School, her husband had given his grudging approval. The lessons, he said, might be "useful and improving," and the required mathematics would do no harm. By fall of that year, however, his attitude had stiffened considerably.

"I told Bob it was time to take my physical examination and start flying lessons," Esther recalled. "He looked at me and said, 'You don't mean you're actually going to *fly* a plane?' I said, 'Of course, dear! What do you suppose I'm taking these lessons for?'

"He seemed to feel better when I came back from my physical. They had found everything fine except my eyes. I am very nearsighted and Bob, much relieved, thought this would finish it off. But the examining physician agreed to send in my application without comment and it came back by return mail, approved. Even I was surprised."

With her instructor, Esther began flying a small trainer plane out of the Roswell airport and around the town. On one practice flight when she looked down from the plane and saw her husband and his crew preparing for a static test, she modestly dipped her wings.

"My instructor was impressed," she remembered, "but Bob was nervous about the whole thing. He asked me please to avoid the tower during firings, as the rocket sent up tremendous drafts of hot air which could be dangerous."

She was within a few hours of making her first solo flight when the Army Air Corps took over the Roswell flying field and civilian lessons were suspended.

"When I told Bob I wouldn't be able to finish my course or get my pilot's license, he was obviously pleased," Esther related. " 'You don't really want me to fly.' I told him. 'No,' he said in a low voice. 'If anything happens to me, you are the only one who can carry on.' "

VII

Late in August 1941, Goddard again set out for the east, this time by train. Following Guggenheim's suggestion, he was still trying to locate an engineer for his Roswell shop. The Navy, he heard from Fischer, would now be interested in discussing a contract. So, said Boushey, would the Army Air Corps. If Goddard's pump-driven rocket was not quite in motion, at least he was. He had no doubt that his personal orbit was shifting.

He found time for New England, for Boston, for a return visit to the past, jotting down in his diary: "Went to Roxbury, walked over to Forest St. to Dudley St. station." On the way he paused to take photographs of childhood scenes, which he showed later to Esther. Forest Street had grown shabby and crowded in the half century since he lived there; his home seemed much smaller than he remembered, as a place revisited often does. He stopped at the corner drugstore where, as a boy, he had bought the new, lightweight metal called aluminum, tried to melt it over the kitchen stove to make a balloon, noting of his experiment: "Failior crowns enterprise." He had not misspelled the word again.

Across the Charles River, in Cambridge, he tried at the Massachusetts Institute of Technology, without success, to find an engineer. Then he went south to Indian Head, Maryland, where Dr. Hickman with his aides, Major Skinner and Lieutenant Uhl, were now seeking to improve his old recoilless gun. He watched their tests in the powder factory's deserted valley, near the small building where he had pressed smokeless powder into discs twenty years before. He still remembered the anguished lieutenant who warned him that he was violating the Navy's safety regulations.

Goddard was fascinated by the new weapon, the bazooka. He congratulated Hickman and his assistants after seeing it take off with its shaped-charge nose and blast its way through several inches of armorplate. The young officers seemed pleased, having that long-distance look about them that he, no doubt, had shown years before.

Unlike his previous trips to the capital city, Goddard, in early September 1941, was preceded by the drumbeating of his young missionaries. Boushey and Fischer had apparently accomplished some results. "They seem to have heard about me," Goddard wrote to his wife.

He was invited to Army Air Corps headquarters, where he was cordially greeted by the young major who had received him coldly only a few months before. The Air Corps officers proposed that they meet for further discussions.

On September 6, Lieutenant Fischer presented the professor to his senior Naval officers, who helped to resolve a few problems. They wanted Goddard to begin work at once for the Navy on a liquid-fuel jet-assist rocket. Negotiations began.

Judging by Goddard's diary of September 5 and 6, Fischer was an active shepherd:

"Sept. 5—Saw Major Chidlaw. Told to call up after lunch. . . . Saw Senator Walsh. . . . Called Air Corps several times in p.m. Lunch at Union Station. Went to dinner at Army and Navy Club with Lieut. and Mrs. Fischer.

"Sept. 6—Called at the Air Corps office at 8 a.m. Conferred with Lieut. Fischer and Capt. Dane of the Air Corps. Contract decided upon. . . .

"Went with Lieut. and Mrs. Fischer to inspect a PBY

scout plane at Anacostia, and went to the shops, etc. at Annapolis. . . ."

On his return to Roswell, Goddard wrote several letters about his negotiations in Washington:

To Dr. Hickman:

"The Bureau of Aeronautics contract went through. It is for a year's work, with six months to deliver the goods. Both Army and Navy contracts were favorably considered. The Navy one went through, as they had first written a letter of intent . . . and they had an immediate plane application.

"Lieut. Fischer was very energetic for the Navy."

To Captain Boushey he wrote twice. On September 15:

"As you may know by this time, I have a contract with the Navy Department on the take-off development, and a tie-up with the Army Air Corps for the delivery of a duplicate unit. The letter of intent was sent by the Navy Department before the Army had prepared a similar letter. . . ."

And, again to Boushey, on October 28:

"I too am sorry at the turn of events, as I had my mind made up for a somewhat different procedure. It is a pleasure to know that you would still like to work with me some time, and who knows but what it may come to pass? There is certainly no one with whom I should enjoy working more. . . ."

Homer Boushey had not met Fink Fischer, nor did he know of his rival's determined and enterprising approach to Robert Goddard. By the time he was aware of it, it was already too late. The men of the sea, not the men of the air, had acquired the man of space. They had acquired him for a somewhat larger fee than the Dutch paid the American Indians for Manhattan Island, and with about as little awareness of the frontiers that lay beyond.

Boushey wrote to Goddard, saying he hoped he could work with the professor on great rockets once the war was over. The Air Corps flier made his last stop in Roswell shortly before Goddard began his Navy work. He landed in a light Ercoupe plane he was taking out to the west coast, assigned to test some small rockets developed by Dr. von Kármán and his Aerojet team. After Boushey's visit, Goddard knew that the young pilot would be willing to fly one day to virtually any destination the professor might make possible.

Later, Goddard heard of Boushey's accomplishment in California. He had attached several of Aerojet's solid-fuel JATOs to his light plane, an Ercoupe, and had taken off successfully. On the last test run, 6 of the 50-pound thrust JATOs were attached to the underside of each wing. To make the demonstration convincing, Boushey had the propeller removed entirely. When the JATOs took hold, the Ercoupe took off and flew a short distance. Boushey became the first American to fly exclusively on rocket power.

The new Navy contract seemed reasonably attractive, and soon went into effect. It provided for payments of $4,000 a month for the first six months and a total of $16,000 for the second six months. The Army Air Corps would share the cost with the Navy during the first half year and receive, in return, full reports and the results of Goddard's work. The Navy would have the option of requiring the professor to move his establishment from New Mexico to Annapolis, Maryland, if it seemed necessary. The professor was expected to enlarge his shop, increase his crew and produce the preliminary model of a new rocket take-off unit, powered by liquid fuels and equipped with his novel system of variable thrust.

The new jet unit, for all the ingenuity it required, was not precisely what Goddard had hoped to offer. Before converting his vertical Nell to the military's horizontal version, he decided to try once more for altitude. It was the week of his fifty-ninth birthday, which the Goddards celebrated with the Marshalls and Paul Horgan in Roswell.

October 1941 began as "the rainiest in New Mexico's history," the professor wrote in his diary. But the skies were clear enough on the morning of October 10 for him to try one more flight. In all too many details, from the jolting trip into Eden Valley to the crew's hopeful wait for Nell's performance, the attempt followed a familiar course, with Goddard's technical notes as its official benediction:

"At the usual time after the igniter key was pressed, a moderately large gasoline flame appeared. There was little or no initial explosion. This flame died down, and a strong flame followed immediately. The white and red lights quickly appeared. After a wait of 4 or 5 sec., the release key was pressed. The rocket rose about a foot and stopped. Something appeared to be wrong, and the stopping keys were pressed, even though the main release lever had operated and the rocket switch and possibly also the jacks in the plugs for short-circuiting had been disconnected. The flame stopped at this time, except for the Dow-metal of the gasoline pump, which continued to burn.

"It was found that the lever on the control that freed the hose pull-off lever was bent. The bending was sufficient to prevent the arm moving out of the two guide or support pieces, and thus releasing the hoses. It seems likely that a flight would have been obtained if the hoses had been released, for the lift quickly exceeded the weight by at least 200 lbs."

There would be no more tests of the pump-equipped rocket. It was now oiled, wrapped, crated and reluctantly put aside.

Some day, the professor told his crew, they would get back to the vertical-thrust rocket. They would eliminate its flaws, assure its reliability. They would try again for great flights that had come almost within their reach. It was still a matter of time, he said, closing his experimental notebook on the P series and turning to the development of the military's rocket.

"I do not think we can carry out further flight tests at present," Goddard wrote to Harry Guggenheim. "I am accordingly storing the rocket and all the flight equipment and shall endeavor to make further flight tests when the Government work is less pressing."

His letter to Guggenheim was dated October 19, 1941. In his diary that night, there is an odd omission. It was one of the few times in forty years that he neglected to write: "Anniversary Day."

Was it, perhaps, a self-rendered verdict? Thus far, this high, for this high man in his lifetime. But higher, a great deal higher, by men to follow. . . .

VIII

He was glad to be counted at last in the hubbub of the nation preparing its defenses. His six-month contract with the Navy and the Army Air Corps would not begin officially until November 21. But in late September, he was already at work on the assisted take-off device: preparing blueprints; assigning models to his machinists; arranging for the expansion of his shop, his testing facilities and his crew.

Earlier, the Goddards had planned to settle permanently in Roswell. They bought Mescalero Ranch, which they had rented for almost a decade, and called on a local building contractor named Swaim to assist in remodeling it. Now the professor asked Mr. Swaim to help him enlarge the shop. When they were done, the building was double its former size and constructed as soundly as a New England church.

The new static test stand, an ingenious array of contrivances, was built to the rear of the shop. Its design was a pleasure Goddard reserved for himself. He hoped to eliminate the time-consuming trips to Eden Valley for static tests. He "doped" out a scheme to muffle the new rocket's roar from his neighbors, a task as formidable as installing a silencer on a coyote. Later, describing his success to the Army Air Corps, he revealed that he had never lost his boyhood delight in contrivances:

"A testing stand has been constructed on which the test unit is placed, free to move horizontally. The jet motor is held by a ring on the open end of the nozzle, engaged by split rings on an 8-inch channel iron. The test unit, integral with this channel iron, is provided with six steel rollers which rest on two angle irons serving as a track. This track is supported by iron posts threaded into I-beams set in a concrete platform. Other I-beams in this platform serve to hold any necessary equipment.

"An underground muffler has been made to deaden the noise when larger thrusts are to be measured. The blast is directed downward, through a hole in a concrete block, into a tunnel formed of 22-inch diameter oil drums, covered with concrete. The tunnel is L-shaped, and 26 yards long.

"The track on the testing stand is provided with two $3\frac{5}{8}$ inches o.d. metal bellows, of 15.6 square inch combined areas, for measuring the thrust. . . . Two threaded brass rods, on the channel iron of the thrust unit, engage these bellows. The entire pressure system, including the pressure gauge, is kept filled with automobile brake fluid."

Before the new project began, the professor hired a design engineer from Chicago, although the man was slightly deaf, not accustomed to rockets and hesitant about joining the project. "His reaction was that he did not see how he could be of use," Goddard wrote to Guggenheim, "as he considered that I had already done 90 per cent of the work. I pointed out to him that the remaining 10 per cent was vitally important . . . involving the factor of reliability, which was decidedly an engineering matter."

Goddard worked with his Chicago engineer through the

final tests of the pump rocket and into the early stages of the take-off device. The chief problem was the man's inexperience with the vital factor of weight in rocket design. After examining his engineer's blueprints, which usually included a few steel reinforcements and bracings, the professor would say, gently at first and then shouting to make himself heard: "It's too heavy! Too heavy!"

"It was about then that I first noticed the huskiness in Bob's voice," Esther recalled. "We associated it, at the time, with his efforts to make himself heard."

When the engineer left, Goddard looked for the sort of recruits he had favored all along—young, practical mechanics and, whenever he could find one, an experienced machinist. For a while there was a lively turnover of talent in the Mescalero shop until Goddard finally took on three novices—Lowell Randall and Glenn Loughner, high school graduates; Randall's friend George Bode, a filling station attendant; and A. P. Freund, an experienced instrument maker from the Iowa Medical School and the National Cash Register Company. These men remained with Goddard until his death.

With an enlarged shop, new crew members and an abundance of ideas, the Goddard establishment in the fall of 1941 temporarily ran out of funds. The Guggenheim Foundation advanced $7,000 until the military's payments would begin, but these funds were soon gone and the first check from Washington was still to arrive. The Goddards arranged personal loans at the Roswell bank to keep the shop going until the government funds came through.

Like the veterans of Goddard's crew, Bode shortly learned that the scientist regarded money solely as a means for rocket research. Nothing was wasted, everything was salvaged in his use of limited funds, although sometimes his administration of finance took an eccentric turn.

"On payday," Bode recalled, "the doctor would call us one at a time to his desk, check his notes to see how many hours we'd worked, and then compute the figures on his slide rule. One week, my pay would come to $24.78; the next week, for the same number of hours, it would be $26.36. When I asked about this, the professor explained that slide rules were not always precise, but that it would all come out even in the end. In fact, it did."

After the promissory missile of her husband's dream, Esther expected that the small aircraft rocket might seem a letdown. Instead, he turned to his military task with renewed vigor, an intensity that increased as the weeks went by.

At the end of November, an experimental model was ready for a static test. Although he modified and adapted devices from his vertical rocket where possible, there were ample and tantalizing problems with the horizontal engine.

For one thing, the liquid fuel and oxidizer had to be force-fed rapidly into the combustion chamber and rapidly ignited. Otherwise, there would be sudden explosions. He solved this problem with ingenious valves, seals, pressure tanks and igniters.

Above all, he considered the safety of the pilot who would operate the unit. For years, Goddard had theorized on safety measures against the day when a manned rocket would take off in flight. Now, turning theory into hardware, he devised a system for flushing out the combustion chamber between runs with carbon dioxide to prevent flarebacks, and a system of cut-off valves and interlocking relays, operated by solenoids, to govern the firing sequence.

Mastering the Navy's requirements was simpler than meeting his own. He could not resist an added refinement. His new model would not merely give the plane an initial thrust. It must also furnish the pilot with controls to vary the thrust as he chose, to turn the rocket on and off, like a faucet, in mid-flight.

He tried his first test run on December 3, 1941. It was

Prior to Capt. Homer A. Boushey's pioneer rocket plane flight in a propellerless Ercoupe powered by 12 solid-fuel rockets; March Field, Cal., August 12, 1941. From left: Clark B. Millikan, Martin M. Summerfield, Theodore von Kármán, Frank J. Malina, Boushey. [65]

Test of Goddard liquid-fuel jet-assisted takeoff unit on a Navy PBY-2, Severn River, Annapolis, Md., September 23, 1942. [66]

At the Naval Engineering Experimental Station, Annapolis, Md., July 1942. From left, front row: Campbell, Ljungquist, Goddard, Alden, C. Mansur; back row: Freund, Randall, Bode, Loughner. [67]

The Goddards at home, Tydings-on-the-Bay, Md., 1943. [68]

ABOVE: Goddard's variable thrust rocket motor mounted for static test, Mescalero Ranch, March 9, 1942. BELOW: The X-15 rocket research plane, with variable thrust, landing at Lake Muroc, Cal., 1961. [69, 70]

The U. S. Army "bazooka," an outgrowth of Goddard's World War I research. [71]

Russian truck-mounted rocket launcher of World War II. [72]

ABOVE: A German V-1 "buzz bomb," captured in Germany before final assembly, April 1945. [73] BELOW: British scientists inspecting a V-2 in Germany, October 1945. [74]

OVER: The Goddard 1935 and 1940 rockets displayed at the National Air Museum, Smithsonian Institution, Washington, D.C. [75]

Robert H. Goddard at Paxtc
Mass., about 1943. [76]

BELOW: Group at dedication of t
Goddard Wing of the Roswe
New Mexico, Museum, April 195
From left, A. S. Campbell, Wer
her von Braun, Lowell N. Randa
Esther C. Goddard, Charles V
Mansur, and N. T. Ljungqui
The structure on the left is a cc
ner of Dr. Goddard's launchi
tower. [77]

promising. He was improving his "variable-thrust" mechanism four days later, when the Japanese struck Pearl Harbor.

While listening to news bulletins on their radio that evening, the Goddards learned that a general in charge of defense projects in the southwestern states was ordering government contractors to post guards at their factories. The inventor needed no such reminders. He had always favored security, suspecting for years that the Germans, in particular, were closely following his work. Starting that night, he and his men took turns sleeping overnight in the shop until a dependable watchman could be hired.

The United States was now at war on two oceans with Germany, Italy and Japan. The New England professor once more stepped up his effort. He built a pump-operated model within a few weeks, tested it, promptly discarded it. However desirable, it would take too long to perfect. There simply wasn't time, he decided with rare impatience.

In February 1942, he was called to the Roswell freight yard to sign for a large crate from the Navy Department. It was part of the hull of a PBY "flying boat," the Navy plane for which he was designing his take-off booster. In a letter to Guggenheim on February 21, he commented:

"I may add in confidence that a portion of a PBY hull was received here yesterday for study. It evidently came from Pearl Harbor, judging from the bullet holes. I can think of nothing that would give me greater satisfaction than to have it contribute something to the inevitable retaliation."

A few days after the Navy's PBY hull arrived, Goddard drew Claude Simpson aside in the lobby of the Nickson Hotel after the weekly Rotary luncheon. Simpson, an executive of the Roswell Chamber of Commerce, years later remembered their discussion:

"Bob Goddard told me he was doing some classified work, that he had to spend all his time now at the shop and wouldn't be able to get to our luncheons. He said he was sorry, and I had no doubt he was.

"He said he would have to drop his membership in Rotary, but didn't want any announcement made, and I shouldn't pass on what he was doing. This was a little strange, because I wouldn't have known what to pass on.

" 'Claude,' he told me, 'this mustn't go any further. Just let me drop out quietly.'

"I told Bob we'd all miss him. I did what he asked about not saying anything, and he didn't show up for meetings after that. After a while, the members didn't ask about him any more."

IX

Goddard had emerged for a while from his isolation. Now he went back to it contentedly. Except for seeing a few close friends, he and his wife returned to the pattern of their early days in New Mexico.

The take-off project now filled the professor's hours. Spring came, but there were no more painting expeditions into the mountains, no more diary entries on the colors of the prairie, or a brook opening up, or the heat striations on a dusty road, or the shades and shadows of the hills.

Goddard was aware of the progress of others, of Aerojet on the west coast with its solid fuels; of Reaction Motors in the east and its "regenerative" liquid-fuel motor, heavier, but possibly more foolproof, than his own. Neither of these motors, he was sure, could achieve the potential thrust of his own. The military was still exploring which approach, if any, would be finally adopted.

For the Goddards, a focus of technical and esthetic pleasures was watching the fiery thrust of the new rockets; the color, shape and size of their flames; the telling signs of successful combustion.

Esther, photographing or watching the trials in her back-yard, looked for what she termed "the beautiful sight of a clean, white, sharply-pointed flame." Of one turbulent, roaring test she remarked to her husband: "What a lovely little flame that is!"

Rather pleased, Goddard devoted a paragraph in his notes that evening to the phenomenon:

"The flame, again, appeared a short time after pressing the starting key, with a quick but gradual increase in length of flame and sound. There was no evidence of an explosion or overshooting of thrust. The flame was steady for the entire 12 seconds, and was about three feet long, tapering to a point, and showed steady striations or standing waves. . . ."

The static tests at the ranch continued through the first five months of 1942. Within that time, Goddard had fulfilled the requirements of his preliminary military contract.

At the end of June, he was able to report that "Test No. 27 meets the requirements of the above contract as to thrust and duration, and possibly as to weight." The Goddard take-off device achieved a run of 22 seconds, with an average thrust of 820 pounds. But he had not yet forgotten another rocket, the one he had crated and put aside. As he wrote to Guggenheim: ". . . the engineering we are doing now will make possible more reliable operation later, if and when attention can be turned to the high altitude problem."

For the moment, Goddard was content with his military work. Based on static tests, his rocket, theoretically at least, could successfully lift a heavily loaded aircraft into flight from a small runway, or from the rolling deck of a carrier or from a restricted body of water. The next stages still lay ahead: to perfect the take-off unit for actual flight, on an airplane with a pilot aboard; and to engineer the device for manufacture, if the military so decided.

In his June 1942 report to the Army Air Corps, he promised a flight demonstration two months hence. Meanwhile, his own plans had undergone a change.

In April, Fischer arrived to inspect the Goddard operation for the Navy. The lieutenant, who would shortly become a lieutenant commander, believed in running a taut ship. In reviewing Goddard's contract with his superiors, he agreed that the Navy's option of moving the professor east should now take place.

The Bureau of Aeronautics, Fischer said, wished to coordinate its individual rocket experiments at the Naval Engineering Experiment Station at Annapolis, Maryland. There, at the Severn River, the professor would have ample space to adapt his unit to Navy seaplanes and also pilots to test it in flight. Besides, he would be nearer the center of things, ready to work on other developments as soon as the opportunity came.

That evening Goddard briskly outlined the Navy's plan to his wife. She was troubled about his health, his growing fatigue, his frequent colds, the persistent hoarseness in his voice. Without consulting a physician, she knew that the humid lowlands of Annapolis would be a poor exchange for New Mexico's climate.

What she spoke of instead was whether the work could not be done as effectively in Roswell, where they were now so well established. She had barely begun to list her hesitations, when he offhandedly brushed them aside with the cliché of that decade: "Esther, don't you know there's a war on?"

Lieutenant Fischer's recollection of Goddard's reaction to the transfer was somewhat different. In retrospect, he also questioned the wisdom of summoning Goddard from Roswell.

"At the time, it seemed the best course," said Fischer. "We needed the JATO and it was all I could offer him. There was no hope then in pressing for a major grant for Goddard and his big rocket, to keep him in Roswell to continue his work.

"During the war, millions were spent on all kinds of projects, but at the time we were still saddled by thinking in terms of minimum budgets, of getting the most for a dollar, of producing immediate, practical hardware. As it turned out, if we had been able to put Goddard on the long-range missile, we would have been years ahead."

As he left Roswell, Fischer was puzzled by the tone of the professor's response to the requested move. Was it, in a way, like that of a football player, long kept on the bench, but finally sent in to play? Or was it that Goddard saw more likelihood of advancing his work in the east than on the prairie? Or was it, perhaps, something more deepseated in the professor's nature, a need to give at last what he had to offer?

What Goddard said was:

"I was wondering when you'd ask me."

X

The Goddards' departure from Roswell was as unexpected in the community as his arrival. He dispatched two letters, the first to his friend and sponsor. To Harry Guggenheim he wrote:

". . . we shall be ordered to move the crew and much of the equipment to a Naval experiment station in the East, possibly sometime in June. I am assuming that you will have no objection to the transfer, and later return, of the equipment.

"I am very proud of the remodeled shop and the new testing arrangements, and would be very glad to have you and Mrs. Guggenheim come here to see them before they are dismantled. Please let me know if this is at all possible."

The second letter, a statement to the editor of the Roswell

Daily Record, went out two days before the Goddards' departure. It read:

"Dr. Robert H. Goddard and the staff associated with him in experimental work for the Guggenheim Foundation will leave shortly for the East to undertake special work. They expect to return to Roswell within a number of months. Both Dr. and Mrs. Goddard expressed regret at leaving even temporarily a place where so many kindnesses have been shown them."

Then, as if fearing to close his statement on an over-personal note, he suggested to the editor: "If you think best, omit the last sentence."

Among those in Roswell who noted the professor's departure was old Dan Wilmot, proprietor of the Mabie-Lowrey hardware store, which had long supplied the rocket shop with its wares. When the account was closed, Wilmot observed that the last item on the Goddard ledger sheets was almost the same as the first, twelve years before:

August 20, 1930	4 ft. chain	$ .80
	1 padlock	1.25
July 2, 1942	4 #500 padlocks	$2.00

By the end of June, Goddard's crew had crated the shop equipment and assorted rockets for shipment to Annapolis. On July 3, Goddard went down to the Roswell freight yard to check the boxcar loaded with his machinery. An engineer pulled back the door and the professor peered inside and then said:

"Fine. Close it up."

The next morning, July 4, 1942, the Goddards left Roswell for the long drive east.

12. THE REALITY OF TOMORROW

From the solitude of the New Mexico prairies, they entered the stream of traffic moving along the continental highways, congesting and funneling into the nation's arsenals, training camps and headquarters cities. Everyone seemed on the move. At a filling station in Fort Smith, Arkansas, the physicist, driving east, met a chemist, driving west, both on military orders. They marveled at the government's penchant for picking up professors and depositing them elsewhere, almost anywhere except where they happened to be. It was seven months since Pearl Harbor.

The roads were especially dense as the Goddards came near Washington. It was Thursday afternoon, July 9, 1942, when they reached the gates of the Naval Engineering Experiment Station in a wooded section of Annapolis, Maryland. A siren sounded a practice air raid alert. They were held back momentarily by a sentry.

For months, Goddard had been disturbed by rumors that his work was being bypassed. There was little comfort in the suggestion of Thompson and others that his own proprietary attitude was possibly hindering him. Perhaps he was proprietary. During his last years in Roswell, he had applied for twenty-two more United States patents on his inventions. But he had not emerged from Eden Valley to be shelved for the war in the stacks of the Patent Office. He meant to be reckoned with.

He had left Roswell with singular expectations, his wife said. "He wanted to help and knew he had something really wonderful to offer. He felt there were barriers not of his own making and he meant to get close to them and try to remove them." Through his modest Navy work, he would show something of the massive power of his liquid-fuel rocket; perhaps, eventually, it would be put to better use. She remembered his saying, with rare truculence: "In the east, I'll stand in the middle of the road. They won't be able to pass me by."

But with all this private bravado, Goddard was now a passenger on the military's wondrous whirligig, and closer to steerage than helping to steer the bewildering mechanism. In the summer of 1942, when he arrived at the naval station, Vannevar Bush was still mulling over proposals for rocket development offered by a variety of advisers. Bush was possibly unaware that, consigned to Annapolis and almost forgotten, was a physicist who had offered most of these proposals through two wars.

Within three years, as the war neared its end, America's rocket development and manufacture would reach an annual expenditure of more than $1 billion. But even this effort was far outdistanced by rocket endeavors long under way in Germany and Russia. In the United States, the greatest research skills and funds were being devoted to the creation of atomic energy and the world's most revolutionary bomb. It was a massive program but it overlooked the rocket as the future prime carrier of an atomic explosive.

In 1942, as Goddard waited at the Annapolis gates, no

one could foretell these events. Young Lieutenant Fischer cleared the professor and his wife into the engineering station. Allowing a moment for pleasantries, Fischer led them through a barbed-wire enclosure to a building on a concrete jetty at the edge of the Severn River. Here the professor was to set up his machine shop and testing stands, where his rocket blasts would carry safely over the water.

Leaving the empty shop, Fischer briskly invited the Goddards to witness a static test of a rocket being developed by the Jet Propulsion Laboratory of Cal. Tech. It was not a solid- but a liquid-fuel device, the first the professor had seen built by someone else.

"We watched the test, but Bob didn't say much," Esther recalled. "He seemed rather relieved. It was powered by aniline and nitric acid, a mixture he never cared for. He felt it was dangerous to handle and that it lacked the power of his oxygen-gasoline. It was a sidestep from what he had already demonstrated."

The lieutenant left them at Carvel Hall, an Annapolis hotel catering to Navy guests. That same evening, though he was barely unpacked, Goddard was projected on what Fischer called "a special Navy mission." He was to proceed at once to New York City to inspect a rocket invention, and then to visit a scientist at the Naval Torpedo Station in Providence, Rhode Island.

His diary for the next few days reveals a willing but bemused scientist, caught up in the Navy's peculiar urgencies:

"July 9, . . . went to Carvel Hall; got a room, had dinner (lamb chops) . . . and went to station B[altimore] & Ann[apolis] and went to Baltimore. Took sleeper to Phila[delphia] to arrive at 3.47 a.m. Blackout, at station.

"July 10, Was awakened at 3.10 a.m.! Sat in station at Phila. until 6.30. Had breakfast in station, and sat until 10 a.m. Went to Navy Yard and met Fischers, etc. Took train for New York; dinner on train. Took taxi and saw Maynor's test. Went to station and took train for Providence. Supper in new, two-table-room dining car, and went to Narragansett Hotel in Providence at 12.50.

"July 11, Had breakfast in Narragansett Hotel, and went out to Torpedo Station. Went over work with Dr. Canfield. Lunch in the cafeteria, and came back to Providence on the bus. Had supper, steak, in station, walked around park near station, read paper, and took 10.7 train for Baltimore. (Good singing in men's room of station.)

"July 12, Sun., had breakfast at B&Ann. station in Baltimore and went to Annapolis in a.m. . . ."

Back at the engineering station, Goddard greeted his crew, newly arrived and housed temporarily in a trailer camp. Meanwhile, Lieutenant Fischer had located quarters for the Goddards on the outskirts of the crowded city, where they lived for three months, before moving to a more commodious house in a nearby community called Tydings-on-the-Bay.

As an independent inventor, Goddard had always set his own pace. Now it was being set for him. When the lathes, drill presses and other machinery arrived by freight from Roswell and were installed in the shop, Fischer urged him to put his crew on a seven-day week. Goddard declined, offering a firm opinion that an unrelieved schedule would exhaust his men and hamper, rather than help, the work.

"It took him time to get used to the Navy," recalled Oley Ljungquist. "We had been there a month and already fired a test run when the doctor got a telegram forwarded from Roswell asking us to leave for Annapolis. 'That's the way the Navy works,' I said. 'That's not the way we work,' he said. He often fretted about paper work and inspections and the time clocks we had to punch."

The Navy assigned formal labels to the crew, but they continued to work together informally, as they had before. Most of his men stayed with Goddard throughout the war: Nils T. Ljungquist, superintendent; Arthur P. Freund, toolmaker;

Charles W. Mansur, welding foreman; Lowell N. Randall, assembly foreman; Albert S. Campbell, special machinist; and George F. Bode, assemblyman.

In August, the take-off rocket was blasting admirably on the test stand, its roar sounding over the Severn River to the Naval Academy and beyond it to the gilt-domed state capitol. The gauges were recording the required 800 pounds of thrust at 20 seconds' duration. Fischer, impatient to display Goddard's accomplishment, pressed at once for a flight demonstration.

"The lieutenant wanted a crash effort, but the doctor wasn't happy about it," recalled Charles Mansur. Goddard wanted to improve, adjust and refine his experimental model before turning it loose. In the military view, inventors needed a firm, practical hand to take charge, particularly in wartime. Fischer declared that the take-off device was to be installed on a PBY for a flight test on September 23. He would fly the seaplane himself.

Goddard's crew and Navy mechanics hastened to install the brazed-nickel thrust unit on the PBY. The professor devised a new safety control, worked on his rocket until the last evening, when the airplane was brought to the river. As he reported to the Navy:

"On September 22 at 3 p.m. the installation was completed by the station crew, and my shop crew gave it a final check. It was found necessary to rebraze the oxygen and gasoline liquid supply tubes between tanks and chamber because of leakage. Only the two helium reducing valves could be removed and checked easily. Both pilot valves of these reducing valves were found to have been injured by heating incident to soldering during the installation. In addition, a number of the tubing lines were found to be under excessive tension, and it was necessary to alter the piping sufficiently to relieve this tension. . . .

"In order to stop the unit if the temperature of the combustion chamber rose too high (normal working temperature being about 150° C.), a special safety device in the form of a thermostatic strip switch was made, to produce contact at the melting point of solder, about 180 degrees C., and was installed on the chamber by my crew on September 21. . . ."

II

Goddard's apprehensions grew on the morning of the flight test when he saw how the proceedings had been advertised. At a dock on the Severn, he was presented to a cluster of Navy officers and two civilian engineers from private industry. He watched intently as Fischer and his co-pilot, Gunner William Gore of the Marines, stowed sandbags in the seaplane to simulate a heavy cargo. Then they climbed in, followed by Charles F. Bellais, a Navy chief metalsmith, and Ben C. Coffman from the Bureau of Aeronautics in Washington.

Goddard, Lowell Randall and a few junior officers boarded a Navy crash boat. Other observers watched from the shore. The heavy plane bobbed on the water, then taxied to the center of the Severn. Fischer fired the jet.

Accounts of the test agree that it was an ordeal from start to finish. The first five runs were summed up in Goddard's laconic report:

"Test No. 1.

"In the first test on the PBY the unit stopped itself after less than 5 seconds. A stainless steel sheet over the chamber, and separated from it by about 2 inches, was found to be hot, and it was concluded that lack of circulation of air caused the chamber temperature to rise and operate the thermostatic cut-off. The stainless steel shield was removed at my suggestion. . . .

"Test No. 2.

"In the second test, the plane was moving at about 5 knots,

and according to witnesses underwent a substantial increase in speed during the 15-second thrust period.

"*Test No. 3.*

"In the third test, the PBY was taxiing, and the thrust unit operated satisfactorily.

"*Test No. 4.*

"In the fourth test, the speed was increased to that required for take-off. The cap which closed the nozzle opening was washed off, taking the igniter with it, before a start could be made.

"*Test No. 5.*

"In the fifth test, with the nozzle cap more firmly fastened, the unit started, but cut itself off almost immediately afterward. This was considered by Lieutenant Fischer and the Station Crew to have been due to the inadvertent operation of the safety thermal cut-off, possibly due to spray forced into the hull around the hole to accommodate the nozzle, and they decided to remove it in order to continue making take-off tests."

Of the sixth test, Goddard's comment was crisp—"The plane took off satisfactorily." It was a pallid description for the thunderous roar of his rocket, the sight of the hull racing above the water, the powerful lift of the heavy plane as it took to the air. In the crash boat, Navy observers heartily cheered. But Goddard remained uneasy as Fischer landed the plane and prepared for another try.

He was troubled by the rapid succession of tests, as his report indicated. His jet unit was still highly experimental. He wanted to inspect it after every two or three runs. His plan was to signal Fischer by radio from the crash boat if he detected any flaw in the shape or color of the rocket flame. But when he tried to summon the flier, the radio was jammed with static from a faulty electrical connection. He was out of touch with the plane.

While Goddard watched, Fischer turned on the booster

full blast. The seaplane once again scudded over the water and was airborne. The liquid-fuel rocket, as someone once observed, is controlled catastrophe. On this final try, it was uncontrolled.

Said co-pilot Bill Gore:

"My job was to check the rear compartment during each run. We couldn't see the rocket from inside the plane, but we could feel it vibrating. When I opened the water-tight door, I saw that the aft compartment was ablaze."

Said Charles Bellais, the chief metalsmith:

"I was sitting beside the dead radio, looking aft. When we were about 150 feet in the air, Bill Gore went past me to the rear and opened the tail compartment. I saw flames and banged Fischer on the foot to get his attention. Then Gore came charging up and hit the wheel to lower us down."

Goddard, in the crash boat, was stunned. At the rocket's first blast, he knew that something was wrong. The jet was yellow and bushy-tailed—an over-supply of gasoline. He wondered how long the chamber could hold the combustion. As he watched, the chamber split open. A moment later, he saw the tail of the plane on fire.

William C. House, a Navy engineer, was standing beside him. House gave orders:

"I said to hell with the medics, they can't help those boys, let's get out to that plane! The PBY was then about 80 feet in the air and coming down fast. We reached it as it pancaked on the water, and got the crew safely into our boat."

Goddard and Lowell Randall were the last to leave the Severn that day, seeing the PBY back to its watery hangar. For the professor, the experience had been a nightmare. They retrieved their rocket unit and stripped it down, searching for clues to the accident. Largely, the trouble had been haste and mishandling. Reporting on the test, the professor tried to submit a well-tempered but forceful warning on the hazards of short-cutting either safety measures or inspections during test runs of experimental devices.

This mishap of September 1942 proved to be Goddard's last flight trial. At Annapolis, no one questioned the thrusting power of Goddard's liquid-fuel motor, but the unfortunate test had scarcely reassured the Bureau of Aeronautics. Shortly, Goddard's take-off unit, as well as the liquid-fuel motors developed by others for jet-assist purposes were superseded by a powerful, cheaper and more dependable solid-fuel booster.

Two years later, Goddard would read in the New York *Times* of September 9, 1944:

NAVY PLANES GET
JET 'CATAPULTS'
Detachable Units Enable
Quicker Carrier Take-offs,
Greater Bomb Loads

WASHINGTON, Sept. 8—The Navy said today that it was prepared to use jet-assisted take-offs, which it demonstrated to a group of correspondents at a naval air base several months ago, for carrier planes and flying boats.

"Jato" units, as the Navy calls them, make it possible to reduce the length of take-off runs by 33 to 60 percent, or to "greatly increase the airplane's load."

At the demonstration, heavily overloaded bombers took off after a remarkably short run.

"Each jet unit," the Navy said in a description of the development, "is an engine in itself—a cylinder full of a solid propellant which includes oxygen in the mixture so it can burn without air. It has an electrically controlled spark plug which sets it off and a rocket-like vent from which the jet gases give their thrust. . . .

Orders had been placed, it was said, for "quantity production."

As it turned out, the Navy's JATO was not used extensively. The aircraft carrier was soon equipped with a mechanical means of catapulting airplanes from its deck, making the JATO obsolete for that purpose—although it is still used for heavy planes taking off from water. As for Goddard's contribution, a rocket engineer later remarked: "Putting his rocket on a seaplane was like hitching an eagle to a plow."

III

In its 1942 crash effort to perfect an aircraft booster, the Navy was beginning to learn its way in rocketry. In similar efforts, the Army Air Corps was also exploring the field. Compared to Germany's massive program, these beginnings were small, yet essential to later progress. They helped develop a nucleus of trained American rocket engineers, the first of the new breed who would follow the professor into the Age of Space.

Shortly after the incident on the Severn, Goddard was ready with another Roswell creation, his rocket for variable thrust. It would give pilots a means to turn on, turn off, idle and vary the blast of the rocket in flight. To witness this virtuoso display on November 13, Fischer invited Gunner Gore, Mr. House, and a few official representatives from Washington. The 13-pound rocket was firmly anchored to the test stand, its nozzle jutting out toward the river.

Fischer asked the spectators to press appropriate buttons on the control panel that varied the thrust. The experimental rocket obligingly roared, cut off, idled and blasted again. Its gauges showed that it surpassed the Navy's requirements for an initial or medium thrust of 600 pounds for 15 seconds; that it reached an idling thrust of 12 seconds' duration, and a full thrust of 1,000 pounds for more than 15 seconds. The rocket behaved masterfully, a Navy commander was heard to remark. "It was like being Thor, playing with thunderbolts."

A few days later, Goddard reported the success to the Navy. Nothing had gone wrong in the test, absolutely nothing:

"Starting occurred at once, on pressing the operating button. There was no exterior flame or explosion, the flame being the normal flame for medium thrust. The idling period also occurred on pressing the operating button. The flame was short, being 6 inches or less in length. . . . The full thrust occurred on pressing the operating button a third time. This, also, was accompanied by no exterior explosion at the beginning or end of the period. Stopping was accomplished by pressing the stop button, and occurred at once, without after-burning or heating of the chamber. . . .

"The chamber, nozzle, propellant storage and supply apparatus, ignition, control system, and safety system were undamaged and unchanged after the run. There was, as usual, no erosion in the chamber or the nozzle, and no evidence of any severe heating. . . ."

With his variable-thrust motor, Goddard had devised the essential control system of the rocket plane, although a plane incorporating this system would not be flown for almost fifteen years, when the experimental X-2 would break aircraft records. In the hard annals of pioneering, however, the test of November 1942 was one to remember.

The Goddards marked the occasion with a rare expedition into Navy social life. On Thanksgiving Day, they attended their first football game, the annual Army-Navy encounter. Navy trounced Army, 14–0. After the game, they joined other celebrants at a cocktail party held by Lieutenant Fischer. A few days later, Fischer was transferred to sea duty. Goddard remained at Annapolis.

IV

In 1943, America's attitude toward jet propulsion was beginning to change. The rocket, to be sure, was not yet accepted by conventional engineers as a prime mover of force and consequence; it was not quite endorsed by elders of the armed services, who persisted in calling it "Buck Rogers stuff"; young rocket enthusiasts, glimpsing the future, still struggled against military and public indifference. But there was a pulse of change and Goddard felt it.

Within the year, ideas he had advocated for a quarter century were coming of age. The portable rocket projector, which he and Dr. Hickman had demonstrated one war earlier, was fired in the deserts of Tunisia. German tank commanders, accustomed to flattening Europe's battalions, were stopped in their tracks by a single American foot soldier, a "bazooka man." In Washington, Army Ordnance celebrated these David-and-Goliath encounters and "discovered" the rockets of inventors and developers everywhere—with the possible exception of those of the Worcester professor who was stationed in nearby Maryland with the Navy.

It was not the first time that the United States looked abroad before finding talent at home. France had proved the merit of the Wright brothers' airplane in the First World War, and in similar fashion Europe demonstrated the importance of Goddard's rockets in the Second World War. As the professor had feared, the principal instruction came from Germany.

In 1943, the United States was also a poor second to its later rival as a space power. As early as 1934, Soviet Russia had undertaken a government-sponsored rocket research program. Stalin himself was interested in long-range missiles, according to Tokaty, the Russian colonel who defected to England after the war. By 1943, the Russians had used rockets effectively in the Battle of Stalingrad, having mass-produced successful rocket artillery since 1940.

But Stalin's Russia, like the United States, was outmatched in rocketry by Nazi Germany, where, in mounting adversity, Hitler was willing to gamble on jet aircraft and even the A-4 rocket. In 1943, this new harvest from German research was reported in the United States by visiting British engineers. They had come to advance the "turbojet" engine of the Royal

Air Force's Group Captain Frank Whittle. The Whittle engine produced a jet blast in an air-breathing motor for atmospheric flight, but it was not a "true" rocket, carrying its own oxygen for higher and faster trajectories. The Germans, said the British visitors, were secretly attempting to build such rockets.

That fall, the Royal Air Force bombed the Nazis' rocket complex at Peenemünde on the Baltic Sea. In November, General Henry H. Arnold of the U.S. Army Air Force at last authorized a survey of the possibilities of high-flying, long-range, liquid-fuel missiles. In the same month, Army Ordnance studied an analysis of long-range rockets submitted by Dr. von Kármán of Cal. Tech. Again Goddard was not consulted. But perhaps it was already too late. The following year Germany's new rockets were dropped for the first time on London, traveling faster than sound.

v

At the outset of 1943, after the Navy renewed his contract, the professor was settled at Tydings-on-the-Bay, a small summer colony overlooking the Chesapeake, some seven miles from the Annapolis engineering station. Among the secluded cottages only two were equipped for winter living, and in one of these the Goddards lived, apart from the military community. It was a roomy, gray stucco house with a coal furnace, a commodious living room with fireplace, and a large screened porch which presented a sweeping view of Chesapeake Bay. At night they could hear foghorns sounding from colliers, freighters and hospital ships setting out from Baltimore harbor to the north for the battle waters of Europe.

That winter and spring, their only neighbors were a retired captain of luxury yachts named Albert Finch and his wife Augusta. Finch was employed by a maritime insurance firm in Baltimore to inspect the loading of cargoes. On weekend visits to Tydings, the captain entertained the Goddards with sea tales, and identified vessels by their configurations as they moved outward toward the Atlantic.

"On weekdays," Esther Goddard said, "there was no one to talk to after Bob drove off in the morning, his headlights on because it was still dark, until he returned at night."

In its remoteness, Tydings was like many of Goddard's other establishments. Goddard described his new surroundings in a letter to Harold Tuson, a boyhood friend in Worcester:

"This is the first time we have spent a whole year in what may be called the South. . . . With the beginning of spring in April, we see the pink peach and cherry blossoms. . . . The dogwood takes up next, most of it white all through the woods and occasionally pink. Then follows the iris and the mountain laurel. At just about this time, the locust trees blossom with a pale yellow flower. The roses also come in the picture at about the same time and they cover the fronts of the houses and even run along the banks beside the road. Several days when the honeysuckle is in blossom, it is like being in a perfumery store where half the bottles have been broken. Just now the tiger lilies are in bloom along with the hollyhocks of various colors in gardens. Whether this will finish the procession or not, I don't know, but it has been quite an experience seeing it pass by. . . .

"The pleasantest time is in the evening, when you can see the lighthouses at various places and hear the bell buoy when it is quiet, which sounds like a church bell on some distant hill in the country. There are many small pleasure sailing boats, and, of course, all the large craft going to and from Baltimore. . . ."

Tydings, Goddard found, was a pleasant retreat from his days at the Naval Station, which were busy and sometimes disquieting. There were a few rewards at Annapolis, however. Shortly after his arrival, he received an inquiry from an executive of the Curtiss-Wright Corporation:

"I would appreciate your giving consideration to the possibility of working out some arrangements whereby Curtiss-Wright could actively push the assisted take-off project by means of some connection with you. . . ."

To the Goddards, the inquiry seemed to mark a turn of events. A reputable aircraft corporation, interested in possible sales to the military, had asked for his services and patents. He replied to Curtiss-Wright and became a part-time consultant, granting it a license to his patents.

Other companies, besieging Washington for war contracts, also discovered Goddard. Linde Air Products, from whom he had once bought his liquid oxygen, now also proposed to employ him. Reaction Motors, Inc., a commercial offshoot of the American Rocket Society, offered a block of stock and its presidency. Toward the end of his Annapolis years, the General Electric Company invited him to work on long-range rockets. They spoke of a new era in which American business would subsidize fundamental research, and time would not matter. The prospect was vastly appealing. But, for Goddard, time was starting to run out.

In 1943, he arrived early from Tydings at his workshop on the Severn, devoted himself to Navy assignments and tried to persuade his superiors that he had more to give them than he was asked to deliver. After the aborted take-off device, his new contracts called on him to improve rotating chambers for rockets developed elsewhere; to increase the thrusts of small motors for small missiles; to perfect his variable-thrust motor; to develop pumps and igniters for the laboratory next door, run by the Navy's young, ingenious Lieutenant Robert C. Truax. In the past, Goddard had created and tested complete rocket systems; now his work seemed repetitive and fragmentary. He fulfilled his Navy contracts but grew increasingly tired and restless.

The Navy, too, became restless with its pioneeer on the premises. Accustomed to working alone, Goddard was unaware that he vexed some of his younger colleagues, who, applying for patents themselves, often found that he had been there first. They acknowledged him as the dean of rocketry, but argued that he was unduly guarded about his work, that he stood apart from them, unteamable, unjoinable.

Lieutenant Truax said later: "He wasn't like the rest of us. Most of us were very communicative. We'd get together and discuss every possible phase of our work. The problem was not in turning us on, but in turning us off. But the doctor didn't care for our sessions. He liked to keep his ideas to himself."

Although he began to feel out of step, it never occurred to Goddard why he should be "like the rest of us." He recognized that the age of the private inventor was passing, replaced by the corporate engineer. The United States Patent Office, extolled by Lincoln because it "added the fuel of interest to the fire of genius," was being deplored as an "octopus of monopoly." In the name of team technology, the maverick inventor was almost lost, although not altogether forgotten, according to A. Whitney Griswold, president of Yale University, who pointedly asked in his Baccalaureate Address in 1957:

"Could Hamlet have been written by a committee, or the Mona Lisa painted by a club? Could the New Testament have been composed as a conference report? Creative ideas do not spring from groups. They spring from individuals. The divine spark leaps from the finger of God to the finger of Adam, whether it takes ultimate shape in a law of physics or a law of the land, a poem or a policy, a sonata or a mechanical computer. . . ."

VI

His Annapolis associates were not the first to wonder at Goddard's interest in patents, to think his behavior odd for a professor of physics. His academic colleagues were long perplexed by his legalistic claims. Dr. William Cole remembered his lanky friend stopping him in the halls of Clark to witness a new affidavit. "When the rest of us had something to say, we tried the professional journals," Dr. Cole remarked, "but Bob wanted patents and affidavits instead. I never knew why, but I don't think he had money in mind."

Businessmen were equally puzzled. For example, the young manufacturer Arthur A. Collins, of Cedar Rapids, Iowa, who had unearthed Goddard's 1912 work in Princeton, had called on the inventor in Roswell in 1936. His company was then being enjoined by the Radio Corporation of America from using conventional oscillator tubes as patented by Dr. De Forest and Dr. Armstrong. Facing possible insolvency, Collins had turned up the early Goddard patent for an oscillator tube. (See cut.)

While Goddard was considering Collins' appeal, RCA sent an emissary to Roswell. "Of course my tube works," Goddard replied testily to the RCA representative.

With his inventiveness assaulted, Goddard grew tenacious in helping Collins. Through Goddard's cooperation, Collins Radio survived and grew from a fledgling into a multimillion dollar establishment. "Dr. Goddard didn't ask a thing for himself," Collins later recalled. "He accepted only a modest consultant's fee, saying it would be enough to pay for another patent he was applying for." Years later Collins amplified the incident, writing in part:

"When I started the Collins Radio Company in a very small way in the early Thirties, I wanted to manufacture radio transmitters. At that time AT&T and RCA controlled the De Forest oscillator patents and had adopted the policy of not granting licenses for the manufacture of radio transmitters. My patent attorney, John B. Brady of Washington, D.C., made a search of the De Forest 'file wrapper' and found that the Goddard oscillator patent had been referenced by the patent examiner as prior art. He advised me that he considered the Goddard patent to be anticipatory and to invalidate the De Forest patent.

"Armed with this opinion, I started manufacturing transmitters employing conventional tubes on the theory that there was no essential difference between the conventional tubes of that era and the Goddard tube as described in the Goddard patent. My little enterprise was promptly sued by RCA and AT&T, charging infringement of the De Forest patent, and the Goddard tube was offered as a defense. . . . The finding of the court was adverse to me and a preliminary injunction was ordered.

"Dr. Goddard told me that he was unaware of the subsequent development of the De Forest patent position, and the fact that there had been a contest in the courts between Lee De Forest and Edwin Armstrong, and that the large electric companies had paid at various times both De Forest and Armstrong amounts exceeding a million dollars for their patent rights in this area.

"The Collins Radio Company, having been enjoined from using conventional oscillator tubes, continued in business manufacturing and selling transmitters using tubes which were physically identical to the tubes described in the Goddard patent. Several hundred of these tubes were used very successfully in broadcasting stations by the (then) Department of Commerce Lighthouse Service and others. RCA and AT&T subsequently modified their licensing policies and granted a patent license under the De Forest patents to Collins and also to many other companies including what is now the entire electronics industry. The contest between

R. H. GODDARD.

METHOD OF AND APPARATUS FOR PRODUCING ELECTRICAL IMPULSES OR OSCILLATIONS.

APPLICATION FILED AUG. 1, 1912.

1,159,209.   Patented Nov. 2, 1915.

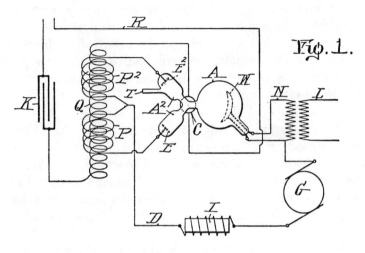

Fig.1.

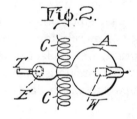

Fig.2.

Witnesses:

C. F. Wesson.
E. M. Allen.

Inventor:
R. H. Goddard
By Attorneys
Southgate & Southgate.

Goddard and De Forest as a result was never adjudicated in the courts.

"It is interesting to reflect that the invention of such an oscillator was the key to the whole development of radio and electronics. . . . Yet Goddard was so absorbed in his experiments outside the field of electronics that, until I brought the subject to his attention, he had regarded his oscillator as one of his less important inventions."

Goddard's ingenious sojourn into electronics had been merely one aspect of his inventiveness. He had been raised in a city which thrived on invention and patent rights. "Without patents, an inventor is helpless," Nahum Goddard had said. Years later, discussing her husband's predilection for patents, Esther Goddard said: "It was New England coming out."

In Goddard's rocket patents, beginning in 1914, he moved, of course, beyond the pedestrian patent practices of Worcester. United States patent examiners have since observed that Goddard's rocket applications were not merely for an invention, nor even a complex of invention, but in fact covered a new area of physical possibility. No previous Worcester inventor had ever set out to encompass so vast a domain, or raised more questions in the process.

The facts are probably clear enough. With the help of Charles Hawley, Goddard's desire for patents evolved, roughly, in three stages. By the time he reached Annapolis, there were forty-eight Goddard patents on rockets, of which eleven had already expired under the normal seventeen years granted by Act of Congress. Among these early patents were his basic inventions of 1914; his later devices for fuel-feeding and cooling; igniters and carburetors; pumps and turbines; gyroscopic stabilizers and landing controls. Through his attorney, he also established in patents his solar and ion-propulsion concepts. (He never told Mr. Hawley where he expected his rocket-landing controls to operate, or that his ion and solar motors, useless within the earth's atmosphere, might be of considerable value in space.)

Goddard's second group of patents were applied for early in the 1940's, until military security banned release of information on further rocket devices. These applications required a preoccupying correspondence to resolve while they were being reviewed by the Patent Office. On one case, Hawley suggested that his client join him in a new march on Richmond, where the Patent Office operated during the war, to talk with the patent examiner:

"It used to be a nice boat trip from Baltimore to Richmond via the York River," said Hawley, "and I believe these boats still run. It is a night trip and they used to serve the best dinners to be found anywhere."

Goddard declined. There wasn't time. A few weeks later, Hawley received another letter from Goddard on a disputed claim involving a liquid storage tank:

"I thought when we ran against vacuum cleaners with the welding patent that we had touched bottom, but the flushing of a toilet, as a reference, is assuredly reaching a new low. . . ."

Goddard's second series of applications, dispatched from Annapolis, led to 35 more rocket patents. Among them were modifications of his air-breathing resonance chamber, a jet-driven propeller and the variable-thrust engine which he had created in New Mexico and later demonstrated to the Navy. Novel methods of igniting, controlling and landing high-flying rockets were also patented.

In one application, Goddard attempted to integrate his years of research into a master patent. Although Hawley tried his best, he was not surprised when the examiner disallowed the petition—it contained too much invention for one patent, probably too much for two, possibly too much for three. Hawley broke the news to his client. "Robert was thrifty," Hawley said admiringly, afterward. "He was always trying to stretch a patent to cover the field. But this time, we couldn't stretch."

The "unstretchable" application was Goddard's amplified design for his evolution of a modern rocket system. This omnibus patent would eventually be issued in three parts. The first two, entitled "Control Mechanism for Rocket Apparatus," were issued in April 1946 as patents No. 2,397,657 and No. 2,397,659. In detailed drawings and claims, they laid out the complete automatic rocket system which he had finally developed in Roswell. The second patent, a "continuation" of the first, dealt specifically with his method of variable thrust.

To the patent examiner, the application still seemed overpacked, like an awkwardly bulging valise. As a result, the "continuation" patent eventually sprouted a "division," which the Patent Office released in 1949 as No. 2,465,526, "Pump Sealing Means." It presented a small but indispensable innovation, which received special attention from later rocket developers. Without adequate seals, the pumps would leak; if the pumps leaked, the turbines would fail; if the turbines failed, so would the rocket.

Goddard's third engagement with patents started at Annapolis and ended years after his death. When military security withheld the issue of rocket patents, a host of Goddard inventions were deflected into the ample safe of Mr. Hawley on Franklin Street. There was little point, the attorney and his client agreed, in sending them on to patent examiners. Instead, they became "Cases in Storage," as Goddard called them.

After the war, when Hawley unburdened his safe, he found 136 Goddard "Cases in Storage." They were, he discovered, sufficiently detailed and precise to enable Hawley to secure 131 more patents, posthumously, for his remarkable client. In all, Goddard was issued 214 patents. He had assigned half interest in most of them to the Daniel and Florence Guggenheim Foundation.

These were the facts, but not quite the answer. What was Goddard's intention? Was it, as Maple Hill believed, to follow his father Nahum's caution, that an idea was only safe when you had an attorney to your front and your rear and on both sides? But many of Goddard's inventions expired before their inventor.

Was his purpose, as Grandmother Goddard had once suggested, to set out flags, to signify to others that one had been here? Perhaps this had cogency. In time, his patents would summon the recognition of his peers, among them Dr. Wernher von Braun of Peenemünde, Germany, and Dr. Jerome C. Hunsaker of the NACA and the Massachusetts Institute of Technology. Considering the rocket patents, Hunsaker would say: "Every liquid-fuel rocket that flies is a Goddard rocket." Von Braun observed: "Dr. Goddard was ahead of us all." In 1950, when von Braun had an opportunity to examine the Goddard patents, he said that he was "virtually overwhelmed by the thoroughness of his [Goddard's] work and found that many design solutions in the V-2 rocket were covered by Goddard patents."

Or did the Goddard patents carry another message, one that Esther Goddard would set down:

"Granted, he couldn't talk about space travel, though he knew it was coming; granted, he could only hint at the moon, though he knew that was coming; granted, then, that he couldn't talk about what was closest to his heart. What outlet, then? First, he could write about it privately, which he did; and he could patent his ideas, which would some day point out to the *cognoscenti* what he had in his heart—which they did. Remember, some of these patents were 'way out':

ionization, use of solar energy, rotating chambers, the germ of inertial guidance. He was sure they would not come in his time. But it was precisely these patents which would tell future scientists that they had a forerunner, who had understood what they could live to accomplish. They were his message to the future."

VII

In 1943, Goddard opened his last assault against sickness, his drive against time. Night after night, before he retired, he continued to record the day's events, but now in a quickened and almost hieroglyphic script. Later, Esther Goddard employed a magnifying glass to decipher and transcribe these entries.

Most of the notes were routine: experiments conducted at Annapolis and their results; trips to Washington to negotiate Navy contracts; communications to Mr. Hawley; descriptions of Maryland countryside; motion pictures they'd seen together; references to quiet evenings at Tydings-on-the-Bay.

In April, she saw passing references to illness, mostly of the head-cold variety, but in May he seemed on the mend. A few weeks later, they went to chapel services at the Annapolis Academy. That night he sketched an iris blossom in his diary and beside it an enigmatic comment: "Note from sermon: 'sun-crowned man.' " "I wonder if he copied this down because he felt himself to be a 'sun-crowned man,' " Esther speculated. "I felt he was."

By the end of June, his voice was husky again. He never wanted to take the time to see doctors. But now he agreed:

"June 23, Tried tanks with shut-off valves for gasoline and water in a.m. Met E at 1.45 . . . and went to Baltimore. Was examined by Dr. Austrian. Had dinner at the Miller Bros. near Lord Baltimore Hotel. Went to circus. Caught the 11.45 train to Annapolis, and came back about 12.30 a.m."

"June 30, Went to Dr. Slack in Baltimore with E in a.m. Came back, and had lunch at Green's Drug Store. Large pump caused suction pressure to drop, because of too small a suction line. Repeated pump tests, with original head; velocity not greater than before . . . and nozzle burned through. . . ."

He had seemed reassured. Of their first trip to Baltimore, Esther added this comment to her transcript of Goddard's diary: "Dr. [Charles R.] Austrian is supposed to be the greatest authority in U.S. on TB. Gave RHG a thorough examination. Said care was necessary, no swimming or sun-bathing, but no immediate cause for alarm. Hence our little dinner-circus celebration. I remember Dr. A. came into his reception room, where I was waiting . . . and said: 'Well, some people *can* live with that much involvement,' in a wondering voice."

Goddard dismissed his wife's concern, enjoyed the circus and afterward wrote a whimsical account of his visit to the doctor. He seemed to treat his next examination in an equally cavalier fashion. To his second diary entry, Esther appended this note: "Dr. Harry L. Slack, Jr. was best throat specialist at Johns Hopkins. He examined RHG and recommended no talking at all, to give throat a complete rest. RHG found this impossible, under the circumstances at the Station. I tried to do what I could, at home, to cooperate. RHG's spirits better, somewhat relieved."

In the next few months, there was no further mention of health. There were references to humid summer evenings at the bay; to seeing "three Perseid meteors at 5 a.m."; to a visit by Colonel Homer Boushey and his bride. The professor and the flier had talked again of space flight, of the day after the war when Boushey would assist Goddard in his rocket experiments.

A few diary items that fall, however, caused Esther to wonder. In September, in Worcester, her husband wrote of a solitary trip to their old house, then rented, on Maple Hill:

"Went out to Tallawanda Drive and had boxes put away in cellar and attic, also launching frame, in cellar. . . . Went back to hotel by bus. . . ."

Afterward, when Esther examined these boxes, she found her husband's first liquid-fuel rockets and the launching frame they had used at the Auburn farm. They were neatly dated and labeled, a scientist's job.

In October they were back at Annapolis. The diary was filled with accounts of new experiments and, among them, these occasional notes: "Worked on write-up" . . . "Wrote on report" . . . "Read theses." Esther had transcribed her way into November before the nature of his "write-up" became clear.

Goddard was taking time to organize his writings on space travel. Shortly after their trips to Baltimore, he had begun to assemble his sealed speculations, his papers once sent to the Smithsonian and the theses of his former students which had taken them, all unsuspecting, to the outer fringes of space flight. One day the essential purpose of their research would be clear:

Donald E. Higgins, June 1924—"A Study of Light Metals and Alloys at Low Temperatures"; Russell B. Hastings, June 1925—"The Emission of Electricity from Substances on Incandescent Carbon"; Lewis M. Sleeper, June 1926—"The Emission of Positive Electricity from Potassium Heated on a Platinum Filament in a Vacuum"; Clyde F. Benner, June 1927—"A Study in Rapid Transference of Heat from Metal Surfaces"; Lillian S. Blomstrom, June 1930—"On the Rapid Absorption of Radiation by Metals"; and Thomas E. Boyle, June 1930—"On the Productivity of Electricity by Air or Steam Jets."

Among these former students, one was surprised by a letter from Goddard in Annapolis, inquiring about a detail of an experiment he had performed eighteen years before. On November 22, 1943, Goddard addressed Russell Hastings without preamble:

"I had occasion to look over your 1925 thesis on Electricity from Incandescent Carbon recently, and noticed that the amount of the vacuum you used was not mentioned. If you happen to remember what it was, on the average, I would appreciate it very much if you would let me know. You may remember that you measured it by means of a short U-tube closed mercury manometer, about 6 inches high, graduated in centimeters and millimeters. . . ."

Unfortunately, replied Hastings, then a professor of physics himself at Macalester College, Minnesota, he had "apparently . . . destroyed the notes after completing the thesis, and thus I am unable to give you the value of pressure used in the experiment."

When Esther reread her husband's papers, she found among them the result of this 1943 "write-up"—a hasty panorama of his space flight investigations which he had called "The Ultimate in Jet Propulsion." He collected many of his ideas, old and new, on the possible use of solar energy in space; the use of ionization for rocket power; the employment of atomic energy "after the problem of atomic disintegration is solved." He also included discussions on space craft and techniques for landing on other planets, on disorientation and weightlessness in space, on re-entering the earth's atmosphere, on methods of freezing protoplasm for man's travel to other galaxies.

In his projections of space travel, Goddard referred to his early reticence on the subject, through which he had "received credit for being a very high-minded scientist, who would not be swerved from the path of practical, albeit rather hum-drum problems.

"Actually," he continued, "this credit was not deserved,

since much time and thought had already been spent on some of the more advanced jet propulsion problems. . . . Slow but sure progress has been made . . . by many workers . . . so that no amount of sensational writing can now retard the development of high altitude rockets. . . ."

"I didn't know at the time, but Bob was obviously finishing up his long-standing chores," Esther said. Except in the United States, the doctrine of space flight was becoming acceptable. Even as he gathered his papers together, the "Ultimate in Jet Propulsion" was coming of age. Goddard, the consummate realist, had obviously saved his greatest fantasy as a curtain line.

Toward the end of 1943, he increasingly spent his evenings at home with Esther, listening to the radio, reading such mystery stories as "The Case of the Fainting Butler" and "The Vanishing Woman." Occasionally, when his voice would clear, he spoke with spurious conviction of future plans. After the war, he said, he would give two more years to Curtiss-Wright. And then they would plan to return to Roswell and to Mescalero Ranch.

Esther heard out these plans and firmly believed that her husband would soon be well. Toward Christmas, she asked him what he would like. "Not a thing, but I'll give you $200," he said, "with the understanding that I will spend the same amount on my 'crazy patent.' "

The "crazy patent" was one of his oldest ideas, his undergraduate vision of an electromagnetic vacuum tube to serve as a transport system between cities. It would perform for surface travel what the rocket would do for airborne travel. One day, Goddard said, men would need such a means to escape from congested roads and highways.

For Bob's Christmas gift, Esther cheerfully gave back her gift money toward the "crazy patent."

13. NEVER AN END

In 1944, as his guarded shop on the Severn became a smaller fragment of the nation's expanding rocket facilities, Goddard showed few outward premonitions of his remaining course. The war had a year and a half to go. Throughout these months, he continued his experiments at Annapolis, dealing with illness as an old adversary, battling it in his characteristic ways.

Early in the year, his crew found it difficult to understand him. With passing weeks, his voice grew huskier and he spoke with more effort. "Some days he could talk pretty clearly, but on others his voice fogged over so we could hardly make him out," said Charles Mansur, his chief welder. "At first, he tried writing out instructions, but that didn't help much. Then he came to the shop with the Morse code typed out for us. For a while he tapped out code messages at his desk with a pencil stub."

In this period, the professor corresponded briefly with the Bell Laboratories, proposing to purchase, or possibly to devise, a portable voice amplifier. He also considered installing a public address system in his shop, equipped with a sensitive microphone.

Now in his early sixties, he learned that the military was making its principal investment in rocket research at Cal. Tech, across the continent. Although there was still little interest in high-altitude rockets, available funds were being committed to Dr. von Kármán's Jet Propulsion Laboratories and his physicists and engineers.

Goddard was not invited to join. Probably he would still have declined, preferring to direct his own shop and crew, few of whom had completed high school. Once he assigned George Bode and Lowell Randall a rather advanced problem in rocket propulsion. "We fussed with it until we came up with an answer," Bode remembered. "Dr. Goddard was delighted. 'It's the same answer they got at Cal. Tech,' he told us. 'And *they* were college graduate students!' "

His men began to detect a change in Goddard, a subsiding desire to tinker with new components, an intensity in assembling records of his past. He appeared to be looking backward. His desk at the shop was cluttered now with folders of rocket photographs taken long before. When they were sorted and labeled, he reviewed his Roswell experimental notes. Once he had been a little dog with a great big bone, but he was unmolested, he told Esther. Now the big dogs, with big-dog manners, had found the bone and were trying to wrest it from him. There was only one possible defense. He stepped up his patent correspondence with Mr. Hawley.

Mansur was puzzled by Goddard's attention to paperwork. "There was a build-up of irritation," said his chief welder. "The Navy's cost accountants kept coming around, although no one was thriftier with government funds. If we needed some bolts or angle irons, he had to fill out requisitions. He began turning over details of his shop work to us, while he worked at his papers."

In January 1944, Goddard saw Naval Intelligence reports on German rocket activity. Although he had predicted that the Germans would outdistance the Americans in rocketry, he was troubled that his prophecy was already true. He read a garbled press account from Stockholm, Sweden, of a German "secret weapon—a giant rocket bomb that climbs to a height of 35 miles." The Swedish account, mistakenly referring to liquid oxygen as the explosive, rather than the oxidizer, minimized the Nazi weapon. But Goddard was not misled.

The Navy meanwhile had asked the pioneer to adapt his pump-and-turbine assembly, the product of two decades of work, for Cal. Tech's nitric acid and aniline, and to develop motors for a small missile called the "Gorgon." Before the end of the year, he reported on and turned over to the Navy his "3,000 lb., four motor unit, for oxygen, gasoline and water, of improved and simplified design."

He was now sure that Lieutenant Fischer's expectation had misfired, that his Navy work would not end in imaginative assignments, but in the merest of finger exercises. His heart was no longer in it. For a while, he continued to visit Washington, arguing hoarsely for his high-altitude rocket. Finally, he abandoned even this mission. "We had the dean of rocketry at Annapolis," said the Navy's Calvin Bolster years later, "but we were not yet ready to develop a rocket for launching masses of explosive great distances, let alone space craft. Goddard was too far ahead of his time."

During the year, Goddard allowed himself a rare admission of discouragement, an exception to his long and deliberate optimism. It took quite a bit to provoke. He was oppressed by German developments. He was being surpassed by younger, team-working scientists at home. The Navy was thinking of ending his contract. His health was fading. None of these discouragements appeared in his diary.

But on March 30, 1944, when Oley Ljungquist, his crew

chief, gave notice of leaving, Goddard's Yankee reserve was finally punctured. That evening, he wrote of Oley's news and the next night, March 31, he mentioned Oley again. Then, as if guarding against possibly excessive emotion, he festooned his diary entry in parentheses and quotation marks:

"(A 'low' day.)"

At the time, Ljungquist was unaware that he had nearly cracked one of the century's granite-like reticences. The Navy had offered him another post at almost twice his current salary. "But, after all those years, I decided after some struggle that I couldn't leave him," Ljungquist recalled. "I had an idea he wanted me. He never said so. In fact he said it was logical to take the offer. But he seemed a lot calmer when I told him I was going to stay."

Goddard, of course, had not taken Oley's news without looking ahead. He felt it was urgent to keep his familiar crew together. Within a few days, he managed to track down Henry Sachs, his former crew chief at the Clark workshop. Sachs, then living in Bladensburg, Maryland, and employed by the Naval Observatory in Washington, was astonished to hear from the doctor.

"One Sunday, he called on the phone. He said he'd been keeping track of my time with the government and imagined I was about due for retirement. He asked if I'd like to take up my old job with him at Annapolis. He was right on both scores. They were going to retire me in a few weeks and I was flattered to go back with him. It was the first time I'd heard from Dr. Goddard in a dozen years."

Goddard's spirits improved when Ljungquist decided to remain. Sachs agreed to come along as chief instrument maker, foregoing the crew chief post. Again, the professor began to plan for the future.

In June 1944, he faced another problem. The small shop on the Navy compound was easily subject to scuttlebutt. The professor, his men were told, was now out of favor and his work would soon be discontinued. . . . Goddard, they heard, had offers elsewhere and planned to leave them behind. . . . Annapolis residents were complaining about rocket firings and the Severn tests would soon be abandoned. . . . The Navy was planning to transfer Goddard and his men to another proving ground—to Turkey Point, Maryland . . . to Cedar Point, Illinois . . . to Banana River, Florida . . . to Point Mugu, California.

When the rumors grew topheavy, the professor gathered his men for a talk. Hearing the effort with which he spoke, they were visibly moved. He delivered a hoarse appeal, based on the following notes:

"Called together to straighten out a few matters that seem to have been bothering you.

"Rumors—Rumors in the station, and even in the town—'barber shop talk' about Cedar Point and even about the work. If there is anything *definite* you need to know, I will tell you in ample time.

"Secondly—some of the men may feel that they are *not* wanted here, and that I have been *dissatisfied*. As a matter of fact, we have the best organization in the station, and I have been *proud* of the work, and know that other men in the station are jealous of the shop and the personnel.

"To have any of you leave would be like losing a member of the family.

"Some of you know I have tried out men and have *not kept them*. You can be sure if any of you were not satisfactory, you would have heard of it.

"If you have anything on your minds at all, or are dissatisfied about anything, come to me about it. *That is what I am here for.*

"I know some or all of you are worried about the future.

"Cdr. Gugg. recently told me, voluntarily, that he planned

to have the foundation finance the work after the war, either in Roswell or where it could be carried out best.

"If anything should happen to me, I am sure there would be openings for you in the Navy Dept. or at a concern like Curtiss-Wright, and I have recommendations in my files for all of you."

"If anything should happen to me . . ." The phrase hung on. His men returned quietly to their work. He did not appeal to them again. When Esther Goddard later gave them her husband's letters of recommendation, they were dated April 1944, a few weeks before he had called them together. They all read somewhat as follows:

To Whom It May Concern:

Mr. Charles Wright Mansur has been employed by me since Nov. 1, 1929, first as an assistant, and more recently as welding foreman on confidential development work, for the Bureau of Aeronautics, Navy Department. Although Mr. Mansur has not received a technical education, other than what he has been able to obtain by correspondence courses in engineering, he has shown very good ability both in machine work and in welding of all kinds.

He is of good character, pleasing personality, a good worker, and gets along well with people. I take pleasure in recommending him highly as a first-class machinist who would be a valuable man in any mechanical development work.

Goddard's talk to his men was the most formal he ever gave them. Later, none of them could recall a single seminar or group discussion on their long and mutual concern—his real purpose in building and flying the rocket.

A newer crew member, Albert Campbell, a science-fiction buff, once tried to sound him out. Leaving the Annapolis shop on a rainy night, the machinist saw Goddard trying to start his car.

"He kept grinding on the starter," Campbell said. "The car had been out in the rain and was flooded. I got a rag, lifted the hood and tried to dry off the wires. But it kept raining and I saw it was hopeless. Finally, I suggested we move the car into the shop so it could dry overnight and offered to drive him home.

"I'd never had a chance to talk to Dr. Goddard alone, and I thought this was a wonderful chance. We could talk all the way to Tydings. Somehow, I figured I'd bring us around to space flight.

"Well, he was worried and wanted to call his wife. He did, and she was worried too. Not about the car, but because he'd left home that morning without his cap and scarf.

"On the way, all he had on his mind was the car. 'I don't know why it should konk out, Al,' he kept saying. 'I just paid to have it tuned up.' I tried to assure him that it would be fine in the morning, and of course it was. It was my last chance to talk to Goddard alone, but we never got around to the rocket or space."

II

In the spring of 1944, space exploration fascinated a few scientists in a few countries. The space that concerned most people was closer at hand, the battlegrounds of the Second World War. At Tydings-on-the-Bay, after his workdays at the Navy, the professor followed the war news by radio, between his favorite broadcasts of Toscanini, Charlie McCarthy and "One Man's Family."

From their front porch that winter, the Goddards watched increasing numbers of convoys—troop ships, supply vessels and hospital ships—proceeding up the Chesapeake. In the news of massive bombings of Europe, they felt the war's quickening pace. The Allied second front was in everyone's mind. The country waited.

Through these weeks the professor's wife was more and more aware of her husband's growing fatigue, although she heard no complaints. Often, when she woke, she noticed his indented pillow on the bed beside hers and then found him outside, well bundled, standing in the grass and watching the skies. In his diary that February, she made out later:

"Saw a meteor, toward the end of path, at 4.5 a.m.; very light, like a car next door. In southeast, about 20 degrees above horizon, end fragment went rather slowly, and 'went out' soon after being observed. . . ."

Esther knew that the damp bay climate hardly favored a dormant tubercular condition. She reminded her husband that his Navy contract, largely at her insistence, authorized his return to Roswell for reasons of health. Goddard overrode her concern. He had come east and he meant to stay in the east. Things were happening. His "laryngitis," as he termed it, would shortly pass.

Reluctantly, as if to please her, he continued his visits to Dr. Slack in Baltimore. After one examination, Esther bluntly raised a question she suspected was troubling her husband. Nahum Goddard had died of cancer of the throat. Did Dr. Slack have any reason to suspect this ailment in Nahum's son? The throat specialist reassured them. "He said he had never heard of cancer superimposed on tuberculosis," Esther recalled. "But Bob, he said, had to continue to rest his voice."

Sergeant Emanuel Gordon and his wife were now their weekend neighbors, living in the cottage next door. Gordon was one of the ingratiating and resourceful mavericks recruited by Colonel "Wild Bill" Donovan for his clandestine Office of Strategic Services. The husky sergeant, who clearly knew his way around, became fond and protective of the aging professor. When he learned that Goddard was foregoing his usual Sunday morning steak because of meat rationing, he showed up on weekends with prime cuts of beef, waving off offers of payment. During the winter, when coal seemed unobtainable, he drove in with a four-ton truckload for their furnace. He was obviously a worker of miracles.

"They were devoted to each other, like newlyweds," Gordon said later, "but they needed someone to see after them. The professor had a wonderful laugh and a real sense of humor. He never used big words to embarrass you.

"He liked to sit on his lawn in the summer, watching the birds, or taking pictures of flowers, or making drawings of the bay. He couldn't talk much, but he always enjoyed a little joke. Once, when they were inside having dinner, I put a stuffed canary on the edge of his stone bird bath. When he came out, he said: 'What a beautiful bird!' I took him over to see how tame it was and, of course, it didn't budge. He saw it was stuffed and had a good laugh."

His voice was failing noticeably. Gordon remembered his gracious but sometimes speechless greetings. At the outset of this decline, when the Goddards were alone one weekday evening, a sudden lightning storm hit the summer colony and the Gordon house caught fire. The professor's party-line telephone was out of order. He quickly got out his car and drove to a nearby village, where he tried to telephone for assistance.

"He must have had trouble getting the operator to understand him, since he could hardly talk above a whisper," Gordon reflected. "Finally, she got him through to the volunteer fire department, but before they arrived the house was already burned to the ground. When I got back to Tydings, they asked me to be their guest until I could get our affairs in order."

In 1944, Goddard's endurance was tested again. His Navy contract was due to expire and now old rumors verged closely on fact. With his crew, he crated equipment for a projected move to Turkey Point, Maryland; then they unpacked. Eventually, when the Navy decided to keep the Goddard shop at Annapolis a while longer, the professor and his wife moved into a more comfortable house at Tydings-on-the-Bay, heated by a convenient oil-burning furnace.

With his crew intact and his living quarters in order, Goddard thoroughly endorsed Esther's desire to enroll at The Johns Hopkins University in Baltimore. Long ago, she had interrupted her undergraduate studies at Bates College to marry the Clark professor. Ever since, she had felt mildly deflated in the academic community for her lack of a degree. Tydings also seemed dull after Bob drove off in the morning. With her husband's hearty approval, she arranged for her mother to keep house while she returned to college. It was their twentieth wedding anniversary. "Do you good to get out for a bit," Goddard advised her. "It doesn't pay to sit by yourself."

III

They were at home on the morning of June 6, 1944, when the major turning point came in the war. They heard the news of D-day on their radio at breakfast. Massive Allied forces had successfully crossed the English Channel, establishing a beachhead in Normandy. The broadcast signed off "with the ringing of the Liberty Bell," as the professor wrote in his diary. He was shortly on his way to his shop, where he was running tests on a small rocket motor, designed for a 500-pound thrust. That night and the next, he recorded tests in his routine fashion:

". . . Had 500 lb. chamber tried. Extending the gasoline deflector caused greater heat, but gave no greater velocity. . . .

"Had cylindrical zone chamber tried in a.m. It burned

through the bottom after about 1½ seconds. Probably it was not enough pre-cooled to have liquid oxygen present. It burned at one of the oxygen entrance holes. The separating ribs were all OK, and each alternate oxygen zone was unheated. It probably needs refractory liners for each liquid, with the high pressure wall outside. . . ."

While Goddard was engaged in his modest Navy experiments, the Germans belatedly unleashed their advertised wonder weapons. Their dire designations—V-1 and V-2—had come from the *Reichsführer* himself. The "V" stood for *Vergeltungswaffe,* or "vengeance weapon." The last of Hitler's technological gambles, they cost $3 billion in marks, six years of intensive development, and the services of thousands of scientists and engineers at Peenemünde and elsewhere. The gamble did not pay off. It proved too little and too late to prevent the invasion of Europe and the eventual defeat of Germany. They, too, Goddard may have reflected, had trouble getting their rockets to follow a timetable.

But he brooded restlessly over reports of these devices. Within a week after D-day, the V-1 or "buzz bomb"—a jet-driven, pilotless aircraft—was launched against London. Four out of eleven struck their target. As well as he could analyze it, the V-1 was powered by an air-breathing resonance chamber, the same type he had conceived at Clark University, patented in 1934, and repeatedly urged the United States armed forces to consider. Now, as the V-1 improved in accuracy, interest of the United States military increased. By the end of June, some 250 of these weapons crossed the Channel from launching sites that pockmarked the French coast. Before the concrete sites were overrun, some 20,000 buzz bombs had exploded, more or less on target. Ground observers said they sounded, in flight, like washing machines gone amok. Royal Air Force pilots eventually learned to fly alongside them, upending their wings and causing them to crash.

American chiefs of ordnance, fascinated by the weapon, spoke for a time of building buzz bombs of their own. They might have looked up musty Goddard references in their files. When a detailed account of V-1 and rumors of V-2 appeared in the press, the professor replied to a request for comments by John N. Wheeler of the North American Newspaper Alliance, on August 24, 1944. He declined to discuss the V-2, but as for V-1 he said tersely:

"The V-1 flying bomb as a flight-controlled plane has already been shown to be an American idea, through patents to Kettering and Sperry . . . and [is] far from new. The general principle of the propulsion unit was described in a U.S. Patent, No. 1,980,266, entitled Propulsion Apparatus, issued November 13, 1934. . . . Features of the patent that appear in the bomb engine are shutter-type valves in a fixed grill; fuel injection orifices incorporated in this grill; combustion chamber; spark plug; nozzle. . . . [The patent] is not at all in the secret category, as anyone could have read it during the last ten years."

Goddard might also have added, if he had known, that his patent had been translated and circulated in Germany in the semipopular aviation journal, *Flugsport,* in January, 1939.

The Germans' second wonder weapon, the 12-ton V-2, blasted off in September 1944. In its initial launching, it exploded on a suburb of Paris; a second hit London. In a few thousand flights before the war ended, it landed frightfully on targets from London to Remagen. As the Allies moved swiftly inland, however, the V-2, like the V-1, was finally put out of business.

If news of V-1 stimulated Goddard, the early reports on V-2 transfixed him—not so much as a wonder weapon, or even as a prodigious technical accomplishment, but for its vindication of his theory that a rocket could ultimately climb to extreme altitudes. The first accounts from England and photo-

GEGRÜNDET 1908 u. HERAUSGEGEBEN VON OSKAR URSINUS • CIVIL-ING.

Illustrierte flugtechnische Zeitschrift und Anzeiger für das gesamte Flugwesen

Brief-Adr.: Redaktion und Verlag „Flugsport", Frankfurt a. M., Hindenburg-Platz 8

Bezugspreis für In- und Ausland pro ¼ Jahr bei 14täglichem Erscheinen RM 4.50

Telef.: 34384 — Telegr.-Adresse Ursinus Postscheck-Konto Frankfurt (Main) 7701
Zu beziehen durch alle Buchhandlungen, Postanstalten und Verlag
Der Nachdruck unserer Artikel ist, soweit nicht mit „Nachdruck verboten" versehen.
nur mit genauer Quellenangabe gestattet.

Nr. 1　　　　4. Januar 1939　　　　XXXI. Jahrgang

Die nächste Nummer des „Flugsport" erscheint am 18. Januar 1939

Anfang 1939.

Die Vorbedingungen für Weiterentwicklung sind im vergangenen Jahre 1938 geschaffen worden. Die vollbrachten Leistungen scheinen, wenn man den Maßstab von vor 6 Jahren anlegt, ~~fantastisch~~ und

ein ~~Schraube antreibt, nachdem das Ventil 32 geschlossen~~
und das Ventil 37 geöffnet worden ist.

Der durch seine ergebnisreichen Versuche mit Abbrandtriebwerken und sein hierüber aussagendes Werk*) bekannt gewordene amerikanische Physiker R. H. G o d d a r d hat in der amerikanischen Patentschrift 1 980 266 (angem. 7. Febr. 31) ein Heizluftstrahltriebwerk (Brennkammer mit konstantem Volumen) dargestellt, vgl. Abb. 41 bis 46. Luftein- und Gasaustritt werden durch die auftretenden Drücke selbsttätig gesteuert, und zwar mit Hilfe einer Feder 36 (Abb. 45) und in folgender Weise: Hat soeben in der Kammer 24 (Abb. 41) bei offenem Schließkegel 26 und geschlossenen Klappen 31 (Abb. 42) eine Zündung

*) „A method of reaching extreme altitudes", Washington 1919, ein Buch, das Anlaß zu der Raumschiff-Epidemie vor 10 Jahren gab.

Abb. 41—44. Goddard 1931: Ein- und Austrittsverschlüsse regeln sich selbsttätig gemäß dem im Brennkammer-Innern vorhandenen Druck.

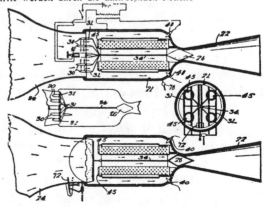

German publication of Goddard's patent 1,980,266, basic to the V-1.

graphs of V-2 wreckage revealed a true rocket, carrying its own liquid oxygen and fuel. At launching, its thrust was said to be 55,000 pounds, more than 100 times that of the smaller motors Goddard had tested in Roswell. The V-2 attained a velocity of 6,400 feet per second. Before veering down in its trajectory, it had soared to an altitude of 68 miles!

If the rocket pioneer was impressed, he was not surprised. Even before he could examine the V-2, it seemed painfully familiar, reminding him of his own experimental models from 1939 to 1941. He waited impatiently until he could study the German machine for himself.

IV

"V-2 type rocket appears to be of interest," he wrote in his diary on November 6. It was a dreary admission that accompanied a profound upheaval in Goddard, a radical new hankering to join, at last, with his American colleagues. He took a train to New York to accept a long-standing invitation from G. Edward Pendray of the American Rocket Society.

Beginning in 1930, when the Society was organized, Pendray had tried, without success, to interest the Worcester professor in joining its turbulent ranks. In the years intervening, the organization had attracted a growing membership of engineers. Pendray, a successful public relations man for prominent corporations as well as an unquenchable rocket experimenter, had recently published a knowledgeable defense of Goddard's status as pioneer. He received an unusually friendly letter of thanks.

Never one to let a warm response grow cold, Pendray had written to Goddard again. He was preparing a book, *The Coming Age of Rocket Power,* and hoped to feature a chapter about Goddard and his work. In addition, the Society, largely an east coast organization, was planning to expand, taking in scattered rocket groups around the country. Would the doctor discuss these matters with him at his convenience?

Goddard at last agreed. He accepted an appointment to the Society's board of directors and met with Pendray. After their first meeting, Pendray dictated a lengthy memorandum:

"I first met Dr. Robert H. Goddard at noon on election day November 7 [Roosevelt's fourth-term election, 1944], in the lobby of the Pennsylvania Hotel. His appearance was very much what I had expected and I recognized him at once. He is of medium height, slender, and gives the appearance of being rather frail. He has a low, husky voice and cannot speak very much above a whisper, owing to an attack of laryngitis he had more than a year ago, which damaged his vocal cords. He tells me he is recovering slowly from this and ultimately should regain his full voice. He turned out to be a friendly, engaging and candid man, capable of considerable enthusiasm and filled with good humor. I suggested that we have luncheon at the Engineers Club and we went there promptly. Dr. Goddard had been in the Engineers Club before but had never eaten there and he was very much interested in the Club and everything he saw. . . .

"Goddard has many unusual gifts; among other things, he can blow glass and in his early days did much experimenting with radio tubes. He patented a variety of oscillating radio tubes before De Forest invented his audion. . . . He blew the glass for the first tubes himself.

"At Christmas time he is fond of Swedish punch, which Mrs. Goddard makes. Mrs. Goddard is a Worcester girl who has been much interested in rockets, and has been of considerable help to him, both in the actual work and also in encouraging him. . . . They have no children.

"Dr. Goddard was a bit scornful of some of the fancy names which have been given to various rocket devices by Aerojet in California. The Aerojet people have one dry fuel rocket motor they call the 'aero-pulse' and one for underwater use which they call the 'hydro-pulse.' Said Dr. Goddard, 'Aero-pulse and hydro-pulse and little lambsie divey.' . . .

"I also suggested that he take . . . part in the American Rocket Society's activities. He seemed agreeable to do so. He asked me to keep in touch with him. . . ."

To keep in touch. . . . It was the first time Goddard had voiced this particular request.

v

By the beginning of 1945, while the rocket was approaching the dawn of its age, Goddard was nearing the twilight of his. As the months passed he tried, with effort, to free himself from a lifelong pattern of reticence. In December 1944, just after a quiet Christmas at Tydings-on-the-Bay, he had met his colleagues of the expanding American Rocket Society at a dinner in New York City, where he spoke hoarsely in favor of a national rocket organization and the great future of jet propulsion. He was considerably warmed at their reception of him, and agreed to write a new preface to his two Smithsonian papers, long out of print, which the Society wished to republish.

After the New York meeting, he went on to the Navy's Mercer Field near Trenton, New Jersey, where Commander Harry Guggenheim was in charge of the testing and commissioning of combat planes. Guggenheim, like Pendray, saw a new cooperative spirit in the now pallid and whispering professor. It was their last conference. Guggenheim was shortly transferred to duty on an aircraft carrier in the Pacific, where he was in combat action from Okinawa to the Ryukyu Islands.

"At Mercer Field, Goddard seemed willing at last, if not eager, to work with others," Guggenheim recalled afterward.

"We spoke first of his immediate plans. Curtiss-Wright bought a license to his patents and wanted Goddard and his crew to join their organization. General Electric was also interested in having him work with them. He sounded pleased with these industrial offers, at least for the immediate future.

"Then we got to talking of the German V-2, which was arousing so much interest. According to highly detailed Allied reports, he said, the German rocket appeared to be remarkably similar to the models he had flown in the prairie and which he had tried so many times to sell our military. Goddard had always played things down and his voice was faint, but what he said sounded historical. I asked him to put it in writing on the back of a photograph of one of his last New Mexico rockets."

Goddard's inscription was firm and unequivocal:

Rocket produced in the spring of 1941, under the Daniel and Florence Guggenheim Foundation.
It is practically identical with the German V-2 rocket.
Robert H. Goddard
Mercer Field
December 28, 1944.

Later, after seeing the V-2, Goddard sent Guggenheim a more elaborate commentary. He knew from reports that the German V-2 components were far beyond his own crude models. The differences, however, seemed less important to him than the striking resemblances of the giant rocket to his own miniature precursors. "I don't think he ever got over the V-2," one of his wartime associates observed. "He felt the Germans had copied his work and that he could have produced a bigger, better and less expensive rocket, if only the United States had accepted the long-range rocket."

Goddard's report to Harry Guggenheim follows in full:

Comparison of the German V-2 Rocket, and the Rocket
Developed by R. H. Goddard in New Mexico, 1930–1941.

	German	American
Fuel	liquid oxygen and alcohol	liquid oxygen and gasoline
Fuel injection means	centrifugal pumps	centrifugal pumps
Pump drive	turbine	turbine
Turbine drive	small rocket motor, using hydrogen peroxide	small rocket motor, using gasoline and oxygen
Lay-out, front to rear	fuel tank; oxygen tank; pumps, turbines, and turbine drive; rocket motor	fuel tank; oxygen tank; pumps, turbines, and turbine drive; rocket motor
Stabilizer	pilot gyro	pilot gyro
Guiding means	stabilizing vanes blast vanes	stabilizing vanes and blast vanes
Rocket motor cooling, general plan	internal layer of fuel	internal layer of fuel

The American rocket was developed through grants from
the Daniel and Florence Guggenheim Foundation, amounting to $190,000, to the point where it [the pump and turbine
model] was given a number of proving stand tests and two
short flights, at which time the shop force began to work on
Army and Navy problems, and the flight rocket tests were
terminated.

Reason for no action on long-range rocket in 1940:
The liquid fuel rocket discussed was for use in comparatively large sizes, and for relatively long periods, hence more

suitable for long rather than short-range rockets. The U.S. had no need of long-range rockets at the time.

U.S. Patents Relating to Features of the German V-2 Design
   Rocket Apparatus, No. 1,102,653, July 7, 1914
      Rocket chamber with nozzle; also step-rocket
   Rocket Apparatus, No. 1,103,503, July 14, 1914
      Rocket chamber supplied by pumps; power plant for driving pumps; tanks containing a liquid fuel and a liquid oxidizer; explosive head.
   Apparatus for Igniting Liquid Fuel, No. 1,879,186, September 27, 1932
      Combustion chamber with outside jacket for cooling the wall; holes in wall introducing liquids so as to have a hot flame in the center of the chamber, spaced from the walls.
   Mechanism for Directing Flight, No. 1,879,187, September 27, 1932
      Pilot gyro; control of directing vanes in blast; and also directing vanes in air stream.
   Seal for Centrifugal Pumps, No. 2,127,865, August 23, 1938
      Pump suitable for pumping liquid oxygen.
   Combustion Chamber for Rocket Apparatus, No. 2,217,649, October 8, 1940
      Cooling of a combustion chamber wall by sprays through holes in the chamber wall.

   VI

   In March 1945, the Allied armies were crossing the Rhine toward Berlin and overrunning the last of Germany's rocket-launching sites. The U.S. forces captured and dismantled an underground V-2 factory in the Harz Mountains. In the general roundup of arms and men, a complete V-2 was shipped to the Annapolis Experiment Station. On an unseasonably warm day, just after its arrival, the professor, with a muffler wrapped around his throat, led his crew into a guarded storehouse where the "vengeance weapon" had been uncrated. At the professor's request, Henry Sachs translated various nameplates on the German rocket. Then Ljungquist, Campbell and Mansur, like skilled pathologists, laid open the shell, revealing the V-2's intricate components. It was a solemn autopsy, conducted with few words.

"I was amazed," Campbell said later. "Of course it was more elaborate and much larger than the rockets we'd worked on, but it seemed extremely familiar—the injection feeding system, the pump assembly, the general layout. The only thing that looked at all new to me was the German design of their turbine."

To Oley Ljungquist, who admired the simplicity of the German pump and "their fine craftsmanship," the V-2 seemed a large edition of the Goddard rocket. "If things had been different," he stated, "we could have flown it before the Germans."

Charles Mansur, the welder, agreed in retrospect that the V-2 was "enough like our Roswell rocket to be its son." But he doubted if the Germans had really copied it, detail by detail. "I thought of the doctor's years of secrecy," he said. "In the early days, he was horrified at the thought of a crew member who drank beer, for fear of what he might say off duty. But with all these precautions, maybe the rocket was still bound to grow up, if not in the United States, then in Germany."

Like many inventors, however, Goddard was reluctant to accept the possibility that inventions and ideas may proceed independently in many places, a point later advanced by the Germans. To Goddard the V-2 merely confirmed what he had been offering for years. Standing in the Annapolis storehouse, he was silent.

"I watched him as he stared at the length and girth of the opened rocket," Henry Sachs remembered, "and went over to him.

" 'It looks like ours, Dr. Goddard,' I said.
" 'Yes, Mr. Sachs,' he answered, 'it seems so.' "

VII

Goddard felt vindicated by the V-2, but he found, once again, that his efforts at home were too early. Many United States strategists would hold that there was no role in the Second World War for his long-range rocket. The Germans of Peenemünde, however, were perplexed at the lack of American interest in Goddard's achievements. A former Army Intelligence officer, Lt. Colonel Ellis C. Vanderpyl, wrote later of an interrogation he conducted in Munich toward the end of the war.

"When we took Munich on 1 May 1945," he wrote, "I was serving as liaison with the infantry, handling top-flight Luftwaffe prisoners as they were turned in . . . they turned over to me a Lt. General Wernher Kreipe, who was the last Chief of the Luftwaffe Air War College. He was a technical officer and apparently had done considerable reading and study on rocketry. It was during my interrogation of him that he blurted out Dr. Goddard's name.

" 'Why don't you ask your own Dr. Goddard?' he said."

Perhaps Goddard was right, that the Germans knew more of his work than his own compatriots. When the war with Germany ended, the scientists and engineers of Peenemünde had a momentary option of moving eastward toward Russia or westward into the American lines. With few exceptions, they chose to move along the war-clogged roads to the West, carrying whatever records they could take with them. Among others interrogated was Dr. Walter Dornberger, commanding officer of Peenemünde, who expressed his views with German assurance:

"I remember that we asked in Garmisch-Partenkirchen and Witzenhausen about Professor Goddard," he later wrote.

"The reason was that Professor Goddard was one of the outstanding rocket pioneers in his country. We could not understand that a man of his genius did not get sufficient support of his government in time. We were interviewed by hundreds of incompetent representatives of the allies. They did not talk our rocket language and could simply not understand us. We wanted to talk to a man who was an expert and a fanatic rocketeer. We never received an answer about what happened to him [Goddard]."

What happened, of course, happened to other American scientists, in the Second World War, but never with more pervasive myopia. In Washington, Goddard and his rocket had been dealt with as a minor distraction. From lack of foresight, perhaps, the United States limited its major wartime research to the atomic bomb in the "Manhattan" project not far from Roswell. The military doubtless never suspected that their atomic warhead would one day be wedded to the rocket in a maximum weapon, or that Goddard's rocket might have given the United States a preponderant lead in the coming struggle for space.

His remaining months passed quietly at Annapolis. Early in 1945, he accepted an additional six months' contract for routine tasks: the development of small rocket motors; a better turbine-driven pump; numerous tests for performance data. Perhaps this offer was meant as a gracious gesture. The Navy had considered releasing him altogether in 1944. Thanks to his superior, Captain Bolster: "We decided to carry him on a while longer."

VIII

Now much of the thrust and intensity went out of Goddard. He kept pace uncomplainingly with the Navy's work. But he was beginning to feel the symptoms of failing

Diagrammatic Comparison

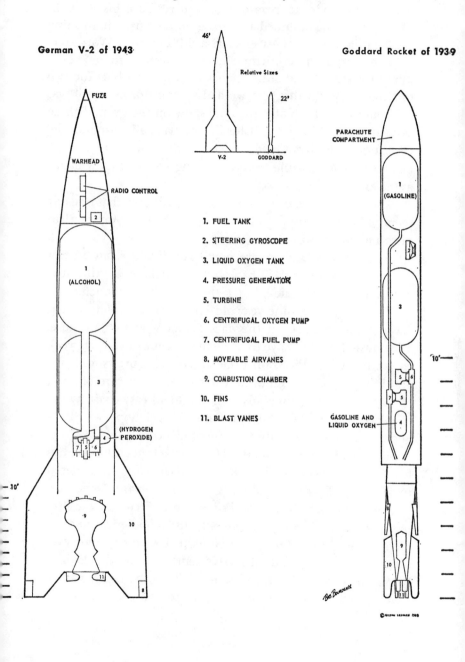

German V-2 of 1943

FUZE

WARHEAD

RADIO CONTROL

2

1
(ALCOHOL)

3

4 (HYDROGEN PEROXIDE)

7 5 6

9

10

11

8

46'

Relative Sizes

22'

V-2   GODDARD

1. FUEL TANK

2. STEERING GYROSCOPE

3. LIQUID OXYGEN TANK

4. PRESSURE GENERATOR

5. TURBINE

6. CENTRIFUGAL OXYGEN PUMP

7. CENTRIFUGAL FUEL PUMP

8. MOVEABLE AIRVANES

9. COMBUSTION CHAMBER

10. FINS

11. BLAST VANES

Goddard Rocket of 1939

PARACHUTE COMPARTMENT

1
(GASOLINE)

2

3

5 6

7 5

GASOLINE AND LIQUID OXYGEN

4

8

9

10

11

health and made deliberate efforts to reassure his wife. In March 1945, he summed up the events of his diminishing season in a last casual letter to Harold Tuson in Worcester:

"It has been a severe winter here, for usually there is only one snow storm of about 4 inches or so, which lasts for two or three days, but this year we had several storms and it was cold enough to keep at least some snow on the ground three or four weeks. The ice in Chesapeake Bay shifts around, depending on the wind, and sometimes there was an ice field, of irregular ice, visible from the living room window as far as the eye could reach. . . .

"We are all quite busy, but it is all routine, so that one day seems like another. . . . I don't see a movie oftener than once a month or so. . . .

"The house where we are now has a living room 40 feet long, and is done in dark panelling throughout. I think it is a bit on the gloomy side, but Esther likes it very much. . . .

"I recently got a nine year old jalopy, a Chevrolet, so that I can come to work on the days Esther goes to Baltimore. Previously I used to have to drive in a night or two each week to get her when the train came in. It rides pretty well for an old timer, 47,000 miles, but has been taken care of. . . .

"By 6:30 P.M. I am ready to flop into an easy chair by the fireplace with a 100 watt lamp and what I hope will be a good book, and wait until the school girl comes in. . . ."

May was an eventful month. Hitler was dead and buried in his Berlin bunker by May 8, when Germany surrendered unconditionally to the Allies. After the news the Goddards, like other proper citizens, went back to their work: the professor to finish his Navy assignment; his "school girl" to complete her studies at The Johns Hopkins University. One evening at Tydings, Goddard inadvertently admitted: "Esther, I don't feel well." If he had sent up flares, he could hardly have alerted her more. Overriding his protests, she unpacked her briefcase and refused to return to Hopkins for her commencement festivities.

"A fellow student reported that I'd won my bachelor's degree with honors," she said. "I called Bob at his shop, something that I rarely did. I heard him sound off to the crew in his cracked voice: 'Boys, Esther has honors at Hopkins!' "

In March there were other cheerful tidings. On one of their usual Saturday drives to the post office, they found a letter from President Atwood of Clark, inviting Goddard to the annual commencement to receive an honorary Doctor of Science degree.

"Bob just sat in the car, looking at the letter and saying nothing," his wife remembered. "I had a queer feeling that it didn't matter much to him now."

At the commencement exercises in Worcester, Goddard's honorary citation was read by Dr. Benjamin S. Merigold, the head of the department of chemistry. Goddard may have remembered Merigold's wry old comment: "Well, Robert, and how is your moon-going rocket?" Merigold was still gently disbelieving, despite his florid words of praise. Solemnly, Goddard moved toward the platform in his black cap and gown to receive the outstretched yellow velvet hood.

Before leaving Worcester, he responded cautiously to requests from the press and gave a brief interview to Anna B. Engstrom of the *Worcester Telegram:*

"I feel we are going to enter an era comparable in its progress to that in which the airplane advanced, although that's saying a good deal. It's just a matter of imagination how far we go with rockets and jet planes. . . . I think it's fair to say you haven't seen anything yet. . . ."

In his hometown, Goddard had now achieved respectability. He stopped by to see Hawley about his latest patent applications. Then he called on Roland A. Erickson, an officer of the Guaranty Bank and Trust Company, who received him cordially. Erickson's brother Albert, who died shortly before the Second World War, had earned his doctorate at Clark under Goddard. Erickson's thesis, "Periodically Interrupted Flow Through Air Passages," was published in the *Journal of the Aeronautical Sciences,* May 1935.

"The professor's voice was very faint and I was concerned for him," the banker observed. "He said he wanted to pass on word that the project Albert had worked on became important during the war, that the Germans had probably followed it in making their V-1. He wanted my parents to know that Al's work had counted."

Back at Tydings-on-the-Bay, Goddard felt extraordinarily tired, but his sleep was unusually restless. He seldom had been so wakeful as he was that spring. On May 9 he had apparently got up early, sat beside his reading lamp in the living room, possibly with a new mystery novel. Later in the day he had written to the American Meteorological Society, describing a predawn phenomenon. Or was it a dream?

"At 3.35 a.m., I happened to be awake, and looking in the direction of this lamp. A whitish light suddenly appeared on the shade, from the window, as if someone were outside with a flashlight. This lasted for about a second, and then a very bright light showed on the shade, such as one might expect from a magnesium flare. This also lasted for about a second. . . ."

Neither Goddard nor his wife were much inclined to interpret dreams. Whatever the cause of this one, he preferred to think of it as an observed physical phenomenon. In any case, he found no logical explanation, nor did the Meteorological Society, which never replied to his letter.

To the scientist, however, facts even now were the most comfortable, sensible means of communication. He turned to facts to persuade Esther, and hopefully himself, of their future. In 1945, he wrote to the Clerk of Chaves County, New Mexico, to maintain their voting rights in Roswell where, he told her, they would one day retire. He also ordered business stationery for the move he said they would make to Caldwell, New Jersey, and Curtiss-Wright. Knowing her husband's Yankee ways, Esther never doubted that an order for printed stationery was an indelible assurance of the future.

IX

Toward the end of May, Dr. Slack detected a small growth in Goddard's throat. It was evidently benign. Slack had "never heard of cancer superimposed on tuberculosis." It was "an unusual and rather baffling case," Slack wrote later.

Within a few weeks, Goddard's health failed sharply. He was sent to Baltimore's Dr. Edwin A. Looper, a throat surgeon.

By mid-June, when summer visitors were once again arriving at Tydings, Esther began to add notes to her husband's diary. On June 14, she wrote:

"Choking spell night of June 14–15, about 1 a.m. . . . vaporizer and poultice . . . helped. Bob slept. . . . When I awoke, Bob was awake, and said, 'I've been lying here watching you. I didn't know anyone could be so beautiful.' "

The next day, Dr. Looper found the growth in Goddard's throat enlarged and made an appointment at the University of Maryland Hospital for the following Monday. In his diary, Goddard made his last entries, writing in his calm and deliberate style:

"June 16, Went to Baltimore, from Annapolis in a.m. with E and saw Dr. Looper. Sat on veranda, etc.

"June 17, Sun., read papers in a.m. Wrote to Brady [at Curtiss-Wright]. Went to post office and to shop, got papers, etc. The Gordons came down, at 11 a.m. and stayed to supper. Finished 'Who Killed Aunt Maggie.' Listened to radio, in eve. E's Ma came at about 8 p.m."

That Sunday, after clearing out his desk at the Experiment Station, Goddard seemed "curiously indifferent—as if resigned that matters were now in the hands of others," his wife wrote. She "explained the situation to the men."

On Monday, June 18, Goddard was admitted to the University Hospital. The next morning he underwent his first throat operation. On his return from the recovery ward, his room was fragrant with flowers.

As the days passed, his spirits improved. Restricted from speaking, he contented himself with scrawling notes on a pad of paper. He was feeling "much better," he wrote to Esther.

"But that evening, as I stood in the hospital corridor," she remembered, "I saw a panel of names on the wall, and his name was there. It wasn't called a 'critical' list, but I said to myself, 'Dear God, it means 'critical.'

"The next morning, Dr. Looper asked me into Bob's room. A number of other physicians—Dr. Slack; Dr. Austrian, the tuberculosis specialist; and several others were there. The growth had been found malignant, although Bob was not told. Dr. Looper proposed another operation to remove the larynx and a decision had to be made. But Bob was conducting matters as if he was running some weird sort of faculty meeting. He pointed his finger at each physician in the room, who indicated there was really no choice, and then he pointed at me. About all I could do was look at the doctors, and nod."

Dr. Looper performed a laryngectomy on July 5. "I felt that things weren't going well," Esther said. "But you couldn't tell this from Bob, except once, when his nurse telephoned me at Tydings about four in the morning. She said he was asking for me. I took the next train to Baltimore and got to the hospital around six. He seemed excited, but when he saw me, he fell back on his pillow and was almost instantly asleep. I saw the pad he'd been writing on. Apparently, the nurse had asked him *why* he wanted me, and he had written: 'About a thousand reasons.' "

Goddard held on for weeks, through July and into August. As he became accustomed to the nature of his operation, he grew attentive to the fact that his crew and equipment were being moved from the Navy to Curtiss-Wright, with Oley Ljungquist taking charge of the migration. Esther, who was seldom far from his bedside, advised him of these maneuvers. Most evenings, she stayed at a congested Baltimore hotel, her quarters somehow arranged by the resourceful Sergeant Emanuel Gordon.

Told of the gravity of Goddard's illness, Oley Ljungquist sent his wife, a retired registered nurse, to help the professor.

"I was with the doctor for about a month," Mandy Ljungquist recalled. "He was different from any person I ever took care of. He never complained, under any circumstance. After his vocal cords were removed, he was still gracious, and would thank me constantly, on his note pad."

There was one remaining task. His wife described it in a few letters to Hawley. On July 4, Independence Day, she wrote:

"I have bad news for you. Bob underwent a throat operation on June 19. . . .

"He cannot speak, but writes notes as to his wants. He signed the Case No. 79 specification on June 29. . . . Bob wrote this on his pad:

" 'Send signed document to Hawley. Explain my situation. Tell him to go over my notes on the subject, and add anything he can think of. Also if he can, add two or three broad or specific claims. The main thing is that it will be a while before I could go over it, and it would be well to file it, in the shape it is, or nearly so, at an early date.'

"Later he glanced over the claims, and wrote,

" 'Add to Hawley's letter that I have read the claims, but under the circumstances cannot add anything. Perhaps he can state the general flow methods in one or two more claims, broadly worded.'

"He asked that I return the enclosed specification to you, so that you could file it promptly, but he wished me to hold the blueprints for a while. He also glanced at them, but he is so weak that he could not really study them. . . ."

The Goddard application resulted in a patent issued in 1951 entitled "Feeding and Cooling Means for Continuously Operated Internal-Combustion Chambers." On August 2, after his laryngectomy, Esther wrote again to Hawley:

"Enclosed is the signed petition for Case 60a. Bob is still very ill in the hospital, so the signatures are shaky, but I hope they will serve. . . .

"We are still hoping and praying for Bob. The old lung trouble has flared up and is retarding the healing of the throat wound. It is a very dangerous situation, but Bob is as usual fighting gallantly. I always knew he was remarkable, but how very much so I never realized until this ordeal. I know it is of comfort to him to have these patents out of the way, for through it all he has asked how they are getting along. . . ."

A day later, she advised the Worcester attorney that "the doctors would prefer that Bob not be bothered with the signing of any papers. . . ."

On August 6, Colonel Boushey called on Esther at the hospital to relay his good wishes and news of recent rocket developments. On July 13, a few weeks before, the Army had established a rocket proving ground at White Sands, New Mexico. They were building a step rocket, as Goddard had advocated, using a German V-2 as the first stage and an American rocket as the second, in Operation Bumper. It seemed likely to achieve the world's altitude record.

"Everywhere, people are becoming conscious of Dr. Goddard," Boushey said. It was an overstatement but she was happy to pass it along, together with the colonel's regards.

While Esther and Boushey were talking downstairs in the hospital, Sergeant Gordon called on the professor upstairs. Gordon was among his last visitors that day. The sergeant brought with him a daily newspaper, its headlines announcing that the United States had dropped a revolutionary bomb on Hiroshima, a principal port of Japan. It was the first public announcement of a nuclear explosion. "The doctor wanted to see the paper," Gordon recalled. "He looked quietly at the headlines, and then, after a long pause, he nodded to me and held up his hand, making a sign for victory."

The professor wanted to see various news editions that day and the next, Nurse Ljungquist recalled. On August 9, he read of a second atomic bomb, dropped on Nagasaki. While President Truman was urging the Japanese to surrender, the rocket professor went into a final coma.

At seven o'clock on August 10, Nurse Ljungquist arrived to begin her daytime shift. "There was nothing to indicate he was going then, or hours from then," she observed. "With most people, you have a clear idea, but with him there was no warning at all. He just passed away." It happened shortly after nine o'clock in the morning.

On August 14, thousands of miles from Worcester, on the battleship *Missouri* in the Pacific, the Japanese signed the surrender, ending the Second World War. On the same day, the professor was buried in the Goddard family plot in Worcester's Hope Cemetery, overlooking Hadwen Park, and not far from Maple Hill.

14. LATER

"Finally, the subject of projection from the earth, and especially a mention of the moon, must still be avoided in dignified scientific and engineering circles, even though projection over long distances on the earth's surface no longer calls for quite so high an elevation of eyebrows. . . ."
—from a new edition of *A Method of Reaching Extreme Altitudes*
Robert H. Goddard
May 1, 1945

So wrote the professor that spring. In the fall he was gone. Once more in Eden Valley, the earth's outlandish creatures took charge, another generation of rattlesnakes, scorpions, vinegarroons and, occasionally, wild rabbits that peered over clumps of mesquite and drummed their feet. Again the prairie basin seemed as remote as vistas on the moon. For a few years a punctuation mark remained. His windmill launching tower still pointed skyward, although it was beginning to flake rust.

After the Goddards left Roswell in 1942, traveling "nesters" camped near the old tower, stripping away some sheet metal at its base and usable bits of wire, unaware that they were poaching on history. They were followed by New Mexico's dry wind and sand, cutting across the flatland, filling in the plank-boarded dugout, burying stones half fused in hundreds of rocket firings, covering cement blocks used to guy up the tower, like some antique memorial to Ozymandias.

Shortly after her husband's death, Esther Goddard sold Mescalero Ranch to friends and the frame workshop behind it to a Roswell laundry proprietor, who moved it down the road and converted it into his home. Before the shop's removal, Esther unlocked it, aired it of musty spirits and retrieved two fully assembled pump-model rockets and "miscellaneous motors, pumps, fuel tanks and valves." These hand-tooled relics were shortly sent on a tour of museums: to New York, Chicago and Los Angeles, and finally to the National Air Museum of the Smithsonian Institution in Washington.

In 1947, Charles Lindbergh was surprised to receive a letter from the Smithsonian asking for his authority to release and exhibit another Goddard rocket, the 1935 model which the professor had sent from Roswell at the flier's urging. With Lindbergh's approval, the false brick wall at the Institution was taken down and the 1935 rocket, still well oiled, was uncrated and mounted for display a few hundred feet from Lindbergh's own *Spirit of St. Louis*.

But Goddard remained little known in these early postwar years. In New England he was largely forgotten, although occasionally a Worcester taxi driver would say: "Goddard? Oh, yes. Didn't he have something to do with rockets?"

In New Mexico, Goddard was also unknown except to a small circle in Roswell. The "Land of Enchantment," however, was expanding in ways related to his work and its various Chambers of Commerce were boasting of new attractions. They spoke with pride of the dry wastelands which became White Sands Proving Grounds for rockets and missiles. A few years after his death, a step-rocket employing a German V-2 capped by an American "WAC Corporal," was fired successfully and made a record ascent from the earth of 250 miles.

New Mexico's second "attraction" was at the northern rim of the proving grounds, a barren nothingness called "Trinity," the site of the world's first nuclear blast. Northwest of Trinity was a third landmark, a mesa called Los Alamos, where an international team of physicists had created the atomic bomb. Like other newcomers to New Mexico, the Los Alamos physicists were unfamiliar with Goddard's work or his vision of the rocket as a spaceship.

The American public was now introduced to space flight not by the work of the Yankee professor but by a wartime foe. After the war, Dr. Wernher von Braun and his team from Peenemünde came to the United States and were sent by the Army to develop missiles at Fort Bliss, Texas; White Sands; and then at the Redstone Arsenal in the small town of Huntsville, Alabama. Among them was the rocket theorist, Hermann Oberth, who had served in a minor role at Peenemünde during the war chiefly in its library where he was assigned to technical research. At Huntsville, Oberth spent a few restless years on advanced space theory, but eventually left von Braun and his team, returned to Europe and retired. It was still an uncertain season for pioneers.

For von Braun, however, American rocket development became a consuming challenge. At Redstone Arsenal, where his team was designing advanced and successful high-flying missiles, he became the most outspoken of rocket enthusiasts, whether native or foreign-born. He repeatedly urged on his adopted country a speedup in rocket technology to match and outproduce America's new competitor, the Soviet Union. He declared there was little technical distinction between the boosters of missiles and of space craft. Heedless of conservative engineers and federal budget makers, who considered his ideas brash and spendthrift, von Braun spoke up with appetite for space platforms, moon landings and planetary probes. His sense of dramatics entranced the motion picture and television producer, Walt Disney, and through him a generation of young Americans, who listened to von Braun and believed that space flight had a Teutonic accent.

II

Esther Goddard's role as her husband's executrix was more encumbered than that of most widows. She inherited an extraordinary mass of papers. She felt summoned not merely to resolve her husband's affairs, but also to establish the scope and importance of his work. In this undertaking, she displayed a persistence that was an easy match for that of the professor.

In 1947, Mrs. Goddard spent nine months with two assistants, transcribing her husband's notes on his experiments. In the living room at Maple Hill, the three women copied some 5,500 pages of notes; mounted and labeled 2,600 photographs; arranged 500 photostat copies of rocket drawings. The result of their labors was twenty-two thick volumes of typescript, to which she later added five more volumes and also a thousand-page transcription of his diaries.

Among the legacy of papers were Goddard's "Cases in Storage," the file of rocket applications he had left with Hawley. When she spoke of these to Harry Guggenheim, he commissioned her to apply for patents on everything that was patentable. "It was a frightening assignment," Esther Goddard said, "but I began working with Mr. Hawley and came across drawings or photographs of devices I remembered. When I learned to put the ideas and the devices together, it became exciting."

The lanky attorney and the determined widow conferred over a period of years translating the "Cases in Storage" into patent claims. When their task was done, 131 more patents were issued posthumously in Goddard's name. The last of these was granted eleven years after his death.

At the conclusion of their work in 1957, Charles Hawley, then in his seventies, retired from legal practice. Before his departure, Esther Goddard parked her car in an alley behind Worcester's Chamber of Commerce Building, where she was presented with two large cartons of Hawley's files. A few days later, she received a gallant letter from the old attorney:

"I share your feeling that our quite abrupt parting in the back alley was hardly a dignified way to close the longest and most interesting experience in my legal career. I feel as if I had been a first-hand observer (and oft-time a participant) in a scientific research project which has rarely been equalled in effort or results. And where may it all end?"

But it was not quite the end of the patent affair. Rockets for defense and space exploration had become a multi-billion dollar industry. In 1951, the Guggenheim Foundation and Mrs. Goddard filed a joint claim for government infringements of Goddard's work. Eventually, in June 1960, the litigation was quietly concluded with an administrative award of $1,000,000, the largest government settlement in the history of American patents. The new National Aeronautics and Space Administration announced:

"Dr. Robert H. Goddard's work as a universally recognized pioneer in rocketry has recently formed the basis of a settlement by the Army, Navy, Air Force and NASA with his widow, Mrs. Esther C. Goddard, and the Guggenheim Foundation. This settlement is in the amount of $1,000,000 for rights to use over 200 of Dr. Goddard's patents which cover basic inventions in the field of rockets, guided missiles, and space exploration.

". . . Upon acceleration of the missile and space program in recent years, production for defense and space use, involving certain of Dr. Goddard's inventions, indicated the need for acquisition of rights thereunder. . . ."

Confronted by the sweeping spectrum of his inventions, the government's attorneys based their settlement on the particular infringement of three major Goddard patents. One was No. 2,395,113, his method of employing pumps, turbines and a gas generator on a rocket. Another was patent No. 2,397,657, a complete automatic liquid-fuel rocket system for a single run or flight, using outside starting devices. The third, No. 2,397,659, covered a similar system for controlled, intermittent operation, with self-starting devices and ingenious pump seals.

It was a lengthy and complex suit, but it established clearly the priority of Goddard's work. Under terms of the settlement, the unexpected return to the Foundation was more than all the funds granted to Goddard during his lifetime. The professor had paid off his debt. The Foundation added these funds to its resources for the continued sponsorship of Goddard professorships at Princeton University, where he had been a research fellow years before, and, perhaps ironically, at the California Institute of Technology, which had become one of the nation's leading schools in jet propulsion.

III

Slowly at first, and then with gathering momentum, a trail of memorials and dedications marked off the places where Goddard had lived and worked. On these occasions, his widow stood on the speakers' platforms, tall and stately, acknowledging tributes to her husband.

One ceremony, in April 1949, was held at Roswell's handsome adobe museum. Mrs. Goddard had arranged for the launching tower to be brought in from Eden Valley. It was scraped, repainted and raised, with a replica of one of the professor's rockets inside.

Other rocket memorabilia were also given to the museum in a later ceremony, attended by many of Goddard's former crew members. Among them were Roswell's "Tiny" Squire, the radio repairman who still liked to lift weights, and his friend Calistro Sanchez, the one-time Goddard handyman. From White Sands came Charles Mansur, Albert Campbell and Lowell Randall, rocket technicians for the Army. Oley Ljungquist and George Bode flew west from the Curtiss-Wright plant in New Jersey, where they were carrying out projects the professor had planned before his death.

After the presentation, Randall spoke for most of the crew to Mrs. Goddard. "We're part of a big team now, with plenty of time and equipment to use," he said. "But it's not as much fun as we had with the doctor."

At another dedication, in June 1957, a Goddard Power Plant was opened on the flatlands of the U.S. Naval Powder Factory at Indian Head, Maryland. This time Esther appeared among a throng of Congressmen and generals to dedicate the building. Behind her the power plant's machinery hummed with energy, above the wooded trail Goddard had followed in 1920, riding a bicycle, an umbrella balanced under his arm, making his way to Indian Head's abandoned powder magazine beside the Potomac River.

In September 1959, the United States 86th Congress ordered a gold medal designed and struck by the mint "in recognition of [Goddard's] pioneering research in rocket propulsion." On the reverse side of the medal, flanking a design of the first liquid-fuel rocket, was a legend taken from his graduation talk in 1904 at South High School: "The Dream of Yesterday Is the Hope of Today and the Reality of Tomorrow."

Another award was given on a spring morning in June 1960, in the courtyard of the Smithsonian Institution in Washington. Goddard became one of the few recipients of the gold Langley Medal for "achievements in aerodromics."

Esther Goddard, on receiving the medal, recalled young
Goddard in Worcester, reading Langley's papers and watching the flights of chimney swifts; read a diary entry recording
his family's astonishment when he received his Smithsonian
grant; spoke of the meetings of Goddard and Abbot in the
red brick tower above the Smithsonian courtyard.

A month later, in July 1960, the scene of dedication
shifted to Auburn, Massachusetts. There a granite marker,
presented by the American Rocket Society, was unveiled at
the former Effie Ward farm where Goddard had flown his
early rockets. The Auburn ceremony, conducted in the bright
sunshine of a New England summer, included a speech by
Dr. von Braun, who referred unexpectedly to Dr. Goddard as
his "boyhood hero." The farm had become the Pakachoag
Golf Course and had been operated by the late Asa Ward,
Aunt Effie's nephew, who once told visitors of the bald scientist's saying: "I'm not trying to hit the moon, Asa. I just
want to get it above the ground." The site of the 1926 launching was now at a midpoint between the tee and the green on
the ninth fairway, a dogleg hole to the left.

A capstone of celebration was held in early 1961 at Green-
belt, Maryland, near the nation's capital. It was attended by
Goddard's oldest friends: Drs. L. T. E. Thompson, Harold
Stimson and Clarence Hickman, his colleagues at Clark; and
by his former sponsors, Dr. Abbot, then in his late eighties,
and Harry Guggenheim.

The dedication took place at the new Goddard Space Flight
Center on a chill afternoon of March 16. It was exactly thirty-
five years since the flight of his pioneer Auburn rocket. The
center, established by the National Aeronautics and Space
Administration as the electronic focus for America's space
venture, occupied more than five hundred acres and employed a team of some two thousand scientific, technical and
administrative young men. Within a few months after its
dedication, the center was commonly known as "Goddard,"

much as Wright Field years before had come to be called "Wright."

In the American Rocket Society, which the professor had joined shortly before his death, Goddard awards became a continuing ritual, bestowed each year upon rocket researchers at the group's Honors Night dinners and announced from the head table by the pioneer's widow.

After one such presentation, Mrs. Goddard turned to Pendray, a founder of the Society and consultant to the Guggenheim Foundation, whose van Dyke beard had grown white with the years. She and Pendray, together, with the aid of Guggenheim, had brought Goddard to public attention. "Ed," said Esther Goddard after bestowing the Society's annual award, "I don't think they really need me here any more. I'm starting to feel like a ghost at the banquet."

v

As Goddard lay dying, astronautics was no longer idle fancy; men would learn to navigate in space as they had learned to navigate on the seas and in the earth's atmosphere. The first successful Sputnik was launched in October 1957, and the race into space was irreversible. Von Braun's Redstone missile launched the first American satellite the following January 1958. Flight into space was becoming the reality Goddard had foreseen.

Perhaps, at the end, Goddard could have foretold that the major difference between the ballistic missile, following earthly trajectories, and the space vehicle, following Keplerian arcs, lay not so much in their thrusts, nor in their angles of departure, but in the nature of man. At one angle of ascent, the rocket was a weapon, at another, a space craft. With a nuclear payload carried forward, it would become the most devastating of weapons and weapon carriers;

with nuclear energy transposed to its rear, it would become the greatest of all prime movers devised by man.

Goddard may have reflected on these alternatives as Esther in her Baltimore hotel room was reading and copying these lines from some book or magazine article, forgetting this time to mark down their source:

". . . When one talks of a man like him, there is no question of defeat or victory. He just is, he goes on. For him there is no victory, immediate or ultimate. He is a factor in education, which goes on and does not cease. . . . It never thinks of itself as victorious, no matter how successful it may be; nor defeated, no matter how it may fail here and there, now and then. It must go on. There is something in humanity that makes it go on. . . ."

SOURCES AND
ACKNOWLEDGMENTS

A. Note on Primary Sources and Method

Shortly after I began work in 1956 on the Goddard biography, *This High Man,* it was evident that there were few published works which would restore to life the man and scientist who died in 1945. This restoration is the primary task of biography. Although Goddard's province was spectacular, he was spectacularly unknown in print and also unknown to me until a few years before I became his biographer.

Aside from the limited published accounts, two other sources were available. They are inevitably part of any biographical research. In the Goddard account, however, they were paramount. First of these were the people who knew Goddard and shared their recollections of him by interview and correspondence. Second were Goddard's own files, almost all of them unpublished, which he left behind.

There always is, in biography, a third dimension: the writer's perceptions which shape, as they record, his materials. In reconstructing the life of Goddard, I have presented thoughts, emotions and viewpoints carefully based on documentary evidence, without interrupting the narrative for attribution.

Fortunately, most of the people involved in the life of the rocket professor were alive during the course of my research. They were interviewed with the aid of a good tape recorder, and their fragments

410

of memory were played back later and transcribed as my primary notes. Almost without exception, the enthusiasm of these allies in my research was an unexpected bonus. With the help of their electronic echoes, an image of Goddard emerged. When it seemed to me that Goddard was himself talking through my tape recorder, it was evident that the time for writing had come.

I have never cared much for footnotes and have done without them in my book. Footnotes usually tell the reader either less or more than he cares to know. What people said about my subject or themselves is either directly quoted or reflected in the body of the text.

I am indebted to many generous contributors for their recollections, chief among them Mrs. Esther C. Goddard, widow of the pioneer. Other vital sources, acknowledged here in approximate categories of Goddard's career, include:

(1) LIFETIME SOURCES: Dr. Charles G. Abbot; Charles T. Hawley; Dr. Clarence N. Hickman; Dr. G. Edward Pendray; Dr. Harold L. Stimson; Dr. Louis T. E. Thompson.

(2) HIS CREW: George Bode; Albert S. Campbell; Albert Kisk; Nils T. Ljungquist; Charles W. Mansur; Lowell N. Randall; Nils Riffolt; Henry Sachs; Calistro Sanchez; Sidney L. Squire.

(3) HIS WORCESTER YEARS: Mrs. Calvin H. Andrews; Dr. Wallace W. Atwood, Jr.; Mrs. William Bennett; Mrs. Carl Berglund; Dr. Samuel J. Brandenburg; Dr. Charles F. Brooks; Dr. Jesse L. Bullock; L. Herbert Carter; Dr. William H. Cole; Benjamin Cooper; Watson Davis; Dr. Richard B. Dow; Franklin B. Durfee; Dr. Rupen Eksergian; Roland A. Erickson; Hugo Gernsback; G. R. Gladding.

Ernest A. T. Hapgood; Prof. Russell B. Hastings; Russell G. Hemenway; John W. Higgins; Mrs. Florence Hyde; Mrs. Anna Johnson; H. Clayton Kendall; Mrs. Amy G. Keyes; Dr. J. A. Knight; Carl L. Larson; L. C. Leach; Hilda Lidstone; Albin Liljehook; Dr. Homer P. Little; Major General Frank E. Lowe (ret.); Dr. Morton Masius; Dr. James A. Maxwell; Prof. Carey E. Melville; Dr. Benjamin S. Merigold; Allan B. Miller; Mrs. Emily Wardwell Mowry; Francis Murphy.

Miriam Olmstead; Roland A. Packard; G. Norman Palser; Dr. Henry C. Parker; A. W. Parkes, Jr.; Douglas L. Parkhurst; Mrs. Inez W. Powers; Dr. Percy M. Roope; Dean Francis W. Roys; Herbert Sautels; Mrs. Walter S. Sherman; Donald Simonds; Harold Tuson; Alma Waite; Asa Ward; Mrs. R. L. D. Whittemore; Mrs. John E. Woodbury.

(4) HIS INDIAN HEAD YEARS: L. P. Johnson; Raymond H. Kray; Grace Lund; Bernard L. Nicholson.

(5) HIS ROSWELL YEARS: Colonel Henry Breckinridge (ret.); Arthur A.

Collins; Roderic Crandall; Herman Crile; General James H. Doolittle (ret.); Mrs. Barry Duffield; Dr. James Edson; Harry F. Guggenheim; Paul Horgan; Peter Hurd; McFall Kerbey; Will C. Lawrence; Charles A. Lindbergh.

Dr. Frank J. Malina; Mrs. May Corn Marley; Mr. and Mrs. Samuel H. Marshall; Dr. Clark Millikan; Mr. and Mrs. A. Peter Nelson; Mrs. Mary Nicholas; Herbert B. Nichols; Effie Olds; H. E. Samson; John W. Sessums, Jr.; Claude Simpson; Dr. John E. Smith; B. Anthony Stewart; Dr. Theodore von Kármán; Mr. and Mrs. Harrison Williams; Dan Wilmot, Jr.; Paul Wilmot; Donald Winston.

(6) HIS SECOND WORLD WAR AND ANNAPOLIS YEARS: Charles F. Bellais; Rear Admiral Calvin M. Bolster (ret.); Brigadier General Homer A. Boushey, Jr. (ret.); Charles W. Chillson; Ben F. Coffman, Jr.; Mrs. William F. Flood, Jr.; Commander Charles Fink Fischer (ret.); Mr. and Mrs. Emanuel Gordon; William L. Gore.

Andrew G. Haley; William C. House; Mrs. Nils T. Ljungquist; Dr. John E. Nafe; Commander Jewett Orth (ret.); Dr. Richard W. Porter; Major General Leslie E. Simon (ret.); Colonel Leslie A. Skinner (ret.); Harry Slack, Jr., M.D.; Captain (U.S.N.) Robert C. Truax (ret.).

(7) GENERAL SOURCES: Alfred Africano; Edwin E. Aldrin; Henry G. Beauregard; Colonel John J. Driscoll; Dr. Eugene M. Emme; Rear Admiral Delmer S. Fahrney (ret.); Clarence M. Fisher; Edward Francisco; Paul E. Garber; William and Lydia Haggard; Roy Healy; Lovell Lawrence; Mrs. Charles Mansur; Hermann Oberth; Wesley Price; Arthur Rudolph; John Shesta; Dr. Ernst Stuhlinger; Major General Holger N. Toftoy; Dr. Wernher von Braun; D. C. Wilkerson.

Next to the above, the second most important source has been Goddard's notebooks, letters, journals, scrapbooks, and memorabilia. Organizations and their members who have generously loaned original material include George Fountaine of the Daniel and Florence Guggenheim Foundation; the Smithsonian Institution; the Clark University Library; Francis De Tarr of the Yale Library; Elizabeth B. Brown of the library of the American Institute of Aeronautics and Astronautics; Science Service; and the National Geographic Society, particularly for use of an unpublished manuscript by Goddard, prepared by its staff writer, McFall Kerbey.

I am grateful to Mrs. Goddard for the loan of much of the contents of three ample filing cabinets which have been by my desk for more than six years. She has patiently explained, as was so often necessary, the circumstances behind the store of personal and technical papers left by her husband. Many of these items will be published in a two-volume edition of *The Papers of Robert H. Goddard,* prepared by Mrs. Goddard and an editorial board. Eventually, the Goddard papers will be deposited at the Library of Congress.

Among the professor's unpublished papers, the following were especially valuable to my study:

"Autobiographical Statement" (around 1921) and "Material for an Autobiography of R. H. Goddard" (July 1927); "Diaries" from 1898 to 1945, as transcribed in 1,003 single-spaced pages of typescript; three volumes of transcribed "Affidavits"; notes on patent applications, and correspondence with the patent attorney, Charles T. Hawley.

Copious files of other correspondence dating from the 1890s to 1945; notes for lectures and talks at Clark University and elsewhere; "Reports" to the Smithsonian Institution, the Guggenheim Foundation, and the United States Navy; volumes of "Experimental Notes"; and a collection of papers, to which, in early form, Goddard gave the "cover" name: "Special Formulae for Silvering Mirrors."

Among the numerous other papers consulted, "Esther Goddard's Letters to Parents (1930–1938)," were of special interest. In this correspondence, a scientist's wife tried to make clear to her parents in Worcester, Massachusetts, what life in the Southwestern prairie was like when shared with one of the first space men of the century.

B. Supplementary Reading List

The list that follows includes books and a few pamphlets which I have used as background. Newspaper and magazine sources are not given here; when pertinent, they are referred to in the text. As further studies of Goddard are made, these publications may be helpful to others as they were to me in the preparation of *This High Man:*

Abbot, Charles G., *Adventures in the World of Science.* Public Affairs Press, Washington, D.C., 1948.

Asimov, Isaac, *The Intelligent Man's Guide to Science.* Vol. 1, Basic Books, Inc., New York, 1960.

Atwood, Wallace W., *The First Fifty Years,* Clark University Library, Worcester, 1937.

Bolster, Calvin M., *The Assisted Take-Off of Airplanes,* Norwich University, Northfield, Vt., 1950.

414 • SOURCES AND ACKNOWLEDGMENTS

Bush, Vannevar, *Modern Arms and Free Men*, Simon & Schuster, New York, 1949.

Clark University Library, *Catalogues*, 1924–1930.

Clark University Library, *Arthur Gordon Webster . . . In Memoriam*, 1924.

Clarke, Arthur C., *The Exploration of Space*, Harper & Brothers, New York, 1951.

Cleveland, Reginald M., *America Fledges Wings, the History of the Daniel Guggenheim Fund for the Promotion of Aeronautics*, Pitman Publishing Corp., New York, 1942.

Davis, Kenneth S., *The Hero, Charles A. Lindbergh and the American Dream*, Doubleday & Company, Inc., 1959.

Dornberger, Walter, *V-2*, The Viking Press, New York, 1954.

Drake, Samuel Francis, *Landmarks, and Historic Personages of Boston*, Little, Brown & Company, Boston, 1900.

Emme, Eugene M., *Aeronautics and Astronautics, An American Chronology of Science and Technology in the Exploration of Space, 1915–1960*, National Aeronautics and Space Administration, Washington, D.C., 1961.

————, *The Impact of Air Power, National Security and World Politics*, D. Van Nostrand Co., Princeton, N.J., 1959.

————, and others, *Aeronautical and Astronautical Events of 1961*, report to the Committee on Science and Astronautics, House of Representatives, from NASA, Washington, D.C., 1962.

Encyclopaedia Britannica, 14th Edition, Chicago, Ill., 1948.

Esnault-Pelterie, Robert, *L'Astronautique*, Société Astronomique de France, 1930.

Goddard, Robert H., *A Method of Reaching Extreme Altitudes*, Smithsonian Miscellaneous Collections, lxxi, no. 2, 69 pp., Smithsonian Institution, Washington, D.C., 1919.

————, *Liquid-Propellant Rocket Development*, Smithsonian Miscellaneous Collections, xcv, no. 3, 10 pp. and plates, 1936.

————, *Rockets* [facsimiles of above two reports with a new foreward by Goddard], American Rocket Society, New York, 1946.

————, *Rocket Development*, edited by Esther C. Goddard and G. Edward Pendray, Prentice-Hall, Inc., New York, 1948.

Guggenheim, Harry F., *The Seven Skies*, G. P. Putnam's Sons, New York, 1930.

Leonard, Jonathan Norton, *Flight Into Space*, Random House, New York, 1953.

Ley, Willy, *Rockets, Missiles and Space Travel,* Viking Press, New York, 1954.

Lincoln, William, *History of Worcester,* Charles Hersey, Worcester, Mass., 1862.

Lindbergh, Charles A., *Of Flight and Life,* Charles Scribner's Sons, New York, 1948.

——, *The Spirit of St. Louis,* Charles Scribner's Sons, New York, 1954.

Massachusetts, A Guide to its Places and People, American Guide Series, Houghton Mifflin Company, Boston, 1937.

New Mexico, A Guide to the Colorful State, American Guide Series, University of New Mexico Press, 1945.

Nutt, Charles, *History of Worcester and its People,* 2 vols., Lewis Historical Publishing Company, Worcester, 1919.

Oberth, Hermann, *Die Rakete zu den Planetenräumen,* R. Oldenbourg, Munich, 1923.

——, *Man Into Space,* Harper & Bros., New York, 1957.

O'Connor, Harvey, *The Guggenheims, The Making of a Dynasty,* Covici, 1937.

Pendray, G. Edward, *The Coming Age of Rocket Power,* revised edition, Harper & Bros., New York, 1947.

Rice, Franklin P., ed., *The Worcester of Eighteen Hundred and Ninety-Eight, Fifty Years a City,* F. S. Blanchard & Co., 1899.

Rockwood, Roy, *Through Space to Mars,* Cupples & Leon, New York, 1910.

Rosen, Milton M., *The Viking Rocket Story,* Harper & Bros., New York, 1955.

Sanford, Edmund C., *A Sketch of the History of Clark University,* Clark University Library, Worcester, Mass., 1923.

Serviss, Garrett P., *A Columbus of Space,* D. Appleton & Co., New York, 1911.

Shapley, Harlow, ed., *A Treasury of Science,* Harper & Bros., New York, 1954.

Simpson, Claude, *People, Incorporated,* Roswell, New Mexico, 1958.

Taylor, Herbert Foster, *Seventy Years of the Worcester Polytechnic Institute,* Worcester Polytechnic Institute, Worcester, 1937.

Tsiolkovsky, Konstantin E., *Beyond the Planet Earth,* trans. from the Russian by Kenneth Syers, Pergamon Press, New York, 1960.

——, *The Call of the Cosmos,* with a foreword by V. G. Fesenkov, Foreign Languages Publishing House, Moscow, 1960.

——, *Na-ootchnoye Obozreniye* [reprinted, with title page in

German, translatable as "The Rocket into Cosmic Space," originally published in 1903], U.S.S.R., Government Printing Office, Kaluga, 1924.

Valier, Max, *Der Vorstoss in Den Weltenraum,* R. Oldenbourg, Munich, 1924.

Verne, Jules, *From the Earth to the Moon,* Charles Scribner's Sons, New York, 1912 edition.

Wells, H. G., *The War of the Worlds,* Harper & Bros., New York, 1898.

Wicks, Mark, *To Mars via the Moon,* J. B. Lippincott Co., New York, 1911.

Williams, Beryl and Epstein, Samuel, *The Rocket Pioneers on the Road to Space,* Julian Messner, Inc., New York, 1955.

World Almanac, New York World-Telegram and The Sun, New York, 1956 and 1962 editions.

C. Photographs and Diagrams

Most of the photographs in this biography were taken by the Goddards, who used the camera to record the development of Dr. Goddard's rockets. Mrs. Goddard made available her complete file of photographs, and these are supplemented by a few pictures from other sources. I want to thank Mrs. Robert H. Goddard; William R. Adam, Department of Defense; Mrs. Henry Breckinridge; Louis Casey, National Air Museum of the Smithsonian Institution; Les Gaver, chief of the Audio-Visual Division, NASA; Max E. Ludwick, Naval Propellant Plant; and Mrs. Rita Riffolt Varney. The following photograph credits are accompanied by the numbers that appear with the captions, and the diagrams are identified by book page numbers.

PHOTOGRAPHS: Frontispiece by B. Anthony Stewart, copyright National Geographic Society; Mrs. H. W. Blakeslee, 41; Homer A. Boushey, 65; Clark University (photo by Bachrach), 11; Clark University, 12–13; Mrs. Robert H. Goddard, 1–9, 18–22, 24–28, 30–34, 39–40, 42–45, 47–54, 57–58, 61–64, 67–69, 76–77; Harry F. Guggenheim, 38; Charles T. Hawley, 14; Paul Horgan, 55; Peter Hurd, 56; Willy Ley, 35; Charles A. Lindbergh, 46, 59–60; Ordnance Museum, Aberdeen Proving Ground, 72; Smithsonian Institution, 15, 75; Sovfoto, 36; Harold F. Stimson (photo by Cameron), 17; L. T. E. Thompson, 23; United Press International, 37–38, 74; U.S. Army, 71; U.S. Navy (courtesy of Mrs. Goddard), 66; Mrs. Rita Riffolt Varney, 16; Worcester Polytechnic Institute, 10. Of the photographs credited to Mrs. Goddard, numbers 9, 18–22, 27, 41, 45, 49–50, 54 and 69 were taken by Dr. Goddard.

DIAGRAMS: Pages 68–69 and 359, U.S. Patent Office; page 83, Smithsonian Institution; page 381, *Flugsport*, German aeronautics journal, issue of January 18, 1939; the diagram in the second section of photographs was drawn by Dr. Goddard for *The Coming Age of Rocket Power* by G. Edward Pendray, published by Harper & Row and used with permission; page 391, Robert Bordeaux, Presentation Associates, used with permission of Milton Lehman.

D. Special Acknowledgments

I also wish to thank those who read manuscript. First among them is John Farrar, my editor-publisher. Others are Messrs. Pendray, Lindbergh, and Mrs. Goddard; Drs. Abbot, Stimson and Thompson; General Boushey; Paul Horgan and Peter Hurd; and Paul E. Garber of the National Air Museum.

There were also others, dissociated from the Goddard story, who reviewed copy with inexplicable cheerfulness and a high degree of historical, grammatical and technological awareness. I want to thank my good and enduring friend, Mrs. Lonnelle Aikman of the *National Geographic Magazine;* Kenneth Clark, Motion Picture Association of America; Dr. Eugene M. Emme, historian of NASA; Allan C. Fisher, Jr., *National Geographic Magazine;* Howard B. Jefferson, president of Clark University; Marvin W. McFarland, Library of Congress.

Edwin L. Peterson, professor of English, University of Pittsburgh; Dr. Albert M. Stone, The Johns Hopkins Applied Physics Laboratory; H. P. Storke, president of Worcester Polytechnic Institute; Stanley Swinton, Associated Press; and Captain Frank B. Voris, neighbor and Navy Research physician with NASA.

My ultimate acknowledgments, however, belong to the amiable foursome who are also mentioned in the dedication of this book: to my children Ann, John and Betsy, who heard about Goddard over the breakfast, lunch and dinner table, long before most Americans of their generation or mine; and, finally, to my wife, Mildred Kharfen Lehman, who in this, as in uncountable undertakings, has been my wisest and dearest collaborator.

I hope these sources and accomplices will enjoy *This High*

Man. They have made valued contributions. For demerits, I am responsible. For merits, they have my gratitude. And may we all have a smooth journey home!

Milton Lehman

Garrett Park, Maryland
June 1963

INDEX

INDEX

Other DACAPO titles of interest